To
Spooge
on your 64th birthday
love
fay xxxx

In this book, Peter Thornton relates a gripping family saga, packed with enough tragedy, triumph and conflict to make many novelists green with envy. From the intriguing opening chapter, I knew I was in the hands of a true story teller who knows how to create a suspense-filled narrative. And it's all set against a fascinating background – the history of the Thorntons' chocolate business, as it grows from a corner shop in Sheffield to a multi-national company responsible for one of the most recognised super brands in the world. Forget any thoughts you had of a dry business memoir – this is a man with a remarkable story to tell, and the skill to do it.

I have to give full marks to Peter Thornton for his honesty about himself, and his relationships – particularly the complex web of intrigue played out over the decades by generations of the Thornton family. At times, the scent of conspiracy rising from the pages was as strong as the smell of chocolate that used to hang over Belper! Sibling rivalries, marital breakdown, echoes of a forgotten age, and glimpses of life in the Peak District - this book has them all. As a lifelong fan of one of Derbyshire's best known products, I'll now be eating Thornton's chocolates with a whole new insight.

Stephen Booth
International award-winning author of the Ben Cooper
and Diane Fry crime series

www.stephen-booth.com

MY LIFE IN THE FAMILY BUSINESS
by
Peter Thornton
With Kenneth Bishton

TOMAHAWK Press

First published in 2009 by

Tomahawk Press

PO Box 1236

Sheffield S11 7XU

England

www.tomahawkpress.com

ISBN 13: 978-0-9557670-3-6

Language and format reviewed and improved by Ken Bishton - kenbishton@talktalk.net
Edited by Bruce Sachs
Designed by Tree Frog Communication – 01245 445377 – info@treefrogcommunication.co.uk
Printed in the EU by Gutenberg Press Limited

This book is based on the recorded notes and recollections of the author. We welcome readers to contact us with any perceived inaccuracies, which we would be pleased to investigate and correct – TOMAHAWK PRESS

Every effort has been made to trace the present copyright holders of photographs used. We apologise in advance for any unintentional omission and will be pleased to insert the appropriate acknowledgement to companies or individuals in any subsequent edition of this publication.

Foreword
by Jo Brand

I am writing the foreword to this book undoubtedly because of my connection to its two great themes: chocolate and mental health issues.

As an ex-psychiatric nurse of ten years' standing, I have come to understand the sorts of pressures in everyday life that can cause problems, and how we all cope differently with these stresses. In the cut-throat world of business, there are many casualties – especially the more gentle souls for whom the rigorous and competitive demands of management can be very personally destructive. And not just individuals, but whole families too, where personal relationships become hopelessly entwined with the business, ultimately causing much damage. This book will give you a great insight into these issues.

I should point out to you that if you were expecting some business wisdom from me, you will be sadly disappointed. I am not the sort of person who is cut out for business. I watch programmes such as *The Apprentice* and *Dragons' Den* with a mixture of horror and antipathy, because the world of business seems to require a great deal of hard work, common sense, certain toughness, a competitive spirit and the ability to gamble – none of which I possess in any shape or form.

I have had business ideas in the past – a human sized hot water bottle being one of the more mad ones. But I wouldn't have any idea of how to put my ideas into practice, and to be perfectly honest with you, I wouldn't want to. No, I prefer to leave it all to those denizens of capitalism like Alan Sugar and Richard Branson, and then just purchase the results of their hard work.

But I do like chocolate! Oh yes, indeed! So how could I resist a book which centres on a chocolate empire such as Thorntons, whose products I have consumed to excess, and have enjoyed over the years to the detriment of my svelte figure as a teenager?

Chocolate sits in our hearts (and on them if we eat too much everyday). We use chocolate to say many things – "I love you," "Sorry" and "Well Done." There is nothing quite like a chocolate to make you feel better at the end of a long, hard day.

So, this fascinating book looks at the life of the man who once ran the Thorntons' empire and also at his family – all involved in the business, and by his account, neither he nor the rest of the Thorntons family had an easy time of it. The stresses of business have caused many tough old birds to go under, and you will find an excellent examination within these pages of how our hero and his family have suffered during their many years at the choc face, as it were.

This book is more than all this though. It reads like an absorbing novel but it is a real life drama. So, put your feet up and stuff as much Thorntons in as you can while reading it. Your enjoyment can only be heightened by doing as I suggest. Myriad pleasures await you as Peter Thornton takes you inside his family's business. Enjoy!

Jo Brand
London, September 2009

Introduction
by Alistair Blair

Thorntons' tiny, busy shop in Grimsby's Victoria Street, was a small but memorable part of my childhood. My mother, who had a sweet tooth and an eye for a bargain, was a regular customer for "misshapes", the not quite perfectly formed chocolates, which tasted "just as good", as she would always say (and she was right). For gifts, she would stretch to a box of Continental Selection. Later, I would often make the same purchases myself.

The shop had a magnetic something; and Peter's book fascinatingly relates exactly how this was achieved by dint of ultra-detailed guidelines set down by his father, Norman. I never saw Norman's Rolls Royce glide down Victoria Street on one of his shop inspections, but I am assured it did so.

In the 1990s, as a journalist on the Investors Chronicle magazine, I found myself covering Thorntons' annual results from time to time. This was eight or ten years after Peter was forced out of the company. His brother John had just relinquished the chief executiveship to the first outsider, Roger Paffard, although John Thornton continued as chairman.

The quality of the chocolates has never been in doubt, but Thorntons' record as a quoted company has been disappointing. Eventually, after yet another announcement from the company that it would not deliver the profits expected of it, I devoted my No Free Lunch column to an effort to get to the bottom of Thorntons' disappointments (Investors Chronicle 16 July 2003).

This resulted in an email from Peter Thornton, then unknown to me. He complimented me on writing the first press article that "comes anywhere near understanding the company", whilst observing that it nevertheless contained some misconceptions. I was pleased to receive Peter's email. Frankly, achieving "near-understanding" and containing only "some misconceptions" is about as good as it can get for a jobbing journalist. Peter and I have been occasional correspondents ever since.

My bookshelves include a large selection of individual and corporate business biographies. These include Jack Welch of General Electric, Roberto Goizueta of Coca-Cola, Akio Morita of Sony and Lord Weinstock of GEC. My "cameo shelf" includes Sir Fred Pontin's autobiography, an account of the Aberfeldy laundry business—Fishers and another of Clarksons, the shipbrokers. Although often heavily nuanced in favour of the protagonist, I find these a rich source of "alternative" information about businesses and business people.

I can assure you that this book is as compelling a read as any of the above and—in a different way from any of them—will give you the same measure of insight.

Thorntons was founded by Peter's grandfather and set on the road to success by his father and uncle. Later, they were loath to give up control to the four sons who went into the business. Peter spent over 30 years in the company and although these included many successes, a powerful undercurrent of frustration was ever-present. Against this background, Peter's book had to be a warts and all account. But additionally, Peter is also a patently honest person. This book surely contains an element of "seeing it my way", but you will not doubt that you are reading an unglossed account of how Thorntons grew from one shop to a £100 million turnover business, in spite of deeply dysfunctional leadership.

This is the greatest insight you will get from the book: how a successful business formula can prosper even if it lacks coherent management. Of course, it wasn't all "in spite of"; there was a huge element of "because of" too. As Peter makes clear, every Thornton involved in the business cared passionately about the company's products and reputation, and laboured hard in pursuit of excellence. Without this commitment, the business would surely never have made it past the first 20 shops. The essential formula of Thorntons was never in dispute. But the detail of how this was to be achieved provoked serious disagreements for more than 30 years. Those wonderful chocolates triumphed nevertheless. You should have this in mind whenever you read an account of "How I made my company a great success". Have an eye on the possibility that public's demand for the business or product is what is succeeding and that the leader's role may be less than it seems.

Peter's book is also a great page-turner. Threaded between the installation of the latest chocolate enrober, inspecting the shops and quarrels about which Thornton is to run which part of the company, Peter turns from a shy youth into a serious Lothario whose exploits and setbacks add an intriguing dimension to the story.

Whether you are a business or a generalist reader, I commend this book to you.

Alistair Blair
Investors Chronicle

Alistair Blair is a past winner of the Business Writer of the Year Award, and has worked in investment banking and fund management.

Prologue

"Clear Your Desk!"

On Saturday, June 6, 1987 I went into my office for the last time. I had left early that morning from my beautiful converted farmhouse in the Derbyshire village of Wensley because I wanted to get to the office before anyone else arrived.

Whenever driving the fifteen miles to the small industrial town of Belper, just north of Derby, where our confectionery business was situated at the time, I always used the quiet country roads so as to avoid the heavy traffic on the A6 through Matlock. From my home I would drive through the old lead mining village of Winster, brimming with childhood recollections, and then left through the sombre steep-sided valley known locally as the Via Gellia after a local landowner, John Gell, who built the original road. This leads to the picturesque and unspoilt limestone town of Wirksworth, on through Idridgehay and eventually along the Ashbourne road to Belper itself.

It was a beautiful morning, with the hills of the Derbyshire Dales rolling off into the distance, the landscape broken only by the centuries-old dry stone walls. All this had been so familiar from boyhood when my family had moved from Sheffield and the wartime bombing raids to the relative safety of Winster and Over Haddon in the Peak District.

I had been crossing the Derbyshire uplands to our confectionery factory in Belper for over thirty years, initially from homes in Sheffield and Ashover and now from Wensley, in all weathers and through all seasons. This daily journey had become an important part of my life, affording me the time to consider the issues ahead or to mull over the events of the day on my way home. It was unthinkable that this was the last day I would be making this trip just as I had no idea what on earth I was going to do with the rest of my life.

By 8.30 I had parked my car directly outside the office on Derwent Street where the family business of Thorntons was based. The road is almost in the middle of the old mill town of Belper, at a right angle to the main thoroughfare, Bridge Street. It leads after a short distance to the meadows on the flood plain of the River Derwent. It is easy to miss the narrow entrance to Derwent Street between what was once Pym's Wine Shop and an old house now that these have been converted into offices. The family business had started in Sheffield and there were offices there still, but the main operation had moved here to Belper in the 1970's.

By 1987 all the buildings on the left of Derwent Street belonged to Thorntons. Indeed a large part of the meadows also belonged to the company. I had bought them from the local Strutt Estate some years before, thinking they would form a perfect playing field for the company's sports teams.

The original main building still looked as it had when I had first gone there with my father in the 1940s. It was a two-storey, dark-red brick building, built right up to the street and, I had always supposed, must initially have been a cotton mill in the late 19th century. There was a remarkably large number of very big windows along both floors of the building, installed, I liked to think, by some altruistic mill-owner wanting to ensure that his workers always had plenty of daylight and inspirational views across the meadows. These metal-framed windows had small panes and, of course, no double glazing. They didn't have straight concrete lintels as one would see today but instead their curved brick lintels fitted beautifully together to support the walls above. The architecture was the kind that looks natural in such a place, almost organic, put there by a master craftsman and not just poured into place by some uncaring concrete mixer as with so many contemporary buildings. It seemed unusual for the place to have metal framed windows at all but it also had some very beautiful cast-iron pillars supporting the first floor, indicating that period of the Industrial Revolution when metal was extensively used in mill buildings. Today the ground floor was almost entirely occupied with offices for reception and secretaries and for the directors.

I opened the door with some trepidation, hoping there would be no one about. I felt utterly ashamed of myself, as if I had been caught in an act of appalling dishonesty. I didn't want to have to explain my state of mind to anyone and rather imagined that any employees would be somewhat afraid to speak to me. I particularly dreaded meeting any of the directors but, this being a Saturday morning, the prospect was unlikely. Fortunately the place was deserted.

My office was at the end of the corridor to the right of the main entrance. No sounds emanated from any of the other offices. Cautiously I approached and entered. Everything was as I had left it four days ago except for one thing. There was a large pile of cardboard boxes in the middle of the floor.

"Clear your desk by the weekend. We have to move on from this," I had been told. Well, I had decided that I would do much more than this. For some reason I felt I must remove all my files. If I could keep nothing else from my 35 years in the company, at least I could take these papers. They contained so much information on what I had achieved over those years. If I took them now, before anybody else had time to think, I could avoid the unpleasant and difficult task of trying to get them later. With this in mind, I had earlier asked my secretary to get a large quantity of cardboard boxes delivered to my office. Also I couldn't bear the idea of anybody else using my office furniture so I had told the other directors that I would take that too.

For a moment I couldn't bring myself to start emptying the filing cabinets and putting the contents into these boxes. Instead I simply sat in my office chair, thoughts of the past flooding into my mind along with a dread about the uncertainty of my future.

Suddenly I could hear machinery running on the floor above me. I realised there must have been some overtime work going on that Saturday morning. It was in the chocolate department, a very long room so suitable for the making of chocolates. This room, with its enrobing machine, was the main reason my father and my uncle Stanley had bought the building in the first place. I instantly recalled the equipment in great detail because much of it I had put together with assistance from our excellent Works Engineer, Colin Bridges, who had been given sole responsibility for the factory machinery for much of the time. We had started with old broken-down machines. We repaired them, rebuilt them, added to and adapted them to manufacture our unique *Continental Assortment* which had become a national best seller. Although it was some years since I had had the pleasure and the privilege of being Production Director, I realised I would know personally many of the people who might be working there that morning.

I stood and went to the window to look out into the factory yard. I always thought it must have been difficult in the 19th century to construct buildings with a wide open space on each floor. Instead, two parallel buildings would be built with a linking shorter building across the ends, giving rise to an enclosed yard between. There was no one to be seen that Saturday morning but I could imagine all the people I had observed milling about in that yard in the past. There would be figures standing about, chatting and smoking during the tea and lunch breaks. I could picture the new starters, just 15 years old, who would be at their playground games as if they were still at school.

"Fall-in, a bottle of gin, fall-out, a bottle of stout," they would sing.

Old Will Thompson, he of the broad Geordie accent and bowed legs, was the first manager of the place. For his office he used a little lean-to building opposite mine. It was there I would eat my sandwiches when taking a break from working as a sugar-boiler. I was in my early 20s and there were probably no more than fifteen people employed in the factory at that time. Mostly, Will stayed in his office rather than on the shop floor because he didn't find it easy to control the workforce, but he was a very kind man and he really knew how to make boiled sweets.

I returned to my seat, filled with a sense of foreboding. How was I going to cope now? What could I possibly do to restore the way that I, Peter Thornton, had felt about my life until just a few days ago? I had reached the age of 54 and had always considered myself to be very successful. My life had been totally dedicated to the Thornton family business. I identified so completely with the company that my own identity and self-respect was entirely dependent on it. Of course, there had been many activities outside the business but these were relatively unimportant. I had no overwhelming hobby to turn to. I had no yearning to go travelling round the world on a lengthy sabbatical. I simply wanted to work, to continue the activity that had given me so much personal satisfaction and a sense of achievement, with the opportunity to learn and develop, to work with good people and to help them to achieve their own goals.

I felt I had been greatly respected in the business world. Thorntons was overwhelmingly respected as a company. It seemed to have everything: a wonderful product, excellent manufacturing facilities, a unique chain of shops, a secure brand name and excellent profitability. What more was needed? I was tremendously proud of all this and of my part in it. Wherever I went the company was admired and, by association, I, too, felt admired. I had been invited to become President of the Confectioners Benevolent Fund and had got a great deal of personal kudos from this. My speeches at seminars and on training courses had received standing ovations.

'Thorntons' was me and I was 'Thorntons'.

It had been so when I was a young boy. That was how I had been regarded at school and I had been brought up to play that role. My father had raised me in the ways of the company from an early age. It was as if I was an extension of *his* life, he being the person who had effectively created the company together with *his* father, and who had developed the perfect business strategy along with his brother. It was bred into me just as with royalty. One couldn't imagine a member of the British Royal Family being suddenly removed and forced to assume the role of an ordinary citizen! So how then was I expected simply to give it all up, and for what?

And then what of the other people in the company? What would they think about me and about what had happened? I felt I had always been very popular within the company due, I suppose, to the fact that I always had a great respect for our employees individually and collectively and had done a great deal to improve their working conditions, representation and rewards. I had spent a lot of time talking to them, encouraging their ideas and involvement. I visited every single shop we owned and had met most of the people who worked in them.

It was painfully clear to me that our employees now would not feel able to speak to me openly. The few people I had seen on that fateful day had mostly turned away, looking sad and saying nothing. However, Doreen, my wonderful and loyal secretary, was completely open and absolutely distraught. She immediately tendered her own resignation. "Mr Peter," she said, "everybody is shocked beyond belief about this. You are the best of the lot and nobody can understand what has happened. They think that if this has happened to you then it can certainly happen to any of them."

But, I wondered, what do they *really* think? This action was so extraordinary that people must surely imagine I have been defrauding the company or perhaps I have committed some other dreadful act. Although nothing could be further from the truth I still felt that I was now regarded as some pariah, almost *persona non grata*. There was no leaving party, no presentation for my 35 years of loyal service and no entry in the company magazine *Sweet Talk*. I never got the chance for a formal talk to any of the workforce although, by chance, I did occasionally meet ex-Thornton employees in the years afterwards.

And then there was my own immediate family? How could I explain this to my children? It was an impossible situation. I didn't really understand why it had happened. Was there really some underlying reason that had not been conveyed to me? Had 'they' secretly thought my performance so appalling that I had to go? What was I to say? If those dealing with me had been anything other than family directors I could have claimed they had their own 'political' reasons for acting as they did and that it was nothing to do with my performance or behaviour.

But these were my close relatives who had acted so hurtfully. No specific reason was given so how could I brush this aside to my children? They had had the greatest respect for my business achievements because of what they could see and because of what I had told them. Now they would think it had all been untrue, or worse, that their wider family was ungrateful and despicable?

And who knows what the commercial business world would think? In such cynical times they would surely conclude that it had all been a front. My public reputation would be instantly ruined and I would be seen as an absolute failure after all. There would be no way anyone else would give me a job. "What?" they would ask. "Fired from the family business? He must be useless!"

And finally I thought of my friends? They, too, would conclude that to be removed by my fellow directors from a company that was clearly doing very well, I must indeed be a worthless and disreputable ruffian of the worst kind. There we go - my reputation, identity and status destroyed in an instant.

So where did this leave me? Shattered and utterly broken, I needed either to re-create myself, to rise Phoenix-like from the ashes of this personal catastrophe or else disappear into oblivion. The latter was an option I simply could not bear. But if I was to forge a new identity for myself what form would it take? At this stage I had no idea and could barely think. I would have to start from scratch and rebuild myself and put the good name of Thorntons behind me. Not for me the comfort of the successful retired Chairman with a big retirement party, presentations and speeches, a lifelong welcome at the company's premises, and maybe continuing involvement as a part-time adviser or non-executive director. No, there was nothing. I was wiped from the company's history book as if I had never existed. At the age of 54, I had to start my professional life all over.

I jumped up from my seat as if waking from a dream. I must get on with this task. Filling the car with boxes of files, I returned to my house and dumped them in the spare bedroom. I then drove back to Belper for a second load. There were now more people about.

Dave Goodwin, one of our great team of HGV drivers, came into my office. A few years ago I had reorganised the Transport Department and the results had been very successful. As a result there was a strong feeling of mutual respect between me and the drivers. They must have seen me on my first trip and, being the sort of gutsy people they are, decided to see if they could help.

"Ay up, Mr Peter, what's going on?" asked Dave. "All the drivers are amazed and very upset. We don't understand how you can be leaving?"

"Neither do I, Dave," I replied. "Neither do I."

"Is there anything we can do to help?"

I thought for a moment. "You could help me carry these boxes out to my car," I suggested, "and the directors have told me that I can take my office furniture so perhaps you could bring it over to my new office in Ashbourne sometime next week." I had discovered a small vacant office situated over the top of a DIY shop on the main shopping street of the nearby market town and had already arranged to rent it.

Despite his short build, Dave was a very fit chap with broad shoulders and immense strength. A few years earlier I had argued that it no longer made sense to make shop deliveries during the day. The shops were too busy and the roads were becoming impossible. It seemed logical to change the working hours and after much argument, deliberation and some extra money, the drivers agreed! They usually started at about 2.00 a.m. on their first deliveries and were well on the way home before the morning congestion started. I accompanied some of them on these delivery trips when we first adopted this routine so I knew what it was like. Not only did the drivers have to get to the right destination but they had to unload their trucks into the shop as well. We were still quite old-fashioned and the drivers always went with a mate to help with the heavy task of unloading each parcel. No wonder they developed enormous muscles and were generally extremely fit!

I had always marvelled at the weights these drivers could carry through the most awkward shop entries. We used to send trays of chocolates in large crates, so-called because they had originally been made of wood. These crates weighed about 30 lbs (about 13.5 kg) each. It was all I could do just to carry a single crate but Dave and many of his colleagues could carry two, one on top of the other. Because he was quite short, he could never see over the top and had to look round the sides! Not surprisingly he made very quick work of carrying my boxes of files out to the car.

On my third session, Eddie Duffy, the transport foreman, was there waiting to speak to me. Eddie and I had had many battles in the past. Originally he had been one of the drivers who was opposed to almost anything I had tried to do. Eventually he did something which had really infuriated me. I had been so cross with him that I had failed to see that it was actually my fault and I had decided to give him an 'official warning'. Later, this ruined my evening because I realised that I had made a mistake. The next day I had calmed down and I called him in to see me.

"Eddie, the warning is withdrawn. You were right and I was wrong."

Thereafter I began to see the real value of this man. He was a Scotsman with a broad accent. Like many Glaswegians he could be quite aggressive but his heart was quite definitely in the right place. He knew everything about all the drivers and he was a very intelligent man. I decided to make him foreman and he was extremely successful at it.

"How's it goin'?" he asked with what looked suspiciously like tears in his eyes.

"Bloody awful!" I replied, "I'm on my way."

He promised to load up my furniture in one of the Transit vans and bring it over to my new office. I arranged to meet him in the company car park on the following Wednesday to go first to my house with a few more items and then on to Ashbourne.

On this third trip, I noticed that Peter Heaps was standing just inside his office next to the reception. Peter had become the Operations Executive of the company and was a person whom I really admired. We looked at each other and I could see in his face that he was very distressed but at the same time did not dare say anything. One look was sufficient to convey what we were both feeling without the need of words.

After these three trips my spare bedroom was completely filled and I had completed the task. I sat down in my kitchen and looked out of the window at the beautiful view across the valley to the hills beyond. This was a bad time and, to make matters worse, my marriage seemed to be steadily disintegrating. Jo, my second wife, and I had become increasingly antagonistic and, in our few years together, we had found it harder to relate to each other. Had our relationship been better we might have said, "Okay, let's make the best of this. At last we now have time together." Sadly that was the last thing that I wanted to do.

Jo made an effort to calm me in my traumatised condition. As we sat at the kitchen table that Saturday lunchtime she came up with an idea. "You are in such a terrible state I think we should get away for the night. Then you can at least try to stop thinking about it all the time."

I agreed. "Yes, thanks for the suggestion. Let's go somewhere."

We decided to go to the Peacock Hotel at Rowsley. Jo telephoned and managed to book a room for the night and a table for dinner. Rowsley is a delightful village situated close to the Estate where the renowned Chatsworth House, seat of the Duke of Devonshire, has stood for centuries. The Peacock is a beautiful old coaching inn, standing beside a bridge over the Derwent and has long been a favourite ever since my parents used to take me there for "a run out into the country" and afternoon tea just after the war when petrol had at last "come off the ration". There is a sign chiselled into the old granite headstone over the door which says 'Johnste Venson'. It was not until much later that I realised this must have been the name of the landlord at some time and the stonemason had clearly not had width enough to get his name more legibly into the available space. There was a wonderful old head waiter there for many years called Larry. He had a really serious limp which seemed to get worse as he got older but he kept going. The food was always the best old-fashioned English fare.

I had been to this hotel on many occasions since those first trips as a boy, then with my first girlfriend when I dared to ask her out for a meal and spent far too long deciding whether I could afford wine, later to family reunions, to company celebrations, wedding receptions and to many other events. Nothing had ever been as sad as this occasion on this evening. We had a beautiful meal and a beautiful room, right on the front corner of the hotel, but I could not sleep. Everything, not least my own mind in turmoil, kept me awake. By the next morning I felt completely depressed and exhausted. I sat on the edge of the bed and did something I had not done for a very long time. I wept.

Chapter 1
Back to the Beginning

Thorntons is not just a family enterprise. It is a public company with both retail and manufacturing businesses, as it always was. It has grown to include 379 of its own shops and cafes with a further 250 franchises and a turnover of £208 million. Today there is Internet trading, mail order and substantial sales to other retailers. The name is still a very strong and widely respected brand, famous for its high quality *Continental Chocolates*, *Easter Eggs* and much more. Thorntons still has a great future. So how did it all start?

I learned the history of the business from my father, Norman, after he woke from his regular lunchtime naps. We would sit before the gently hissing gas fire in our comfortable sitting-room at Greenways in suburban Sheffield. We also made visits to our shops throughout the region, not just nearby Chesterfield and Rotherham but further to Manchester, Leeds and Leicester. Thus, from an early age, my understanding of the business grew and my future was assured. These memories, together with a few family papers, have helped me piece together the whole story.

"Our family came over with William the Conqueror. That is why I was named William Norman." This was my father's grand statement, based on no evidence whatsoever, but the claim to Norman ancestry has been passed down through the generations. What we know for certain is that the Thorntons lived in Leeds for many years under various occupations from shopkeeper to innkeeper until eventually Joseph Thornton, born 1832, moved south to become a railway storekeeper in Sheffield. In 1868 he married Ann Gibbins at Pitsmoor, and two years later my grandfather, Joseph William Thornton, was born. Young Joseph grew up to become "a commercial traveller (or 'book-keeper' according to some records) with the Don Confectionery Company" and opened his first shop in 1911 on the corner of Norfolk Street and Howard Street in Sheffield. At that time the family was living in rented property in the nearby Derbyshire village of Hathersage.

Joseph William was the true founder of the company. He had the vision to believe that a high-class confectionery shop could do well in the city centre. It proved to be profitable from Day One. He obviously was more than just a salesman and understood the manufacturing side of the business well enough to teach my own father how to make confectionery. His acumen was such that he soon opened a second shop in another successful location, this time with room for in-store production and accommodation for his family. This may have seemed a risky enterprise at the time but he was a true entrepreneur with a definite goal in mind. He wanted to establish a commercially viable manufacturing and retailing confectionery business. There were few precedents and none of the spreadsheets or business plans required of the modern businessman.

Sheffield at the time was a boom city, famous for its steel and silver plate. The cutlery capital of the world had grown as a result of the water power from its many rivers and from the iron ore, grit stone and coal in the outlying regions. The valley of the River Don to the north-east had hundreds of iron and steel mills, such as Vickers and Firth Brown, belching out smoke and heat, working night and day so that the noise could be heard even in the smart residential areas to the south of the city. From the surrounding hills it was possible to observe the permanent pall of black smoke covering the city from the blast furnace chimneys and the tenement workers' coal fires, and the elegant city centre buildings were soon covered in the black grime of soot settling from the atmosphere.

By 1911 Sheffield's population had reached 400,000 but, in the days before Trades Unions, the Labour Party or the welfare state, many people lived on survival wages in dreary back-to-back terraces while the few who had had the opportunity to create and own successful businesses could lead the grander life in the leafy suburbs of Nether Edge, Fulwood, Ranmoor and Broomhill. Nevertheless, most workers still took a pride in their work and shared their company's goals and interests. Many wore uniform clothing, usually made up of trousers hitched to the knee, a cloth cap and a white neckerchief. Passers-by could look through the wide open doors of the factories, feel the searing heat of the furnaces and see the small shapes of the workers standing dangerously close or, in the smaller production shops, they could observe grinders, sitting hour after hour legs apart, straddling the wheels and manually sharpening knife blades on large grinding stones. There was always great danger from the stones themselves, the fast-moving flat belts and pulleys or the flying sparks from the wheels. In those days it was "work or perish" but companies such as Mappin and Webb were so successful with their hand-engraved Sheffield Plate that most workers felt secure in their employment.

Against this industrial background you would think my grandfather was taking a huge gamble in starting a confectionery business, particularly in investing so much of his own money. He prudently retained his job as a commercial traveller until 1913 to guarantee himself an income but, more importantly, he had assessed the needs of a community thriving on its new-found wealth where people would be looking for quality goods on which to spend their money. He correctly reckoned that high class confectionery would definitely be on the list.

Everywhere, the city displayed its new prosperity. A traveller from out of town would be dazzled by the riot of colour at the annual Sheffield Fair, swept up by the noise and mingling crowds of the shoppers at Smithfield Market or tempted by the proliferation of goods on the High Street. He or she could take one of those new electric trams or walk the gentle slope, passing the Rag 'n' Tag market on one side and the elegant Walsh's department store on the other, up to Cole's Corner. The Cole brothers, John and Thomas, had established their silk and hosiery business in 1847 and their beautiful Victorian store had become a popular meeting-place for thousands of Sheffielders over the years. Here the smart set would parade: parasolled ladies in tight corsets and hair piled high under large wide-brimmed hat, the gentlemen in high-collared jackets and bowler hats. The working people would wear their finest clothes too, suits and waistcoats with perhaps a gold watch chain on display in imitation of their richer neighbours. At night the streets were gas-lit and the shop displays would be illuminated by bright electric arc lamps. Omnibuses and horse-drawn carriages were being outnumbered by the newest vehicles rolling off the assembly lines of the Ford Motor Company, just opened in Manchester's Trafford Park. British cars from Morris and Austin were competing for a share of this new road traffic, despite the difficulty for motorists of negotiating a safe drive between the tram tracks.

Our traveler might then pass along Fargate with its small businesses and local grocery chains and be tempted by the rich aroma of roasting coffee from the machine in the window of Field's, the tea and coffee merchants. After the large Yorkshire Penny Bank building and newspaper offices, he or she would come to the imposing Town Hall, built in 1890 at the top of Pinstone Street, with the Church of St Paul beyond it. Around this central area were the many music halls and theatres providing the only type of mass entertainment then available.

Our visitor could move on to Moorhead, known now simply as The Moor. This was the main shopping area, filled with small traders of every description catering to the needs of the local citizenry. It was a street of great character and colour, full of busy people matching the style and attractiveness of the various shops. The tram tracks ran down the middle of the road and the power cables were suspended over them, crackling and sparking as the electricity was collected by the trolley heads. The street was narrow and the shops stayed open till 9.30 in the evening and even 10 o'clock or later on Saturday night.

This was the milieu into which my grandfather launched his business, the Chocolate Kabin, on Norfolk Street running parallel to Pinstone Street and The Moor. It was just behind St Paul's Church on the corner with Howard Street which itself led directly to the Midland Railway Station. Next door was the showroom of silversmiths Mappin & Webb and this, combined with the passing rail travellers, guaranteed a certain number of interested parties, essential to the success of the new business. There were not many sweet shops in Sheffield at that time, nor was the confectionery industry particularly well developed. Joseph realised that the city's growing population of affluent business and professional classes, together with a large working class who might be persuaded occasionally to provide treats for their family, would welcome a sweet shop of high quality. It was his intention to offer the nicest sweet shop in Sheffield.

The walls were covered in fashionable cream anaglypta wallpaper. There was a beautifully shaped glass case from which *Kunzle cakes* were served individually with tongs. These were small chocolate covered cakes manufactured by the Birmingham firm of Mr Christian Kunzle, a Swiss chef who had originally worked at the House of Commons in London. Trays of Mackintosh's *Toffee Deluxe* were broken into pieces by assistants using toffee hammers and pincers and put into waxed bags on the brass weighing scales. Mr John Mackintosh had invented his famous toffee in Halifax in 1891 while running a pastry shop in Calderdale in Yorkshire. Toffee had been around before then but certainly his version made it more popular. Like fudge, it was made by boiling a sugar and glucose solution, then adding condensed milk to caramelise the mixture. After adding a little butter, it was poured into tin trays and, just before consumption, would need to be broken in the shop into small manageable pieces for customers. Behind the counter there were mirrors from floor to ceiling, giving the shop a classy air and making it seem much bigger than it actually was, with glass shelves for the knock-stoppered jars of caramels and boiled sweets. Other now-unfamiliar products included *Cachous*, *Violet Cachous*, *Sweet-Lips*, *Phul-Nanas* and the descriptively-named *Curiously Strong Mints*.

Joseph couldn't afford to give up his job at the Don Confectionery Company at the time, so he decided to take his son Norman out of Abbeydale Secondary School when still only 14 to become manager of the shop when it opened in October 1911. The other members of staff were two young ladies "of a very superior type" who doubtless gave the shop the necessary atmosphere of quality that Joseph sought. There must have been great relief in the family when the shop opened successfully, taking £20 a week which my father told me was "quite a lot of money… in those days". It was successful enough to persuade Joseph in 1913 finally to leave his job and risk opening another shop.

He couldn't afford the higher costs of the more upmarket Fargate near Cole's Corner but decided that a shop on The Moor would be the next best place because the rents would be lower and there were considerably more passers-by. It also had the added advantage of extra space. The new shop had the same décor as the first, and it was here in the basement that Joseph began some simple manufacturing of his own products, using techniques he had learned in his former employment. He would demonstrate to Norman how to make simple boiled sweets such as Fish Mixtures and Mint Rock. The boiling of the sugar was done in a copper pan over a gas fire and the shaping of the sweets carried out with hand rollers. No thermometers were available, so the hardness of the solution had to be tested by dipping fingers into cold water and then putting them immediately into the boiling syrup, a procedure which occasionally caused severe burns. In a back room on the ground floor of the shop there was sufficient space to start manufacturing chocolates. The chocolate was melted in a *bain Marie* and the centres were made in the basement on a marble slab, then flavoured with Otto of Violet or Essence of Rose and cut into oblongs before being dipped into the chocolate and left to set on wax paper.

The family left the rented house in Hathersage and moved into rooms above the shop, thus efficiently combining retailing, manufacture and accommodation under one roof. There were four children now in the family: Constance, born in 1898 two years after Norman, Frank who was born in 1900 and Stanley born in 1903. When Stanley was 11 years old he obtained a scholarship to the Sheffield Central Secondary School where he stayed until he was 18. The school had a very high reputation and it was a measure of Stanley's ability that he gained a place there. He obtained a further scholarship to Sheffield University to study Chemistry and Physics but this did not provide him with sufficient income to be financially independent and he was under pressure to relinquish his university place and join his brother Norman in the business. Helpfully, the University allowed him to attend on some evenings and on Saturday mornings to study food technology and this later became a very valuable asset to the business, but back when he was a small boy things were very different. Life must have been extremely difficult in the family's cramped quarters particularly as Constance was now starting to show the first signs of the illness that led to her later incarceration in a 'mental establishment'.

It was no time for the family to put up with more difficulties but it was the beginning of a time of great suffering for all because the year 1914 marked the start of The Great War. My father, to his everlasting guilt, didn't join the Armed Forces even though he volunteered for the Royal Flying Corps. He was rejected on account of his poor eyesight. For the family this was extremely fortunate because he soon became the only competent wage earner, supporting everybody until 1921. The economic growth in Sheffield continued as steel was in even greater demand for armour, shells and shipbuilding, but alas, sweets, chocolates and raw materials were in very short supply. For the family business there was plenty of demand but it was difficult to satisfy.

Grandfather Joseph became ill in 1917 and eventually died in 1919. Norman, just 21 years old, took over the business along with the care of his ailing mother and his three siblings including the disabled Constance. Sadly, despite Joseph's importance in founding the firm of Thorntons, he subsequently became a forgotten figure, largely because of the shame and ignorance surrounding his illness. It remained a matter of great family disgrace to acknowledge that he had become syphilitic. Today he would have received a discreet course of anti-biotics and no one need be any the wiser, but back then he was sentenced to a lingering decline in disgrace and isolation, spending his final two years in a nursing home in Newton-le-Willows.

Norman was desperately ashamed of his father and would only mention in whispered tones: "He died of that dreadful sexual disease, you know." Joseph's illness greatly affected the whole family. It could have been contracted at any time in the twenty to thirty years before his death. He may even have had it at the time of his marriage and it was thought it might even be a cause of Constance's mental illness. Whether the family visited him in his final years or stayed away through the shame and horror of it all, there is no doubt the stress of the situation made life increasingly difficult for them all.

By 1919 the family had become exhausted with living over the shop at No. 107 The Moor. The constant rattle of tram cars outside the window seven days a week until midnight and the cramped conditions had all become too much. Norman felt he could now afford to buy a house and No. 68 Southgrove Road was in a respectable residential area and not too far from the company's shops. In spite of the poor trading, and given his anxiety and constant fear of bankruptcy, this was a bold move. Maybe after the death of Joseph they all desperately needed a change and a new environment, and this large newly-built house with its four bedrooms and lovely garden became the family home from which all the brothers later were married and where their mother, Kate, lived with their sister Constance until her death in 1938.

Norman worked very hard during the war trying to consolidate trade in the two shops. Conditions meant it was impossible to increase the turnover from confectionery alone so he decided to try his hand as a fruiterer. In 1920 he bought an existing fruit business, also situated on the Moor, and then opened another shop in 1923. Sales were about five times those of the sweet shops but the profit margin was much lower. It created a lot of extra work because he had to go to the fruit and vegetable market at Smithfield early every morning and bring the produce back in his father's handcart. Eventually he employed two young lads to work part-time in these shops. The first, Arthur, stayed on for quite some time and features in the company's early history. The other, Leslie Charlesworth, also played a significant part over the next 60 years. These two helped to transport the produce but there was a terrible amount of waste as, with no refrigeration, everything had to be sold on the day or else thrown away.

I never learned much about my father's other brother, Frank. He, like Constance, became one of those family secrets that my father didn't wish to talk about or the world to know about. All I know is that Frank worked in the factory for a time, didn't settle to it, was asked to leave and was given a lump sum and a life pension. This all happened before younger brother Stanley joined, leaving the way clear for the pair to work in partnership. Perhaps Norman felt that 'three would be a crowd'? It is a measure of the trust that Norman had in Stanley that in 1921 they formed a limited company called J.W. Thornton Ltd with themselves as the two shareholders. Here were two good partners working together, establishing a secure prospect for the future growth of the family business.

What sort of image did these two businessmen present to the world? My father was an upright young man of medium height with a deep broad forehead topped with a mass of dark brown hair. His protruding lips rather detracted from his pleasant but sober-looking face and his horn-rimmed glasses gave him an even more serious look. Throughout his life he was very shy and introverted. My uncle Stanley was a few inches taller, much better looking with slightly lighter hair always smoothed back with hair cream. Both brothers dressed very well in the stylish manner of the time and preferred handmade tweed suits with waistcoats and smart, almost flamboyant ties held in position by a gold tie chain.

Stanley's personality was the exact opposite of my father's. He was outgoing, warm and friendly. It would have been easy for Norman to feel some resentment towards his younger brother. After all, he'd had to leave his secondary school very early, his education incomplete, to help his father to start the new business. His brother had managed to get a scholarship to the best secondary school in the city and had completed his schooling. It seemed Stanley must be the favoured son. It is little wonder that there was some impatience, frequently anger, between them as each possibly envied the other's qualities. On the other hand, the difference in their age and personality meant that Norman had already established the business and was head of the family, leaving Stanley feeling somewhat inferior to and intimidated by his elder brother. Just before Stanley joined the business in 1921, Norman had purchased a 'Model T' Ford van but Stanley immediately, and rather grandly, became its driver and mechanic. He was also appointed to the high-sounding position of 'assistant fruit buyer' and it then became his job to go and buy the fruit and bring it to the shops in his van.

After the Great War the country's economy went into a sharp decline. The workforce had been swollen by a corps of returning soldiers yet the demand for armaments had dramatically decreased. The result for Sheffield was high unemployment and low wages. Finally in 1923 local conditions started to improve and the Thornton brothers decided to open two more shops. The first of these was on London Road just where it joined the end of The Moor, and the second was at nearby 194 Rockingham Street, both being very busy locations. This doubling of outlets meant a doubling of stock for which the new London Road shop had production space. All chocolate and Easter egg manufacture was transferred there with only the production of sweets continuing in the cramped basement at The Moor.

They had not been at London Road very long when they were told that the property had been put up for sale and they would lose their tenancy unless they could purchase it themselves. This included not only their premises at Nos. 1 and 3 but also four other shops and four houses. The asking price was £5,000 but the brothers took a chance and were offered what seems like a very good business deal. They paid £250 there and then with an agreement to pay a further £250 in March each subsequent year. Understandably, this then put great pressure on the business to increase earnings in the early part of the year and the selling of Easter eggs became the obvious solution. They were desperate to do whatever they could to keep the new premises because they now had an excellent shop. Their manufacturing facilities were well established and, despite thinking of themselves as 'young and ignorant', they knew they would have to meet this challenge.

Writing people's names on Easter eggs doesn't seem to have been a particularly original idea but it did prove to be a very successful one right from the start. Orders for named eggs were taken daily and the brothers would then hand-write these in the evenings, often working till midnight to ensure delivery to the various shops the next morning. Unfortunately, the decorated eggs sometimes went to the wrong shops, causing much confusion for staff and customers alike. Stanley suggested that the solution was simply to write the names on the eggs while the customers waited. This idea worked well enough until the egg was then placed into the customer's paper bag whereupon the writing would often be smudged into an illegible mess. Norman came up with the answer – rather obvious to us – that the finished product should be supplied in a rigid box. The extra cost could be added to the price of the egg. They correctly reckoned that customers would pay this, a mere 4½ old pence for egg and box, to preserve their unique confectionery, at least until they ate it.

Norman was good at promotion and advertising. He put up a huge illuminated sign, three metres square and visible to everyone coming down The Moor, offering 'ANY NAME WRITTEN FREE ON

EASTER EGGS'. This had a considerable effect. He was extremely keen on window display and once made a huge chocolate hen, covered with icing, with eggs moving along a platform to a little chocolate house and then coming out the other side as woolly chicks. These imaginative efforts produced the desired boost to their Easter sales and they were easily able to find the £250 that they needed every Easter.

The mechanically-minded Stanley started buying small-scale production machines from bankrupt auction sales and would restore and maintain them himself. As the company mechanic, he was faced one weekend with the job of repairing the broken back axle of the 'Model T' Ford van, not a job often undertaken by a contemporary motorist but a commonplace occurrence back then. He jacked up the vehicle, dismantled the axle including the differential, fitted the new axle and put the whole unit back into position. However, when he put the clutch into first gear for a test drive, the van went backwards. He had replaced the differential the wrong way round and had to start the job all over again.

In 1924, a once-in-a-lifetime opportunity arose when, out of the blue, Norman received a telephone call from a local Belgian chef inviting him on an expenses-paid trip to Belgium and Holland to learn how to improve his chocolate making. Norman jumped at the chance and visited a number of small continental family firms where, as traditional *pâtissiers*, they made cakes and chocolates in the back of the shop. He learned a great deal about continental methods of production and their range of products, and was able for the first time to arrange the purchase of high quality Dutch chocolate.

The economy had been gradually improving until, in the 1924 Budget, the Chancellor of the Exchequer in Stanley Baldwin's Conservative government, the recently-appointed Winston Churchill, announced his decision to return Britain to the so-called Gold Standard whereby the exchange rate of the pound was linked to the value of gold. This led to deflation, increased unemployment and industrial unrest, first among miners and then to the General Strike of 1926. The private owners of the coal mines, finding they could only sell their coal at a reduced price, attempted to pass on their losses to their employees in the form of reduced wages. The miners were having none of it. However, despite the spread of industrial action to other groups of workers, the public as a whole didn't fully support the strike and turned their hands to all sorts of labour to keep the country going.

Around this time Thorntons were still selling Mackintosh's *Deluxe Toffee* but with only modest sales. The two brothers felt they could make something better than this and at a greater profit. Stanley started to experiment, first at home in the kitchen and then in the basement of the shop on The Moor, using his university experience to produce a home-made toffee that everybody seemed to like. They sold it for the relatively high price of 6d (2½ p) a quarter – a quarter pound being roughly the equivalent of 114g. It became so popular that it soon made up half of the total sales of the business and remained the company's pre-eminent product for the next 50 years. It was sold at that same price for 15 years, indicating the negligible inflation in the national economy until the outbreak of the Second World War. This product was the engine that drove the business for many years, and in many people's minds the words 'Thorntons' and 'toffee' became synonymous.

How the toffee was sold soon became a matter of critical importance. Stanley had developed a top quality product with little thought for its saleable shelf life. This was of little concern when the toffee was sold on the day of manufacture but Norman found that, once exposed to the air, the broken toffee would absorb moisture, become sticky and would start to congeal into a solid lump once more. It became prudent to leave the toffee unbroken in its tray until required and this actually worked better as a selling format. The appearance of this beautiful mouth-watering confection in the shop window, together with newly-broken pieces on display behind the counter, suggested freshness and a wholesomeness that customers rightly assumed was the result of the product being made in the back of the shop.

Sales rocketed, even during this difficult period of the 1920s, and an even better Special Toffee was introduced along with an increasing variety of chocolates. Vigorous promotions, such as the 'Saturday Specials', a precursor to the 'Buy One Get One Free' offers of today, ensured that customers were reminded of the excellence of the brand. A further two shops opened in 1926, the year of the General Strike, one in neighbouring Rotherham and the other on Union Street. The Rotherham shop was the first outside of Sheffield and was a great success but the one on Union

Street was less so and became the company's first shop to be considered a failure. It closed within a year.

In the same year Stanley had a little adventure with the Ford van. The basic chocolate was now being imported from Holland through the docks at Hull but, with the dockers now on strike, there was no one to deliver it to the company. Stanley, in urgent need of this basic ingredient, was not going to let a little problem like that halt the company's activities and decided he would fetch the stuff himself. In those days, having no bridge across the River Ouse on the northern side of the River Humber, vehicles would either use the river ferry or go the long way round to the west of the river.

Things did not bode well from the beginning. The weather was dreadful. The van suffered a puncture so the spare wheel had to be fitted. Then there was a second puncture. Now Stanley had to remove the tyre from the wheel hub, somehow mend the inner tube, replace it and inflate it with a foot pump, all in the pouring rain. On reaching the river, he found that the ferry had sunk in the appalling conditions and there was only a much smaller boat available, usually used for small cars and foot passengers. The ferryman was willing to take the risk of transporting the Ford van if Stanley was, and amazingly this tiny boat got them both safely to the other side. He eventually reached the docks and, after some persuasion, the dockers allowed him to load the chocolate onto his van.

But, as many a Yorkshireman will tell you, "it never rains but what it pours". Stanley didn't want to risk the small ferry a second time so he reluctantly had to face a much longer journey back to Sheffield. No motorways, by-passes or dual carriageways, just lots of small roads up and down hills. The overloaded 'Model T' struggled to climb these gradients and, in some places, Stanley actually had to drive uphill backwards as the reverse gear had a lower ratio and could just about cope. Naturally, all this put a great strain on the engine; the radiator boiled over several times and was repeatedly refilled with cold water from horse troughs. Few people enjoying this chocolate at a later date would have had the faintest idea of the effort undertaken to procure it. Such were the perils and pitfalls confronting the confectioner of the 1920s.

Despite such determination, the brothers found their sales steadily falling between 1922 and 1927 by as much as 50%. Further effort was required to survive. Stanley continued the process of mechanisation of the two small factories, very much helped by Leslie Charlesworth. Of crucial importance in the production of the *Special Toffee* was the design of the boiling pan to prevent the mixture from burning and there was much trial-and-error and a lot of improvisation. However, necessity remains the mother of invention and there was continuing improvement in both products and their manufacture. In 1927 a small factory on Penistone Road was rented for £35 a year to cope with increasing production. This was independent of the shops and much of the London Road manufacturing was transferred to it. The company was now trying its hand at ice cream along with the traditional boiled sweets, toffee and chocolates. Mechanisation continued and a small chocolate 'enrober' was installed upstairs for covering the chocolates automatically.

The brothers now had to split their responsibilities: Norman managed the shops and did all the administration, Stanley oversaw all the manufacturing. They still took important decisions together following what were described by Stanley as "heated but friendly arguments". Later I was to observe these arguments as heated and *un*friendly. They had a simple procedure for selecting new shops. Norman would hear about an available property when travelling around or perhaps would be contacted by an estate agent. If it was felt to be suitable, Stanley would go to check it, usually on a Saturday afternoon, their busiest day. They would compare impressions and make a decision. This arrangement worked four out of five times, Stanley said. As it was then a buyer's market they could always get short leases with a three-year break clause. A successful format had been established and in 1928 a new shop was opened in Castle Street followed in 1930 by shops in Leopold Street and in Spital Hill, all in Sheffield. The latter soon closed, but a very successful shop appeared in 1931 in the heart of the city at Fitzalan Square.

By 1931 the tiny factory on Penistone road was already too small so production moved to a larger and cleaner factory on Stalker Lees Road in the less industrialised south of the city, allowing for a further increase in production, range and mechanisation. By the early 1930s Thorntons were aware that their successful formula could be expanded over the North of England and maybe even to Scotland. They remained unsure of the South, believing that the consumption of confectionery was linked to average ambient temperature. Their theory, partly correct, was that in cooler regions people needed more sugar, less so in warmer climates. They concluded, somewhat erroneously, that consumption of confectionery was likely to be less in the South. With true Northern pride they saw their products as part of the culture of the region and were not convinced that effete Southerners would ever want to buy a product such as *Thorntons Special Toffee* from Sheffield. The Scots, on the other hand, were known to have a very sweet tooth and perhaps would buy even more than the Sassenachs. It goes without saying that their assumptions about Southerners proved to be completely unfounded.

Mindful of the dictum not to run before you can walk, the brothers felt it would be wise to expand first into adjacent towns rather than some far-flung corner of the Kingdom. A shop in Manchester, just an hour's train ride from Sheffield, was easier to supervise than one, say, in Glasgow. Delivery costs rather than brand reputation were foremost in their thinking. No one in Manchester would have any idea who 'Thorntons' were but the excellence of the product, along with the quality of service and presentation within the new shop, would soon establish the popularity of the brand. Of course, much later Thorntons' reputation *was* able to precede it into new markets and a customer base would already be present, just waiting for their new shop to open. Mancunians got their first taste of Thorntons' products in 1932 with a shop on Oxford Street, only the second branch to open outside Sheffield. It was followed by a shop at 37a Boar Lane in Leeds, appropriately the area in which the family had lived for centuries. The Thorntons had come home.

As quaint as it seems today, the strong social belief at that time was that you shouldn't take a wife unless you could afford to keep her. Now their increasing prosperity induced Norman and Stanley to take unto themselves a marital partner. So it was that in 1932 Stanley married Netta Jamieson, but my father Norman beat him to the altar by three years when he married my mother, Muriel Illingworth. In this way the Thornton 'family' started to extend.

Britain in the 1930s was once again engulfed by economic difficulties as the Great Depression hit the world. Economies declined, unemployment increased, wages and salaries were reduced. Through all this Thorntons' business continued to grow and, despite national trends, the brothers decided in 1934 on a purpose-built factory instead of relying on rented premises. They chose Archer Road, surrounded by new suburban estates designed to re-house council tenants from the slum clearance programmes after the Great War. This site was about four miles south of the city centre with cleaner air and closer to the countryside. Its one big disadvantage was that it was a former quarry, merely 20 metres deep with a vertical quarry wall behind it, making construction work very difficult. On the other hand it was dirt cheap and there was a first-class workforce on the doorstep. The new factory cost £4,000 and was finished in 1935. To both my father and my uncle these premises must have seemed enormous when compared to their earlier factories. In fact there was a modest 2,000 sq. ft. on each floor. Two years later they built a similar-sized extension for roughly the same cost.

Once again the dogs of war were about to be loosed upon the world. The German Chancellor Hitler, riding a wave of unprecedented national fervour in his homeland, decided to exercise his expansionist foreign policy and had invaded Poland. Britain felt obligated to honour its mutual defence treaty with the smaller country. More importantly, a palpable sense of threat was engendered by the rise of National Socialism and, despite Prime Minister Chamberlain's attempts to appease the Führer, the terror of an invasion of Britain remained. Accordingly, war was declared in September 1939. Suddenly the steel works in Sheffield were busy again. This led to a boost in other regional businesses, including Thorntons, although this was short-lived, offset by other negative factors, chiefly the shortage of raw materials, particularly cane sugar which of course always had to be imported. Confectionery was quickly rationed to a mere two ounces a week. Staffing in the retail shops was reduced as individuals, male and female, left for Military Service.

The company had opened eight new shops in the year before the start of hostilities with a total of 35 shops in 18 towns, but Chancellor Hitler, now in conflict with our old friend Winston Churchill, put paid to any further expansion for at least ten years. Indeed, some shops were actually lost, either through expired leases or air-raids. There were at least 30 instances of retail premises suffering war damage. The night of the 1st and 2nd June 1940 was just such an occasion when three of Thorntons' shops in Manchester were heavily bombed and reduced to rubble. The branch on Mosley Street in the heart of the city was a particular loss as the brothers were extremely proud of this very successful large branch with its five display windows.

Later that year in Sheffield heavy bombing took place on the night of the 12th and 13th December, destroying much of The Moor including the shop where the family had once lived and the shops on London Road. A hundred thousand houses were destroyed that night and thousands of people lost their lives. The steel works were very badly damaged but within a fortnight were restored almost to normal production. The Thorntons factory on Archer Road was only superficially damaged but gas, electricity and other services were lost for seven weeks. With some remarkable forethought, the brothers had anticipated such a contingency and had recently acquired a small bankrupt factory in Lancashire to transfer production there if necessary. Leslie Charlesworth was dispatched to Bury and set up production of the *Special Toffee* so that the shops could at least get some supplies.

Thorntons, its premises and people, mostly survived the war. Now it was time to look forward and consider further expansion. An application for a building licence to extend the Sheffield factory on its quarry site was refused because of the very great shortage of building materials and skilled labour. It was felt that repairs to existing buildings, roads and railways, damaged by enemy action, took priority over developing the nation's sweet tooth. However, one of the brothers saw an advertisement in a local paper offering a factory in a place called Belper in Derbyshire about 35 miles to the south. This was unexplored territory in the back of beyond as far as they were concerned, but the building was relatively very large, with a 150 foot long room suitable for making chocolates and with the advantage, they thought, of even cleaner air than still grimy Sheffield. They also had the romantic idea that they would buy milk from local farmers and condense it for use in their toffee. This never happened, they successfully acquired the building in 1948 for £8,400 but signally failed to notice that Belper had the lowest rate of unemployment in the country.

At this stage in their lives, Norman and Stanley could look back at their humble beginnings with some justified pride. From the two small sweet shops started by their father in 1911 they had taken Thorntons through two World Wars and the Great Depression and now had a very profitable company with about 32 shops, two factories, an excellent reputation for quality and value, first-class products and an almost unique business model that could be expanded profitably across the whole country. At this stage my father was just turning 50 and my uncle was still in his 40's. They had achieved considerable status for themselves and their families, living in beautiful homes, enjoying golf, bridge and other social activities. The social disgrace of their father's demise and an institutionalised sister were completely suppressed.

Between them, Norman and Stanley Thornton fathered four sons who, right from the start, were set up to shoulder the responsibility of keeping Thorntons at the forefront of the confectionery business. There was never any option for the boys, no other career choice. Yet, at the same time, the two fathers had no intention whatsoever in relinquishing any control to their successors. Ominously, they insisted that all control remained with themselves and were determined to keep hold of the reins until they died, firmly in the belief that no one else could ever be trusted with their business empire.

Unwittingly, the seeds of discontent were being sown.

Chapter 2
A Boy's Life

There were several new arrivals in the world in 1933. *The Lone Ranger* was first heard on American radio, *King Kong* was first seen on cinema screens. In Germany, the *Gestapo* was established and Anne Frank was born, and Albert Einstein arrived in the US as a refugee from the Nazis. And on May 5, the day radio waves were first detected from the heart of our galaxy, I came along as the newest member of the Thornton family. My brother Tony had preceded me by four years, my sister Gill followed in 1937 and then younger brother John in 1943.

The first home I remember in Sheffield was a 1920s semi-detached house on Carterknowle Road. My memories are few, but I distinctly recall being very poorly there when I was about four years old. Probably I had one of those serious childhood illnesses – measles or scarlet fever – and was lying in a darkened room, curtains drawn, convinced that I was already at death's door. I had a strange out-of-the-body experience and sensed that I was flying around the room, looking down upon my prone form in the bed.

This is it, I thought, my time is up. Somehow I survived.

The world at that time was a very exciting place for a small boy. The streets were alive with traders and vendors of all kinds. I can clearly see the Wall's ice-cream man in his blue and white blazer. He pedalled a two-wheeler bicycle with ice-cream, packed in a container of steaming dry ice, perched on his handlebars. He would dismount on the pavement corner below our house and he really did shout, "Stop me and buy one!" All the children rushed out when they heard him.

There was also the knife-sharpener with a pedal-driven grinding wheel on the front of *his* bicycle. He would prop up his bike on the same corner, shout "Knife grinding!" and out would come all the housewives with their bread knives and carving knives. I watched with fascination as he applied each knife to the grinding wheel, causing sparks to fly in all directions.

There was a particularly hot summer's day in 1937 and the family was having its usual formal lunch in the dining-room. The French windows were thrown wide open onto the garden and a brave, or foolish, wasp decided to enter, unannounced and uninvited. Its presence at the dinner table was not at all welcome and my father, quick to anger, suddenly leapt to his feet, brandishing a rolled-up newspaper and proceeded to pursue the hapless insect around the room. The effect on the wasp was, of course, terminal but not as long lasting it was on me. I was really frightened by this display of intemperate rage, not for the first time and it would certainly not be the last.

Later we moved to *Greenways*, a much bigger house in the grander area of Whirlow Lane. My father still wanted to remain within walking distance of his new factory on Archer Road, but this now meant a walk of 2½ miles each way. To his credit, he often did the downhill walk to the premises but the chauffeur would usually drive him back up the hill afterwards. The move had been prompted by the improvement in his business fortunes. He later told me that his income had now reached £5,000 a year, quite substantial for the time. We moved from Carterknowle Road one evening with me reclining in the fold-down exterior seat, a feature of many pre-War cars known as a 'dickey-seat', at the rear, watching the gas lamps flashing above me through the dark streets.

We children rushed around the new house. It seemed huge after Carterknowle Road. There were six bedrooms, a very large sitting room, a dining room and even a playroom. We raced in and out of them all excitedly. There were two kitchens, one with a cast-iron range, a yard outside and a range of sheds. The next morning we explored the gardens, ran over the huge lawn bordered by beds of antirrhinums and lupins and up to the field above. From the top we could see far over Sheffield to the countryside beyond. *Greenways*, we decided, must have been formerly owned by a serious drinker. The garden was filled with discarded gin and beer bottles.

Here was a modern house, no more than 15 years old when we moved in. There was a sort of art-deco feel to the place, all plywood panelling and a bay-windowed tower at one end. My father had already done some work on it by extending the main bedroom to form a private wing complete with *en-suite* facilities, an innovative idea at a time when it was customary to leave one's bedroom at night to find the bathroom somewhere off the landing. This wing was closed off to us children so that he had a little sanctuary of peace and quiet. Of course, we had our own family bathroom but with no shower. Indeed, we hardly ever used the bath. Once a week was quite enough, thank you very much.

It was 1938 and time to start school. I was enrolled at a dear little place called Broad Elms High School run by Miss Handley and Miss Greaves in an old cottage about a mile and a half from home. The two teachers had about 30 to 40 pupils in mixed classes and it was around this time that I made a discovery. Little girls, it seemed, could be rather nice. While sitting next to one of them on our bench in the classroom, our knees would occasionally touch and I found this to be strangely exciting.

As war clouds gathered over Europe, my father was one of the few people who shared Churchill's view that war with Germany was very likely, almost inevitable. Shortly after arriving at *Greenways* he had a large pit excavated at the end of the drive and built a concrete air-raid shelter into it with a double garage above. I can recall the steps down to its heavy iron door and my curiosity as to its purpose. I was soon to find out what it was for in no uncertain terms.

I don't really remember the actual start of the war. It was the little things that showed that something was up. All the windows were criss-crossed with sticky tape to stop them shattering if bombs fell nearby. Blackout curtains were put up with very strict regulations to ensure that no house light escaped through them at night. My father joined the ARP, going out in the evenings in his Air Raid Warden's helmet and his blue tunic. The few months at the end of 1939 were actually rather quiet, what came to be called "the phoney war". Everything changed when the Germans swept into Western Europe and occupied Belgium, Holland and France, all within a few weeks, and by 1940 the bombing of Britain had begun. London was first to be blitzed, followed by intensive raids on all the other major British cities. Sheffield was not to be spared.

I awoke with a start. It was the middle of the night. Air raid sirens were wailing all around me and my dad came into my room. "Come on, Peter, we have to go into the air-raid shelter. The Germans are bombing Sheffield and the whole city is on fire already."

He picked me up, wrapped me in a blanket and carried me downstairs into the cold night. I heard his feet crunching on the gravel drive as we approached the cold concrete steps into the shelter. There were loud explosions and the sky was as bright as day with the flames from the city just beyond the hill. To me, this was incredibly exciting. My father said that the centre of Sheffield was under attack. I don't remember being at all afraid, but clearly my parents had been very fearful of this happening.

"Can we go up to the top of the field and have a look please, Daddy?"

"No, of course not. We must get you into the shelter."

My father put me into one of the wooden bunks. It seemed that half the population of the Lane was already there. I could see Mr and Mrs Kelk from the house above, and there was my mother's great friend Elsie Nunweek from the house below, with her husband Bobby, puffing on his cigarette as usual. My parents had equipped the shelter very well with double bunks around the sides and a supply of emergency lights, food and water.

When eventually the noise had died down, we all left the shelter and trooped to the top of the field. The city centre lay before us with black smoke billowing from the intense heat and flames of the devastated buildings. Sheffield, like Rome, stands upon seven hills and, just like the Roman capital under the Goths, it had been thoroughly sacked. From our distant vantage point we could see the conflagration, with flames reaching hundreds of feet into the night sky, and we could hear the clanging of the fire engines as they raced to the scene of yet another outbreak.

This was too close for comfort, my parents decided. Even the quiet suburbs of Sheffield were becoming unacceptably dangerous for young children. My dad, together with Uncle Stanley, decided to look beyond the county border and find somewhere in neighbouring Derbyshire to which both families could move in safety.

They first rented a small cottage in Over Haddon while they searched for a better property to buy. The cottage was in a spectacular location, overlooking Lathkill Dale, still one of the most peaceful and unspoilt of the Derbyshire limestone dales. We stood in the front room of this tiny house, now a part of the Lathkill Hotel, and looked over this wonderful landscape. We were right on the very edge of an extremely steep valley, almost a ravine. It was no more than a mile across, but it must have been over 350 feet deep, so deep that you couldn't actually see the Lathkill River flowing through it. The sides were lined with trees, rocks and the characteristic dry stone walls. This was like nowhere I had ever seen before. The beauty of this country environment overwhelmed me. I knew instinctively that here was a place just waiting for me to explore.

One day we were out walking. My brother Tony was slightly ahead of us when he suddenly came back, shouting excitedly, "I found a crashed plane! I found a crashed plane!"

"What is it? What is it?" I shouted. "Is it a German bomber? Are there any bodies in it?"

"No, it's a Lancaster, I think, and the bodies have all been taken away."

We all decided that we liked living in Derbyshire after this.

Eventually, with Stanley, my father purchased a house in the nearby village of Winster. It was on the main village street, was grandly named Winster Manor, and all of us – my mother, brother and sister, my aunt Netta and her children, Shirley, Michael and Sandra – moved with them into this new home with lots of bedrooms and other exciting places to discover. We children had great fun playing together in the house and exploring our new surroundings. Winster had once been at the centre of the Derbyshire lead mining industry before it had become uneconomical in the early 20th century. The village had developed at an astonishing rate during the 17th century and had been one of the largest settlements in the county. There had obviously been some money around to judge from the style of the houses, built without frontages to the edge of the street. Most of these had been 'Georgianised' by their wealthy owners.

Derbyshire villages, indeed all villages in Britain at that time, had to be self-sufficient. Shopping was done locally so there was a good grocery shop and a butcher's shop together with four public houses, all for a population of about 1500 people. There was little evidence of newcomers to the village as, for many years, the community comprised simply a handful of large long-established families, resulting in a plethora of common surnames.

Memorably, a small earthquake occurred while we were resident in Winster. The village was built over a small geological fault and there was a heavy rumbling noise one night, loud enough to wake everyone and send us all rushing out into the road. There was no damage to structures but a small crack appeared down the centre of the street itself. However, a larger division was occurring within our household with Dad and Stanley having their own seismic disturbances. Their constant arguing at work soon started to make life disagreeable for the two families at home. My mother and aunt were also having problems trying to live under the same roof. It soon seemed preferable to my parents to risk being bombed in Sheffield than to persevere with this fractured domestic situation.

It was all a great shame as far as I was concerned. I had had great fun running around this big house with my various cousins, playing 'Hide and Seek' in the secret places that only seem to exist in an old Manor, running up the hillside behind the house, daringly entering the abandoned lead mines. I liked Uncle Stanley and Auntie Netta – they were fun. Stanley had converted a large ballroom at the end of the house into an air raid shelter by bricking up the big window onto the garden. He then used it for a cinema and would show us old silent films of *Charlie Chaplin*, *Laurel and Hardy* and *Popeye the Sailor*. Even at that age, I recognised the different temperament of my uncle. He was always happy and cheerful. Little wonder then that he and my father were always arguing.

So my family moved out, leaving Stanley and Netta and the children in this large house where they remained for many years. I remember my father being upset that he didn't get back his share of the investment in the property until much later on. Yet he retained an indulgent attitude toward his younger brother and let him get away with things.

Now, back in Sheffield, our parents were still anxious about our safety while the bombing raids persisted. Their solution was simple. Tony and I would be dispatched to a boarding school. I was still only seven years old, far too young to understand what was happening to me, or why. Being unable really to fend for myself, I found it to be a very frightening and rather detached experience. We went to a huge old stately home, Thornbridge Hall, with a dormitory in what was called the 'Long Gallery'. The beds were crammed tightly together in order to make enough room for everyone. I put up with this for a year until I locked myself in the outside toilets one day in an attempt to escape.

To my blessed relief, my parents brought me back home again after that. Now I was to attend a local private preparatory school, Birkdale, where I stayed until I was 13. I used to take myself to school right from the first day. I walked down the lane, got the bus from Dore that took me to Ecclesall tram terminus, and then boarded the tram down to Hunters Bar from where I would walk up the hill to the school. This was my routine every day unless I could get a lift from Graham Gillott's father. Graham lived about half a mile away and, if I walked to their house, I could travel with him in their Vauxhall right to the door of the school. This was quite exciting because his father seemed to me to be an extremely fast driver. Sitting in the back seat of the car, staring with a mixture of excitement and trepidation as the speedometer reached, then exceeded, 50 mph through the 30 mph limit, I felt that Mr Gillott was most daring, complete with his trilby hat and always with a cigarette hanging from his mouth.

Riding the tramcar was an experience in itself. After school I would board the tram at Hunters Bar, leaping on to the rear platform and rushing up the narrow spiral stairs to the top floor. My friends and I would always sit in the bay window at the front or the back. The tram was always full, most of the other passengers smoking heavily. If there was no room on the upper deck I would have to stand downstairs and the conductor would shout, "Pass along the car please. Move right up to the front." The tram would then heave and buck its way up the steep road from Hunters Bar to Ecclesall Terminus where I would then be on the bus back home again.

Later, in 1946, I again went away to boarding school, this time to Repton in Derbyshire, and I did reasonably well, getting acceptable School Certificate results and 'A' levels, but for now there were still the tribulations of the war to endure. Crazy things were happening in the world. Everyone followed the course of the war by listening to the wireless and reading the newspaper and I was no exception. Of course, at that age I had no understanding of the tens of thousands of people being killed, but I would listen to the news every evening, just after the recording of the chimes of Big Ben was played. The real thing had been silenced "for the duration".

"This is the BBC Home Service. Here is the news and this is Alvar Liddell reading it". I had no idea who "Alvarly Dell" was, but I followed his crisply enunciated reading. It all seemed like an exciting story being played out for my entertainment. We listened to Winston Churchill's stirring speeches, sitting in silence in our blacked-out lounge. The end of the war in Europe came in 1945 on May 8, just after my birthday, and the world began to put its fear of the Nazis behind it.

However, the fear of my father remained. I grew up very frightened of this tyrannical man. He seemed remote and distant. He frequently shouted at me, criticising my apparent ineptitude, such as not knowing my times tables. His values were typically late Victorian, embodying that particularly British attitude of 'stiff-upper-lip'. It was paramount that you should not display your feelings, not cry or get angry. On the other hand, he was a man who definitely showed anger himself at his children's behaviour. I can well remember being very upset about something and running upstairs to my bedroom, screaming, whereupon he chased after me, dragged me from under the bed, in a furious mood, hitting me as he went. He was always and incontestably right. There was never any questioning of that, and he could never accept an opinion from me, either then as young boy or later in life.

My mother on the other hand was a very loving warm personality and full of fun. I am sure they were unhappy together because, even when I was very young, my mother used to confide her feelings to me. I was sitting on the playroom floor one day and thinking what a beautiful woman she was with her long black hair. She wore a light green dress and to me she was the most beautiful person in the world.

We snuggled up and she said, "Your father is so mean to me. Do you know he doesn't give me a regular allowance? I don't even have a bank account of my own. I always have to ask him for money, even for a small amount. He is always telling me how short of money he is and how the firm might go bankrupt at any time. He is always getting angry with me for spending too much money. What can I do about it, Peter? I just can't do anything right. Did you know that I once had such a lovely boyfriend before I met your father? He had a motorbike and he used to take me for such exciting rides. He was so dashing and good-looking."

Feeling distraught in the face of such sorrow I said, "Well, what happened, Mum? Why did you not marry *him*?"

"He got ill, darling, with a terrible disease," she answered wistfully, "and so my parents stopped me seeing him. He had been going out with other women and hadn't told me, but I still often think about him."

I felt desperately sad for my dear mother, whom I loved very much, after that conversation. There were many others like it, but what could an unhappy woman do in those days? Everybody deserves happiness and yet divorce was not an easy option. For my part at that age, I felt I was some sort of surrogate partner.

My father had many sayings that he would repeat over and over without ever realising that he had ever said them before. Meal times were quite formal in the dining room of *Greenways* with him sitting at the head of the table. We had a maid to bring in the meal, at least until the end of the war. I remember one girl called Ruth Taylor who had become quite disconsolate. I asked my mother why, and was told, "Her brother has just been killed in the war. A few months ago he had his finger shot off. He got better and went back to the front line and this time they killed him." For weeks afterwards I had a vision of this poor boy lying dead in the trenches, his hand lying lifeless on the ground with the finger missing. I was finally beginning to understand the implications of warfare.

Dad would sit very slowly and deliberately eating his meal, telling us that we should always chew every mouthful 38 times in order to help the digestion, that we should never over-eat and should always leave the table feeling that we could eat a crust of bread. He came home from the office for lunch and so this was quite a formal meal too. He would usually spend some time talking about the things that had annoyed him that morning in the office, particularly if Stanley had irritated him again. That was often the case as Stanley seemed to have such crazy ideas, according to my father, but then he would finish his tirade by saying, "Oh well, Stanley is very good socially and he did invent the *Special Toffee*, you know!"

He came home early one lunchtime in a particularly bad temper, desperate to tell us what had happened now that Stanley had moved from Winster to Matlock. My uncle had become very enthusiastic about the place and had actually become a councillor for a short while.

Father said, "Stanley really is the limit! Sometimes I think that he is not quite all there. He said to me this morning that we should open a shop in Matlock! Matlock! Well, it is obviously far too small, isn't it? What a daft idea!" Then the inevitable, "Oh well, Stanley is very good socially and he did invent the *Special Toffee*, you know!" If my mother ever started to discuss problems in personal relationships – anybody's relationships – my father would close the conversation by looking at us all grimly and saying, "Sex is dynamite, you know. Sex is dynamite!"

After lunch he would retire to the little sitting room, formerly our playroom, and sit in front of the gas fire with his newspaper. He would then doze for an hour before eventually returning to the office. Later on, when he was older, he would take himself off to bed for a couple of hours and would not re-appear until the late afternoon.

My older brother Tony was a very good friend and we played many imaginary games together. We loved to play war games on the garden pond where we had our own naval fleet of warships fashioned from twigs. This pond was actually a concrete static tank that Dad built as an extra water supply for the fire brigade in case of an air-raid. We both gave our younger sister a hard time, as brothers do, often carrying out important surgical 'operations' on her dolls.

John was ten years younger and this big age gap made our relationship more like parent-to-child than brother-to-brother. From a very early age Dad decided that John was the most intelligent of his children and, oblivious to the psychological effect of this on the rest of us, he made his views known. In truth, John did prove to be better academically by gaining a degree at Cambridge but we didn't really have the same chance. University education was very much a decision made by our father in relation to the needs of the family business. Dad continued to treat John quite differently from his older children. Maybe his attitude had mellowed slightly with his increasing years and John was the lucky beneficiary.

Immediately after the war we began taking family holidays at the seaside. Dad found a house close to the beach on St Andrew's Drive in Skegness. He had bought it before the war and but kept it closed until peace was restored. It was a quite boring pseudo-Tudor house called *The Lea*, semi-detached and built on the dunes. He had also mothballed a beautifully upholstered Austin 16, finished in grey leather with three seats in the back along with a further two fold-down rear-facing seats. It was full of the latest refinements such as a knob positioned centrally under the dashboard which, when turned every few thousand miles, did the 'greasing' which was so necessary in those days. If there was a puncture, you could actually raise the car from the inside by using the built-in jack in the floor beneath the front seats. The enormous boot would be filled with everything needed for a wonderful holiday and off we'd go, driving down Whirlow Lane in the early morning with our father turning from the driver's seat to say, "Have you remembered the kettle, Muriel?" and suchlike, to which she would reply, "Of course I have, Norman!"

My dad had a strange habit whilst driving of continually looking at his face in the driving mirror as if to check whether he had put in his teeth or shaved properly. My parents always made a full day of the journey and had their favourite place to stop for a picnic on the way. Eventually we would reach *The Lea* and then rush madly around the place to check it all out. Our first job on arrival was always to mow the lawn and after that our mother would get out the bed linen and make up all the beds.

My father was at that time still a keen golfer. He belonged to the North Shore Golf Club, just five minutes' walk away at the end of St Andrew's Drive. He would let me accompany him around this typical seaside course and hoped I would learn the game. There was the time when he gave a tremendous slice from the elevated ninth tee so that the ball flew over the bordering gardens and through a bedroom window of a private house. A woman came out and shouted at my father, "What do you think you are doing, you idiot."

He made his way through the rough ground and peered over the hedge into her garden, and for the first time in my life I heard him apologise. "I am extremely sorry, Madam," he said. "My son moved when I was taking the shot and it put me off. Let me arrange to pay for the repair."

Once we were out of earshot I proclaimed my innocence.

"I know that," he admitted, "but I couldn't very well tell her it was just a bad shot, could I? I had to have a reason!" This was probably the only time I ever heard Dad apologising sincerely to anybody.

Shortly after this my father bought a second house in Skegness for his in-laws, Joseph and Eva Illingworth. My mother's parents had run a newsagent's shop at Banner Cross in Sheffield and Joe was a lovely grandfather. I was very fond of him. He had originally been an engraver working for many years in the silver industry. He was a true artist and would have preferred a career as a fine-art painter but there was little money in this. I'm still very proud of the paintings he gave me. Joe and Eva took up the news agency in their later years and lived in the little room behind the shop with further accommodation above. I can still picture that living room with its open fire and china in glass cases. I can hear the ticking clocks and recall how cosy and welcoming it all was.

They lived in Skegness for about ten years but, I think, in some misery as theirs was not the happiest of marriages. Incompatible personalities once more seemed to lie at the heart of the issue. Joe was intelligent and sensitive; Eva seemed to be quite the opposite. Separated from their old friends, neither gained much comfort from their union. Joe joined a local amateur artists' society and continued to enjoy his painting, Eva simply faded into early senility. They finally returned to Sheffield, poor Eva to a mental hospital and Joe to live with us. Eva died not long after in 1957. Joe passed away four years later, aged 83. I was heartbroken at my loss, having been much closer to my grandfather than to my own dad. I could talk to him as an intimate friend whereas my father remained only an intimidating 'superior' individual.

Father sold the Austin and bought a pre-war Rolls-Royce complete with a chauffeur by the name of Eddie Unwin. He often invited me to accompany him in style in the back of this huge old car while Eddie drove us to visit some of our shops. He even installed a very large radio set on the back of the driver's partition so that he could listen to the news at every available moment. I can picture him now getting very agitated when Sir Stafford Cripps, the new Labour Chancellor, introduced a new 'wealth tax'. We would visit up to seven shops on these outings but he always included a lengthy lunch break in some hotel where we could have a decent meal and a little snooze in the lounge before continuing our rounds.

The routine for these shop visits was always the same. He would ask Eddie to drop us off close to the shop with instructions to come back in half an hour or later as required. We would spend some time looking at the window display where he took note of all the things that displeased him. Muttering to himself, he would then stride into the shop where the assistants, all prepared for his coming, would present themselves behind the counter. They were always dressed in smart white aprons and little white maid's caps. The confectionery was behind the counter in knock-stoppered glass jars and in square tins on the display shelves. His first task would be to check that the weighing scales were properly balanced. The equipment was quite unsophisticated with its brass weights and polished brass scoop.

Then he would move behind the counter, hold out his hand and say, "Cash book, please!" and the manageress would nervously pass it to him. There would be a pause. "Hmm, last week wasn't very good. What happened.?"

She would look at him apologetically. "We had the window out to dress it on Thursday and Friday, Mr Norman."

"What? You were dressing the window on a Friday?" he would ask incredulously. "You should never do that."

Next he would look at the *Special Toffee* on sale. "How long has this been chopped?"

"Trade has been a bit slow today, Mr Norman, so it was done this morning."

"Scrap it!" came the response. "It's all sticking together. You can't sell it like that."

Next he would turn to the boiled sweets in their jars behind the counter.

"The top is loose on this jar. Make sure that they are always tight!"

"Yes, Mr Norman."

Eventually we would sit down in the back of the shop, the manageress would make us a delightful cup of tea and the mood would ease. We could now be treated like old family friends and enjoy a pleasanter general conversation.

"Is this location still as good as it was?" he would ask.

"Well, no, not really, Mr Norman," she would explain. "You see, the shop next door has changed hands and is not as popular as it used to be. And the bus stop that was three doors away has been moved closer so that the queue is often right in front of the shop door."

"I see. Have you got a cat to keep the mice down?"

"Well, Mr Norman, we did have but it died last week, so we had to get a new one."

As the tea was finished my father would lead the manageress outside to look at the display window.

"Who has done this window?"

"I've done it, Mr Norman."

"You should have put the toffee in the middle, unless there is a promotion on. Or if it's summertime you need the best-selling product there in the middle." He would study the toffee closely. "I see that it's melting. When was it last changed?"

"Two days ago, Mr Norman,"

"I thought as much. In this hot weather it should be changed every day. Change it immediately we have gone."

This conversation could last up to half an hour until my father was satisfied that everything was right. He set huge store by the quality of his window displays, quite correctly seeing them as artful in their own right and the means by which passers-by would be tempted into the shop. Once he had finished we would stride off through the streets to the next shop, my little legs struggling to keep up with his brisk pace. There, the entire routine would be repeated, and so on until at last we could settle back into the comfortable seats of the car and let Eddie take us back to *Greenways*.

Before my adult life could properly begin I was conscripted to National Service like all other young men of my generation. I received my call-up papers and had to report to 7th Training Regiment at Catterick Camp in Yorkshire. There, we were herded into a large chilly Nissen hut and immediately issued with our kit. Named after their designer, Major Peter Nissen of the Royal Engineers, these huts were the first prefabricated buildings, patented in 1916 and constructed from semicircular metal frames covered in sheets of corrugated iron. A hut could be delivered in one small truck and erected in under two hours. It came with oil-cloth windows instead of glass and no insulation, just a coke-burning stove in the middle. The Army used thousands of them, often joined together into 'spider-blocks', a collection of Nissen huts joined at right angles to a main building known as an 'ablution' block.

They were not pleasant to live in, particularly in the depths of winter. We needed to get the stove red hot just to keep warm, huddled around it, cleaning our kit or listening to Radio Luxembourg, the first commercial station to broadcast to the UK. Condensation dripped at night from the corrugated walls on to our beds. In the morning it would be pandemonium with everyone trying to wash in the ablution block at the same time, all desperate to be on time for parade. A full shower or a bath meant a long walk to different barracks so this luxury was reserved for weekends only.

There followed eight weeks of basic training, an experience I shall never forget. We marched up and down, up and down endlessly on the parade ground, while the sergeant-majors and corporals screamed and shouted at us. We were subjected to a tirade of abuse because our boots were not quite polished enough or our uniforms not perfectly aligned. We were taught field craft, map reading and basic tactics, and how to shoot and clean our weapons. Having been to public school I had not the first idea of the kind of people with whom I would be sharing this experience. You can imagine that it took me quite a while to get used to the language, dialects and mannerisms of these everyday recruits. However, to my great surprise, I was soon on very friendly terms with them all, suffering together and then enjoying a beer together in the NAAFI, helping each other with kit cleaning, sharing our problems about girl friends and families. Despite our differing backgrounds we soon became the best of friends.

Towards the end of the eight weeks we were selected for ongoing training. I was moved into another hut with about twenty others who had been selected as potential officer material, all of them ex-public school or ex-grammar school boys. Now the training became more strenuous and constant: spit and polish, marching, cleaning of brasses and boots every night until midnight, ready for the minutely detailed inspection on the parade ground at eight every morning. You simply had to accept the aggression, the criticisms and the insults for even the slightest misdemeanour and remain rigidly at attention.

"What's your name, sir?"

"Thornton, Sergeant."

"Am I hurting you, Thornton, sir?"

"No, Sergeant."

"Well, I should be, Thornton, sir! I'm standing on your hair! Get a haircut!" The Sergeant would turn to the next trainee.

"Your boots are filthy, sir. Get them clean for tomorrow morning or – I will put you where the crows can't shit on you!" The last bit would always be shouted at you as if you were in the next field.

After training we were sent to the War Office Selection Board. It was utterly intimidating for an extremely shy youth, as I was then, to stand in front of twenty or thirty very self-confident other young men and give an impromptu five minute lecture. There were intelligence tests and initiative tests ("Now, tell us exactly how you would cross a river with the minimum of equipment.") Finally came the hour-long interview with two officers.

"Good morning, Thornton. Please sit down."

The two officers, a major and a captain, were already pacing behind their table. My heart was in my mouth with fear. They both carried their officers' leather-bound silver-topped canes which they occasionally slapped on the table for emphasis.

"What newspapers do you read, Thornton?"

Immediate panic. I hadn't read a newspaper for months apart from the occasional *Daily Mirror* in the NAAFI but I knew that wouldn't do for an answer. I remembered the *Daily Telegraph* in my House Library at school.

"Well, er, I read the *Daily Telegraph* sometimes."

"Sometimes? SOMETIMES? Don't you read it every day?"

"Well, you see, it's a bit difficult in the Army. There isn't really the chance."

"Not that difficult," they contradicted. "You can always order one through the NAAFI. What do you think of their political stance? Do you support it?"

The rest of the interview became a haze of total embarrassment because of my failure to answer anything intelligently. Afterwards, I felt like a spy who had been subjected to a gruelling interrogation under a harsh spotlight. I was not at all surprised to be told that I was 'NY 3' which meant 'not yet ready, come back in three months'. A further twelve weeks of training followed, as before, and then I had to go through the entire W.O.S.B. process once more. Again it was a humiliating experience, again I failed and my self-regard sank ever lower. There was little to be done about it. It was the just the way I was, nothing more, but it was hard for me to see that at the time.

There seemed little point in trying again so, when offered a choice of what to do next, I elected to go on a cipher course. This attracted me because, on its completion, I would obtain the rank of corporal with better pay and higher status, and to this end I spent a further twelve weeks at Catterick learning how to encode and decode messages, the first really interesting thing that I had done since I had joined the army. Here, at last, was a role for me in the Service. Suddenly we weren't raw recruits any more, not just 'squaddies' to be shouted and sworn at by every other NCO. We were learning an important technical job, one that I could actually do and which wholly fascinated me.

Then came my first posting. Thank goodness, I thought, I'm off to Malaya and not Korea. In readiness for this, we were transferred to a Transit Camp near Newton Abbot in South Devon where we stayed for three weeks, awaiting our trip abroad and receiving countless injections against the various tropical diseases we might encounter. The National Service Army seemed to be incredibly good at wasting their soldiers' time.

There were even more injections on the day before departure to the point where none of us could raise our right arms. This seemed to be typical Army organisation as, the next day, we had to march from the camp to Newton Abbot railway station carrying our bags, complete with tropical kit, along with haversacks and rifles to board a train with no corridors for the journey to Liverpool docks. This train was probably the slowest I had ever travelled on. Leaving mid-morning, we eventually reached Liverpool at about six in the evening, bladders bursting and our arms extremely painful so it was quite difficult to carry our belongings. We were marched up the gangway to board our troopship, the *Empire Georgic*, which had been converted from its previous life as a combined cargo and passenger vessel.

Our sleeping quarters turned out to be hammocks slung closely together on a deck surrounded by the massive open space of the hull in which cargo had previously been stored. There was no room to store our kit apart from on the floor. We were shown around the ship with its enormous dining room and a few simple recreation rooms. I was given the job of ship's announcer probably on account of my nice public school voice. The job necessitated standing in this very small cabin with a microphone, reading reams of instructions to the troops all over the ship. I had to do this five or six times a day.

We set sail from Liverpool that same night out into the Atlantic and turned south towards Gibraltar. The ship heaved violently in the rough sea and, as we hit the Bay of Biscay, the weather worsened and the ship heaved even more. I lapsed into an immediate and permanent state of seasickness through which I was obliged to continue my duties as announcer. The announcer's cabin made me feel even more nauseous and occasionally I had to stop mid-sentence to open the door and vomit over the ship's railing, conveniently close by. There was no way at all I could eat anything and, in a day or two, I started to weaken. Three days of this misery ensued until I decided that the only thing for it was to force myself to eat. I began gingerly with a bread roll. This seemed to do the trick and I started to become accustomed to the motion of the boat. I was able to eat a little more and the vomiting ceased. By now we were approaching the calmer waters of Gibraltar and, once through the Straits and into the Mediterranean, the swell of the ocean ceased and it would have been quite a pleasant cruise, were it not for our basic living conditions.

Back in my school days at Repton, I had had very little interest in the opposite sex, unlike some of my friends who boasted of exciting interludes with female friends during the holidays. Some even continued these extra-curricular activities during term time, creeping out at night for secret trysts with local girls. But for me, apart from a certain prurient interest in the pictures of bare-breasted native women in the school's *National Geographic* magazines, I had not really had the chance to get to know many women. Now, on board ship, there were quite a number of service women around and I felt very aware of my lack of experience with them.

"Very boring here, isn't it?" asked a sergeant in the Women's Royal Army Corps one day. "What do you do with yourself all day?"

"Nothing much," I answered, trying to appear nonchalant, "apart from being the Ship's Announcer and standing around talking to my friends, Sergeant."

"Oh, so *you* are the person who keeps telling us over the loudspeaker where to go and what is going on, and so on."

"Yes, that's right," I said, beginning to get slightly apprehensive about her interest.

"Well, you've got a lovely voice, did you know that? Where do you come from?"

"I come from Sheffield."

"Oh," she said, rather taken aback. "You don't sound like a Sheffielder."

Trying to avoid mentioning public school, I said, "Well, I got it from my parents, I think. They speak like this all the time."

She smiled and said, "Would you like to come and have a drink in the Sergeant's Mess?"

"Thank you very much," I mumbled, "but I don't really think I could manage it. You see, I am constantly on call to make announcements." I felt a bit out of my depth here and hoped that this might deter her. I happened to see one of my friends a few yards away. I said "Oh, there is my friend, Rodney. I'm sure that he wants to talk to me. I'll have to go. Bye!" and with that I rushed off with a great sense of relief. At this stage in my life I was not prepared for what she may have had in mind and I did my best to avoid her from then on.

One evening I was standing alone at the ship's rail looking out to the distant coast of Spain. It was a beautiful night, the sea was calm and there was a gentle swishing as the ship cut through the water. The lights on the far shore mirrored the stars above. Under this perfectly cloudless sky I considered where Fate had brought me thus far. A member of the ship's crew came to stand beside me.

"Hello, mate," he said good-naturedly. "What are you doing here all by yourself?"

"I was just enjoying this wonderful evening and thinking, for the first time, how lucky I am to be in the Army, enjoying this special moment, courtesy of His Majesty." He nodded in agreement, and I returned his enquiry. "Who are you and why are you here?

"I am one of the stewards from the Officers' Mess. I'm off duty this evening."

"Are you on this ship permanently?"

"Yes", he answered, "I was in the Merchant Navy during the war and decided that I liked the life."

After a while he asked me if I wanted to come to his bunk room and share a bottle of whisky. This seemed a very attractive idea and I agreed. We made our way down to his room. He then shut the door and got out the drinks. Suddenly, to my utter and total bewilderment, he turned off the light and started groping me in the darkness. I was not prepared for this at all. The implications were far more disconcerting than when the young sergeant had tried to chat me up. Fortunately my eager friend had not locked his cabin door. I managed to scramble out into the light and made a hasty and somewhat relieved exit.

We finally docked at Singapore and set off to the transit camp at Kuala Lumpur, about 200 miles to the north, travelling overnight on an another painfully slow train. On boarding we were told that it was subject to frequent ambushes by communist terrorists and therefore we must take turns to mount guard in readiness. The carriages were ancient with an open platform at each end. Our guard duty consisted of standing on one of these unprotected platforms alone, waiting to be shot. I assumed that any would-be attacker would pick off the guards first, leaving the carriages defenceless. When my turn came, I felt a new understanding of the words "sitting duck". In other circumstances, it would have been quite pleasant in the cool air outside. The darkness of the jungle rushed close by, huge leaves hanging near enough to touch. An occasional glimpse of movement in the depths of the trees furthered my trepidation, but it was probably nothing more threatening than monkeys.

To our collective relief, the terrorists must have had something better to do that night and we arrived unscathed at Kuala Lumpur station, disembarking from the train into the back of the inevitable Bedford trucks for the rest of the journey to the transit camp. There we stayed for another month, doing nothing much in particular except, of course, parading and waiting to be posted on, like packages in a storage depot. Eventually I learned that I was destined for the Rear Divisional Headquarters (XVII Division) at Seremban, wherever that was.

The camp in Seremban consisted of the inevitable spider huts just as at any British military camp from Catterick to the Far East except now there was no need for windows at all, nor even complete walls as the hot moisture permeated the air. I was allocated a bed and the all-essential mosquito net and settled down in my place in the *basha*, the local name for these huts, ready at last to fulfill the purpose of my National Service. Now I could contribute to the British military machine by handling encrypted messages.

Walking around the camp that first day, we observed how the jungle crammed in on us on all sides. We were separated from it only by a high fence topped with barbed wire. If we went out beyond the Guard Room we could walk right into the dense undergrowth. So that's what we decided to do. A narrow path led through the trees, almost hidden by the foliage. We walked for about a mile in the heat and oppressive humidity, huge flies that we called 'buzz-bombs' flying madly around us, sometimes in our faces. Monkeys swung and chattered in the branches above us. Although we had been told that the terrorists did not operate in this area we were still somewhat apprehensive. Finally we broke out on to an open hilltop and there, in a small clearing, was an abandoned Buddhist shrine, and beyond it a wonderful vista over jungle-clad hills. In the far distance, we could make out a squadron of RAF Mosquitoes engaged in an air-attack.

This was 1952 and we were based in Rasa Camp with men from the Gurkha Signal Regiment. My duties were undertaken in a little concrete building behind the main signal office. The Gurkha signallers manned the office and were extremely efficient and hard working. We worked very closely with them, sitting in our little sweat-box translating messages in twelve-hour shifts, night and day. The work wasn't onerous and we never built up any great backlog. In truth, I became very skilled at it and found the messages themselves to be quite exciting. It gave me a real insight into what was happening all around me – how many CTs (Communist Terrorists) had been killed or captured, where our patrols were engaged and so on – and I was grateful not to have been on the frontline out in the jungle, squelching through mud, bitten by lice, waiting with pounding heart to be shot by some terrorist sniper. I didn't feel guilty, just full of admiration for these National Servicemen and their extraordinary and outstanding bravery.

My time at Seremban was uneventful apart from two memorable occasions. We were told we would have some infantry duty and were sent to defend a local village against a possible terrorist attack during the Chinese New Year. The population of Malaya then consisted of the indigenous Malays with about 15% Chinese. The terrorists were from this minority group and would murder their fellow civilians if they were not given food. Part of the strategy for dealing with the insurrection was to move most of the Chinese population to *kampongs* (villages) rather than leaving them vulnerably dispersed throughout the jungle. This successfully reduced the murder rate but led to further antagonism between the terrorists and the locals.

We were taken to this particular *kampong* in our Bedford trucks. We surveyed the area, roughly three acres surrounded by a high wire fence. The jungle had been cleared for a distance of 20 metres but beyond that was an impenetrable wall of trees. Within the compound were rows of small thatched huts, on stilted platforms well above the ground. At the centre was an open area, almost like a village square, where a crowd of soldiers and Chinese civilians had gathered, looking intently at the ground.

As soon as we had unloaded the trucks we put up tents for the Company Headquarters. This gave us a little time prior to the Briefing at 16:00hrs, so I suggested to my two firm friends, Ginger Haythornthwaite and Jock MacDonald, that we should cross to the centre of the *kampong* to find out what was going on. Jock pushed his way to the front of the crowd. "It's ower-ere," he said in his rich burr. By the time we pushed through to join him, Jock was already looking pale and needed a smoke. "Gie'us wan o' yer fags. Ah've ran oot," and Ginger handed over his packet of Craven A's.

We looked to the ground and I immediately had to turn away. Six tiny, emaciated bodies, clad only in Chinese loin cloths, lay there, each with bullet wounds. Suddenly all those deciphered messages came back to me. 'Objective achieved. 6 CTs killed. No casualities.' No longer would I think of these reports as simply a cause for celebration. Here were real people, most of them just teenagers, who had been alive a few hours ago. Now they lay ingloriously on the floor of the compound, their lives taken forever, and for what? I turned to a soldier from an infantry regiment and asked, "Where did they come from?"

"One of our patrols just brought them in," he said matter-of-factly. "We caught them napping, having their lunch – if you can call it that." I turned away and went back to our Company HQ, feeling shocked and sickened.

At the briefing the Commander Officer addressed the company. "Intelligence has told us to expect CTs to attack in force during the night, hoping to break into the *kampong* with the objective of killing all the Chinese and stealing their rations. You will all take up defensive positions, to be allocated by Sergeant Jackson, around the perimeter and shoot on sight when you see the enemy or any movement beyond the wire during the night. Go to it, chaps. I know I can rely on you for a good performance."

I didn't think the attackers would have had any real chance of getting into the village because of the formidable surrounding fence but it was still thought necessary to defend the place. I was placed in a trench position with twenty or thirty clips of live ammunition. That anything could actually move out there seemed highly unlikely because the jungle was alive with other defences – Bren guns, rifles, the occasional mortar and flares from Very pistols – illuminating the no-man's-land between the fence and the jungle. During one of the quiet periods between the flares I thought I detected something moving about ten metres in front of me. With bated breath, and fearful of attack from some fierce Chinese adversary, I raised my rifle to firing position and quietly released the safety catch. Then something moved and I squeezed the trigger. The shot rang out followed by a loud squealing noise and the pig that I had *almost* hit ran as fast as any pig can run. This porcine encounter aside, nothing happened and at about seven in the morning we gratefully queued up for a rather good breakfast out in the open.

I discussed the night's excitement with Jock and Ginger. "I saw something moving and shot at it. It might have been a pig. What about you? Did you see anything? Did you have to fire?"

Jock said "Ah'm fair scunnert! Nowt!" which was his way of expressing dissatisfaction at seeing nothing.

Ginger simply declared, "Reet champion! I saw nobbut a chicken."

During my stay at the Rasa camp I had to be appraised by the Squadron Commanding Officer, Captain Beauchamp, to see whether I had matured enough to be an officer. I was ordered into his office and stood smartly to attention.

"Right, stand easy, Corporal. You can sit down. I am going to interview you." I sat down on the hard chair opposite his desk. "Well, tell me what you think of your work here. It seems pretty routine to me but Sergeant Jackson tells me that you do it competently."

I immediately had this rather ribald picture in my mind of the aforementioned sergeant of whom it was said he was so "well endowed" that he had a special dispensation to wear extra-long shorts. I immediately cast this absurd image from my mind lest it should affect my reply. We had always been advised not to tell the officers too much so my responses remained fairly non-committal.

In concluding the interview Captain Beauchamp said, "Well, Corporal, I am going to fill in the appraisal form now but I must tell you that I will need to write 'This man has no initiative'."

What? I was aghast. I felt very indignant. How on earth am I supposed to show any initiative in a routine post like this, I thought to myself. Don't they recall the night I walked a mile and a half with an urgent message for the General and delivered it personally to Divisional Headquarters? I determined from that point never again would anyone charge me with being unassertive. My future life was going to by a model of bold decisiveness, I promised, to show this Captain just how wrong he was.

The second memorable occasion came when I had the chance of a three-week furlough by travelling to Hong Kong and back on a troopship. Reflecting on that, it seems incredible that, in my two years of Army service, I was only on active duty for nine months and was still allowed a three-week holiday.

I returned home on the *Empire Windrush*, another converted passenger ship and far less comfortable than the *Empire Georgic*. I can still feel the surge of emotion as we sailed past the Isle of Wight and into the dock at Southampton. Britain certainly was a green and pleasant land and I was very pleased to be back on home soil again. A few years later, in 1954, on a return trip from Japan there was an explosion in the engine room of the *Empire Windrush* and the ship was lost.

Even today I still value the experiences I had in Malaya. I was fortunate to have met such genuine people, and the lessons learned then stood me in great stead for the life ahead of me. I was able to relate to and respect people of all kinds when they were deserving of that respect. Many of the names of friends known at Seremban have faded in time but I will never forget Ginger and Jock. They were both what we called "characters": Ginger Haythornthwaite was a very tall Lancastrian, a gangling character with a great sense of humour; Jock MacDonald was a short Scotsman who seemed to be dangerously obsessed with attractive women – "I love them," he sometimes told me, "and I just can't resist them" – but we liked him nevertheless. In many ways, he was quite ordinary and with very little education. We must have made an odd couple, the ex-public schoolboy and Jock the Glaswegian, yet our friendship was solid. I was never teased or held at distance on account of my background. The reverse held sway in that the experience of military service and the common experiences shared with your companions, each reliant on the other, never knowing when you might be in a life-or-death situation, dictated that social barriers should fall. Military rank was about the only division: social class and background became irrelevant. If your life depended on your comrade, who cared what family he was from?

From Southampton we trundled by train back to South Devon and to the same camp at Newton Abbot where it had all begun. In the lumbering manner of all military organisations, it actually took four weeks for the army to discharge us, but at last I was a free man, my service complete and civilian life awaiting me. I returned to Sheffield and was welcomed home as a military hero although I knew I was nothing of the sort. My parents even had the Union Jack fluttering from a flagpole in my honour.

My previous A-level results from Repton had been good enough to gain entry to Sheffield University. My father had wanted me to study chemistry despite the fact I wasn't very keen on the subject. In fact, Chemistry was my least favourite and it was no surprise that I failed the A-level exam. The sole reason behind my father's thinking was that he thought it would be good to have a chemist in the business. Anyway, I decided to have another shot at the exam and started a correspondence course, thinking that I might understand it all a bit better now.

I'd been studying steadily for a few weeks when, after lunch one day, my father invited me to join him in the sitting room. "There is something I want to talk to you about." He continued, "I realise that Chemistry is not a good subject for you. It is a waste of time trying to study it again. I think you should drop the correspondence course and do something else."

"Something else at the University?" I wondered.

"No, I have found a course for you at the Borough Polytechnic in London. It's in 'Chocolate & Sugar Confectionery'. I think you should do this rather than stay in Sheffield. You could take the course there and work here in the holidays for the business."

I was used to him making such decisions for me. That's how it always was for me. There was no question of my having a choice in my higher education or career. It was entirely my father's decision and he didn't even seek my endorsement. So I jumped at the chance. There was no point in arguing. I reckoned two years in London with a small company income, studying a course that would probably not be too demanding, would be quite relaxing after my two years in the Army. I said, "That sounds like a very good idea."

I was formally taken on to the staff of J. W. Thornton Ltd in July 1953 for the grand sum of £5 per week which was considerably better than the £1-10s a week I received as a corporal in the Royal Signals. Thus was my career choice made. No other consideration was given. The boy was fitted to the career, not the career to the boy.

Chapter 3
A Promising Start

My career with Thorntons began on the factory floor at Belper in the summer of 1953. This little Derbyshire town had been at the forefront of the revolution in industry and manufacturing from the mid-18th century. Originally known for the manufacturing of nails, it soon changed to become the hosiery capital of the region. Jedediah Strutt, with his brother-in-law William, invented what was known as The Derby Rib, an attachment to a stocking frame that allowed the production of ribbed cotton stockings. These were cheaper than silk, more comfortable than wool and became very popular, allowing Jedediah to open his first mill in 1777 beside the Derwent. The site was expanded to six water-powered mills, the last of these rebuilt after a fire and still in use today as the Derwent Valley Visitor Centre. Other spinners and hosiers set up mills, allowing the community to thrive and, as these businesses were classed as light industry, Belper retained the feel of a market town, a 'clean' environment in which a confectionery company could do business.

My brother Tony had been with the company for 4½ years, having already completed his National Service. He had had to serve only 18 months rather than the full two years of the later conscription term. He was not just older than me. He was taller, broader, had many friends including a regular girlfriend, and he had a TR2 sports car. Naturally, he was my hero. Although we had always been on good terms, there was no way I could be his equal. Everything that had happened to us since childhood meant that I looked up to him in every sense.

We still lived with our parents in Sheffield and had to drive early every morning to work, leaving around seven o'clock in Tony's bright red Triumph and travelling at breakneck speed over the moors into Derbyshire. We careered through the beautiful park at Chatsworth, narrowly avoiding the sheep, deer and cattle which roamed freely over the road, on through Matlock and Matlock Bath, former spa towns still inviting visitors to 'take the waters', until we reached the factory. We set a record for this journey of 28 minutes, astonishing when you think that some of its 30 miles was through built-up areas. There was a straight stretch of road on the moors between Sheffield and Baslow called Stony Ridge where Tony usually managed to get the TR2 up to 100 mph. These morning drives were very exciting, if somewhat reckless by today's standards. I enjoyed the throaty rasp of the exhaust and, when we had the hood down, the wind in the slipstream ruffled our clothes and hair. Of course, conversation was out of the question.

On my first morning at the Castle Factory on Derwent Street, Tony gave me the grand tour so that I could familiarise myself with the site. As with many others, this building was a former cotton mill which, during World War II, had been taken over by the famous aero-engine manufacturers Rolls-Royce Ltd. as their Performance and Stress Office. They had evacuated some of their workforce from the bombing in Derby, but they did very little to maintain the Belper premises. The front building was in a very poor state with whitewashed walls, dirty windows and dust everywhere. The dimly lit ground floor was stacked high with packaging and raw materials and, in one of the rooms, we met Mr Taylor whom Tony introduced as the storeman and boilerman. The long room on the first floor had been partitioned and the area beyond was filled with furniture, all covered in dustsheets, from our now-sold holiday home at Skegness. The rest of the room contained some huge galvanised tanks that Tony said were for 'crystallising'.

We went through to the rear building and upstairs we came to a long, beamed room. Nothing was happening there but downstairs we found activity. As Tony slid back the door, I was immediately hit by the noise and heat of the Boiled Sweet Department. On the left was the clanking *Rostoplast* from which was pouring an endless stream of unwrapped sweets onto a rotary cooling table. On the right was a 'cut-and-wrap' toffee machine from which wrapped toffees were flowing faster than the eye could see. Beyond these were several long metal slabs, some bearing huge mounds of toffee which slowly flattened as it cooled, others had similar mounds of a multi-coloured substance that resembled a huge plastic jellyfish but which was in fact the mass from which the sweets would be formed. Further on were the boiling pans, some with vertical stirrers mechanically mixing the sugar and glucose, others were just large copper bowls in which syrup bubbled as it boiled over a gas flame. Once the syrup had reached the correct temperature, one of the sugar boilers would pour it onto a water-cooled slab to be rolled out for the adding of colour and flavour. The slightest slip or unsteadiness and the syrup would spill over the side of the bowl with the risk of a serious burn to hand or arm.

Tony introduced me to Will Thompson. "This is my brother, Peter, who will be working in the Boiled Sweet Department for a bit."

"Pleased t' meet ye, I'm sure," replied Will. He was very short, in his 60s, bald and slightly bow-legged. He was in a white coat covered in bits of sugar and toffee but wore no hat. At that time the women had their hair completely covered but the men had no such headgear, just white coats and ordinary trousers covered, like Will, in toffee, sugar and grease.

Tony took me outside and showed me the antique vertical boiler which had to be coal-fed by hand to supply heat to the boiling pans. It looked at least 75 years old with steam hissing from various leaks and smoke pouring from its short chimney. By this time Mr Taylor was stoking it up. The coal lay in a huge heap at the end of the yard so he had to fetch it in a wheelbarrow and tip it just in front of the boiler, open the fire-door and start shovelling. I asked Mr Taylor what sort of a job it was. "I've 'ad a raight ta-tar wi' it. I'd gorra lo' on today. Ev'ry half hour it needs coal." He pondered a moment, then said, "Yer'll 'ave to ask yer Dad to buy another!"

Most of the machinery had come from a bankrupt factory in Newcastle. My father, together with Uncle Stanley, had bought it, partly to get hold of that factory's sugar allocation. Will had been its manager, already skilled in making boiled sweets, and had moved down to Belper to continue in that role. However, I later learned that he not been given any real authority and, as with much of the workforce, had been left more or less to do as he liked. He had a tiny office in an adjoining wooden shed and seemed to spend most of his time in there. Tony, despite not being appointed to any managerial duties, soon assumed some control over the unit and, by the time I arrived, the place was working more efficiently.

I took up my new job with no real idea of what was expected of me. Apart from a few suggestions from my brother, I was left simply to work out my own position within the company. There was no job description, no induction and no way to measure my progress. My father had said, "Do some work in the Belper Factory," and that was it. During my first few weeks I just helped where I could in the Boiled Sweet Department, usually weighing out the raw materials in a small extension to the building. On the roof was a galvanised steel tank containing the liquid glucose, an extremely viscous material that ran through a pipe to a large valve over the weighing scales. I had to put a metal bucket on the scales and open the valve, allowing just the right amount of glucose to fill it. Imagine how bored I got, just standing there waiting for the stuff to drip from the pipe. So I started to 'multi-task', I found I could open the valve, go away to do something else, like weighing the sugar, and get back just in time to stop the glucose overflowing. This was fine until I was called away one day to do something quite distracting and forgot all about my bucket. You can picture the scene when I returned. The floor was two inches deep in liquid glucose. It was a rather expensive mistake and very difficult to clean up, a job which, it goes without saying, was left entirely to me as the person responsible. It took two days, but it did prompt me to invent a switching device which sounded a bell the next time the bucket was almost full.

My new working routine was quite exhausting – up at six in the morning and not back home till six in the evening. Yet I still found time for a few social and sporting activities. After some experience in sailing while on holiday in North Wales, Tony had joined the

South Yorkshire Sailing Club, and I started to go out with him in small boats on a reservoir north of Sheffield. This was all very enjoyable… and then I met Mary.

I had not shown much interest in girls while in the Army – everyone said it was the bromide "they" put in our tea in the canteen – but in later life there was no such repression. I had first met Mary when straight out of service and had immediately been struck by her charm and beauty. I was still a bit reserved and it was she who shyly suggested that I might like to visit her at home "to watch television". Very few families had a TV set in the early 50s so this was rather an exciting invitation. I accepted and walked to her house where she opened the front door and smiled. "Hello, Peter. Come in, we are going into the living room."

I sat down next to her on the sofa and there was her father, Freddie, sitting opposite us in his armchair. Her mother came into the room. "Hello, Peter," she beamed. "Would you like to have a coffee?"

"Yes, please," I said, and there we all sat, primly watching this little box with its tiny black-and-white picture and chatting occasionally. After twenty minutes, Freddie fell asleep, her mother left the room and Mary and I snuggled a little closer. I soon had no interest in the broadcast at all. Things got very exciting and quite daring, considering that Mary's father was right in front of us, fast asleep. However, we were both mindful of the instructions given to young people of the dangers of "going too far". The few girls of that time who would sleep with a man were still thought of as 'fallen women' although this didn't deter most of the other young men from wanting to go out with them. On the other hand, the vast majority of girls heeded their mothers' advice and knew exactly how far to let things go. Mary was certainly one of those girls but we did enjoy a measure of intimacy that was bold for the time. She soon became my regular girlfriend and we went to parties and dances together. I would collect her in my mother's Hillman Minx and afterwards we would park in a secluded spot somewhere for one of our regular sessions of "getting to know each other". Still, mindful of whose car we were in, we always exercised enough self-discipline not to misbehave too much.

September arrived and I was ready to start my term at the London Borough Polytechnic. The Poly had its own arrangements with recommended bed-and-breakfast accommodation and I was placed in a freezing cold bedroom in this fairly dingy turn-of-the-century house in Streatham with a young man from Northern Ireland called Oliver. Olly's father ran a bakery business in Londonderry. The room was poor but we did at least get a decent breakfast and evening meal. The rent was roughly £2-10s (£2.50) a week which left very little from the weekly £5 I was getting from Thorntons. The course itself was undemanding – we studied Confectionery Manufacture, some Science and Design – and I concluded that the whole thing could have been done in about three months, but I decided to make the best of it and enjoy myself on the couple of pounds I had left to spend.

As the main summer vacation approached we were encouraged to get some work experience in the local confectionery business and I was offered a temporary job at a firm called Candycraft. I quite enjoyed this and was given the chance to do all sorts of manual tasks. One day I was chatting to Cliff, the manager, and mentioned my poor digs in Streatham. I said the rent was too much for what we got and I would like to find somewhere else. He immediately invited me to live with his family in their small terraced house in Clapham. He could only offer a tiny back room but, with a rent of just £1 for everything including meals, I was not going to refuse. His family was extremely kind to me and my one abiding memory is the smell of the egg-shampoo that my new landlady used on her hair before going out every Saturday evening.

My father's stories and my own experiences had already provided me with a measure of understanding even before I started the Polytechnic course. Although I found some of the Design lessons uninspiring I did have the opportunity to look through several useful books which made me realise something important – the Continentals, particularly the Swiss, were superb at creating beautiful-looking chocolate confectionery. One book, published by the Coba School, had some really exciting designs and I mentioned this to my father during one of my visits home.

"Oh yes?" he said, "Tell me more about it."

"Well, first of all, the appearance of the pieces is so attractive," I enthused. "They have so many different shapes, some like globes, some covered in icing sugar and others beautifully decorated. The descriptions of the centres are so mouth-watering: all sorts of truffles, some made with fresh cream and liqueurs, some made with nut pastes, roasted almonds, hazelnuts and walnuts, plus something called *ganache* which is a mixture of chocolate and cream. Delicious!"

"Hmm. Well, Peter, that sounds interesting. I will have to get Stanley to find out more about it."

"Yes, I think that would be a good idea. No one makes anything like it in this country. Here, it's all the same old boring stuff: just creams, toffees and jellies. We could beat all the others if we could develop our own range of Swiss-type confectionery."

Before long my father and uncle were off on one of their joint car holidays to Europe with their wives and they visited the Coba School with the intention of finding their own Swiss confectioner. This was quite an innovative thing to do as there was no market yet in Britain for continental-style confectionery but I felt pleased that my remarks had prompted them to action.

My two years at the Borough Polytechnic were soon at an end. I easily obtained the relevant certificates and, in the process, had a lot of fun which was very welcome after my two years in the Army. I kept in touch with only one person, Dick White. Dick was an Australian with an impish sense of humour. He had been my best friend in London and we had had a lot of fun together, souping up old 1930s Ford 8s to make them go as fast as possible. Mine eventually broke its rear axle when I was driving along Oxford Street, causing an enormous traffic jam with hundreds of enraged taxi drivers hooting their horns at me. Fortunately, Dick was with me and we managed to tow it to the side of the road. His father had a confectionery business in Melbourne called Small's. He told me the story of the time when he had been on work experience in a chocolate factory there. It involved a chocolate *mélangeur*, a huge mixing and grinding machine about 20 feet wide that has two large granite rollers suspended from rotating arms. These slowly crush the chocolate to a finer texture.

"An old chap who looked after the chocolate *mélangeur* was peering in over the side to see how the mix was going. His spectacles were not too securely fixed to his head and he was concentrating so hard on the chocolate mix."

"Yes, well, what is the point of the story?" I asked.

"Well, you see, his spectacles suddenly fell off into the mix and, before he could grab them, they went under one of the huge rollers."

"Well, what then? Did they have to stop the whole machine and try to find them?"

"No, the old chap just said, 'Never mind. They'll get ground up so fine that no one will be any the wiser'!"

Dick and I corresponded for a while and some years later I actually went to Melbourne and stayed with him for a few days. I regret that I have not seen him since then. 'Olly' Oliver returned to Londonderry and started work at his father's bakery. He joined the Territorial Army and, about 30 years later, I read that he had been shot by the IRA in front of his family as he was getting into his car to go to a T.A. parade. Not surprisingly, I found this news to be very upsetting.

After the Borough Polytechnic in mid-1954 I resumed my job for real at the Belper factory. Tony was still unofficially running the place though without much enthusiasm. Much of the factory was disused and filthy, and it bordered a large area of overgrown land to the rear which we were obliged to cut down regularly to discourage the rats and mice. We were producing mainly boiled sweets and still only had one delivery van to supply all our shops. In theory, Will was in charge of the manufacturing but, as observed before, he confined himself largely to writing on bits of paper in his office. The place was really run by Betty Hall, a wonderful woman who, without title or status, simply got on with the job. She was most perceptive and purposeful, and was extremely good at organising people to get the best out of them.

We did produce a small range of crystallised fondants such as *Savoys* and *Maple Brazils* as an extra line, but these were almost impossible to manufacture successfully. We started with a centre, for example a brazil nut, which had to be dipped by hand into the fondant mixture. This was a solution of sugar and glucose, partially crystallised, which sets to a hard cream with a pleasant eating texture. The process was then completed by leaving the fondants on stacked wire mesh trays in the upstairs galvanised tanks so that sugar crystals would form within the syrup. This was such a critical job that only Tony was allowed to do it. The syrup had to be boiled to a very precise temperature and the tanks were then left for twelve hours but, if we were lucky, the result was a beautiful piece of confectionery. Unfortunately, at least half of each batch wouldn't crystallize properly or turned unattractively white and would have to be scrapped. The process was such a headache that in the end, after much head-scratching and deliberation, Tony persuaded my uncle to drop the product.

Now that I was back permanently at Belper I extended my range of involvement in the manufacturing – boiling the sugar, dealing with the crystallised syrup – but the daily journey from Sheffield and back was becoming exhausting. Tony suggested that we find an alternative, and occasionally we stayed at the Lion, a small pub in the centre of the town, but they only had one guest room and it only had a double bed. Sharing a bed with my brother was an experience neither of us particularly relished. Prior to this, Tony had set up a camp bed in the office but the idea of 'sleeping over the shop' wasn't too popular either. It would have made sense for the company to purchase a small town flat, just right for two bachelors, during the week but this never occurred to anyone.

It was soon obvious to me that we did not have the best workforce available, largely because we were paying the lowest wages in town. Most people could get much better pay working in the many cotton and hosiery mills in the neighbourhood and, even though national figures were high at this time, Belper was largely unaffected by the spectre of unemployment. I felt this had been a major oversight when acquiring the factory and it was an issue that was destined to trouble me in the future, but back then I had my own problems to deal with.

I was well aware that I was unusually shy and self-conscious. I was starting work in a commercial business without any real confidence in my own abilities. This had manifested itself on several previous occasions. There was the time my parents had given a party some months after I'd left the Army and I met a young man, John Tyler, who had just completed his National Service after a year in the infantry in Malaya. He had been commissioned, I believe he'd reached the rank of Captain, and he'd been highly successful in the Army, winning the Military Cross for gallantry. Against this brave and outgoing young man I felt myself to be so small and worthless I could barely speak to him. My lack of confidence, the result of my father's overbearing manner, was such that I was convinced of my inferiority in relation to any man older than myself, especially those in positions of authority such as doctors, lawyers and military officers. This definitely included my brother Tony.

One day I was returning in the TR2 from Belper with him when our talk turned to the subject of girlfriends. He said, "It seems to be getting very serious with Mary. What are you going to do about her? Are you going to get engaged?" This was very much the social expectation after a year's courting, but I was not up for that at all.

"Certainly not," I replied in no doubt. "There's no way I want to marry her!"

This caused me to think about our relationship and do something about it. Mary was indeed a very attractive girl but I knew deep down that we were not in love and didn't really have that much of a friendship. It had been nice while it lasted but it was unfair to both of us to keep going out when I had no intention at all of getting married. So, choosing the worst possible time just after the T.A. ball at Christmas, we sat together in the parked car and I told her as gently as I could that I thought it was time we stopped seeing each other. Unsurprisingly, she was terribly upset and I felt an absolute heel about it, but it was time for a fresh start in our lives.

"Freshness and quality, Peter. That is what sells." This was the strong conviction upon which my father based the success of his company. "Freshness and quality. Other companies don't bother. When you go round our shops for yourself, you must insist on this." We were undoubtedly in the better position of being able to make our products and get them to our outlets the next day, long before Marks and Spencer pioneered the concept of chilled delivery. It was common practice among our rivals for confectionery to travel in hot vans to over-heated wholesale store-rooms and then in to stuffy shops with no air-conditioning. Little wonder that their stock sometimes was often in an unfit state when it reached the customers. Chocolate does not stay at its best in such conditions.

"We must never sell our products to any other retailer, Peter. That's the road to nowhere." This was another of my father's business principles. Thorntons had indeed achieved regional pre-eminence and brand recognition by following this policy. It was clear that for our own shops to remain profitable in their own right we must maintain a steady supply of product to them and not compromise their volume of sales by selling to non-company owned outlets.

My father also believed in the importance of the right location, a strategy which had been successful from the early days. "You see, Peter, this is an impulse business. We have to catch the passing trade. People see our beautiful window displays as they walk down the streets and, even though they may have no intention at first of buying, they are attracted to the mouth-watering confectionery on display and will go in and purchase something. Besides that, for the cost of one large central shop, we can have four or five in secondary areas with far more exposure to passing trade."

The contact with the Coba School in Switzerland had paid off and, in early 1954, Walter Willen, a young Swiss confectioner, came to work for us. Tony and I went to pick him up at Derby Station and brought him to the factory to introduce him to everybody. He spoke virtually no English and we lodged him at a boarding house in nearby Allestree. Walter was a charming, fair-haired young man and was probably able to earn more in England than he would have at home although the situation changed later when the Swiss became one of the more affluent European nations. I think he came originally just to learn English, possibly to stay for a year and then go home. Fortunately for Thorntons he remained until his retirement.

Walter set to creating a new range of handmade confectionery which we called our *Swiss Assortment*. It was really exciting to see those pictures from the Coba School book materialising in front of me. Such beautiful pieces, round spiky milk and plain chocolates, slices with layers of nut paste, pineapple *fourée* and everything so delicious. We eventually had to change the name to the *Continental Assortment* for reasons which will become clear later. Stanley worked closely with Walter during this period so that we could adapt the recipes more to the English taste. Stanley's daughter, my cousin Shirley, came in during her university vacations and a lab was established in one of the downstairs rooms for her and Stanley to work out how to extend the delicate short shelf life of these recipes. Tony was working on improving the shop displays to bring the new chocolates to the public's attention. With no market research whatever, assumptions were made that this range would sell. If it didn't, the company would have an expensive failure on its hands, but it was profitable enough to afford the risk.

As for me, I felt I was simply getting nowhere. I remained the company dogsbody and wondered how much longer I could stand this. Then Fate stepped in and everything changed. In July 1956 Egypt nationalised the Suez Canal which had previously been jointly controlled by the British and the French. The Prime Minister, Sir Anthony Eden, considered invading Suez, a concept that aroused international consternation. Everybody feared another major conflict which, in this new age of nuclear missiles, gave rise to all sorts of nightmare scenarios.

Not only were young men still required to do two years National Service but afterwards were supposed to serve for a further two years on the Army Reserve. This meant that, in cases of national emergency, they could be re-called into the Services. Shortly after leaving the Army I had received an invitation to apply for a Commission as a full Lieutenant Cipher Officer which seemed to me like a very good idea as it would certainly be more pleasant to serve as an officer if I had to return to the Army rather than to continue as an 'Other Rank'. I decided to accept this offer and, much to my surprise, I was quickly commissioned as a full Lieutenant. When an invasion of Egypt was under consideration the government recalled many Reservists to provide them with a sufficient number of troops. I duly received my call-up papers and was required to report to Aldershot.

Tony did his best to get me out of all this by writing to the War Office and telling them what an absolutely essential worker in the confectionery business I was. This seemed to make no impression on them, so I soon found myself accommodated in the pleasant surroundings of the Officers' Mess at the Signals Squadron rather than, as before, a barrack room with 20 or 30 squaddies. Shortly after my arrival I was allocated a truck filled with cipher equipment together with a group of men who were to be my Cipher Liaison Troop. We were given no instructions whatsoever and all we ever did, in fact, was to open the truck once a week, check the equipment and lock it up again. After we had spent a few such weeks of indolence at Aldershot we were suddenly informed that we were going to the Middle East with orders to drive our trucks in convoy to the docks at Barry in South Wales. We did this at a very slow pace only to be told upon our arrival at the docks, that our Embarkation Order had been cancelled and we were to return to Aldershot.

In due course, as well as checking the truck and its equipment, I was unexpectedly put in charge of the Cook House. I had absolutely no idea what was involved in this job either. Possibly they thought that my background in the confectionery business would make me an adequate catering manager. Anyway I soon learned the routines of ordering food and devising suitable menus. To my astonishment, everybody said that I was the best Cook House Manager that they had ever had. Well, I thought, I might as well enjoy myself while I'm here and I had my mother's car, a long-suffering Vauxhall Velox, brought down to Aldershot to allow me to get out and about. Dances were held on Saturday evenings in Guildford and I would go along with a friend to see if we could meet a few girls. One such was Stancie, but it was the usual thing – some dancing cheek-to-cheek and a bit of cuddling in the car – but nothing serious ever happened. It was simply a pleasant diversion from the complete boredom of being a Cipher Liaison Officer.

I did have fun in the Mess with my fellow officers and I felt like a guest in a rather good hotel for a while. In time I succeeded in completely smashing up mother's Vauxhall. I was driving back from a dance late one Saturday night and was going up a hill known locally as the Hog's Back. The otherwise-straight road had a left-hand bend at the top and, for some unfathomable reason I got into a rear-wheel slide. The offside wheel hit the adjacent kerb and the car did a total somersault, flipping on to its roof and skidding back down the road for some distance. Apart from bumping my head against the roof, I was apparently quite unhurt although it took me several days to get over the headache – and the embarrassment. Anyway, I was immobilised for a short period and resorted to going to Guildford on the back of a friend's motorbike. He drove at a frightening speed and Stancie was most concerned for me. She gave me a St Christopher medallion to protect me from further accidents. I carried this with me everywhere until it, together with my wallet, was lost somehow at Castle Donington airport in 1991. Unbelievably, about two weeks after, Stancie managed to track me down and we met up for old time's sake. I had mentioned over the phone that I had just lost the medallion so she thoughtfully brought along a replacement.

I was finally released after nine boring months in the Reserve Army in December 1956 and, shortly afterwards, I received a telephone call from David Ward, an old school friend who was organising a skiing party after Christmas to Arosa in Switzerland. I felt in need of a break before returning to work so I said that I would be absolutely delighted to come. We were to travel by rail all the way from Calais and this proved to be an interminable journey on a series of very slow trains, especially as we didn't have sleeping berths. My alternative was to climb into the overhead luggage rack and use it as a bunk. However, the trip was made much more bearable by my meeting with Alice Riley, a girl with whom I fell instantly in love. She was vivacious, with curves in all the right places and so completely attractive that I was hooked. This was the first time I had ever felt like this. We idled away the long hours, enwrapped in conversation and oblivious to our fellow travellers. We were all booked into the Crystal Hotel, ostensibly to share twin rooms with same sex colleagues, but inevitably there was some moving about between rooms. Alice and I did not let the presence of her room-mate prevent us from expressing our feelings towards each other.

By now I was beginning to feel the need to shed some of my inhibitions. Alice came from a fairly free-thinking family and it was time, I felt, for me to act likewise. During one of these occasions, when I was engaged in a programme of passionate kissing on her bed, she suddenly said to me, "Darling, is there something the matter? I've got blood all over my face. Is your nose bleeding?"

"Oh dear!" I apologised in some embarrassment. "I'm really sorry. I often get nosebleeds. You see, I have had them ever since I was little. Honestly, it's nothing."

Alice just happened to be a nurse, working exclusively at that time in tonsillectomies and she responded at once with a medical remedy.

"You must do something about it," she said, taking a look inside my mouth, "and what's more, your tonsils are in a terrible state. You really need to have them taken out, particularly if we are to be going out together. I don't want you being ill all the time."

"Oh," I murmured, "am I really in such a bad state as that?"

"Yes, you are," she declared. "You can see my uncle when we get back. He is an ENT specialist and he will operate on you. I expect that both operations can be done at the same time."

"Really?" I said, imagining the unpleasant experience I had let myself in for as a result of meeting Alice. "Do you think that is really necessary?"

"Yes, it is. If you want to go out with me regularly, you are going to have to do something about it."

The skiing in Arosa at the time was fairly elementary. We spent most of our time going up and down on the ski lifts and falling over. Yet I enjoyed this holiday enormously, spending all my spare minutes with Alice, dancing closely every night in the little bar-restaurant that we found, playing liar-dice uproariously with our friends, chatting intimately. By the end of the holiday we had decided to get engaged immediately.

I returned home late one evening and decided not to tell my parents about the engagement until the next day. In the morning, they were sitting up in bed having their tea from the *Teasmaid* in the bedroom when I looked in on them. I perched on the edge of the bed, gave them a big smile to put them into a relaxed mood, and told them all about the holiday. At the end I announced that I was engaged to Alice Riley.

"Who is Alice Riley?" they said almost in unison.

"Well," I replied, feeling very nervous, "she is a lovely person. She is always bright and jolly and full of fun. In fact, she is just like your friend, Mum, Elsie Nunweek. I've never yet found her to be miserable. She is beautiful, friendly, everybody loves her and I love her very much. And I want to get married."

"But," and there was a pause, "we have never heard of her before. What sort of a family does she come from? What does she do? What does her father do? Do they have any money?"

I didn't know which question to answer first.

"She has one brother called Robert," I said, trying to paint the best picture of her I could. "Her family lives in a lovely old Victorian house in a nice district, and her father is the General Manager of a steel mill in the East End – and they are a very happy family."

My mother now relaxed slightly, but my father was still clearly shocked. We started to discuss other things, such as how long would it be before we got married, and so on. I left them both rather taken aback by all this. They were obviously far from satisfied. Their unexpressed question was that of all parents faced with the prospect of their child's future marital happiness. "Would this girl, about whom we know nothing, be the right partner for our son?" It seemed to me they couldn't think of Alice, a nurse who worked in a children's hospital, as that person.

Once we had recovered from our holiday Alice invited me to meet *her* parents whom I found to be quite delightful, relaxed and amusing people. Her father was a real character with an obvious fondness for the bottle. He treated me as an equal straight away. This was an immediate relief after the relationship I had with my own father. Alice's mother was the same and I at once felt I was part of their family. Her dad had a massive diamond that had once belonged to his mother and I had this set, at some expense, into a lovely gold band, surrounded by smaller diamonds, as an engagement ring.

We had been out one evening and, back at her parents' house, Alice introduced me properly into the erotic arts. I was really a beginner when it came to sex, and I could imagine my parents' disapproval if such a liaison had been taking place under *their* roof, but Alice's parents seemed openly to encourage us. There were many such occasions when we would return to her home after they had gone to bed and continue our lessons in love in their living room. I would even stay over on some nights, sharing Alice's bed, and would be aware that this was something virtually unheard of in those puritan times.

On our first Saturday morning back in Sheffield after our holiday, we went to The Stonehouse, a pub for the young socialites of the day. It was next to the famous Cutler's Hall on Church Street in the city centre. The Cutler's Hall was a very impressive and beautiful building, home to the Cutler's Company of Sheffield and the place where many wonderful balls and parties were held. As we walked into The Stonehouse I was bursting with pride having this wonderful girl, wearing her sparkling engagement ring, hanging on my arm. Everybody immediately wanted to talk to us and to know all about the engagement: was it sudden, how and where had it happened, and when would we get married? For some months I felt enormously proud of myself. I had managed to capture this delightful and vivacious person and make her my fiancée. It all seemed perfect – until things started to go wrong.

Chapter 4
Rise and Fall

In early 1957, shortly after returning from the skiing holiday, I had my first lucky break in the family business.

"Pete," said Stanley to me one day, "can you come into my office? I want to ask you something."

There was only the one office. We all used it. It was on the first floor, overlooking the yard. He sat at the desk and looked at me. I had no idea what he was about to say, but he was always pleasant to me, more of a friend than a senior member of the family business.

"We are having serious problems in the Chocolate Department in Sheffield. I wondered if you would like to take it over and become the manager."

I could hardly believe my ears. I was actually being given a post of responsibility. It had been so frustrating over the previous five years, having no real position in the company, that I'd seriously been seeking a way out.

"Of course I would," I replied eagerly. "I've been fed up with having nothing to do. I promise you that I will make a great job of it." I was already thinking of the benefits of having my own company role, not the least of which was the end of the daily journeys to Belper with Tony.

The Chocolate Room in the Sheffield factory took up the whole of the first floor and, despite being only twenty years old, was already beginning to look shabby. The pine floors were badly worn with repeated cleaning, the white paint was flaking from the brick walls and the green metal window frames were starting to rust. The low ceilings gave the place an air of cluttered oppression and allowed no space for overhead wiring or pipes. There were two offices beyond a partition: one for my father and the other for his secretary, the now-married Miss Cutts who, with a small clerical team, dealt with all the administration.

Thankfully, there was one very competent person there and that was Iris Muddiman. I had just three weeks to learn as much as I could from Iris before she left to have a serious operation. I got on famously with her. She was one of those wonderful employees, dedicated utterly to the business. She was in her late 30s, tall, slim, outspoken and would do everything possible to achieve success for the firm. At the end of the three weeks I said to her, "Iris, I think you are an incredible person and you have been a big help to me. I couldn't have asked more from anybody. I do hope the operation goes well and that you'll be back soon."

"Thanks, Mr Peter, it has been great working with you. I hope to see you again." Clearly she was apprehensive about her forthcoming treatment.

As I walked around my new department on the first Monday I could see some of the problems at once. Much of the working space was taken up by our two large chocolate enrobers. These, as the name implies, covered the fondant creams and marzipan centres in chocolate as they passed beneath on a long conveyor belt, but they were pre-war models, second-hand and very decrepit. They were not independently powered but were linked by an arrangement of line-shafts and leather belts which came up through the floor from the ceiling of the floor below. They took up the full width of the building so it was really difficult to move around them as the belts flapped noisily above.

In between the enrobers I found a figure dressed in a white boiler suit all covered in chocolate. This was Bill Jones, the manager. As he heaved slopping buckets of chocolate around from kettle to enrober, he was perspiring heavily. I told him that I had been asked to take over as manager.

"Ye are welcome to it, man," he replied in his rich Geordie tones. "This place is a reet bugger's muddle! Gandie at that, will yer! There's not enough room to swing a moggie! These machines are in a dreadful state. That Leslie Charlesworth seems to be struck by the moon, an' Stanley is always yakkin' on about what he used to do when he ran the machines but I does no' think tha' he knows *what* he's talkin' about."

"I see," I said, trying to mollify him a little. "No wonder they have asked me to take over. I'm not sure now that I am looking forward to this quite so much!"

It was obvious that something needed to be done to improve the efficiency of the department. Things were not working well and we were failing to deliver adequate stocks to our shops. I decided not to bother asking my father or Stanley for permission to make changes. They would only say no, especially if it meant spending more money. Dad was particularly adverse to any expenditure on capital. His constant fear of financial collapse confined his spending to the opening of new shops and improving the existing ones. In reality, Thorntons was far from impending bankruptcy as it was a profitable, cash rich business with high sales, particularly of its *Special Toffee*, and had never made any loss nor had debts. There was always plenty of money in the bank. However, there was absolutely no question of buying a new machine. Thorntons had never bought new machines. We only bought second-hand equipment, usually very old and virtually for nothing and then we refurbished it at low cost.

Leslie Charlesworth was the unofficial manager of everything except the Chocolate Department. He'd never been formally appointed to the position; he'd simply just taken charge. I was very afraid of him as he tended to get angry when things weren't being done properly. He was a very tough character, in spite of being short and quite bald, and most of the workforce was scared stiff of him. There were times when he was very difficult to talk to and, although he was an intelligent and highly driven individual, most people agreed with Bill Jones when he said that Leslie was "touched by the full moon". This refusal to communicate was a big problem for me because Leslie was in charge of producing all the chocolate centres needed for the enrobing but, when I took the list of all the centres I required for next week's work, I could never get a word in against his constant toffee boiling and fondant making. I would stand around each Friday, feeling rather like a spare part, just waiting to be noticed and observing all that was happening in the Toffee Department. This was on the ground floor and much more than just toffee was made there. Different chocolate centres, fudge and nougat were all produced in an area half the length of the Chocolate Department.

There was a section at the back full of clanking cast-iron boiling pans stirred by a device that moved up and down independently as the toffee cooked. When it looked about ready, the operator would stop the stirrers, stick a metal spatula into the mix, draw it out and then rush to the sink to run the semi-liquid toffee under the cold tap. This was how we knew if the batch was at the right consistency or perhaps needed further boiling. It was hardly scientific but certainly better than the original method of sticking our wet fingers into the mix. Here, too, was the fondant machine in which a solution of boiled sugar and glucose was passed through a horizontal screw to form a crystalline paste. This was used to make 'chocolate cream' centres and the like. Pouring the mixture into the feeder trough over the revolving screw was an extremely dangerous job which Leslie always did himself to avoid injuries to anyone else. He would tip the syrup from one of the boiling pans into a large bowl and carry it up a set of wooden steps to the fondant machine. I watched him do this in dread anticipation of his falling with all the appalling consequences of such an accident. If only I could supply him with a simple mechanical pump this risk could be avoided, but it was not my place yet to suggest such a thing.

The main part of the room had a series of cold metal slabs where melted toffee was hand-poured into tin trays. This whole area, with its concrete floor and higher ceiling, was bustling with people putting trays into racks, operating the noisy cutting machines and all under the watchful eye of Mr Charlesworth. He seemed to be able to spot a slacker without even turning his head. "Don't just stand around! Get on with your job!" he would bawl across the room. He made certain that I had little or no opportunity to speak to him. On the few occasions when I managed a quick comment I would get a very gruff answer. He seemed absolutely determined to be difficult with me, and you would suppose that his attitude would prevent him from working to the company's best interests. But no, he always produced exactly what I wanted, when I wanted it and to the highest quality. He would grumble and complain in his begrudging way but he always came up with the goods.

I agreed with Leslie that it was time for one of the chocolate enrobers to go. He was delighted if he could "get one up on Stanley" who had always argued in their defence.

"I keep tellin' Stanley it's nowt but a nuisance to have them machines in the department. You should get rid o' one of 'em." They were both in poor condition with narrow conveyor belts, the standard size when they were made, and it was a constant struggle to keep them in operation. This seriously limited our levels of production. Scrapping one machine, I thought, would give us more space and make it easier to get the remaining machine to work properly but there was one big operational problem. It would have to be changed from milk chocolate to dark chocolate and back again at least once a week. This was a difficult and messy task which involved partly taking the machine to pieces and getting inside to clean it thoroughly so that each type of chocolate did not contaminate the other.

Having decided which of the lumbering old machines was beyond restoration, Leslie and I, together with several strong men, came in one weekend to do the job. As we employed no engineers, it was up to us to dismantle the thing and drive it off in a hired truck to the scrap yard. Then, although I had no engineering experience to speak of, I set about trying to modernise what was left. I found some suppliers in Sheffield to provide all the bits and pieces I needed and spent a weekend drilling holes in the remaining enrober and bolting my new inventions to it. I stripped out the old line-shaft and had Mr Monks, a local electrician, connect up the motors. To my astonishment and great pleasure it all worked.

Despite my initial efforts our manufacturing levels still fell short and I knew that more was needed if we were to raise production further. We didn't have the benefit of computers or calculators but I acquired a little manual adding machine and devised a new approach to some of our systems management. The first thing to be changed was the Friday cleaning. For many years it was the custom that there would be no production at all on that afternoon and every member of staff would pick up a mop, bucket or a brush and try to clean the place. All we ever achieved was chaos and poor hygiene, so instead I brought in a couple of early evening cleaners and saved half a day's production.

Iris Muddiman now returned after her operation and was quickly helping to get things moving again. She had tremendous energy and we often had vigorous rows over the best ways to increase production, but she was usually right and together we made great improvements. We bought our raw chocolate from Cadbury's and they provided us with a consultant. He was Jim Nolan and he was bursting with ideas about how to cover our chocolate centres. Some of his suggestions were unusual, to say the least, but by taking a few of his ideas on board we started improving both the quality and quantity of our output.

Jim took me to Cadbury's factory at Bourneville on one occasion and showed me into an overwhelmingly noisy room filled with chocolate enrobers, all greatly enhanced versions of our old equipment. There were about thirty such machines, operated by around 500 employees, and I took note of all the little devices and modifications they used to save time and make a better product. This visit had a profound effect on me, and I remember sitting in my car for an hour afterwards writing down everything I had seen before returning to Sheffield.

The next production issue to be tackled was that of automation. Our equipment had always been started manually but it took an hour and a half before the machine was fully operational. I re-designed the entire system to get everything running automatically.

Then there was the laborious and messy method of filling the enrobers with chocolate. I approached Ashtons, a local engineering company, to supply a special type of pump which I fitted with a motor and installed into a frame. Iris's new husband, Walter Smith, was a plumber and he helped me to connect it to the equipment by a special pipe. This was a very effective innovation that allowed us to get chocolate into the enrobers more quickly and without the spillage we'd had previously.

Sometimes chocolate would get everywhere and I remember a lovely young employee called Margaret who tried hard but who wasn't exactly 'the brightest button in the box'. I once gave her the job of cleaning out the large kettles which could hold up to three hundred pounds of liquid chocolate. I left her to it, and when I returned she was covered from top to toe and standing in what could only be described as her own personal lake of thick melted chocolate.

"What on earth have you been doing, Margaret?" I asked her in astonishment. "You've got the stuff everywhere!"

"Well, I am very sorry, Mr Peter," she said in her nicely-rounded tones, "but I was only doing my best." I sent her to the cloakroom for a complete change and wash. Iris took charge of the situation to get everything cleared up and gave me one of her withering looks.

"Now then, Mr Peter," she said. "I hope that you have learned a lesson from that!"

I could now afford the luxury of not coming into work until 7.15 each morning in the full knowledge that everything would be up and fully running when I got there. We were turning out five tonnes of high quality merchandise each week instead of the previous one tonne. We no longer short-supplied our shops and presumably our gross margins and profits had increased to match. Life seemed to be getting better at last. I was enjoying my work and took immense satisfaction from watching the serried rows of beautifully finished chocolates coming from the cooling tunnel to be packed into trays and sent to our shops. I felt I was not only making improvements in the Chocolate Department but also in my social life. I now had my own Merlin Rocket racing dinghy to use at the club, and Alice and I were spending our weekends together, sailing and wondering how many such blissful interludes lay ahead of us.

My reward for all this effort was to be allowed at last into the inner sanctum of Leslie Charlesworth's tiny office for the thrice-weekly meetings between him and Stanley. My uncle would arrive at about 10.30, walk through the factory despite not wearing any protective clothing, and would assume his position in the single office chair at Leslie's desk. Leslie would stand in his white boiler suit, his arms folded impassively, and I would have to squeeze into the corner behind the door. The conversation was invariably about the toffee recipe.

"I was having dinner at a friend's house last Saturday evening," Stanley would say, "and someone told me that they thought the toffee flavour wasn't as good as it used to be."

"Well, it don't taste right t' me neither," grumbled Leslie in reply. "It's that there butter you bought. Right rubbish it is."

Stanley always ignored Leslie's outspokenness. "I had to get it from another broker," he explained. "It's not the usual New Zealand stuff that we generally get, but it was still expensive enough."

"That don't mean owt. It's still rubbish."

"Well," remonstrated Stanley, "we are going to have to use it. I can't very well send it back."

"I could put more of it in until the next lot of 'New Zealand' comes."

"How much more, do you think, Leslie?"

"Maybe a pound, and take out two pound of the margarine."

Stanley considered this. "No, I think that's too much. How about take out one pound of margarine and put in half a pound of extra butter?"

"Aye, I s'pose that'll do," agreed Leslie.

"No, hang on a minute. I'm not quite sure that's right..."

This conversation could easily last an hour and a half by which time Stanley would have smoked an awful lot of cigarettes and done most of the talking. At the end he would say something like, "Well, strike a light, Leslie! We could go on all day like this. Look, OK, we'll take out one pound of margarine and put in half a pound of butter – and that will be that!"

As far as I could tell these conversations and recipe changes were never written down. Everything was simply retained in their heads. I made no contribution to the discussions and I suppose I was allowed to stand there mainly for the benefit of my education. As pointless and time-wasting as these meetings seemed, I still had to admit that we had established and maintained a fantastically successful product. Making the *Special Toffee* was a very simple process anyway.

Although some parts of the business were inefficient, particularly the chocolate production, Stanley and Leslie had a very effective method of costing the manufacturing process.

"How much do we pay for the raw materials?"

Leslie would have the answer already worked out. "About £20 a batch."

"And the labour? About the same, isn't it?"

"Aye."

"So that gives us £20 for profit and we should be able to sell it for about 1/7d a quarter. Yes, I think that's about right." Stanley would be satisfied as this allowed for the straightforward development of new products without too much concern for their profitability. As a small business, we simply used our own shops to test out a new line very quickly.

"There's this great pile of walnut powder," said Leslie one day. "It's from chopping walnuts for the walnut truffles. It's daft to just leave it there. What do you want us to do with it?"

"Well," I pondered, "we don't want to chuck it away. Besides, we'll just keep making more of it while ever we continue with *Walnut Truffles*."

"Aye, I know. Tell you what," he said, having already got an idea in mind. "I'll mix it up with marzipan, then you can cover it with chocolate, stick a walnut on top of it and we will call it *Walnut Marzipan*."

"Yes, that's a great idea," I said. *Walnut Marzipan* became a best seller and we were soon grinding walnuts just to make the powder.

Despite these occasional inspired ideas, Leslie remained both overbearing and uncommunicative and there had been too many Fridays when I had been kept waiting overlong in his Toffee Department just for him to take my list of required chocolate centres without a word beyond the usual grumbles. This made our working relationship very strained and I was determined to do something about it. We were, when all was said and done, both managers of our respective departments with comparable responsibilities. As with all the other domineering adults I had encountered in my life, I resented being humiliated in this way. I decided to get even with Leslie by deliberately provoking him into an argument. I reckoned he would be so taken aback that I could assert my right to be treated as an equal, not as some inferior underling. I wasn't at all sure of how I was going to do this and I worried about it for days beforehand. There was a central staircase in the Chocolate Department coming up from the Toffee Department and I seized my opportunity when he came up the stairs one day to speak to me.

"Look, Leslie," I said, "I have to tell you that I've had quite enough of your ungracious behaviour!" I raised my voice uncharacteristically. He looked very surprised. "I refuse to spend my Friday afternoons standing around in your department waiting for you to give me the courtesy of a few moments of your time!"

The girls who were placing centres on the enrober all looked up in amazement. They'd plainly never heard anyone speak to Mr

Charlesworth like this before. He stood there blankly, seemingly lost for words.

"In the future I expect you to behave civilly towards me," I continued. "You'll agree that we'll be able then to do our jobs much better."

At last Leslie seemed to recover from this unexpected onslaught and said, "I'll be obliged to ask you to show me some respect. I've been in the firm for nigh-on twenty year – an' you've not been here five minutes!"

I stood my ground. "I'll treat *you* with respect when you start to treat *me* with respect." I manoeuvred him into the tiny upstairs office to continue the conversation until we had reached an agreement. This seemed to change his attitude and he suddenly began to see me in a new light. After that things became much easier between the two of us.

However, I was still left with the thorny problem of my father's attitude. I still couldn't challenge *his* dogmatic self-assurance, his absolute conviction that he was right in all things, and I was aware that everyone in the family was being regarded in a similarly dismissive way. We were treated to the regular 'Monday morning row' in which Stanley would meet with him in his oak-panelled office at about ten o'clock. My father would have walked there from home and Miss Cutts, his faithful secretary, would have prepared the room by putting the mail on his desk and warming his cushions from the willow-backed armchair in front of the gas fire.

On entering the office, he would immediately telephone the bank for the account balance although he usually knew this from the running totals he kept on the back of envelopes in his pocket. His telephone manner belied his normally brusque exterior as he tended to let the mouthpiece slip under his chin while talking so that the other party could hardly hear him. I remember the times I had phoned him from school at Repton only to listen to his voice fading in this seemingly shy and reclusive way.

Stanley would give him time to settle and then come in at about 10.30. They would sit facing each other to talk business and I was sometimes called in to witness the proceedings. It could hardly be called a discussion because mostly it consisted of my father merely telling Stanley how wrong he was and how stupid were all his ideas. His voice rose as his anger increased, and this ritual was enacted every Monday morning, for who knows whose benefit.

Through all this, I had had no time to think of my engagement or whether I should perhaps be looking for a house for myself and Alice. Not surprisingly, she eventually raised the issue and started to urge me to look at properties, but I felt quite unhappy about this, particularly as we'd not yet agreed a wedding date. I felt I was just not ready to settle down and, besides, I didn't really have the money. All the houses she wanted to look at were far too big and expensive. She also kept holding me to the promise to see an ENT specialist about the regular nose-bleeds and tonsil problems and eventually I heeded her advice. I was told that the specialist could perform a nasal skin graft to stop the bleeding and take out my tonsils at the same time. Iris Smith, formerly Mrs Muddiman, was now completely recovered from *her* hospital admission and was fully capable of running the department in my absence, so I decided to take some time off in October 1957 to have my operation.

The procedure went well enough but the after-effects were pretty shattering. I was left with a very painful throat, a completely blocked nose and it was extremely difficult to breathe for quite some time. I was so weakened by the operation that I had to have three weeks off and, in my convalescence, I started to get depressed. I had no idea why as I'd never suffered from this before and I was aware that in my life there were many reasons to be cheerful. However, Alice's decision to leave her job at the Children's Hospital in Sheffield to work in London wasn't one of them. I couldn't work out why she was doing this. Was she simply trying to get away from me?

This depression deepened and took on an air of permanence. I would wake in the morning, feel OK for about ten minutes and then the blackness would hit me. It was completely irrational, or so it seemed. I didn't know what lay behind it and I felt terrible all the time. Alice couldn't understand me and seemed indifferent to my situation. Before the year was out, we knew that something had to be done about both my condition and our deteriorating relationship. We decided to take a few days off after Christmas, drive over to the Lake District and stay in the Old England Hotel at Lake Windermere. We set off in the company's Morris Minor and drove first up the east of the Pennines to call on one of Alice's old friends. Then, after tea and some delicious cake, we crossed over to the west and reached our destination.

The hotel was in a spectacular location, right on the edge of the lake. We checked in and were given a beautiful room overlooking the water. Here, we thought, we could have some privacy and put things right between us but, for some reason, we were both now suffering from stomach ache. We couldn't eat much dinner and, before long, we were so ill that any ideas of passion and rapprochement went straight out of the window. In the morning I knew that we had something serious and I asked the hotel to call a doctor. We both had food poisoning – could it have been Alice's friend's cake? – and our weekend was completely ruined. We stayed on a few days until we were strong enough to return home, but our journey back was a miserable affair.

A few days later, Alice phoned me at work and asked if we could meet at lunchtime. We went to a pub at Ringinglow on the outskirts of Sheffield and here she declared her position.

"I want us to finish. I want to call off the engagement and I don't want to see you any more". I was dumbfounded. "Anyway," she continued, "I have decided to go to America for a year on an exchange-nursing visit." This was devastating news to me. I was still deeply and utterly in love with this girl, almost obsessed.

"But – I am madly in love with you," I protested. "I couldn't bear to live without you. I want to spend the rest of my life with you. What's the problem? Is it because I have this awful depression?" She didn't answer. "How could you do this to me when we have had so much fun together?"

"I just don't want to go on with it," she said after an awkward silence. "Do you want your ring back?"

She had no explanation for her feelings however desperately I pleaded. "Keep the ring," I said ungraciously and left the pub in a complete daze to drive back to the factory. I couldn't do anything more that day and just sat in the office until it was time to go home. My grief was such that I thought I would never be able to fall in love ever again. The loss of this special love was just too painful.

The weeks after Alice went out of my life were among the most miserable in my life. I was now suffering from depression and a broken heart as well. I made a few pathetic attempts to get her back. I wrote to her in America but had no reply. Nothing I did could dispel my grief.

Mental illness was something of which one was greatly ashamed. You didn't talk about it and you tried to hide it. I didn't tell my parents nor did I ever see a doctor. My depression stole away all enthusiasm I might have had for anything. Everything was a great effort. It was easier just to curl up into a little ball and do nothing. I had to force myself to every action because it all seemed so pointless. The world was a dull grey place and I was a dull grey person in it. I was beginning to feel suicidal. Alice had been the only one I had spoken to about this and even she had not been fully aware of the depth of my feeling. However, by the start of 1958, Iris had recognised my state of depression and guessed how distraught I was over the broken engagement. She became quite maternal and would direct me to do some work in the office rather than just stand around looking miserable in the Chocolate Department. I came to believe that the only way to cope was through work – complete and total distraction by using every hour that God sent me, from dawn to dusk, every day of the week.

I was already working very hard when I met Roger Baker, a friend who had been on the skiing trip. We were in the bar at the Sports Club one evening and he told me that I ought to do something different to get over the break-up, something like joining the Territorial Army. I thought he was probably right.

I volunteered for the T.A. and started to spend all my weekends, plus two evenings a week, being a soldier once more. There was a routine to be followed in the T.A., and wonderful friends with whom I had to be cheerful, so there was no way to continue drowning in a sea of self-pity and misery. The hectic activity pulled me out of my depression even though it took at least two years before I felt fully over it. Although I have had minor recurrences, I have not been afflicted in such a deep way since then.

My new Territorial Army unit, the Hallamshire, was an infantry battalion, part of the York and Lancaster Regiment with a very distinguished record during the last war. I was taken on despite my lowly commission in the Royal Signals and my lack of infantry training. In the Mess I was soon mixing both with senior officers who had distinguished war careers and with younger officers who, like me, had recently joined after their National Service. In the light of my long-standing feelings of inferiority and my newfound depression, this was a challenging experience.

I very much admired Colonel Nicholson, the Commanding Officer, for his ability to think on his feet and make difficult decisions. On his retirement he was succeeded first by Col. Newton and then Col. Hutton. To me, these men represented 'the best of British' and my ego received a welcome boost from the fact that they were quite prepared to accept me, to relate to me and to encourage my self-respect. I soon found my feet in their company and I worked hard and learned quickly.

The monthly Mess Dinners were enormously enjoyable. I loved the traditions, the friendships, the games, the drinking and joking. It all helped me to forget about Alice for a time and I slowly started to gain some confidence. I found myself doing things I had never imagined. I once went as part of a group to a social evening organised by another T.A. unit and at the end I was urged to take the stage and give a speech of thanks. To my great surprise I managed this quite easily, with no planning and none of the usual paralysing fear. I was not yet fully aware of the powers of the mind to overcome the emotions but I was beginning to suspect that I was capable of much more than I'd realised.

My work with Thorntons still took up most of my time. I felt that I had made significant improvements in the department and I now turned my attention to the preparation of truffle chocolate centres. These were being hand-made by a small team of women headed by Rose Lister. They started with a mass of truffle paste and had to knead it and squeeze it through a dough roller to get it to the right thickness. It was then divided into individual pieces with metal cutters and the whole lot dusted liberally with powder to prevent the pieces from sticking together. It was a fairly intensive manual procedure and I asked Rose about it one day.

"This is a laborious job, isn't it, Rose? Surely there's a better way. What do you think?"

Rose was in her mid-50s and was a jovial and hard-working employee. She considered my question for a moment.

"Mr Peter," she said after a pause. "I've been tellin' Leslie for nigh-on two years to get a bar with ten cutters on it. Then, by 'eck! We'd cut ten pieces in one go!"

"What a good idea," I said. "I'll try to get one for you."

This made things a lot better but I still thought there was more we could do. An obvious improvement would be to use what is called an extruder but I knew nothing about them or where I could get one.

I then happened to be talking one evening in the bar of the Abbeydale Sports Club with John Mickelthwaite, a friend who owned a meat products business. I knew he made sausages so I raised a query with him.

"John, I've got a problem in the factory. I think I need some sort of extruder. Do you use anything like that in your business?"

"Of course we do," he said with a grin. "How on earth do you think the sausages are made?"

"To be honest, I've really no idea," I replied.

"Well, with a sausage machine, we use a screw-type extruder. Would you like to come and try your truffle paste through it?"

I took a tray of truffle mix to his factory and tried it out. It wasn't entirely successful because the screw churned the paste and squeezed the fat out of it onto the floor. However, I didn't abandon the idea and on a visit to Bassett's factory in Sheffield I saw a liquorice extruder in action. It had four horizontal screws and forced the liquorice through a plate into the required shape. This seemed more promising and I started looking through the *Confectionery Production* magazine and eventually found one for sale at a bankrupt liquorice factory in Pontefract, a Yorkshire town well-known for its liquorice manufacturing as the plant root used to be grown there.

It was always disheartening to go to a sale at a bankrupt factory. I would walk round all the echoing hollow rooms and imagine the activity which must have taken place, thinking of how that business would have developed, and yet now its employees would be sitting at home facing unpaid bills and no future. There was always a dead atmosphere when you had an assembly of idle machines, no sounds, no buzz of production, no deadlines and no customers. What use were such places without the people, their plans and schedules?

Anyway, I found what I was looking for and bought it for £20. I had to arrange transport to get the extruder back to Sheffield and then spent several weekends working on it in the factory garage. I stripped away the ancillary equipment, mounted it over a roller conveyor and made some wooden boards to slide beneath it. Once this was done I asked Leslie to get Tom Rich and some other muscled chaps to help me move it in the lift upstairs to the Chocolate Department. There was some shaking of heads but they all set to the task in earnest, and my new contraption was soon in position, ready for Nellie and her team to continue making their *Nut Truffles*.

She put a large lump of truffle mix into the hopper of the extruder. I switched the machine on and there was a sudden loud clanking noise immediately followed by a jet of truffle shooting out of the extruding nozzles. Alma Pashley, who usually hand-dipped and rolled the truffle centres, looked alarmed. "Mr Peter!" she exclaimed. "Slow it down! Us'll not keep up wi' that! You've got it going too fast."

I quickly switched the thing off and Alma, Rose and the other ladies got down to clearing up the mess. I changed the geared motor to run at about one-tenth of the speed and tried again. This time, perfection; everybody cheered as we started producing very neat lines of truffle paste. All Rose and her team had to do was cut across the boards with a long knife, saving a great deal of time and reducing much of the boredom. She looked after the new system well and production was increased almost a hundredfold. Alma was happy too as she didn't have to wait for her truffle centres anymore.

Our father was well into his middle age by 1958 and contented himself with occasional visits to the shops just to see how things were going. There were the inevitable criticisms of changes and interminable conversations with Stanley about business strategy. These two were the only directors at that time, with sole controlling interests, which meant that Tony and I had no real say in the company's future plans.

Tony was spending less time at the Belper factory because he preferred to be more involved in managing the shops. Like the rest of us, he wasn't doing this with our father's blessing but rather because he felt it was what he should do. He was quite right about this and was highly successful. He gradually took over the whole management of the retail side and Dad seemed content to leave him to it. His first major improvement was in the presentation and layout of the shops and their window displays. He designed a simple glass counter in which Walter Willen's hand-made *Swiss Assortment* was presented in a very mouth-watering way. Sales soon began to increase. He took over new shops as and when suitable premises became available. The Thorntons network was spreading.

By now we had a huge range of chocolates but some sold less well than others and I felt it would be practical to dispense with them. I did a bit of elementary market research and Tony and I agreed to cease their production. We didn't consult with Dad or with Stanley. We just went ahead and did it, but Stanley didn't seem to mind as such decisions helped to improve our business efficiency. He only came to Sheffield three mornings a week so he really didn't have much time to notice.

One day in October I was busy in the chocolate department when Stanley came up to me. "Have you ordered the Ritchie boxes?"

I had no idea what he was talking about. "What do you mean? What Ritchie boxes?"

"You know, the picture boxes that we buy for Christmas. We usually have about 500 of them."

"No," I said, "I don't know anything about them, but leave it with me. I'll see to it".

So I found one of Ritchie's catalogues full of florally-decorated chocolate boxes that I personally felt were just about the most boring presentation boxes I'd ever seen. They looked more suitable for packing table mats than chocolates. Anyhow, I went ahead and ordered a thousand, double the usual quantity, so that we could offer a variety of designs to the fifty or so shops we were currently maintaining. They'd get around twenty boxes each which I felt was enough to meet our Christmas market.

We also had a seasonal item which we called *Candies*, a selection of chocolates and fondant creams, and probably sold about two thousand of those in their distinctive round boxes with a transparent lid. No one else had thought of selling confectionery in such boxes but they sold very well because people could see "what they were buying". I had initially designed a selection of chocolates which Dad thought should be called our *Oxford Assortment* and Tony and I decided to stick our necks out and pack 10,000 of them for the next Christmas together with 10,000 boxes of *Candies*.

We got these ready for Christmas 1958 and they were a huge success. They sold out well before the holiday season so we knew that we would need to increase the quantity the following year. This was the start of Thorntons' successful Christmas chocolate box trade and they were packed in a very tiny department in Sheffield. One packer per table could do about fifty one-pound boxes a day, selecting from the trays of different chocolates in front of her. Once I had installed a conveyor belt to supply an endless stream of confectionery, the packers were able to double their output. The shortness of the room meant that the conveyor had to be U-shaped but this was just another of the specific technical challenges that I had to solve to improve our business.

Then there was my cousin Michael. He was Stanley's son and, like me, he joined the business after completing his two years of National Service. He, too, started at Belper and initially worked through the production departments while completing a Company Secretarial Course at Chesterfield Technical College. As soon as he was qualified, he took over much of the administrative work including the buying of raw materials. I never really got to know him properly even though we knew each other well enough from childhood. As he was four years younger, we never established any close friendship. I could definitely see Uncle Stanley in him. He was fun-loving and looked like a rugby player which was just as well as that is exactly what he was. He had a big frame and a loud voice, very useful for singing rugby songs in the bar after matches. As Tony had moved on to retail management, Mike gradually assumed overall responsibility for the Belper factory.

Tony, Mike and I made many trips to Germany during this period. Our first was in 1958 and we went to investigate German confectionery. We were curious to see what products they sold and how they displayed them in their shops. It was quite a squeeze in the little Morris Minor as Tony and Mike were big men and had to sit almost doubled up for the duration of the journey. I was driving rather fast along the *autobahn* which, in light of the still-weakened German economy, was largely empty of other traffic. There were no speed limits and the road was like a racetrack. I had nearly reached 90 mph, very fast for that tiny engine, when I suddenly noticed the oil pressure drop. We pulled over to the side of the road and raised the bonnet. The dip stick revealed that there was no oil in the engine. I looked under the car and saw the last few drops of oil trickling out from where the engine's sump plug was meant to be. The vehicle had just been serviced before we left and I guessed that, after the oil change, the plug had not been properly put back in. In the true spirit of British ingenuity, we walked into the adjoining woods, found a small branch of a tree and cut off a piece of wood with a pen-knife. This fitted perfectly into the empty screw hole and, by sheer good fortune, we had a reserve can of oil in the boot, so we were able to continue our journey. A British Leyland agent in the next city looked at the engine for us and confirmed there was some damage but, amazingly, the engine survived until we got back to England.

We learned a great deal from this foray into Europe and we also had a fabulous time living like lords in the Palace Hotel in Aachen. The deutschmark was extremely weak and so with a very small amount of money we could afford a suite with three separate bedrooms while thinking of all the ways to improve our *Swiss Assortment*.

At the end of 1958, just before Christmas, I was feeling pleased with what I'd been doing in the Chocolate Department. My father called me into his panelled office, the 'holy of holies', and I thought maybe he was going to congratulate me on a job well done.

"Oh, sit down Peter. I have something to tell you." He looked pale and not particularly happy. "Peter, I have decided that you have more than your share of the family business. For the sake of the others you are to give up the Chocolate Department and take over Quality Control."

I was flabbergasted. I stared at him in complete amazement for a few moments.

"But – I have made a great success of it, wouldn't you agree?" I demurred. "Surely I should be allowed to continue or, better still, be given a better job. Look at the Belper factory. That is a real mess."

"That is neither here nor there. We need someone to look after Quality Control and, besides, Michael is running the Belper factory."

"But what is there to do on Quality Control?" I argued. "Nobody really does any Quality Control. Stanley replies to the complaint letters and does a bit of investigating to find the source of any contamination. That takes about an hour a day at the most!"

I looked at him. He remained unmoved by my argument and I couldn't bring myself to get angry with him.

"When do I start?" I asked, resignedly.

"Straight after Christmas."

I went into the factory and found Iris. "Do you know what that father of mine has just done?" I asked her, making no attempt to conceal my exasperation. "He's just ordered me to give up the Chocolate Department for Quality Control."

Iris turned and stared at me in blank amazement. "With all due respect to your Dad," she said, "how stupid is that? Can't he see what a difference you've made to the department?"

"I don't know. I don't understand it at all."

"Maybe Stanley got to him," she wondered. "Perhaps Stanley thinks Michael's not getting a good enough opportunity, or possibly he's had enough of dealing with the complaints?"

"But Dad takes no notice of Stanley," I said, thinking that any persuasion from my uncle was most unlikely.

Iris, shrewd as ever in her observations of people, remarked, "Well, there may be more to it than that, but I wouldn't be at all surprised if Stanley is behind this. You just wait and see."

"You know, Iris, you may be right," I concurred.

There was no happy Christmas at home for me that year. My father had removed me from the first job I had ever really enjoyed. I had no enthusiasm for taking over Quality Control and I no longer had Alice to comfort me. I felt that I couldn't bear to live in this house much longer. Instead, I spent the holiday enjoying the company of my new friends in the T.A. and tried to forget about it all.

Chapter 5

The Man from PERA

Today it is more likely to be called Quality Assurance and to have Accreditation from the British Retail Consortium with specific standards to maintain, but the importance of Quality Control was not really recognised when I took on the job in 1959. Procedures were not written down anywhere and there was no audit trail to follow the stages of production and use of materials and so isolate the exact cause of a faulty product or contamination. For me, any such system would have to be developed from scratch. There were very few complaints anyway as everyone involved in the manufacture and retail of our products would automatically check everything as they went along. Perhaps later there were a few more problems when we started to bring in automation but not at that time. It seemed like a 'non-job', somewhere to sideline me, perhaps permanently for all I knew despite everything I'd achieved in the Chocolate Department.

Nevertheless I tried to take the job seriously and make whatever improvements I could. There had been an ongoing problem of contamination of the *Special Toffee* with an average of two complaints a week, mentioning such indigestible extra ingredients as paper clips, drawing pins, glass and metal. It was impossible to understand as these materials were banned absolutely from our factories and shops alike. We even had metal detectors on all the packing lines but I investigated each complaint anyway and always drew a blank as to the cause. The customer would receive a polite letter of apology and a replacement box of toffee but I eventually came to suspect that the contamination might, so to speak, be 'self-inflicted', so I decided to make a few home visits.

My first was to an elderly couple in Leeds who had complained of finding a pin in their confectionery. They had sent a letter accompanied by the offending article in a half-chewed piece of toffee wrapped in wax paper. I went without invitation to their small terraced house in Bramley, wondering if I was to find it awash with pins. I knocked gingerly on the front door and, after some shuffling inside, an elderly lady opened it and peered out.

"Can I help you, luv? Are you selling something?"

"No," I replied quickly. "I'm here to talk to you about your complaint to Thorntons."

"Don't know what you're on about, luv," she said, looking puzzled.

"Well, I'm Peter Thornton and I've come to talk to you about the pin that you found in some of our toffee. I'd like to apologise to you for it."

She continued to stare at me in blank amazement, then half-turned to shout something into the small room beyond. "'Enry, 'Enry, there's a bloke here. Says he's from Thorntons. He wants to talk to us."

A voice boomed from the parlour. "Be civil then if he's come all the way to see us. Tell 'im to come in, Gertie."

They asked me in to sit in their tiny front room but, as ''Enry' was already in the one armchair and the sofa was covered in Gertie's sewing, I remained standing.

"Well, Mr and Mrs Ramsbottom," I said, "I'm extremely sorry that you've had this unfortunate experience of finding a pin your toffee. I was so concerned about it that I thought it was only fair to come here to apologise to you personally."

"Eee, that's reet good of you," Gertie said.

I continued, "Where do you normally keep the toffee once you've brought it home?"

"Well, we usually keep it on the mantelpiece. Then, when I'm doing my sewing, I bring it down here on the sofa next to me so I can take a piece when I am feeling a bit peckish."

I tried hard to keep a straight face as I said, "I suppose you use pins to hold the sewing together before you do the stitches?"

"Of course I do, Mr Thornton," she said, looking at me as if I were an idiot not to know that.

"I see. Well, I don't want to seem rude, Mrs Ramsbottom, but I don't suppose there is smallest chance that you might have dropped one of your pins yourself into the toffee box, is there? You know, while it was lying open on the sofa?" I tried very hard not to sound accusing or patronising.

"Oh, dearie me, Mr Thornton, I would never be as careless as that!"

Henry, having been silent for some time, put down his *Sporting Times* and opened his mouth. "Come on, Gertie, I've seen you do that meself!"

There was a moment of awkward silence. Gertie looked somewhat abashed and decided to change the subject.

"Would you like a cup of tea, Mr Thornton?" she said, clearing the sofa to make room for me to sit.

"I'd love one," I said. I accepted the tea graciously, feeling that my concerns were vindicated and my journey had been worthwhile. The Ramsbottoms probably meant no harm but it had been instructive to discover exactly what happened sometimes to our product once it had gone from our shops.

As well as dealing with customer relations, I also inspected the general upholding of quality standards in all our shops and factories despite finding the work boring and frustrating. Some of the toffee manufacturing and Easter egg production had transferred to Belper so I returned there for a while to assist. Even with Walter Willen's hand-made *Swiss Assortment*, the factory's output remained low. I observed that the manager, Mr Hudson, didn't always seem to be using his time efficiently. Indeed, many of his staff of 35 were often under-employed and lacked direction.

In January 1960 I went to Kitzbühel in Austria for a fortnight with three T.A. friends: Tim Wish, Roger Baker and Ted Hobson. We went intending to have a riotous time filled with sun, sex and skiing. The sun failed to appear and we turned out to be quite useless at the other two, but we had a laugh anyway. Skiing was more difficult than I'd imagined, and the fact we were staying in this awful barn of a hotel meant that any *entente* with the ladies was not as *cordiale* as we would have liked. My one liaison with a young American girl was hindered by the prodigious amounts of alcohol I'd consumed merely to summon up the courage to ask her in the first place.

Ted Hobson and I became so disenchanted with the whole experience that we decided to go off by train to Vienna for a few days. This was much more fun and Ted caused considerable mirth in the Austrian *pension* where we stayed by striding into the breakfast room saying "*Morgen früh, Morgen früh*" to everybody, completely unaware that this actually meant "Tomorrow morning". So much for his claimed ability to speak German.

Despite these linguistic shenanigans we returned home convinced that riotous bachelorhood was not all it was cracked up to be, and we felt we'd be better off settling down with our girlfriends into conventional married life. I was still missing Alice dreadfully and had abandoned any hope that she would one day return to me. I knew that she was back from America and had even heard of her engagement to a charming and debonair older man named David Smithers. This simply re-inforced my lack of personal esteem, and it was around this time that I first met Janet.

Janet was extremely attractive, tall with long black hair, and very reserved. She was from a solidly respectable old Sheffield family of lawyers and businessmen and, as I felt certain that I was not going to fall in love with her, I deemed it 'safe' to take her to parties and other social events. She introduced me to her father, Walter Elliott, who had been in the Army during the war and the TA after it. He'd seen action at Dunkirk and had risen to the rank of Colonel. Now, as director of a large Sheffield brewery, he was yet another older man whom I both respected and feared in equal measure.

Janet and I saw a lot of each other but maintained quite a distant relationship in most respects. One night, early in 1960 just after the skiing holiday, we were snuggling in front of a glowing fire in her parent's living room and I got rather carried away. Out of the blue, I asked her to marry me and she accepted. As I drove home afterwards I suddenly realised what I'd done and immediately regretted it. I hadn't been thinking rationally and had just popped the question without any real forethought or consideration. It's hard to explain the cultural landscape of those times to a contemporary observer but, back then, a gentleman's word was his bond and to go back on a decision or an agreement was fraught with dishonour and shame. Even so, I knew I had made a terrible mistake. A little voice inside pointed out that she would make a very good wife and, in going through with the marriage, I would be able to escape from my father's bombastic ways and establish an independent home for myself, but somehow it didn't feel right. I knew I had been utterly foolish.

Everybody else was absolutely delighted about the engagement. My parents felt that she was 'their sort of person' and, against my own better wishes, I knew I simply could not go back on my word. By April we had made arrangements for a September wedding to take place at St. John's in Ranmoor, Sheffield, followed by a reception in a marquee in Janet's garden.

In July 1960, Janet became seriously ill with a disabling attack of colitis. I wasn't allowed to see her, she suffered a dramatic weight loss and the wedding had to be postponed. Any thoughts of breaking the engagement now were completely out of the question as it would seem I was being unsympathetic to her condition. I was in a trap of my own making and I faced the eventual prospect of marriage, now moved to November, with no enthusiasm and a large portion of regret. Perhaps, I wondered without any real conviction, our relationship might improve once we were actually wed and I went so far as to arrange a honeymoon in Sorrento in Italy but then decided to cancel it. I knew that Janet would not be up to the rigour of foreign travel for a while so instead I booked a few days for us in the Hyde Park Hotel in London.

The marriage took place as originally planned at St. John's and we had the reception at our Regimental Headquarters at Endcliffe Hall. I suppose everything went well but, as Eddie the chauffeur drove us in the Rolls-Royce to Chesterfield Station for the train to London, I was still convinced that I had done the wrong thing. In retrospect, it would have been fairer to Janet, even in the circumstances of her illness, to have broken off the engagement. There would have been a dreadful fuss, of course, and I would have radically upset a great many people, but in the long run it would have been more honest. Unfortunately, the 'stiff upper lip' and 'gentleman's word' behaviour that was so instilled into young men like me from our childhood created a moral paralysis in which both head and heart are overruled and I acted irrationally for fear of shame.

Janet and I checked into the London hotel. The room was very pleasant but Janet was still quite unwell. Any wedding night consummation was rejected out of hand and I was beginning to fear that a consoling physical relationship was not going to be any part of the deal. I was newly married but found myself sitting alone in the bar in the hotel or going off for walks on my own.

We returned to Sheffield and moved into the house that I had bought and furnished on Rushleigh Drive in Dore on the outskirts of the city. Dore was a quiet rural village, not the commuter suburb it is today. Janet and I settled into this modern house which I had been able to purchase fully from my savings, remembering another of my father's maxims – "Never borrow money, never have a mortgage" – and we tried to establish some sort of reasonable working arrangement between us. It was great to have a place of my own and sufficient income to have no money worries, but our married relationship remained uncomfortable. My misgivings were proving to be well founded. A marriage without the shared joys of intimacy was totally unsatisfying. Worse, I found myself grieving for Alice even more than before and this heartache began to disturb my rational thinking.

Undoubtedly, Janet was very unhappy too. I'm sure she had come to a similar conclusion about our union and I had no wish to hurt her personally. I did everything I could to make her happy but in so many ways we were completely incompatible. For example, I had put my wonderful new FM radio in the living room and thrilled to the pure sound that came from it but, as soon as Janet saw it, she said "I'm not having that ugly thing in the living room. Put it in the attic." So into the attic it went along with my love of classical music.

Janet wanted a dog. Now I'm not really a dog-person but I bought one for her to keep her happy. She also wanted children and I thought, in my naïve way, that children might help to create a bond between us. However, she wasn't at all keen on the preliminary necessities for 'making babies' and the whole process was undertaken in a most perfunctory and loveless way. She became pregnant but then, to our mutual devastation, the baby miscarried at about seven months. Another bout of colitis followed but she stubbornly refused to seek medical treatment. I had to send for the doctor secretly and ask him to call in, as it were, on a surprise casual visit as otherwise I knew she would neglect herself. The ensuing lengthy period of disability made us both even more miserable.

During May of 1962, around my 29th birthday, I went to see my father in his panelled office in Sheffield, ostensibly to express my frustration with the Quality Control job and to discuss the shortcomings of the Belper operation, but the conversation soon came round to the subject of my marriage.

"How are you two getting on now you are settled down in your new home?" he asked.

"Fine," I lied. It never did to blurt out the truth to people such as my bossy father. "Yes, we've got the place organised now. Janet has made it look very nice and we've bought a Labrador puppy which makes her very happy."

"I hope you are going to continue coming round to see us now that you are independent. We don't want to lose touch." We were regularly expected to go for Sunday Lunch though this was becoming a real bore as I much preferred to go sailing or to immerse myself in the world of the TA.

"Yes, yes, of course, it's lovely to see you," I said through gritted teeth.

"How are you getting on in the business?"

At this point I decided to be absolutely frank. "I am unutterably bored," I told him. "I really can't stand this for a job. I look around both factories and I see such inefficiency. We have people standing around doing nothing and materials being wasted and thrown away. I'd love to get my hands on the production side of things. I could put things right straightaway but I have no authority to do so. I know you want Michael to do it though, so I feel there is nothing I can do about my own position."

"Surely it's not as bad as that, is it?" he asked. "After all, you have the Quality Control to do which is very important."

"Oh, I hate the Quality Control job! I can't possibly fill more than two hours a day on that. In fact, I've come here today to tell you that I want to leave the business. I have no idea what I want to do with my life but doing nothing would be far better than this total frustration!"

Dad looked rather shocked and surprised but I felt he wasn't really taking on board what I was saying. I think that he had seen this coming and already had his answer. "Look, Peter, you are now 29. Tony was made a director when he became 29 so now we are going to make you a director as well."

I was completely taken aback. I had absolutely no idea that this was coming. The wind was taken out of my sails and my words of resignation simply evaporated into it. I admit that I had not been entirely serious about quitting as there was no way I could have matched the income from Thorntons in any other job. I would in all probability have ended up on unemployment benefit. Instead I was locked in to the family business in a way which forced all of us to remain even through the bad times.

"Oh, all right," I said, "but that still doesn't give me a better and more useful job to do. The directors here don't do anything special, you know. We never have any Board Meetings. You and Stanley have entire control of the voting shares and make all the Board decisions."

He had no answer to this.

"Well, anyway," he said, "you can't have any other job. Quality Control is very important and you must keep on doing it. That is why I wanted you to do the Course at the Borough Polytechnic so that you'd understand all about it. Also Michael is looking after the Belper factory as we have to make sure that Stanley's side of the family has its fair share of the business. Remember, with Tony running all the shops now, it would be too much if you had any more responsibility."

I went away somewhat deflated but with a modest tingling of pleasure that I had been made a director.

I came across an organisation known as PERA – the Production Engineering Research Association – and I discovered that they had a very strong work-study department available to members. I suspected that I would have difficulty persuading Stanley and my father to join, despite the low cost, as it was unlikely they would have even heard of work-study and certainly wouldn't recognise the need for it. I decided on a different tack and suggested that membership would help meet our need for engineering expertise, but secretly I intended to use PERA's services to sort things out at the Belper factory. To my amazement, they accepted my proposal and agreed to join.

Accordingly, I arranged for the head of their work-study department, Edgar Chase, to visit us. Edgar, an articulate and verbose individual, seemed eminently suited to the task. I well recall the day of his arrival. I was with Stanley and cousin Michael in the first floor manager's office overlooking the yard at Belper. Our secretary, Mrs Beachim, showed him into the office and he immediately went into full flow.

"Ah, delighted to meet you all," he said, beginning to pace around the room with a huge smile across his face. "I must say that I admire your wonderful products. I was only saying this last night to my wife. We'd just shared a box of your new *Swiss Assortment* and we were remarking on its outstanding quality. I've really been looking forward to this meeting." Without pausing for breath and oblivious to our reactions, he went on. "Of course the Production Engineering Research Association has the most outstanding range of engineering services specifically designed for the Engineering Industry but there is absolutely no reason why a company like yours shouldn't take full advantage of the possibilities. For instance, our Work Study and Work Measurement Department could provide you with a first-class and hard-working consultant who could come to this factory and measure your production processes over, say, a period of a week. He would then prepare a full report with different charts showing any levels of efficiency against the standard rates, and measurements of the level of productivity in your various departments. Additionally, there would be bar charts...."

At this stage Stanley decided he had to ask a question. He tentatively raised his hand like a nervous schoolboy.

"Excuse me, Mr Chase," he said, "I wonder if you could explain to me what a bar chart is. I'm not really very familiar with these terms. Is it perhaps a chart you would find in a pub to show how many drinks you've just consumed?"

Mike and I laughed out loud. We weren't sure if Stanley's ignorance was genuine or whether he was simply trying to make a joke. Edgar continued, having hardly noticed the interruption.

"No, no, no. A bar chart is simply a graphical interpretation of the differing work rates that we might find on a particular job. We measure the minutest detail of every operation. For instance, if your operator throws his arm to the side like this," – he demonstrated by violently throwing his right arm out as if to pick up something from the top of the filing cabinet – "then we put down a specific symbol on the worksheet and measure the precise time with a stopwatch, or if the operator has to bend down to pick something up," – again he mimed the appropriate action – "then we write down another symbol."

Seeking to keep the flow going, I said, "Well, that's really impressive, Mr Chase. I can see that you could have a major impact here on this business."

"Oh, yes, I think so. In fact, I'm certain of it. We never get less than a 40% improvement in productivity regardless of the type of business, so I'm sure we can do the same here." As he made this remark, he moved towards Stanley who was standing with his back to the open bay window. He had been completely bowled over by the force of Edgar's discourse to the point where I was afraid he would actually fall back through the frame.

"Well, Mr Chase," he said, "I've been very impressed by all this and I suppose that we'd better go ahead with it."

Edgar returned to the centre of the room, clearly relieved with his reception. "Well, thank you very much indeed, Mr Thornton," he said. "I'm sure you won't regret this. All I have to do now is send you a short agreement showing the work that we will do and the cost of it all. Then you simply have to initial it and return it to us and we can get started! Once you've received our full report you'll be able to consider whether you want to proceed to the implementation stage which will take a few further weeks. I think I can guarantee that as a result of our service you will find a big increase in productivity and profitability and thus pay the cost of our fees many times over."

A short while later Edgar returned to the factory with a young consultant named Peter Crook. As the Quality Control Manager I had no role of authority to work with Peter but I took it upon myself and nobody objected. Peter was a very pleasant individual with an incredibly quick brain and a marvellous way of cutting corners. A small and wiry man in his early 30s, he always wore a smart dark blue suit and everything that he did was in fast motion. He would suddenly materialise in the office, having donned a white coat over his suit, and would announce, "Right! I've got standards for the toffee-boiling now!"

"What? Already?" I would gasp. "You only started an hour ago."

"Yes, yes, yes, I know," he would reply, "but I have developed my own shortcut methods, you know. I don't do it exactly by the book. It would take years if I did that."

Within a week he had completed his study of the Toffee Department and produced a set of Standard Times, these being the amount of time each element of a job should take. Using these figures we learned that the department was actually running at about 50% of its potential efficiency. We initiated a project, based on incentives, where we would pay a bonus if production in the Toffee Department met the 60% of the Standard with pro rata payments for further increases. By now Peter Crook and I were getting on like a house on fire and of course he became well aware of my serious frustrations.

My old friend in the Boiled Sweet Department, Betty Hall, had become my secret spy and informant. As I walked around the factory looking at 'quality issues' I would always find time for a chat with her and a few other confidantes. On one occasion she asked if she could come up to see me as there was something she wanted to talk about.

"Mr Peter," she said, once we were in the secluded confines of the office, "the management of this factory is dreadful."

I sat in the chair behind the desk and looked at Betty. She was a strong woman, used to heaving huge masses of boiled sugar around on the slabs. She had taken unofficial charge of this work and poor old Will Thompson had normally withdrawn to his office and left her to it. She kept an eagle eye on everybody and if she ever saw people slacking she would rush in, brush them aside and start throwing sugar around. As a heavy smoker, she suffered from bronchitis and the climb up the stairs to the office had left her rather out of breath. Nevertheless, she lit up another cigarette and continued.

"When I was at Belper Mill it was pretty bad, but it is much worse here. There are people hanging around in the toilets all the time doing nothing, just talking and smoking. It's very difficult to get the others to work properly because there is absolutely no backup from senior management. We hardly ever see Mr Hudson and when we do, he does nothing about it."

"What can *I* do about it?" I asked her. "I'm not in charge here and my father won't let me take over. He wants Michael to do it and I'm stuck with doing the Quality Control."

"Well, somehow you'll have to get him to change his mind. There aren't too many good 'uns workin' here and far too many bad 'uns because the wages are so low. But I can't put up with it anymore and, unless something is done, I'm just going to have to go back to Belper Mill again."

"Thanks, Betty," I said. "I really appreciate your openness and honesty. I'll to try to do something about it if I can."

In the light of these comments Peter Crook and I discussed how we could achieve some sort of managerial change as any initiatives of mine were pointless if I didn't have the necessary authority to implement them. We felt that we had no alternative but to persuade Stanley that I be allowed more control of the factory. I didn't really know Michael well enough to predict what he would think about all this. I didn't discuss these matters at home with Janet very much but she was clearly aware that things were on my mind.

"Why don't you just talk to your cousin about it?" she asked one day, getting exasperated with me. "Ask him outright whether he really wants to run the factory or not?"

"That's not the sort of question I can just go up to him and ask, can I? I don't know him well enough!"

"Well, it's time you got to know him better. Why don't you take advantage of the current circumstances? You've got the perfect opportunity now."

"What opportunity is that then?"

"Look, he's broken his leg, hasn't he? Why don't you offer to pick him up from his home in Matlock while you're on your way to Belper and you can ask him if there's any way you can help. That will allow you to get on friendlier terms and you will have plenty of time to talk things over." I hadn't considered this possibility at all, but it seemed a sensible thing to do and I was grateful for the suggestion.

Michael had broken his leg playing rugby in a County Trial in September and couldn't drive. I suggested that I give him a lift each morning and he was very pleased to accept. After a few trips I broached the subject of the Belper factory and its day-to-day management. Wouldn't he be happier, I ventured, running the financial side of the business and taking on the duties of Company Secretary for which he was well qualified? He readily admitted that this was what he would really like to do. Together we agreed a proposal to put to Stanley where Michael would give up this pretence of running the factory to take on this alternative important role and that I should step into his shoes.

We went off to see Stanley at his home, the grandly-named *Stanley Lodge* in Matlock. He always claimed it was so called before he bought it but few people actually believed him. He'd had a serious bout of the 'flu and was resting in a bed that had been made up for him in the small conservatory. He looked to be in no state to make business decisions.

Mike stumped into the conservatory on his crutch. Father and son looked at each other wryly, recognising that neither was in the best of conditions.

"I don't know how you managed to do that, you chump," said Stanley. "It's a good job you've got Peter and your sister Sandie to drive you around."

"How are you, Dad?" asked Mike. "You look awful?"

"Yes, I feel awful," he admitted. "What do you want with me? What's so urgent that you had to come here to my sick bed? I really don't feel up to talking much so make it quick."

I jumped in. "Well, Mike and I have been talking things over, and we both agree that it would be a big improvement if Mike was to move to Sheffield to look after the administration and the accounts, to become in fact the Company Secretary, and I was to take over his role in overseeing the Belper factory."

Stanley was too poorly to take in what we were saying. All he could say was, "Who's going to do Quality Control then?"

"Oh, that's no problem," I said. "I'll continue to look after all that at Belper and I would suggest that Mike does the same at the Sheffield factory. That would be all right, wouldn't it, Mike?" I asked, turning to my cousin who agreed immediately, of course.

Stanley considered things for a moment. "Well, I can't see Norman will object to this really. What do you think, Mike?"

"No, I don't see why he should either."

"Well, that's OK then. If that's what you want, then I suggest you both get on with it! Now, if you don't mind, I would like to get back to sleep. I've got this terrible headache," and he rolled over with his back to us and we crept out of the room.

This is how I came to be in charge of the Belper factory. It was October 1962, a month after Mike's rugby injury. Now all those concerns that had previously been academic to me were suddenly a real responsibility. Betty Hall came back to me again and said I must now do something about Mr. Hudson. Until this problem was sorted I couldn't begin to tackle any of the others. I felt there was no option but to dismiss the man. We didn't have to follow any employment rules here. An employee could simply be dismissed with no regard to the fairness of the procedures. I hated the idea and worried terribly about the prospect of sacking him but I couldn't see any alternative.

The inevitable day loomed in front of me and caused me much anxiety. I knew that I had to do this even though I had hardly ever disciplined anybody before, never mind actually dismissing someone. I was fully aware of the effect this would have on his life and his family. I had to steel myself for the moment when I invited Mr. Hudson to meet me in the office. I decided to cut to the chase and told him straightaway that we felt he was not satisfactory as an employee and that he would have to go. Astonishingly, he didn't seem too surprised. He must have seen it coming, but it was a very unpleasant thing to do. I was only able to deal with it because it was for the benefit of the business.

As soon as he was gone, I had a clear field to start managing the place according to my own ideas. First, I introduced the new production incentives to the workers in the Toffee Department. We suspended production one lunchtime and everybody gathered around in the department packing area. I had to raise my voice to be heard over the fans and still-clanking machinery.

"From next Monday we are going to start a new bonus scheme," I announced. "This is Peter Crook. He's a professional work-study engineer. He's measured all the jobs and produced what we call Standard Times. You can see what these are if you like. They are posted up on the notice board. The scheme means that you get a bonus for all output over 60% of Standard, and if you achieve 100% Standard you will get 20% extra in your wage packet. This bonus is for the whole team in the department of course, not just one section of it."

There was a stunned silence for a few moments and some looks of total disbelief. Gordon, a stalwart of the Toffee Department, spoke up "Ay up, mi ducks, that's a belter of a job. We shall 'ave to do it." There were some mutterings of agreement and then a cheer went up. "Good on yer, Mr Peter! Us has needed that for years."

Mr Crook and I retired to the office feeling rather pleased with ourselves and couldn't wait to see the difference in output, if any. He drove up from his home in Northampton a week later, arriving as always at eight o'clock, and we calculated the results manually as there were no calculators or small computers in 1962. At last Peter sat back, brandishing his slide rule.

"They've achieved 110%." he said.

"I don't believe it," I said. "Let me see the figures".

I had to agree that this was right. We had effected a dramatic increase. Productivity had gone up over 50% and the earnings of the staff in the Department went up by over 20% as agreed. Everyone was delighted and the knock-on result was that we were now able to attract a more motivated class of employee.

After the great success of the incentive scheme in the Toffee Department we moved into the other departments with similar results. Within a few weeks we had increased productivity throughout the factory by at least 40%. Neither Stanley nor my Dad seemed to notice and unsurprisingly I received not a word of thanks.

From this time my experience of the business became, on the whole, much more satisfying and I was now more fully occupied. The incentive schemes were up and running throughout the factory and this created a huge change to our profile as employers in this small Derbyshire town. Everything changed dramatically: the factory, the development of new products and methods of manufacture, the expansion of the retail outlets, the entire nature of the business and my role within it. I had gone from being an extremely frustrated Quality Control Manager to sharing full control of the business with Tony.

At this time my history of emotional conflict and confusion with all paternalistic figures began to create an ever greater problem for me. All five senior members of the family had to work together but I saw my relationship with my father as an all-consuming and unresolved difficulty. It was not that we had great rows as any show of antagonism of opposition was out of the question. It was more the constant suppression of one's feelings, always having to bite one's tongue, the perpetual feeling of being ignored and under-valued. Such emotional dissonance is not helpful in the objective business of running a successful company. We all had differing levels of emotional maturity, and we all came to our jobs simply as members of the family, not as trained executives who were head-hunted for our specialist expertise. It is a matter of conjecture whether in fact we could have held such positions in an outside company. We were, of course, in our various ways extremely competent and there was no disputing our obvious success in establishing and maintaining the principles upon which Thorntons was based, but equally we each had weaknesses that were difficult to come to terms with in a family-based business. We lacked the usual hierarchical structure of independent executives who could support or ultimately dismiss those who were failing to contribute as they should.

Stanley, for example, was very involved in his extra-curricular duties and had eased back considerably in his company role since I had taken over at Belper. He was Captain of Matlock Golf Club for some years, Chairman of Sheffield Bridge Club, Chair of Governors at the local girls' school in Matlock, always very outgoing and friendly in public and at parties, the antithesis of my father. In a confrontation he was inclined to concede rather than take a hard line. As time went on, however, he became increasingly less aware of what was happening in the business.

My cousin Michael, too, was and is a charming individual. Since I got to know him better I have always liked him enormously. He has a great sense of humour allied to a bold, some would say brash, personality, and was generous to a fault through thick and thin. His strengths lay in his ability to deal quietly and efficiently with the administration and financial management. He was not particularly creative or dogmatic. Like his father, he was good with people although probably a little too lax. He avoided conflict by refusing ever to take sides.

Tony remained my hero-figure, still more like a father than a big brother. We were always good friends and worked extraordinarily well together for quite a long time. His understanding of the retail business was superb. He was one of the first people in Britain who really maximised the concept of multiple retailing. His particular strength was in merchandising and display. He could dress a shop window beautifully and set the standard that became the hallmark of Thorntons shop business for many years. What he couldn't do was deal with disciplinary matters. He was such a kind and generous individual, a real charmer as far as the female staff of the shops was concerned. They would certainly do anything for him and he treated them with great respect. On the few occasions that he needed to assert company policy, he hated it so much that he inevitably passed the job on to me!

Dad was very sound with the company finances. His decisions must have been entirely based on information in his head because he never had any management accounts. He would always know exactly what each shop was taking, what all the rents and general outgoings were, and particularly what the bank balance was. His economic understanding was somewhat basic and was predicated on a firm principle that no monies be expended except on new shops. He was continually haunted by the spectre of financial collapse even though this phantom was entirely of his own imagination.

Dad would never agree with any of my suggestions, almost as a rule-of-thumb. Any financial concessions I got from him had to be so miniscule as to remain unnoticed. This explains my necessary skill in the purchasing of useful second-hand equipment at auction. At Belper we were lucky to have our own small engineering shop that Stanley had set up with Colin Bridges, a superb engineer who, despite his dour exterior, was extraordinarily competent with the limited tools and equipment we had. He could rebuild and maintain even the worst old wreck of a machine that I would bring him and sometimes get it to do things it was never intended to do in the first place. He was particularly inventive with wrapping machines. After an hour's frustration with a machine in the Boiled Sweet Department I would go to him and say, "Colin, please will you come and look at the cut-and-wrap? I just can't make the damned thing work!" Without a word he would pick up his tool box, go off to the department, say something like, "Oh, yes, the knives need sharpening," and within ten minutes it would be pouring out wrapped sweets again.

In the decades before the 1960s employment laws didn't really exist as we know them today. People were desperate for jobs and would often accept positions with very low wages in dreadful conditions and then be dismissed at some later stage when they were no longer required. That all changed when the jobless figures fell and people could be more choosy over whom they would work for. Belper had always been an area of low unemployment because of the town's cotton and hosiery mills. Those choosing to work for Thorntons came, I always believed, because they wanted to. I felt that the majority of our employees were wonderful, highly motivated individuals who wanted to share in the company's success. There were some real characters that I got to know and respect well.

There were the Falconbridge brothers. Ivan was a tremendously hard-working and competent chap who took on many different roles in my time as manager. He, along with most Belper people, would always address everyone as 'youth', pronounced 'yowth'. (The normal greeting was "Ay up, youth", though they were always careful not to address me as such.) Ivan came from a family with a bit of a reputation. His brother was in trouble with the law but I would readily have employed him on the strength of Ivan's qualities.

Unlike the Sheffield workforce, the Belper factory workers could easily get agitated if something didn't suit. With plenty of other work in the town they were liable to walk out of one job and into another, especially if it was better paid. The incentive schemes were providing a deserved financial benefit but we knew that we still paid lower than the average. I began to realise that we had to do something to recruit and retain better quality workers other than paying even higher wages. The first thing that I did was to start to install a lower tier of management. There were two junior managers when I first got involved, one being Trevor Fleetwood who ran the Toffee Department and who had come over from Sheffield to live and work in Belper; the other was Walter Willen who was running the small chocolate department, hand-producing what was now called the *Continental Assortment*.

Fortunately I found there were many others on the shop floor with intelligence, potential management skills and other abilities that I felt could be developed. Betty Hall was one of those. Nobody officially ran the Boiled Sweet Department now that Will Thompson had retired and Betty had just taken on the responsibility herself. She was fully competent to do this, having a strong physique and a personality to match. She was not an overbearing, autocratic person but she would stand no nonsense. I don't know how long she had been with us but she was certainly an asset. She understood exactly how her department ticked and had great initiative. I officially appointed her as manager of her department.

Many of our employees had simply not had the education to bring out their innate skills. They'd been allowed no real chance to move from the bottom of the ladder. Today, they would have gone to university and on to some high level administrative or executive job. If these people could be constructively directed towards a greater sense of professional responsibility they would be less likely to channel their energies into disruptive activity.

Walter Willen was, of course, the wonderful Swiss craftsman who had created the most beautiful product line for us. He was not really a manager by temperament – he was an artist – but he had taken on the role naturally. The product name had changed to the *Continental Assortment* during the period when I was doing the Quality Control job. The Swiss Embassy in London had written to us complaining that we could not use the name *Swiss Assortment* as the product was not made in Switzerland. If this had occurred today we would probably have employed an expensive creative design agency to brainstorm a list of hundreds of potential names for us, but I simply came up with the new name without the benefit of any focus group. My suggestion was immediately accepted and the name change had no detrimental effect on sales.

The *Continental Assortment* was unique to Britain. Our methods of production and supply, overseeing all the conditions imposed by its short shelf life, meant that we were the only confectioners able to make such a product, long before Marks and Spencer developed their "cold-chain" idea allowing susceptible foods to be stored, transported and delivered in chilled conditions. Walter was a highly creative person but he wasn't really up to managing people. He was getting headaches, leading to frequent absences, and I proposed that he should stick solely to research and development. He agreed and I took over management of the Chocolate Department because there was no one else to do it.

Where the crystallising tanks used to be, the department now had this large mixing machine, a chocolate *mélangeur* which ground hazelnuts and almonds into paste 24 hours a day. As the rotor arm turned within the giant mixing bowl it made such a noise that the vibrations could be felt through the floor and must easily have been noticed in the adjoining terrace houses beyond the party wall.

One morning our receptionist called through to say that I was needed downstairs. I found a very tall, elderly gentleman waiting to see me.

"Ay up, Mr Thornton," he said.

"Good morning, how can I help you?"

"There's summat up wi' your fact'ry. I live in t' house next door, and my missus and I can't sleep anymore because there's this dreadful rumbling all night long. Can yer do summat about it, please?"

Realising immediately what was causing this trouble I said, "I'm terribly sorry about that, but there is a machine running all night and it must be shaking the floor and wall between our building and your house. I'll see what I can do about it for you." We had to suspend night-time production from then on.

Another priority was to standardise the recipes. These were constantly changing as a result of those mid-morning discussions in Sheffield and nothing was written down. Leslie was now coming over to Belper regularly to check that the toffee was being made correctly. This caused further complications and Trevor ended up not being sure for whom he was actually working. Was it me, Stanley or Leslie Charlesworth?

I wanted to publish definitive versions of the recipes for the whole of the factory. The problem was where to find them. I had heard on the grapevine that Leslie did actually have some toffee recipes written down somewhere in his office in Sheffield. I felt certain he would never just hand them over so I decided to go on a secret Sunday raiding expedition and look through his filing cabinet. Like some undercover spy, I parked my car some distance from the factory to avert attention and crept quietly through the silent factory. Fortunately his office was not locked but I still felt very guilty going in illicitly. I found a whole pile of handwritten recipes in an old cupboard. I took them all to the photocopying machine in the general office and copied the lot, being most careful to put them back exactly where I had found them. Later I had them typed up and officially distributed. Neither Stanley nor Leslie ever asked where I had got them from.

By the spring of 1963 I was feeling much happier. I was having a great time at the Belper factory, productivity was up, quality was up and levels of waste were down. Tony and I were working well together with able assistance from Mike. There was still much more to do and a need for greater mechanisation. I wanted to make myself responsible for all the production management so that I could be the Production Director. This was not a job that anyone would hand to me on a plate. I basically had to get on with it, in *fait accompli* style, and avoid confrontation.

My father was still my biggest problem, always criticising and complaining, moaning to me about Tony or moaning to Tony about me. My marriage was still unhappy and I still grieved for Alice. I used to imagine myself seeing her near her new home or perhaps meeting her at a party or a dance. I pictured her falling back into my arms, telling me that she too was desperately unhappy. We would look into each other's eyes. "How did we ever allow this to happen to us?" we would say. "Let's throw all caution to the winds and get back together." This fantasy was quickly smothered by the reality of Janet's new pregnancy. A baby was to be expected in September.

Chapter 6
New Arrivals

Life everywhere had noticeably changed by 1963. Post-war affluence had increased significantly with modern housing replacing the old industrial slums and with a big rise in the ownership of cars, televisions, washing machines and other consumer goods. Unemployment and inflation had been low for some time and there was a general feeling of well-being throughout Britain. People were beginning to put the dull, dark days of austerity behind them. That symbol of the British war-time spirit, Winston Churchill, was now redundant and the country lent its support instead to the Labour Party, giving it a landslide victory in 1945 under Clement Attlee. A second election win followed in 1950 but with a reduced majority and a year later the Conservatives were returned to office under Harold Macmillan who was moved to remind his mid-50s electorate that they "had never had it so good".

The Labour government had presided over a programme of radical nationalisation: the Bank of England, the coal and steel industries, the major utilities and transport, all came under government control. However, the Conservatives reversed much of this policy, and growth in the British economy compared less well in the 1950s to that of other industrialised nations such as Germany and Japan. So much for their having been on the wrong side of the War. The decline was partly the result of inefficiency and poor management in British companies which, combined with low unemployment, poor wages and insensitive worker-owner relationships, created a feeling of restlessness and agitation among the nation's workforce, leading to a greater militancy within the Trades Union movement and ultimately to strikes. The jewel in Labour's crown had been the creation in 1949 of the National Health Service, an aspect of the Welfare State which the Conservatives did not dare to dismantle.

However, on the world stage peace and security remained elusive. It is hard to recall now the levels of Cold War paranoia and hysteria, particularly in the USA, prompted by the isolationism and political ambition of the European Communist bloc and the setting up of the so-called Iron Curtain. For a time East and West truly looked as "never the twain shall meet".

For Janet and me, things were rather different. Our union had indeed been fruitful. In September 1963, we were both blessed by the arrival into our lives of our daughter Sarah. Immediately I discovered the joys and responsibilities of being a dad and soon learned that these far exceeded any of the inconveniences which parenthood brings. Janet was now a mother as well as a homemaker, and the presence of this new small person gave us both a renewed sense of closeness. I put some of the unhappiness of those first years together behind me and hoped that little Sarah could dispel some of that longing and emptiness that remained in my heart.

In December Janet and I went with a party of friends to the annual dinner and dance at the Abbeydale Sports Club. As we stood drinking and making small talk before the meal I suddenly realised that Alice was also there with her husband. Later that evening I went out of the clubroom to 'pay a visit' and, walking along the corridor, I almost bumped into her as she came round a corner. We stopped and smiled.

"Alice," I said, "how wonderful to see you. How are you getting on?"

"Oh, very well, thanks," she said with a big grin that made my heart melt. "We are settled down now, you know. We have a lovely house…and a family on the way. What about you? You are looking very well. I hear that you are married now. To Janet, isn't it? She's such a lovely girl. I'm sure that she's just right for you."

I grimaced at this remark. "Oh yes," I said, not sounding wholly convincing. "She is, as you say, a very nice girl but, you know," – and I hesitated a moment – "I can't get you out of my mind, Alice. I'm sorry, but I'm still in love with you."

"Oh, don't be silly, Peter," she said with a broad smile. "That was years ago and we were both very young, weren't we? We didn't really know what we were doing, did we?"

"Well, *I* knew what *I* was doing," I replied, sounding in deadly earnest. "I was madly in love with you and I still am. Whatever went wrong, Alice? Why did you give me up? I'm sure you were mistaken. You knew how much I cared for you," I blathered. Then, in for a penny, in for a pound: "I would give up everything I've got to be together with you again."

"Peter, how silly you are," she said, as if this was all just a trifle to her. "Things changed for us, didn't they? Surely you realised that."

"No, I didn't," I protested. "I never understood why you wanted to leave me. Don't you still love me, Alice?" I must have sounded a bit desperate.

"Of course not, Peter," she said with a big laugh. "I love David and I'm very happy with him and that is how things are staying."

Those words, said so matter-of-factly, crushed any hope I'd harboured of a possible reconciliation. She suddenly became just another young woman whom I had once loved but no longer. That evening I accepted that it was over and I would never again seek her out to talk to or look for her when driving near her house.

In mid-1964, nearly a year after I had taken over at Belper, I decided to see for myself how things back in Sheffield were progressing. At my insistence, Stanley had clarified Leslie Charlesworth's position as manager of the rest of the factory two years earlier but the Chocolate Department was, in effect, still leaderless. I found Iris and asked her how everything was.

"Well," she replied, rather exasperated, "it's very difficult really. Nobody is in charge. I look after the enrobing. Alma and Nellie just manage by themselves. It's been like this ever since you went to do Quality Control. I'm not really sure where I stand with Leslie. I ask him to make the centres for us, just as you used to do, but he really doesn't take any notice of me. He knows I'm not really in charge."

"That must be a bit awkward for you," I said. "Doesn't Stanley get involved?"

"No, not really," she answered. "I see him on those occasions when he comes to speak to Leslie. He strides through the factory but doesn't seem that bothered about how things are going here." She fixed me with a persuasive grin. "Look, Mr Peter, why don't you come back and take over again?"

"That seems quite a good idea," I said, feeling flattered. "It would be quite useful because I could then co-ordinate things with the Belper Chocolate Department."

She gave a rather satisfied smile. "I think that you have just taken charge!"

She was very happy indeed to work with me once more. I told Leslie of my decision and informed him that Iris was in charge of the entire Chocolate Department under my supervision and she would be giving him the regular weekly list of required centres.

It became quite a logistical problem, juggling my time between our two factories, and I felt the need to introduce further mechanisation. Belper still didn't have an enrober as most of the chocolate products there were hand-made. I wasn't even certain that the complicated Swiss-style chocolates *could* be made by machine. How were the centres to be properly shaped? Where could I get the money to purchase suitable equipment? It seemed to be an impossible situation.

As usual I had to fall back on the old method of doing everything on the cheap. I went to yet another auction sale and bought a very old and basic chocolate enrober. This particular machine had a narrow conveyor band – 16 inches wide rather than the standard 48 inches used today – and had been built by an American company, W.C. Smith. They tended to build lightweight structures rather than the heavy cast-iron models made in Europe. I can recall every detail of its pre-war design and, in some ways, it was an improvement on the machine we had in Sheffield. For example, it was easier to open up and clean which saved a lot of time. The liquid chocolate was raised for pouring over the centres by a simple wheel system, and it had what is known as a 'pre-bottomer' which simply gives the chocolates an initial coating underneath. Colin Bridges and I added to it with improved conveyor systems and a long cooling tunnel built out of plywood.

The main problem was that no one at Belper had the slightest idea of how to operate it. I asked Iris to come over and instruct the staff which she did for a time.Despite her teaching, the initial results from the new enrober were not good. The equipment was crude and the staff's inexperience showed through. Finally, I asked David Varney, a young man working in the Boiled Sweet Department, to take charge as I reckoned he might be able to fathom the workings of this basic equipment. It seemed to take a year before we had it up and running properly.

"How's it going, Dave?" I would ask him on those mornings when I went over early to Belper.

"Ay up, Mr Peter. Couldn't you sleep?" he'd reply. "Well, I 'ave to tell yer, it's a right mess today. Heater's gone off on chocolate tank so it's all set hard. I'll 'ave to melt it all again afore I can do owt wi' it."

Around this time I became aware of George Belfield. He was working on the centres for the *Continental Chocolates*. He'd be rushing around on his own between the *mélangeur* and the mixers, pouring in cream, chocolate and flavourings for the nut pastes, truffles and marzipan. I was intrigued with this energetic man, a former milkman, constantly moving, switching equipment on and off, as if he were still hurrying round from doorstep to doorstep delivering his daily pintas. I remember our first conversation when he was busy filling up the *mélangeur* with roasted hazelnuts and icing sugar while whistling the melody from a Beethoven symphony.

"Good morning George," I said, "It's very unusual to hear Beethoven's Fifth on the shopfloor."

"Hah! Yes," he said, "I love Beethoven, particularly the last movement of the Ninth, of course."

"Oh, indeed, the Choral. Yes, I love that myself," I said with great enthusiasm. "What else do you listen to?"

"Mozart, of course. Who couldn't like Mozart?" he said with conviction.

"Well, lots of people have never experienced that joy, I'm sorry to say." Then, to change the subject, I asked, "How do you like this job?"

"Well," he mused, "it's great at the moment. This company has obviously got a good future ahead so I'm hoping to work my way up. I've not got much education but my ambition is to earn £1000 a year." I was impressed with his candour and determination.

"I'd love to be able to help you do that," I said, being reminded again that our employees were, by and large, our single greatest asset.

After my experience in Sheffield with the liquorice extruder I wondered if I could devise a similar thing for our truffle and nut products. I experimented for a while but, because of the high levels of butter fat and nut oil, it simply didn't work. Any pressure on these materials just squeezed the fat out in the way the sausage machine had. The shapes had to be formed gently by taking the mixture and hand-rolling it before dipping it into the chocolate.

The biggest demand was for *Rum Truffles*. George would tip a huge mound of truffle mix from the bowl on to a metal slab. A group of six girls would pick up amounts between their fingers and work on them. This was not very productive and was hardly hygienic. Our first attempt to mechanise this process came when Walter Willen and I obtained some small extruding guns from Switzerland. These consisted of an alloy cylinder on wheels, about 8 inches long, with a removable plunger on one end and a nozzle at the other end. We'd fashion a 'sausage' out of the truffle paste and stuff it into the cylinder. By fitting the plunger on one end and turning a handle the extruding gun would produce a thin rope of truffle.

I had seen a picture in an American magazine of something called a 'balling machine'. This consisted of two grooved rollers running at slightly different speeds which would spin a rope of truffle into small ball shapes. We copied the picture and placed two large rollers of our own on to a frame over the enrober's feeding belt. All that we had to do then was put the strips of truffle from the little extruding guns between the rollers and, hey presto, the resulting truffle balls would drop out onto the conveyor belt.

This was innovative stuff, and it was with improvements such as this that we continued moving forward. Of course, the routine was much more mundane and 99% of my time was spent on consolidating what we'd already established, but I am a great believer in the possibilities contained within that other 1%. By being open to the opportunities for wonderful and far-reaching things to happen, particularly when you're not really expecting them, all sorts of unexpected benefits can accrue. One such instant presented itself when I was back at the Sheffield factory one day. A representative from Baker Perkins had dropped in. Baker Perkins was probably the foremost manufacturer of confectionery machinery in Britain at that time. We, of course, never bought any brand new machinery so I'm not really sure why Geoff Cliffe, their representative, had bothered to call, but out of courtesy I sat down with him for a chat. I just happened to ask if he knew of any machine that would form chocolate centres from very soft truffle paste.

"Oh, yes," he replied quickly. "We represent a company in Germany called Otto Kremmling. They're based in Darmstadt near Frankfurt and they make a machine called the OKA which is supposed to do that sort of thing." He went on, "We've never actually sold any of these machines in Britain but it is supposed to do what you want. I don't know really that much about it."

I took OKA to stand for *Otto Kremmling Automat* and Geoff provided me with a brochure containing details of the machine which intrigued me no end.

"How much would one of these cost?" I wondered aloud.

"Well, for a single-head machine of 16 inches belt-width, it would be about £5,000."

I swallowed hard. This was an enormous amount of money at the time, about £75.000 at today's values, and was not one that I believed my Dad would be prepared to spend in any circumstances. However, I said to Geoff, "What can I do about this? Is it possible to try out one of these machines?"

"Yes," he replied, "but you'll have to go to Germany to do so."

Ever since my skiing holiday in Austria in 1959 I had been embarrassed by my inability to speak German properly and I decided it was high time I did something about this. I approached Viktor Waldispuhl who had come to run the Sheffield Chocolate Department in my place. We firmly believed that European-trained *chocolatiers* were the best and, as there were certainly none to be found in Sheffield, we returned to the same confectionery school from where we had employed Walter Willen and there we discovered Viktor. I said to him one day, "Viktor, I want to learn to speak German. What's the best way to go about it?"

"Well," he replied, "I am staying in digs just up the road with a family called Taylor. Mrs Taylor is from Germany. Her name is

Lisalotte. She is not only a fluent German speaker of course, but also she teaches it. I'm sure she would probably help you."

So I set about learning the language and had private tuition for about six month with Lisalotte who turned out to be an inspirational teacher. The lessons were conducted exclusively in German – *"Kein Englisch sprechen!"* – and I achieved a reasonable standard over this short period, sufficient to allow me to undertake a trip to Darmstadt. I asked Geoff to arrange a visit to Kremmling's so that I could 'have a go' on their machine.

I flew to Frankfurt with two suitcases filled with truffle paste. The customs officers were completely bemused by this and decided to levy a steep import duty (about £30) on it all. Renting a Volkswagen Beetle, my plan was to drive straight down the autobahn to Darmstadt and stay overnight before visiting the Kremmling factory the next morning. I had never driven on any motorway by myself yet and found the prospect exciting but a little intimidating. The signs were largely unintelligible and, of course, I was on the 'wrong' side of the road, so there is little wonder that I missed the exit junction and went sailing past Darmstadt for another 30km before I was able to turn round and come back.

Darmstadt is twinned with Sheffield's near neighbour Chesterfield but is much larger. Eventually I arrived at my hotel and had a restful night. The following morning I travelled out of the city to where 'Otto Kemmling' was beautifully situated among woodland. This was my first experience of an authentic German factory and, as I passed through the Reception, my nostrils were filled with the aroma of coffee and good cigars. The offices and factory were spotless and looked to be models of Teutonic efficiency. I met Herr Kremmling himself and his son Andreas and I was relieved to be able to communicate quite well with them in their native tongue. We took my suitcases into the factory to try my truffle paste in their demonstration machine.

Before they started it up, they wanted to show me how it worked. I love machines and this one, with its incredible interconnection of levers, arms, wheels and controls, was truly marvellous. Everything was designed to take the fragile truffle mixture and ease it with the utmost tenderness through an extruding plate. To my absolute amazement and joy it all worked perfectly and out came beautifully shaped truffle pieces, all neatly arranged in rows on a conveyor belt. I knew then that we just had to have one of these wonderful inventions. Somehow or other, my father had to be persuaded to part with £5,000. I didn't feel that that was an unreasonable proposition but, knowing my father's disposition, I was not optimistic.

Whilst in Darmstadt the Kremmlings took me to several other factories in the locality to see different installations of their equipment. This was particularly useful as it gave me an insight into the practical possibilities that these machines presented. Otto Aribert Kremmling, together with his wife Elizabeth, his father Otto and his mother, had escaped from East Germany, literally overnight, in 1948 at the time of the Communist takeover, leaving his factory and business behind him. All he had been able to bring were the machine drawings of the OKA Extruder. The machine had first been developed in the early 1900s and had been refined over the years to become the sophisticated creation that now impressed me so much. On my return to England I went to see my father at the earliest opportunity.

"Dad, I've seen this most amazing machine that can form virtually all the centres for our *Continental Chocolates* and our other truffle products," I enthused. "It only costs £5,000 and somehow we have to buy one."

To my utter astonishment he replied straightaway. "Yes, that's a good idea."

The sound of my jaw dropping must have been audible outside the building. I don't know whether the takings had been good that week or what, but my father was convinced that this was a good idea and I wasn't going to argue. I had the greatest pleasure in placing an order for the first new machine that Thorntons had ever bought but, as I'd not been anticipating such a positive response, I hadn't really thought through the practicalities. For example, where were we going to install it? This was a real issue because we had to accommodate the existing enrober. We didn't want to move the whole production line as we were already short of space. Walter Willen came up with the answer to that particular problem.

"Ve have to have an extra house!" he said, and that involved a small extension over the top of the loading bays at the back of the premises which saved us moving the enrober and provided a solid new concrete floor which could support the new machine and absorb the vibration.

The OKA eventually arrived in a huge packing case together with a rather elderly German engineer who would help us to build it and set it up. I felt that the complexity of this machine required an operator with slightly more intelligence and application than the average employee and I sought out a young man named David Oliver straight from the local Grammar School to do the job. The engineer took about four weeks to assemble the machine properly and, as he had not a word of English at his command, I became resident interpreter for the duration. I would hear him approach with cries of *"Herr Thornton, bitte...,"* usually followed by some urgent request. *"Könnten Sie mir bitte einige Seegeringe kaufen?"* ("Can you buy me some spring clips please?") Then came The Big Moment. Would it work? It was put into operation and – everything was just about perfect.

One minor problem was that the machine was still not up to forming the round *Rum Truffles*, one of our most popular confections, but then you can't have everything. We considered changing the traditional shape but this was the very thing that made these Swiss truffles unusual for the UK market. I decided to ponder on this for a while but no solution immediately presented itself.

Then, as with so many things that one puts into the mind's pending tray, the answer just popped out when I was least expecting it. My 'Eureka' moment came when I was at home, fast asleep in bed. It was about 3 a.m., and my head was suddenly alive with an idea. I leapt from under the covers and shouted, "That's it, that's it!"

Poor Janet woke up alarmed. "That's what? What's the matter? Has something happened? Are you having a nightmare?"

"No, no!" I said excitedly. "I've just made an important discovery!"

"What, in the middle of the night? How could you? You were fast asleep. How can you make a discovery when you are asleep?" This seemed a reasonable question.

"It just came to me," I said. "I just saw the answer while I was asleep." There were historical precedents for great ideas coming to people in their dreams, but I never expected to be one of those people.

Janet turned over. "I'm going back to sleep," she yawned. "Please don't make any more discoveries!"

I drew a diagram in my bedside notebook and rushed early into work the next morning to find Colin Bridges.

"Colin! Colin!" I said. "Would you please make an extrusion plate for the OKA extruder with holes that are 1/8 of an inch in diameter?"

He looked at me quizzically. "What on earth for? Are we suddenly going to start making spaghetti?"

"No, no," I replied. "It's to make the *Rum Truffles*. The idea is that we blow the truffle paste out under pressure through these small holes so that the truffle then swells up like a balloon to its normal diameter!" (This was about 5/8".)

He was extremely sceptical. "Hmm," he pondered, "I bet you a pound that it doesn't work."

"Yes, it will, it will!" I almost shouted at him. "Just make it for me as soon as you can. Please!"

As usual he indulged me and quickly produced the plate to my specifications. I asked David Oliver to fit it to the OKA and then put some *Rum Truffle* mixture into the extruder hopper. It usually took a minute or so for the paste to appear through the extrusion nozzles. David twiddled all the controls to get the right settings and, as if by magic, thin ribbons of truffle started to appear. I gabbled instructions to him.

"Get the head down, David. Increase the pressure. Lift the head up slowly. Look, the truffle is forming into ball shapes." To my complete delight perfectly spherical truffle balls were now processing down the conveyor belt and we could say goodbye at last to all that previous laborious manufacturing. The word 'manufacture' means 'to make by hand' but there was no reason now for us to apply it literally. It was innovations like these that gave Thorntons the edge over our rivals in the confectionery trade and our *Continental Assortment* soon became the leading brand in our shops and throughout the country.

The second trip I made to Germany was to visit the Interpack Exhibition in Düsseldorf. I went with Leslie Charlesworth in 1964 although, for some reason, we travelled in separate cars. En route we intended to call on a machinery manufacturer in the small Westphalian town of Bottrop (twinned with Blackpool) for the purpose of seeing his machine for making *Chocolate Nut Clusters*. We currently didn't sell these as they had to be entirely handmade using two teaspoons and were therefore very expensive to produce. However, I felt sure they would be very popular if we could make them economically using this machine. I thought it might not be too expensive and had persuaded Leslie to come and see it with me.

We drove in convoy through Holland and then, for some reason, I was held up at the next border. He went on into West Germany, blithely unaware that I was not following, and with no real idea of where we were going. All details of this machinery-maker were with me. He knew it was in Bottrop and that we were going to visit the next day, but we'd not yet decided where we were going to stay overnight. I had all the cash. He had only a few travellers' cheques. Of course, today we would have soon been on the mobile phone to each other. Leslie could probably have paid for some accommodation ahead of me by credit card. As it was, he was well and truly on his own.

He soon realised that we had lost contact with each other and knew he would have to find somewhere to stay by himself, hopefully using his traveller's cheques as payment. The trouble was that most small German hotels in those days knew nothing of traveller's cheques. All they understood was cash. He went to check out the next morning and tried to explain his situation to the hotelier. Unfortunately, Leslie spoke only English, the hotelier spoke only German. This nonsense about having no cash and only cheques aroused the hotelier's suspicions and, accompanied by a bulky hotel porter, he insisted on marching poor Leslie to the local bank. Leslie did not appreciate these strong-arm tactics, being an old soldier who had previously fought his way through Germany in the last war. The bank cashier was no better informed about traveller's cheques but eventually accepted enough to give Leslie sufficient cash to pay the bill and make his great escape. He was then able to proceed to Bottrop in the hope that we would eventually meet up.

When he arrived I was still conspicuous by my absence so he decided to ask at the local police station for the whereabouts of this machinery manufacturer. The police didn't have a clue but instead they called in the local newspaper. A reporter turned up and suddenly Leslie was news. The story of the lost Englishman in Bottrop appeared in the local paper together with a photograph of him standing forlornly outside the police station. By one of those happy chances that rarely occur in real life, the journalist had a friend who knew where the small garage factory was based and was able to give directions.

I arrived at the location on its quiet suburban street just as Leslie turned up from the police station. I howled with laughter when I heard of his misadventures and the poor German proprietor, who didn't speak English, must have wondered what on earth was causing such mirth. *Crazy Engländer*, out of their minds. After all that, this extraordinarily clever machine was far too costly for a product that we didn't make. My father would have looked at me with the same expression as this puzzled German. Instead, we drove on to Düsseldorf and, as it was getting quite late now, we turned off the main road looking for somewhere to stay. We found a small place called the Hotel Schutzenberg in the village of Burscheid, checked in and stayed for a few days.

Visiting the exhibition was perhaps the most exciting experience I have had since I joined the business. I couldn't believe the range of wonderful machines that could do almost anything. Unfortunately we were in the embarrassing position of not being able to talk serious business to any of the suppliers. We were there just to browse and pick up information where we could, but we returned regularly every two years thereafter. We always stayed at the Schutzenberg and became well-known to the staff. Our group increased in size year by year as we would invite departmental managers, engineers and buyers to come with us so that everybody could learn from the experience. Not surprisingly, we had a lot of fun on these occasions, playing skittles in the *Kegelbahn*, and consuming vast quantities of German beer. I was even obliged to drink the '*Brüderschaft*' with the hotel owner by linking arms and knocking back a litre of lager, thereafter remaining her 'blood-brother' although, I have to admit, I turned down the invitation to go skinny-dipping in the local ice-cold reservoir.

On another occasion I took Janet with me for a few days. Lisalotte Taylor had suggested that we stay the night with her parents in the small village of Lüdenscheid near Wuppertal. We arrived in the late afternoon and I soon discovered that my language skills were not up to the challenge as I had to act as interpreter for Janet while listening to an entire household chattering away nineteen-to-the-dozen in a foreign language. Lisalotte's father was a dentist and, as there wasn't really any room in the family home, we were invited to sleep in his adjoining surgery. This was not so bad except that there were only two places to sleep: the couch and the dentist's chair. Being the perfect gentleman I let Janet have the former while I tried to make do with the latter, not too easy with all the drills and dental implements hanging over my head. I can't say that I had a restful night.

Next morning we were served an unusual breakfast. Instead of English bacon and eggs we were given large helpings of goulash soup to be washed down, not by tea or coffee but by cognac. The mere sight of the soup made Janet feel ill but we didn't want to offend our hosts so I had to eat hers as well as my own *and* drink two lots of cognac. The moment I'd gulped the last mouthful of soup our host put his head round the door and asked in German, "More, Herr Thornton? You would like more soup – and more cognac?"

I felt obliged to say "*Ja, bitte!*" and was thus condemned to even more of the stuff so, despite their generous hospitality, or perhaps because of it, I was really glad eventually to get away and continue on our journey across Europe although what state I was in after all that brandy is anyone's guess.

– ★★★ –

Our factory at Belper was very old and the area where we made our Easter eggs was tucked away upstairs at the back of the building using primitive equipment. It was an imprecise method of manufacture and an awful lot of egg shapes had to be scrapped and melted down for re-use. We wouldn't start production until after we'd finished the Christmas chocolate boxes which could take us right up to late December. We sometimes wouldn't get started on the eggs until January which was cutting it rather fine, especially if Easter fell early that year.

Unemployment remained very low in the Belper area and we still had difficulty attracting enough people to work for us, even with our generous bonus schemes. One year we faced a particular problem when asking employees to transfer from the Chocolate Box Department to the Easter Egg Department. Everyone we approached said no, and I really couldn't understand why. Eventually I had a quiet word with Betty Hall to see if she knew why the girls were so reluctant to move.

"Oh, that's obvious," said Betty. "I thought you knew. The supervisor up there is well-known as a lesbian and the other girls have been told by their mothers not to work with her. The only ones who will are probably lesbians too."

This came as quite a surprise to me and was a departmental setback which needed resolving, but how? Fortunately, the situation sorted itself out when the individual concerned committed a serious indiscretion and definitely had to go. Whatever next? I thought to myself. Who would have guessed that someone's private preferences could impact so much on the making of our famous *Easter Eggs*.

We were so far behind in production that we had to start up a night shift. The main problem here was that there was no one available to come in at night, so I ended up doing this myself. For two whole weeks I would work through until 6 a.m., go home for breakfast and a short nap and be back again at 9.30 for the day shift. This was a totally punishing schedule and I was left shattered, but at least it meant we met our targets for that year.

There were claims that parts of our factory, like most old buildings, were supposed to be haunted. During those night shifts I often wondered if I was truly alone. It was a very eerie thing to be in such surroundings late at night, and I was indeed visited on several occasions by unwelcome guests. However, there was nothing spectral about them. These were our resident mice, and our high-tech solution for dealing with them was to run about after them wielding a broom, hoping to commit acts of extreme violence upon them. However, our attempts at eradication were probably less effective than those of the farmer's wife in the nursery rhyme and I surmised that we really needed some proper effective pest control. This led to a contract with Rentokil and we never saw our little rodent friends again.

In 1964 the constant shuttling between Sheffield and Belper was starting to get me down. It was very exhausting and it occurred to me that things would be easier if Janet and I moved over the county boundary into Derbyshire. I was working in the front garden of our house at Dore one day when one of our neighbours walked past and spoke to me.

"I hear you're thinking of selling up and moving to Derbyshire."

"Yes, that's right," I answered, wondering what his interest was in all this.

"Well, I would like to buy this house," he said. "How much do you want for it?"

I considered the facts. I'd paid three-and-half grand in 1960 and had improved it extensively. It seemed that four-and-a-half grand would a reasonable asking price now.

"£4,500," I replied.

There and then, over the garden wall, he said, "Fine! I'd like to buy it." We shook hands and that was that!

Now, of course, we needed to look for a house in Derbyshire. Where to start? I decided to let Fate lend a hand and put a pin in the area on the map between Sheffield and Belper. It landed on a little village near Matlock called Ashover. We scanned the *Matlock Mercury* and found a place for sale by auction on the edge of the village. The house was called *Over Asher* and it was in a magnificent elevated position on the hillside overlooking the village. It was a three-storeyed semi-detached stone-built house, ladled with charm, and I secured it for £4,800. We moved in a few months later and joined this charming community with its three pubs, ancient church, garage and shops. Imagine the radio village of Ambridge, home to *The Archers*, made real before your eyes and that was Ashover. We quickly felt at home there and my commuting time was drastically reduced.

But in tackling one inconvenience I created another. It was now quite impractical for me to continue with the TA in Sheffield and regretfully I resigned in November 1964. To my amazement I had reached the rank of Major and had been commanding an infantry company in Rotherham. The TA life had been of enormous personal benefit to me and it had allowed me to mature and gain much-needed confidence.

So, having given up the military life, I decided to return to my other leisure pursuit: sailing. Fortuitously, there was a local sailing club within fifteen minutes of our new house. Members used the reservoir at nearby Ogston and I started sailing there in 1965. This became, after the job with Thorntons, my main pre-occupation and gave me something to take my mind off all my other stresses and strains. Unfortunately, Janet had no wish to share this interest with me and that was one of the problems. So I'd be out on the water on my own, trying not to dwell on the unhappiness I felt about the state of my marriage.

One Saturday morning in early 1965 I went over to the Sheffield factory to discuss with Tony some ideas I had concerning sales and production. I started cheerfully.

"Good morning, Tony. I've been thinking about the *Rum Marzipan* in the *Continental Assortment.* It'd be a lot easier if we could put the marking on the other way, that is, lengthwise. It would reduce the labour quite a bit."

"I don't like that idea at all," Tony said. "It doesn't look half so good."

"Oh, all right. Well, here's another thing. We've changed the flavour in the *Coffee Truffles*. See what you think?"

He tasted a sample. "No, no, that's not right at all. I think you'd best stick with the old one."

And so it went. All my ideas seemed to be rejected. I went back to Derbyshire feeling very deflated and depressed. This mood remained with me for the rest of the day. By Sunday I started to crawl out of my 'slough of despond' and asked myself, why was I feeling like this? After all, it's perfectly reasonable for Tony to have a view. In fact, it's a good thing that he has opinions, so why should I feel so bad about this? Am I being irrational?

I was beginning to understand a little about human behaviour and it suddenly dawned upon me that my sense of rejection and depression probably lay in the fact that my brother tended to dominate me, and that I *allowed* him to dominate me in the same way that my father had. This could not go on, I suddenly said to myself. My life will be a constant misery unless I do something about it – and soon.

After mulling this over for two to three weeks, I resolved to have a showdown, not with Tony but with Dad as I felt that he had been the cause of all my emotional difficulties from the beginning. I would pick an opportunity to have a row with him just as I had with Leslie Charlesworth. It had worked before, and hopefully would work again. If I could get to an understanding with my father that allowed me equality and respect, I could surely achieve the same with any other senior men I encountered instead of my usual feelings of inferiority.

I occasionally went round to my parents at *Greenways* after work in Sheffield. We'd have a drink and a bit of a chat before I went home to Ashover. On this particular occasion, I went fully prepared to have it out with my father once and for all.

"Look, Dad," I said, after the usual pleasantries had been exchanged. "I have something to say to you. This is not easy for me, but please hear me out." I swallowed hard. He said nothing.

"I've been in the business quite a number of years now and I think I've done some pretty good things. I'm getting absolutely fed up of being pushed around by you. I just can't go on any longer accepting that everything you say is right and I am always wrong. From now on I think it is fair that I get treated properly when I am in the right, with respect paid to me where it's due. I am an adult and I demand to be treated as one and not as a child!" Then I added, "And I also think you should start to treat Tony properly as well. He is as completely fed up with it all as I am…"

My father immediately exploded in a fury of rage and indignation. His face turned bright red, he leapt up from his armchair and shouted, "I'm not having you talk to me like that! Who on earth do think you are? I am your father – I am much older and more experienced than you! I'm not going to stand for it!"

This provoked me into an even greater determination. "Well, you're just going to have to accept it because I'm not going on like this any more."

"That's enough!" he yelled imperiously. "I've had enough of you, Peter! I don't want to see you any more! Get out of my house and don't bother ever to come back!"

I could say nothing except "Fine!" and I stood up to go.

My mother had overheard the row from the other room and came out into the hallway. She whispered to me as she guided me out of the front door, "Well done, Peter! Don't you worry about it. He'll change his mind, I'm sure of it. He'll come round in time."

I drove away feeling not distressed as you would suppose but rather satisfied with myself and wondering why it had taken me till the age of 31 to do what I should have done years ago. I didn't hear from my father or speak to him for quite some time after that.

It was about eight weeks later when he called me up.

"Peter," he said, his voice trailing away as the phone did its customary dip beneath his chin. "I'm sorry about what I said to you before, about telling you never to come here again. You were quite right and I was wrong. I'd like you to come round and see me again, will you?"

I was delighted and relieved. Naturally, I still had greatest affection for him and respect too. He was my father, after all, and the last thing I wanted was that we should become permanently estranged. I had no hesitation in replying, "Yes, of course I will, Dad."

I went round to see him shortly after. He apologised again and I accepted, and from then on we maintained an open man-to-man relationship. I was accorded much more respect and was more acknowledged for my contributions although he always made it clear that he thought that my younger brother John was intellectually superior.

Nearly all my adult relationships improved after this, the two notable exceptions being Janet and Tony. Communication with Tony almost broke down completely and, in fact, he hardly ever spoke to me which is not really practical when you are trying to run a business together. I still couldn't understand the reasons for this unless it was that he envied me for having stood up to our father, something that he plainly couldn't do for himself yet.

I wanted to achieve a similar autonomy as manager of production for Thorntons as I was aware that Leslie Charlesworth, despite his great technical knowledge and imagination, was not really management material. He was a long-standing and loyal employee, having started working for the business in the 1920s making deliveries in a hand cart between the two shops. He had moved into the tiny unit in the cellar beneath one of the shops and stayed on the production side ever since. He was a bit of an institution and I had come to admire and like him a lot, for all of our earlier clashes. He was certainly not 'struck by the moon', whatever that meant, and I felt in essence he was an intelligent and creative man but ultimately he seemed frustrated in his ambitions and had little time for his colleagues when things weren't done as they should. This was revealed when a little incident occurred that involved our company rule obliging all women and girls to wear hair nets and head-dress to enclose their hair. The anomaly was that no such rule applied to the men and I saw this as illogical and a breach of principle. Men's hair was just as likely to fall into our products as women's hair. Anyway, one day I was in the Chocolate Department and a young woman walked through, having been to the ladies' toilet without wearing her head-dress. She was under Leslie's supervision and I told her that I would have to mention this to him. When I did, he fired her on the spot. I thought that this was really quite extreme. I felt that she had made a simple mistake, but employees had absolutely no workplace protection in those days. Instant dismissal was, therefore, quite common.

Leslie used to complain to me endlessly when he got the chance. He would often catch my ear at the end of the day and go on and on about various things, but his main grumble was over my uncle Stanley. There would be nothing I could do for him apart from stand there, letting him get all this off his chest. If it helped him to go home in a somewhat happier state, I suppose it was worth it, but I felt that he would feel more settled if his role within the company was made more interesting and creative. I managed to persuade Stanley that perhaps Leslie would better off concentrating on the development of products (except the chocolate confectionery which we left to Walter Willen). Thus I took over Leslie's duties and became the direct manager at Sheffield with responsibility for production for the whole company.

This was too much for one person to handle so I looked around to see who we already had at Sheffield who could be appointed as factory manager. Dad was never keen on the idea of employing someone from the outside just for their managerial skills – they had to be making confectionery at the same time. It would have to be someone on the existing payroll, but I had no real experience in selecting people for important posts. That needed special skills and training. Then, as often happens, the answer presented itself.

I had been developing an interest in personal, social and industrial psychology and had developed a contact with the National Institute of Industrial Psychology. Jamie Dodd, one of their representatives, came up to see me in Sheffield and I was immediately impressed and amazed by his knowledge. He said he would do some psychometric testing of everyone in the factory to see if anyone might be suitable. In this way I learned a lot about the people in our employ that I had not known before. Unfortunately, it seemed that none of them were really fitted to the post I was hoping to fill.

Then Jamie also persuaded me to do the tests myself. Although I had done these in the army nobody had ever really given me any results. I knew I'd done reasonably well at school but I never thought of myself as particularly intelligent, rather the opposite if truth be told, but I was very surprised to learn that, according to the results, I was in the top percentage of the population. This band was rather small and to be told that I was a part of it gave my confidence an enormous boost. I had always been put down by my father, told constantly how much brainier my younger brother was, and had failed to get my army commissions in a way that pointed to my not being very bright. I'd not really questioned that, and had simply adopted a philosophy which argued for the right of an individual to be informed equally of his or her limits and potential, believing that most people had more of the latter than the former.

Viktor Waldispuhl, our Swiss *chocolatier*, had left Thorntons to pursue a career in the United States and we replaced him with Hans Hanneman whom we found not in Switzerland or Germany but on our doorstep in Sheffield. We had not asked Hans to take the tests as they had been designed for subjects whose first language was English. However, he did come with managerial experience and, as beggars can't be choosers, I felt I had no alternative but to appoint him as factory manager. This turned out to be a serious mistake. I was still in overall charge of production and gave myself the title of 'Production Director'.

Domestically, things continued to be very difficult. Giving up the TA had actually made things worse as I was now at home more. On Saturdays I would work on the house and garden and I looked forward to my sailing each Sunday in order to get away from things. We both loved *Over Asher* and I did quite a lot of home improvements with the unpaid assistance of Tom Taylor, Lisalotte's husband.

The idea was that they should come over in the evenings from Sheffield and Tom the builder could work on the house while I continued my German lessons with Lisalotte. I repeatedly offered to pay for all this but they would have none of it. It seemed that they were extraordinarily generous and it would have been churlish to refuse. A small space at the back of the house was converted and extended into a personal study and here at last I was able to accommodate my new hi-fi system without encroaching on Janet. Tom made a complete new bay window for the living-room and insisted on fitting it one evening. He brought the window over from Sheffield on the top of his car and we carried it down to the front of the house. We took out the existing window, removed a substantial part of the wall, put in a new beam and installed the window, all in the one evening. It was hardly surprising when, at two o'clock in the morning while we were still hard at work, our neighbour, Ted Bond, knocked on the adjoining wall. Janet had gone to bed and Lisalotte was fast asleep in a chair and we had just worked on regardless. Ted, usually the kindest of souls, then telephoned through to us.

"For God's sake, stop making this terrible noise!" he demanded, expressing a sentiment with which I could wholly sympathise. Ted was the assistant headmaster at the local comprehensive school. This had formerly been a highly-respected grammar school and he had been devastated when its status had changed. He mourned the loss of an establishment with such an outstanding educational record. Ted was a lovely person and he and his wife Freda were the best of neighbours, always friendly, generous and ready with helpful advice to younger man like me.

I still held on to the notion that having children would help ease my marital difficulties. I adored the idea of a loving home, filled with youngsters, and I was delighted when our second daughter Samantha was born in 1965. Unsurprisingly this did not create any more instant wedded bliss than before and I really wondered what more could I do to achieve the happiness I so craved.

The problem seemed to be insoluble. Janet continued to dislike intimacy between us. At her insistence our occasional love-making could only take place in the dark wearing full night clothes. She seemed far more at ease cuddling dogs and horses. The colitis kept returning, bringing her more misery and yet she still wouldn't seek proper medical attention. She had a serious bout just after Samantha's birth, and I wondered if it would help to have some further distraction. She loved our dog and I thought that maybe having a puppy at home would give her some additional thing to care for. The Labrador was mated, produced a lovely litter and we kept one of the puppies, a cute black bundle of canine fun, and this certainly helped her for a while. For me, having our two beautiful daughters Sarah and Samantha was a great delight to come home to.

But generally my home life remained a source of dissatisfaction. My only fulfilment came through my work. This imbalance had profound implications for me, and I was always fearful of things collapsing around my head. Tony continued to be uncommunicative and I still found myself 'out of the frame', as it were, having to follow his leads with no real information to go on. There was no discussion or planning as to when and where we would open shops. I would be told at the last minute that a new shop was being opened somewhere on a certain date and that I had to produce merchandise for it. The demand for our products was being constantly stretched and there was never any advance notice. How long could this unhappy state continue?

Chapter 7
Extensions and Indiscretions

In 1963 I started waking in the night with an uncontrollable wheezing and coughing. My doctor diagnosed asthma. He prescribed cortisone which suppressed the effects for a while but as soon as I stopped the medication the symptoms returned. I endured this dismal and distressing condition for 30 years until a better treatment came along. During those three decades I was permanently on prescriptions of very large quantities of cortisone and antibiotics for up to four weeks at a time. It was something that I just had to live with, but I had Thorntons to distract me. As soon as Mike had taken full responsibility for the financial side of things, Tony and I could at last be brought more into the picture. In 1967 we had nearly 90 shops making a profit of almost a quarter of a million pounds on a turnover of over £1.7m. (That would translate in today's finances to a profit of almost £3m compared to Thorntons' profit of £8.47m in 2008.)

From 1962 to '67 I enjoyed a marvellous time as Production Director but then things started to deteriorate once more. Although our family dynamics were improving, particularly with

Dad and my cousin Mike, the relationship I had with Tony was quite unsatisfactory, indeed non-existent. Nevertheless, the company was expanding fast and, to cope with the expansion, creating more space through increasing mechanisation and improving efficiency.

It had not always been so. When I had first seen the premises at Belper I had thought the place to be so huge we could never fill it, but by 1965 we were getting as cramped as we were back in Sheffield. In truth, the shortage of space was exacerbated by the fact that so much of the production in the city was being transferred to the Derbyshire factory even though the latter site had its own storage and overheating problems, especially during the summer months. We had long been aware of the potential damage and loss as a result of the flat, uninsulated roof at the Sheffield centre and often dreaded a long hot summer. I once sought Stanley's advice about this.

"Oh, don't worry about it," was all he said. "We always have this problem. Just take a hosepipe up on the roof and completely flood it with water. That will evaporate in the sun and cool the room down below."

His suggestion wasn't of great use, partly because the roof leaked, so the solution simply added to the problem. All we could do was halt production until a cooler spell came but that then left us with an under-occupied workforce.

My father was equally unhelpful. He seemed perversely cheerful about the situation. "Well, you'll simply have to lay people off," was his pragmatic response. This was something that I really wanted to avoid as we had no arrangements for interim pay and the staff would not be eligible to claim unemployment benefits for these temporary periods. I felt that we were being unfair as a company and we should have better arrangements for what was, after all, a perfectly normal aspect of our British climate.

As soon as we commenced chocolate production at Belper, I was aware that we had the same seasonal problem and was determined to do something about it – without spending too much on the solution, of course. We built a small storage room cooled by an ancient, massive and noisy ex-War Department air conditioning unit. It was not terribly reliable but it did at least get us through one hot summer without damage to our chocolate stocks. Eventually I realised that the entire chocolate department needed to be air-conditioned and a new and efficient system was installed at some cost. This expense was justified as it completely revolutionised the manufacturing of our high-quality chocolates.

The old mill site at Belper was bounded by other properties. On the east side up Derwent Street to the High Street there was a place known as Pym's Buildings (Pym had a wine shop on the main road); to the south there was Brettle's, one of the many hosiery companies (now with a sizeable lot of vacant land), and on the west there were various small buildings. The north side was Derwent Street itself with our factory fronting directly onto it. Immediately opposite was a chemicals business housed in an ancient stone mill next to an old wooden dance hall called the Assembly Rooms, now occupied by 'Fisk Tyres'. The Assembly Rooms had also once housed an impressive restaurant overlooking the Derwent meadows where Tony and I had sometimes dined in the past but, when we heard that the property might be for sale, we saw it as a potential storage facility for our own packaging.

I telephoned the owners of Fisk Tyres to tell them that we were interested in buying this building and immediately agreed over the phone to buy it for £7,000. I didn't have my father's permission but things had improved between us. I knew that he liked property and considered it the next best thing to spending money on expanding our chain of shops. The opportunity seemed too good to miss and fortunately our cash flow was strong enough to allow for it.

Earlier, in the mid-1950s, Stanley had bought some land from Brettle's to extend the open space at the back at the factory. This gave us enough space to construct a new building adjacent to the Boiled Sweet Department which moved into the ground floor of the new building to make way for production of the chocolate centres in the vacated space.

Upstairs in the new building was a big factory canteen. Improved working conditions were just as important as levels of pay, and I felt that a first-class staff canteen with subsidised meals would be a big asset. We employed a proper chef and his high quality lunches were appreciated by one and all. This was one of the factors that helped us increase our workforce over five years to three times its original size. We were constantly reminded that Belper's employees could be choosy when it came to finding work as there were many other well-paid opportunities for them elsewhere in the town.

Working conditions were changing dramatically everywhere and we had to acknowledge this. When I first entered employment the convention was that children left school at 15 and went straight into work, the average adult wage being well under £5.00 for a 48-hour week. At Thorntons we offered a fortnight's annual leave but included Saturday mornings in our working week. Wages were set at a national rate by a Joint Industrial Council for the Confectionery Trade but this wasn't wholly satisfactory as the rate didn't reflect the varying costs of living in different parts of the country. Once the Council had been dismantled we were able to set our own rates of pay but felt that we couldn't necessarily offer different levels to our Sheffield and Belper employees. Incoming legislation on age and sex discrimination meant that eventually everyone was paid the same except where they had extra responsibility or special skills. What this meant in real terms was that no one ever left our Sheffield base voluntarily but in Belper the turnover was constant and I really wanted to tackle this problem of motivation and retention. Improving the old building, providing the canteen and offering excellent changing room facilities were all part of my strategy to make our employees more comfortable and willing to remain with us.

It was 1965 and I asked George Belfield to come to the office to discuss matters with me.

"George, I can't go on doing everything myself," I explained. "I need someone to be Factory Manager. You have worked in every department here and you're now running the Chocolate Department. I think that, with some proper training, you could do the job. What do you think about it?"

He pondered for a moment. "I would need to know what the arrangements were for the job and what specifically you have in mind regarding training," he said, "but yes, of course, I would love to do it."

"Oh, that's good because I've been looking into management training courses at Derby Tech for you. They run a two-year works management evening course followed by a further one-year course to get the diploma."

"Could you get me more details of that, please," he asked, "and let me know what the salary and conditions are for the job?

Then, if it all seems satisfactory, I'm sure I'd like to do it." Thus within a couple of weeks George became Factory Manager.

A problem had arisen among the girls who packed the chocolate boxes. Although the installation of a conveyor-belt system made the packing more efficient and the incentive scheme made the work potentially lucrative, something wasn't right. There were constant stoppages and clearly the girls were unhappy. This was a mystery to me but the chance to get to the bottom of it all came when I was approached by someone from the Medical Research Council from Sheffield University who wondered if there might be a project that one of their Ph.D. students could work on.

"Yes," I said, "we have an issue in our Chocolate Box Packing Department. For some reason, we have people constantly leaving, being absent and fighting. I don't know what on earth is causing this."

A young student, Denys Cross, was dispatched to study us. He had started on the shop floor in industry, realised that he had ability and got into Work Measurement, eventually doing very well at university where he had earned his doctorate. It was a great sadness to me and others when, some two years after completing his Thorntons project, he was killed in a car crash in his mid-thirties.

After two weeks spent observing our production methods Denys told me that he was ready to present his findings. George Belfield and I met up in the management office and we asked him to summarise his report.

"There's a whole range of problems but the main one is to do with the social mix of the women you have working in the department."

"What exactly do you mean?" I asked.

"Well," he replied candidly, "it seems that the individual members haven't been very carefully selected. You need to understand that these packing teams have to function as a social group. The job itself – sitting there all day putting the same chocolates into the same place in a plastic tray – is inherently boring. No intellectual effort is required. The women do at least have the satisfaction of doing a good job but they need social satisfaction as well. This is very important."

"I see what you mean," I said. "You think we have the wrong sorts of people working together."

"Yes, definitely. They all talk a lot together and this helps to pass the time, but they do need to have some shared interests. A teenage girl doesn't have much in common with a more mature woman. She will want to talk about boyfriends, pop music, films, you know the sort of thing. The older person will have quite different interests."

"I can understand what you're saying," said George, "but this is hardly a reason for them to be physically fighting each other."

"No, it isn't," Denys agreed. "The team incentive scheme is the main reason for that. The younger women are much more interested in earning the maximum bonus than the older ones. Many of those older women are there just to earn a bit of 'pin-money' and for the social occupation. If you have a mixed age team such as this the younger ones are bound to get fed up. They feel the older ones are preventing them from earning their maximum bonus. Also, the younger ones generally are much more dextrous and can work much faster."

"I see. And is there anything else?" I asked.

"There are a couple of other things. Your department manager isn't really up to the job. She doesn't know how to deal with people and sort out their problems when they arise. And your incentive scheme has become ineffective. Haven't you noticed how the department is always achieving 100% performance?"

"Oh. Do you think there is some fiddling of the figures?" asked George, not entirely in surprise.

"I don't think – I know," answered Denys emphatically. "By the way, during the last few weeks while I've been watching things closely, I've been chatting to Betty Hall and I can tell you that she understands these problems very well. I'd say that she would be a great manager."

I turned to George. "What do you think about all this?" I asked.

"I agree that the incentive scheme now seems to be doing more harm than good," he concurred. "I can't prove it but I'm sure there's been some 'massaging' of the figures recently. That's what's been undermining the Packing Department and, I guess, causing fall-outs elsewhere. As for Betty, I agree with your observation, Denys – she'd be ideal for that job. She's got great people skills and I think she's just what we need to take charge there."

It was time to make a few decisions. I put it to both of them that we drop the incentive schemes altogether and consolidate the bonus payments into the normal wage. We would still measure output and report back to the production teams. They were in full agreement. As Denys pointed out, we had already created comfortable and secure working conditions. "Now," he said, "let your teams get on with doing a good job and, most importantly, *tell them* they are doing a good job! It is patronising to think that people will only ever work harder if they are paid more. Human behaviour is governed by more than money, and rewards need not always be financial."

We implemented these changes, improved our selection procedures and re-organised the workforce into teams of similar abilities. Most importantly, we asked Betty Hall to take charge of the department. The results were outstanding – productivity increased still further and labour turnover dropped almost to nothing.

Betty came to see me one day in the office. I always knew when she appeared at the door that she had some important confidential knowledge for me:

"Have you heard about Pym's?"

"No," I said. "What about Pym's?"

"Well, the Wine Shop on the corner of Derwent Street and Bridge Street has gone bust and I expect that Mr Pym will want to sell the whole property."

"Thank you, Betty," I said. "Thank you very much."

I called Mr Pym straightaway. "I'm very sorry to hear that the Wine Shop has closed down and I wondered if you might be interested in selling the property."

"I'm glad you called," he said. "Yes, we *would* like to sell the whole property that goes from your factory wall up to Bridge Street and including four houses along the main road. If we can negotiate this privately then we can avoid agents' fees."

I swallowed hard, thinking this would be quite a chunk of real estate to administer and would probably be quite costly. "How much do you want for it?" I asked.

"Well, I think that £12,000 would be a reasonable amount, don't you?"

I actually thought that it was a *very* reasonable amount and wanted to buy it there and then, but I restrained myself, recognising that I should first talk to Stanley who would then speak for my Dad. Stanley was in the building at the time so I called him over.

"Stanley," I said, not able to contain my excitement, "we could buy the whole of the Pym's buildings for £12,000! It would open up the whole of the side of our property and, you know, there are some useful buildings on it and we could rent the shops off. So – what do you think?"

He was quite impressed but his first response was financial. "Don't you think that you could knock him down a bit?"

"Well, I'll try to get a bit off," I replied.

I talked to Mr Pym again and we settled on a price of £11,500. I was delighted with this marvellous opportunity but I realised it was at the expense of the Pym family in their misfortune.

Anyway, we *were* able to rent out the shops on Bridge Street, we converted the 18th century former nail factory into our new engineering shop and demolished the old cottages where once had lived the elderly neighbour who used to be disturbed by the nocturnal rumblings of the *mélangeur*.

Behind the Assembly Rooms was a large hosiery factory belonging to the Sylcoto Company, another family-owned business. However, we felt that they invested less of their time and effort into running their company than we did in ours. Walter Willen and I would often stand in the Chocolate Department and be distracted by the sounds of a loud exhaust and the braking of a souped-up XK 150 Jaguar outside.

"He's there again with 'is racing car," Walter would comment drily.

"Who is?"

"Young Squires, that's all he is interested in, I think. Almost every day it is the same."

Looking out of the window, I would see the XK accelerate madly and then, just as violently, brake with a loud squeal of tyres. It was no surprise to us when their business failed but, although I was keen to add their site to ours, my father was less so and we missed that particular opportunity. However, its new owners, Maystock, were willing to sell us some adjacent land behind the Assembly Rooms, which we used as a car park, as well as a small modern block which we acquired for use as a Personnel Office. In this way, we gradually increased our overall site and our range of properties. This was something my father had never foreseen but was fortuitous nevertheless.

I wondered if I might be able to buy the beautiful flat meadow running down to the edge of the River Derwent. Here was an area of roughly 12 acres which I thought would be ideal for our ever-growing Sports Club. As an added possible advantage I thought that at some time it might be possible to develop the land. This meadow formed part of the Strutt Estate and I entered into persistent negotiations with their Land Agent to acquire the rights. We eventually paid £12,000 – a high price for agricultural land – but given its potential value to the company I thought it was money well spent.

Somehow or other the local building company of Bowmer & Kirkland always seemed to finish up building our extensions for us. The company at that time was run by an old bounder called Jack Kirkland, an individual who was more than capable of calling a spade a spade. I really enjoyed working with him because we were able to have a flaming row about something, anything, and then shake hands and remain good friends. He would get on with the job with tremendous determination. The work was always done on time, to a very high standard and at a very reasonable price. I remember a story about Jack: he went to look at one particular job and saw one of his workmen digging a trench very lazily by hand.

"Get a f***ing move on! Is that the best you can do?" he thundered. When nothing much happened Jack himself leapt into the trench wearing his best suit, grabbed the shovel, and proceeded to dig at a frenzied rate. He finished the job very quickly, got out of the trench and fired the offending labourer. I can't really defend treating an employee like that but it certainly showed the spirit of the man. The Bowmer side of the business had no real involvement in the company. It was definitely Jack who was in complete charge. He brought his son John into the firm and he was quite a different personality. Between then they built the business up and we had a successful commercial relationship with them for many years.

With Colin Bridges and others we developed a good engineering department. I was always going to bankruptcy sales looking for suitable equipment. Often accompanied by Leslie Charlesworth, we continued buying broken-down old machines for next to nothing and then Colin and his team would restore them to something like working order. On one occasion Leslie and I went to a filthy old factory in Glasgow. This involved an overnight stay in the city and Leslie had booked accommodation for us. It turned out to be an extremely down-at-heel boarding house with water leaking through the ceiling and down the walls, damp and dirty bedding and mice playing in the rafters overnight. I decided to make all the bookings in the future.

At the sale I purchased a utensil-washing machine, an ancient thing for which I paid £50. However I soon realised my mistake when I had to bid separately for its driving motor. This cost me another £50 and then we had to get the whole thing back to Belper. It was a very solid chunk of machinery and it took a rather large truck to move it. That involved a further £250 so the acquisition was not quite as cheap as I would have liked.

I remember feeling very nervous at the very first machinery sale I attended. I started bidding on some pieces at a very low price, probably at about £5, but was quickly outbid. I felt the eyes of the auctioneer staring at me, prompting my next move. I took forever deliberating on whether to proceed and, in incremental stages, the price reached the dizzy height of £10. My rival immediately bettered that and again I pondered for what seemed an age before making my next small bid. After all, I was new at this game.

"Come on, young man, hurry up," urged the auctioneer. "We haven't got all day."

Afterwards he had a quiet word with me: "There's nothing that irritates an auctioneer more than a bidder who cannot make up his mind and wastes time." Oops! I decided thereafter that I would do the opposite and try to please the auctioneers so I always bid very quickly, being absolutely clear what my upper limit was, and I would seek to demoralise the opposition by bidding in large jumps rather than small ones. This strategy proved to be very successful and I compounded the effect by always going to auctions in my shabbiest clothes thus convincing my fellow buyers that I probably wasn't capable of bidding very highly.

I spent a lot of my time discussing machines and gadgets with George Belfield and, if there was some technical problem, we would usually come up with a solution. I remember one of those 'eureka' moments when we hit on a way to cut our *Hazelnut Slice*. This product, made from hazelnut paste and then covered in chocolate, had always been cut by hand and we felt there must be a less laborious alternative. The task required a very slow guillotine which could do the job without cracking the chocolate coating.

"Let's go down to old Robinson's in Derby to see what he's got," I suggested to George. We often went down there on Friday afternoons when all was quiet and we could walk round his confectionery junkyard without being disturbed. 'Old Robinson' was a delightful Irishman who seemed to do extremely well from buying and selling all this old equipment.

"Have you got a guillotine?" we asked.

"Aye, oi tink dat dare might be just such a machine out in the yard round the corner," he replied in his rich brogue. We were shown a very simple device covered in bits and pieces of other machinery and rubbish.

"How much do you want for it?"

"30 quid," he said immediately.

"We'll give you 20 for it," we stated, and the deal was done.

We took it back to Belper, Colin cleaned it up and, to our absolute amazement, it worked perfectly – another example of constructive labour-saving. Not long after that Colin Bridges left to take up a job elsewhere but, in his time, he had achieved minor miracles for us in his sparsely-equipped workshop with all the old machines we brought to his attention. However, we were fortunate to have another excellent engineer, Ron Marsh, who was able to take over and provide the service that we needed.

The confectionery business is seasonal with a huge peak for boxes of chocolate just before Christmas. We coped with this in two ways: we employed extra people on a temporary basis, and we manufactured sufficient product well in advance and were able to freeze it. I learned about freezing from an article in an American magazine and knew that confectionery with a short shelf-life could be kept for up to six months if properly frozen. The secret was how to prevent the chocolates from gathering humidity when they came out of the deep freeze. The answer to this was quite simple – we packed the boxes into sealed polythene bags which were not opened until the packages had defrosted for about 48 hours. I then discovered that there were several ex-Ministry of Food long-term deep freeze stores around the country which had been built for storing emergency rations during the war. We managed to rent freezer space at a very low rate and so in our now air-conditioned factory we were able to start making chocolate boxes for Christmas sales in June.

Next, I had to calculate how many additional employees we would need for all this extra demand between June and

December. Peter Crook and I worked out a production planning system and, on the first occasion, we concluded we would hire about 20 temps but by the time I was Production Director we were employing up to 200 extra workers. One of these, Eva Kent, stayed with us and eventually became Personnel Manager. She was superb at selecting the right sort of people and was kept extremely busy during June and July recruiting for us.

I have already said that the secret of attracting and retaining staff in this high-employment environment lay in making their work enjoyable, but I realised there was more to be done. We had to ensure that everyone was treated equally and this meant setting up Terms of Employment which, although it is hard to believe today, we had never done before. Prior to the introduction of the Contracts of Employment Act there were no formally binding agreements between employer and employee. The bosses could take whatever action they wanted without any fear of retribution. This was against a background of aggressive Trades Unions, endless strikes, very poor quality management and very low unemployment. I was firm in my belief that unionisation resulted in strikes and conflict and was determined that we should resist it. The whole country was affected by the politics of it; there was generally a very negative attitude towards companies, employers and profit. The latter was a dirty word implying that 'profit' was stealing money from the workers. The staff in Sheffield seemed to present no threat but I was concerned that the highly-strung Belper workforce would seek to become unionised and we would then be subject to strikes and massive wage demands. We had just such an occasion one day and it made me realise that something had to be done to mitigate against this in the future.

Once again it was Betty Hall who brought the news to me. She knocked abruptly at the door and came into my office, out of breath as usual.

"Mr Peter, Mr Peter, can you come to the canteen straight away please? Everybody has stopped work and they're all there saying they'll walk out unless something is done about it."

This was alarming news. "Oh hell," I grumbled, "this is just what I was dreading. What's it all about?"

As we rushed toward the canteen Betty gave me an outline. "It's the alleged unfair treatment of Phyllis in the Toffee Department. She was stopped half an hour's pay for being late but there are others who claim they've been late and never had pay stopped."

The adrenaline kicked in and I moved to face the crowd with a perverse feeling of excitement. The room was crammed with about 150 agitated individuals, some standing, others sitting on canteen chairs, all talking at once.

"Can we have a bit of quiet please, and can someone tell me what the problem is?" I implored.

Phyllis spoke up at once. "Yeah, I'll tell you what it is! We've been stopped 'alf an hour for being ten minutes late – and they don't do that to them what's in HB." (That was the Boiled Sweet Department, imaginatively referred to as Hard Boiled, or HB, alluding to the product, not the employees!)

"Well, I'm sure we can sort that out quickly enough, but there must be some more general problem for you all to come to the canteen like this?"

Then the floodgates opened and I was up to my neck in a stream of angry statements – questions about bonuses, pay rates, break times and just about anything else that might cause conflict. I did my best to answer these grievances in the 20 minutes that followed and eventually everyone returned to their work stations feeling somewhat ameliorated for having aired these comments, but I was left in no doubt that more definite strategies were now required to deal with such issues if they arose again.

In the days before the Internet and Google you had to find things out by reading newspapers and magazines, by going to libraries and talking to people. I heard about the Glacier Metal Company Project and the work of Wilfred Brown and Elliott Jaques, an organisational psychologist. They had gone to enormous trouble to set up fair terms of employment and to establish a stable working environment with the full participation of the workforce in order to prevent conflict and to treat people fairly. I felt that we could set up a Works Council on similar lines.

First of all I made sure that every department and every employee level would be represented. To Stanley's great concern I established the principle of unanimous voting which meant that every single person had to agree everything. This was at the heart of the system set up by Brown and Jaques to ensure complete involvement and agreement of everything under discussion. Stanley was unconvinced.

"We'll lose all control, Peter," he warned. "They'll want to decide the wages as well and they'll set them far too high."

"Well, actually I think it would be a good idea if we got them involved in agreeing the premiums for various skills," I said. "That way there wouldn't be all the arguments about whether they're fair or not."

I went ahead, by-passing his reservations. I was so certain that it would work. I commenced by drafting a very detailed set of Terms of Employment and then sought the necessary agreement of the Works Council. So that the various representatives could feel that their views were taken fully into account, we even paid for a lawyer of their choice to advocate independently on their behalf. We spent many, many hours in those Council meetings but we achieved our mutual aim: Terms of Employment that all parties were completely happy with and which worked. Everybody was treated equally and we had a system of warnings and appeals long before these came into general industrial practice. Our workplace atmosphere became benevolent and positive with all employees pulling together even though in the rest of the commercial world management and workers remained at constant loggerheads with perpetual disputes and strikes.

I had been an absolute novice as a manager at the start as there was very little precedence for it within the company, but we ended up with an excellent management team. Our system was built on what I had gleaned from books and the various seminars I attended. I consolidated my own experiences by talking to other people. I had always appointed existing staff to managerial positions but now I realised that I needed to scan a wider field of potential candidates if I was to secure the best individuals for important posts.

This rule was not fixed in stone, of course, and I still made some appointments intuitively when I simply had the feeling that a certain person was the right one. George Belfield was an outstanding example of someone who I felt sure was capable of better things and he went from manufacturing chocolate centres to running the whole of the Belper Factory. He was first-class at everything he did and, after some management training, his skills and knowledge improved enormously.

My younger brother John joined the business in 1967. This was entirely the decision of my father and Stanley. At first I had no reason to oppose it as I had yet no idea of the risks it would present. He was ten years my junior and I felt a certain involvement in his future. He was in his final year at Repton when Dad had asked me for my thoughts on his next move. "Well," I replied, "he obviously ought to go to University and study what he is good at – engineering." So that was what he did. He got a good degree at Cambridge and then had a further two years' practical engineering in order to complete his studies. By this time we had purchased the OKA extruder and were on very good terms with Baker Perkins here in Britain and Kremmling in Germany. I was able to arrange a year's apprenticeship for him at the former followed by some time overseas. This allowed him to go straight into the Engineering Department once he formally joined the family business.

It didn't take long to realise that potentially I was going to have a difficult working relationship with John. Dad had always had a high opinion of him so this gave him quite an edge of authority even though he was new to the company. He was definitely a chip off the old block, very reserved, self-assured and soon prone to changing things over to his way. This quickly had implications for the way our production was being managed. In fairness I suppose that John felt he would have to fight to make his mark in the family business as there were already three very well-established family members in senior positions.

As Production Director I have to admit that, were John not my brother, he would not have lasted more than two weeks, behaving as he did. However, I also knew that I would get nowhere if I voiced my concerns to our father. He and my uncle still had this vision of themselves in complete control when it came to decision-making. I would probably have been thrown out on my ear if I had dared to challenge the status quo. Besides, I did feel a fraternal obligation to help John if I could. I recalled an incident when he was only six and we had been chasing each other around the house as youngsters do. I was sixteen and much stronger and, when he ran into the kitchen, he had to put all his weight against the door to stop me from pushing it open. Well, I stopped pushing and the door suddenly shut tight with his fingers caught round the edge. I was horrified when the end of one finger fell to the floor on *my* side of the door. My parents rushed both him and the severed digit to the hospital but it was too late to be re-attached successfully and he was left with a finger about half an inch shorter than it should have been. Few people ever noticed but I always did, feeling an unassuaged measure of guilt that I, as the older brother, should have pre-empted this accident and prevented it.

– ★★★ –

We had learned a lot about European methods of manufacturing and retailing of confectionery from our visits to Europe but we still knew next-to-nothing about our counterparts in the USA. The American confectionery business had developed quite separately from the European industry and we were eager to check out the competition. However, going to America was a big thing. I knew no one who had ever been there. I read avidly their trade magazines such as *Manufacturing Confectioner* and could tell that in many respects their approach was quite different regarding machines, methods and products. What *was* similar was the number of companies which operated within the same manufacturing/retailing structure that we did.

I decided to go to America to find out for myself, there being no Internet, e-mail or cheap and effective telephone networks. I made only one prior arrangement for a visit with a confectionery technician in New York. The rest I would sort out when I got there, using my list of addresses and telephone numbers.

I flew into John F. Kennedy Airport on a BOAC Vickers VC10 on November 7th 1967 in the late afternoon and took the airport bus to the Grand Central Hotel in New York. Suddenly arriving in America like this was a real culture shock: the airport bus had taken me through the teeming, busy streets of New York jammed with yellow cabs and bustling people. I gazed in complete amazement at the skyscrapers which created a palpable feeling of claustrophobia within the streets below. I entered the foyer of the Grand Central Hotel, expecting to go straight to the check-in desk. I found a solid mass of people all trying to do the same thing so I had no alternative but to join in the crowd, feeling completely exhausted after my flight. I stood there for the next three hours before finally getting to my room at about 8 p.m.

My first night in New York was not a good one. I should have realised by the name alone that the hotel would be close to Grand

Central Station. The US railway network was still very active in the 1960s and my sleep was filled with loud clanking noises as freight trains were assembled and steam trains chugged nearby. Added to the cacophony was the continuous sound of sirens from the patrol cars of New York's finest.

I crawled out of bed the next morning and went ahead with my plan. I telephoned the presidents of the confectionery companies on my list and, to my complete amazement, I was put through, received an extremely courteous response and, in all cases, was invited to visit. There was a fairly 'open culture' in the European confectionery industry at that time, but here I found that the American companies were not only open but were very proud to show me their businesses and factories. I travelled across the States for the next two weeks, having the most amazing experience. Simply to get on an aeroplane and fly a thousand miles and still be in the same country was so different from life on our tiny island. Their infrastructure, highways and air traffic systems were all so advanced. I received outstanding hospitality wherever I went but none greater than at the Sweets Candy Factory at Salt Lake City on November 16th. There I was met by Jack and Tony Sweet who showed me not only their entire factory in the greatest possible detail but, after taking me to lunch, they delivered me to another candy plant for my afternoon visit. Then they insisted upon collecting me from my hotel that evening to take me to their club.

The club was situated on the 25th floor of one of the tallest edifices in Salt Lake City. It seemed to occupy the whole of one side of the building. I looked out at the spectacular view over the city and away to the mountains in the distance. There is a strange sense of calm and hush in these tall structures, way above the noise of the streets, safe behind the huge double-glazed windows. Jack explained things to me.

"Well, you see, you can't just go into a bar in this town and buy an alcoholic drink. It's against the State Law. So the only way that you can have a drink is in a private members' club like this one."

"That must make things very difficult," I said.

"Yes," he replied, "but it doesn't really stop people drinking, you know. They just find ways to get round the laws. Even in this club I can't buy alcohol across the counter – we have our own locker stocked with our own bottles of spirits. We have to buy them in the State Liquor Store, bring them in here and give them to the barman who locks them away for us. He then gets them out when we come in and need a drink."

"What a ridiculous set up," I suggested. "Whoever made laws like that?"

"Well," replied Tony, "this *is* a great city, beautifully situated. You can see the mountains in the distance from here where we go skiing and it has a wonderful climate. So we put up with the laws. The city was founded by the Mormons and they are still very strong here. There are a lot of good things about their religion but also some very strange things." He didn't elucidate further.

Jack went up to the bar and asked for his bottle of whisky. We sat round a table looking out at the fantastic night-time view and chatting. The whisky soon seemed to disappear and Jack was up asking the barman for another bottle which was consumed as quickly as the first. I knew I was getting drunk but to hell with it! I was having such a good time. It was great whisky and good company. I was taken back to my hotel around 10:30 although by whom I'm not sure as I don't think anyone else there was fit to drive anymore than I was. I collapsed into bed with no thought other than the fact that I needed to be up at 7 in the morning for my flight to San Francisco. Of course, I didn't wake till 10. I'd missed the plane and gained a serious headache. Fortunately, I was able to take a later flight. When I returned to England a few days later I had enough ideas to fill a 40-page report for our business.

– ★★★ –

The state of my unhappy marriage was still a constant source of stress. In 1967 I had gone to Frank Kershaw, a senior partner in the company's law firm, to ask for advice on divorce. As a much older man he was not really the best person to have consulted over this issue. We sat in his over-heated office in Sheffield and he advised that a divorce would break me financially, that there was an unbearable stigma attached to it, that I wouldn't be able to afford to live properly, that there would be serious ramifications concerning the ownership of my shares in the company and so on and so forth. What he was really saying was "Don't even think about it!" Even as late as 1967 divorce was something that one shuddered to consider. It was frowned upon and you were supposed to put up with a marriage, however bad it was. Furthermore, I dearly loved my children and could not bear the thought of leaving them. I left Frank Kershaw's office after that interview feeling that I was stuck. As I obviously couldn't get out of my marriage and, since there was no real satisfaction within it, I deliberately decided that I needed to have an affair.

In June 1968, my son Miles was born in Claremont Hospital in Sheffield, a joyful event for me as I was delighted to have a son. We took him back home to Ashover and installed him in the little bedroom that had become the nursery. A German au-pair named Sonja had been engaged to help with the new baby. Janet was already suffering from colitis once more so we had decided to send Sarah and Samantha to my parents' holiday home in North Wales. Clearly she couldn't cope with them as well as the illness and the new baby. I was very concerned for her because her own suffering and unhappiness were not eased.

Janet's condition deteriorated and she became so ill one night that I thought that she was going to die. I phoned her specialist at home at 1.00 a.m. and was told to get her into hospital immediately. She was admitted to Worksop hospital in the middle of the night and remained there for about three weeks. Naturally, she was extremely concerned about Miles being left alone with Sonja, so I asked a local woman who was very competent with young children to look after him for a few weeks.

This left me alone in the house with Sonja. This had not been my intent but I wasn't going to object. Sonja was delightful and lightened my days, particularly as I could speak German with her despite the fact that she was meant to be practising English. I was still going to see Janet every evening in hospital but she remained utterly and completely miserable.

After a few days I was sitting in a meeting in the office with George Belfield, Betty Hall and Trevor Fleetwood but my mind was not focussed on the discussion. I was thinking about Sonja, what a beautiful young woman she was, the fact that she loved classical music, spoke the language that I enjoyed, was bright and cheerful and happy and full of fun. After work I went straight to hospital to see Janet but my feelings for Sonja were taking over. She had made a beautiful meal which we ate together in the kitchen, laughing and happily conversing in her native tongue.

I suggested that we move to my little study where we could listen to some music and I would show her the photographs of my trip to America. We started on the sofa and ended up on the floor. I told her I was interested in psychology and she corrected my pronunciation of the equivalent German term. I loved the way she shaped her mouth as she kept saying this word, over and over, as we kissed.

At my suggestion we moved to the bedroom and this was the pattern every night for the next few weeks until Janet came home. However, there was no way for the relationship to be complete as Sonja was already engaged to a dentist in Germany and had promised to be faithful to him. Even so, this brief affair brought the most intense relief to me. I was now 35 and she only 23. Despite myself, I fell deeply in love with her and wondered how I could hide all this from my wife.

Janet eventually came out of hospital and eventually, to her deep distress, I had to tell her the facts. Miles came home and Sonja was sent back to Germany two weeks early. Janet assumed that it would be all over now but it wasn't, or at least not for a while. I still longed to see Sonja again and I found it almost impossible to think of anything else but her. I felt that I just had to see her again.

I found an excuse to go to Germany for a long weekend although Janet probably guessed what I was up to. Sonja's home was in Bremerhaven where her parents had a riding school and she had a tiny flat in the city. She picked me up at the airport in her parents' Audi and we drove to her student accommodation. It was a single room on the top floor of the house with the ceiling sloping down to the single bed. Most of our time was spent lying on that bed together and listening to her recording of Tchaikovsky's *Pathetique Symphony* by Herbert von Karajan and the Berlin Philharmonic, a piece of music that I find deeply emotional. She even took me to a local record store so that I could purchase my own copy.

After three almost idyllic days I came back to England with a heavy heart. That was the last time that I ever saw Sonja. She sent a parcel to the office a couple of weeks later containing a personal letter and a copy of a Bruckner Symphony all wrapped in a pink ribbon. I replied with great passion but, after a few more weeks had passed, I received a 'goodbye' letter. She said that she was ruining both my marriage and her own engagement and that the only sensible decision was to stop.

I put both letters and the pink ribbon into my briefcase. The next day I took them with me on my drive to Sheffield from Ashover. On the way I found a secluded spot on a quiet lane on the moors and made a little pile from these things and put a match to them, and that was that. I kept both LPs though as I couldn't bear to burn those. I thought that this little ceremony might excise the longing from my mind once and for all. I was determined not to be afflicted by unrequited love ever again – and I wasn't, at least for the next five years.

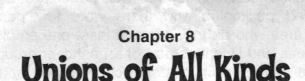

Chapter 8
Unions of All Kinds

We had reached 1968 and the working relationships within the family were no better. Over the next few years this had a serious effect upon our turnover and profit margins, despite the fact that we had even more outlets and franchises. We had even set up a successful arrangement with Marks and Spencer. Dad had finally relinquished the Chairmanship of the company – he was 77 after all – and Stanley had taken over as Joint Managing Director with Tony. At last, we could have proper directors' meetings with a chairman, but there was still no co-ordinated central management and the business continued to drift. The figures on the balance sheets looked worrying. I was very concerned but was not in a position personally to do anything.

From the first I had sensed that there would be problems for me with John. I tried to work with him positively. I did my best to assist him within the company, but he was very much his father's son. He shared that same aggressive introspection, was always dogmatic in his thinking, and we found ourselves at constant loggerheads while I was Production Director. Tony, too, did not make things easier for me. He was having serious difficulties with his marriage. Judith would regularly interrupt our business conversations with phone calls, seeking comfort and reassurance from her husband. This, combined with his secretive and uncommunicative nature, would make things very awkward. Most of the day-to-day management had followed the production activity to Belper but he was reluctant to move and maintained his control of the retailing from Sheffield. This put quite a strain on my ability to co-ordinate the two aspects of the business – production and marketing – and this lack of communication took a heavy toll on my effectiveness as a director.

When Christmas finally arrived that year, it was with some relief that I went to the annual charity ball organised by the Chesterfield Red Cross. It was generally held at the Bradbury Hall, a social venue owned by one of Chesterfield's most successful business families, the Robinsons. Their stock-in-trade was paper products, surgical dressings and packaging and there were few people in the Chesterfield area who did not know at least one employee of the company. Janet and I went as part of an Ashover group and I fully expected the usual tedium of polite conversation and obligatory dances with each lady in turn. However, things brightened up when it was time for the tombola. All eyes, at least those of the men present, were on the gorgeous blonde operating the draw. The idea that had been fermenting in my head for some time – that of having an affair – now seemed tantalisingly possible, and I determined to make myself known to this attractive creature there and then.

Her name was Charlotte Nicol. She was married and had three children. This information did not deter me. When I learned that she was a member of the badminton club I determined that I, too, would start to play badminton. I persuaded Janet to join with me so as not to make things look too obvious, but my real intent was to get to know Charlotte better. The sight of her swinging her racket and wearing her sexy little skirt certainly stoked the passions at the time. I wondered if I could get her involved in the social scene back home in Ashover. There was always a party going off somewhere in the village. All the young marrieds would attend and it was deemed perfectly acceptable to go off smooching with each other's partners to the sounds of Jane Birkin and Serge Gainsbourg as they breathed "*Je t'aime*" at each other from the record-player.

Charlotte was there one evening at just such a party, held in the home of a local solicitor. The conservatory had been rendered intimate with low lights and soft music and there was very little difficulty in persuading the delectable charity worker to put some of her charitable intentions my way. We must have spent an hour and a half in each other's company and we didn't waste the time merely on small talk. Of course, this did not go down well with Janet and I was in the proverbial dog-house for several days, but my enthusiasm for Charlotte was undiminished. I had to find some plausible excuse to talk to her on the telephone to ascertain for sure whether or not my approaches were really welcome.

It seemed a good idea to organise a charitable event as I was sure that Charlotte would be able to help me with her list of contacts. I found her phone number and dialled it, hoping that her husband wouldn't answer. He didn't.

"Hello, Charlotte, it's me," I said tentatively. "I was wondering if you'd be able to let me have a list of your guests at the Red Cross ball as I'd like to invite them to my own charity fundraiser."

"Yes, no problem," she replied.

"Oh, great. I was thinking to call round and pick it up if that's possible. I'm always having to drive between Sheffield and Belper so I could easily pop round to your place on the way. Perhaps one lunchtime?"

"Yes, that'd be fine. How about tomorrow?" This was an open invitation and I looked forward to the encounter with great anticipation. I'd never been to her house but I knew where it was.

The following day I parked nearby and walked to her front door. She welcomed me in to her sitting-room where we sat together chatting on the sofa and drinking coffee. She was very amiable and said she preferred to be called 'Charlie'. She produced the guest list for me and I moved closer to read it more carefully.

As I glanced at the names she suddenly announced: "I'm not going to go to bed with you the first time, you know!" This rather frank admission took me aback. Was I being *that* obvious?

"No, no, of course not!" I protested. However, it did lay open the intimation of what might happen the second time.

"Why don't we meet at a pub for lunch in a few days' time?" she suggested.

"Yes," I agreed, unable to curb my enthusiasm. A date, time and place were fixed.

The next few days passed excruciatingly slowly and I just couldn't wait to see her again. We met as arranged and had a drink although that wasn't really what I wanted. Then we drove, each in our own vehicle, to a secluded country lane. We parked discreetly behind a hedge and Charlie joined me in my car for an hour spent in mutual absorption. However, the circumstances were less than ideal and we both knew it. "This is no good," she averred. "You'd better come to my house tomorrow."

Well, that night I couldn't sleep. The longing to be back with her again was overwhelming. When tomorrow came I went through the same pantomime in parking the car and knocked on her front door. This time there was no small talk on the sofa and no coffee. She led me straight upstairs and within two minutes there was a heap of our clothes on her bedroom floor. We embraced with the passion of two teenagers who had discovered physical love for the first time. This was an all-consuming, totally overwhelming experience, way beyond the perfunctory love-making I'd known before. Everything about Charlie – her shape, her scent, the touch of her skin – engulfed me and I surrendered to the experience, helpless to do otherwise. I knew from Charlie's smile that she also was achieving the fullest pleasure from our being together.

An hour passed but it was a timeless moment for me until I suddenly looked at the clock. "Oh my God, Charlie! I must go. I'm supposed to be in Belper!" That was hardly the most romantic line after such a union, but it was probably not one she'd heard too many times before.

And so it went on. Twice a week through that summer we would meet at lunchtimes, either at her home or a local pub, and drive to some idyllic country spot for a torrid session of consensual bliss. At least, that is how I saw it, and I was becoming increasingly obsessed and distracted by it all. When the time came for Janet to take our children off for their annual break with her parents at Sandsend in North Yorkshire, I sensed that Fate was handing Charlie to me on a plate. We could see each other far more often.

One evening I picked up the phone and heard Charlie's breathless voice. "Darling, he's gone out to play squash. Can you come round?" She even said "please". How could I refuse? Time was short and in our desperation we felt we had to make every moment count.

Janet brought the children back after a few weeks but my clandestine meetings continued. This affair was beginning to overwhelm me. Charlie would even ring me at the office and I was sure that sooner or later someone would catch on. We were playing a dangerous game and I sometimes tried to refrain from taking her calls, but my willpower wasn't strong enough.

"Look, Charlie," I said to her when we had been seeing each other for well over six months, "we really must stop this, at least for the time being. It is taking over our lives."

She understood and agreed, and we had a temporary cooling-off for about a month. But Charlie was as caught up in this as me. She called me one day, using that velvety, seductive voice which I found irresistible. "Peter," she purred. "I'm desperate to see you... I *must* see you. Please, come and see me as soon as possible!"

I relented, as she knew I would, and so our illicit union went on in this way for several years. We were helpless in the strength of our feelings for each other. I genuinely believed that this was helping my marriage as it provided me with an outlet and eased my frustration with Janet. Outwardly, the two of us could share our marital home as if everything was fine and dandy, at least on the surface. We could even contemplate moving to a bigger place and when a dilapidated farmhouse came up for auction in the village I went along to bid for it. The surprise of the occasion wasn't the fact that I successfully outbid all others there but that Charlie and her husband were present. We all met up afterwards for a drink and I had to be really careful about what was said between us.

Bath House Farm needed a lot doing to it. It was built entirely into a hillside and I asked Jack Kirkland if he could help with the necessary excavation. With his digging machinery we cleared away all the land behind the house and replaced it on the slope at the front. We altered the old stone barn that had been blocking the view and completely re-landscaped the property. An architect re-designed the entire building and converted it into a splendid home, full of old stone and beams and new oak panelling. These changes were not achieved overnight and for nine months after selling Over Asher we had to live in two rented caravans until the make-over was complete.

The women in my life were not the only ones giving me pause for thought. Peter Crook had moved on from Thorntons by this time and his duties had been taken over by a ginger-haired

Sheffielder named Graham Tidman, another consultant from the 'human dynamo' mould. He was always popping into my office, full of ideas and energy, and I asked him one day where his career had first begun.

"I was looking to join a better consultancy firm than the one I was at," he told me. "So, when I was out in California one time, I just presented myself at one of their big engineering companies and asked if there was anything I could do for them."

"What? Just like that?" I asked, impressed by his initiative. "What did they say?"

"I was taken immediately to their top man, the president, in his office. 'Gee, we sure could use you here,' he told me. 'We've got at least six weeks' work that needs doing. When can you start?' Well, right away, I told him, and I stayed for six months. That's how I got my business started."

"Wow," I said, unable to conceal my admiration. I felt that Thorntons could tap into some of Graham's 'get-up-and-go' as we were having problems with our Sheffield manager. Hans Hanneman was the type of manager who was not really helpful. He always told you what he thought you wanted to hear instead of giving you the honest picture. Glossing over the difficulties was not really a satisfactory way of dealing with them, and Graham had already sussed out the situation.

"Things are in a mess in Sheffield, you know," he said. "It's a shame, Mr Peter, but Hans is not really up to the job. It seems that he is not too popular."

"Why do you think that is?" I asked him. "Could it be anti-German feeling perhaps? There's still a lot of prejudice about."

"No, I don't think it's anything like that," replied Graham, "although some of his mannerisms and speech conform to the stereotype. It's just his ineffectiveness. I think I could improve things for you if you let me take over his duties until things get better."

I was grateful for his offer but couldn't understand his reasons. "Graham, what about your own business? You employ a lot of people yourself. How are you going to keep all that going?"

"Oh, that's no problem, Mr Peter. I can do that in the evenings and at weekends."

Graham's enthusiasm was genuine but he proved to be no better at working with the Sheffield workforce than Hans. However, he had done some terrific work for us and taught me a great deal, and his name has to be included in the roll-of-honour of individuals who have contributed significantly to the company's success: Jim Nolan, Jamie Dodd, Peter Crook and Geoff Cliffe among others.

Next I decided to let Dennis Beard have a go. Dennis had been running the Boiled Sweet Department at Belper and had indicated his willingness on several occasions to have a crack at the Sheffield factory. He accepted and became a first-class manager, moving to Sheffield in 1971 with his family to make the position permanent. One humorous aside about Dennis centred on the fact that he had no middle name which meant that he was referred to in minutes of meetings simple as 'DB' (initials were used to identify all individuals in minutes) and I felt this didn't seem enough. When I appointed him to the manager's job, I raised this minor issue, saying it would be better if I could list him with three initials.

"All right," he said. "You can put DMB."

"DMB? I asked. "What does the M stand for?"

"Mutt!" he replied, and he was known as 'DMB' ever after.

By 1972 John had reached the grand old age of 29. He came up to me one day with an announcement.

"I've been appointed a director of the business. As such I am going to be Director in charge of the Engineering Department. This will now be separate from the rest of the business and I will not be taking instructions from you any longer regarding the engineering requirements of the factory!"

This took me completely by surprise. If our father had consulted John and Stanley over it, he certainly hadn't consulted me. I immediately started to feel angry.

"How the hell am I supposed to run things if I can't get the engineering work done when I need to?" I asked. He didn't answer. "We've had a successful system in place since I took over this factory ten years ago, although," I couldn't resist adding, "since you have been in charge, it has been much more difficult. Now it looks as if my job is going to be impossible."

"Well, that can't be helped. This is the way things will operate from now on."

My job was indeed made extremely difficult. Together with a non-existent relationship with Tony and the stresses of my marital dilemmas, I was in for several years of sleepless nights. I felt that there ought to be something I could do to restore the status quo but this rather depended on the doubtful support I needed from the others in the family. That was likely to be unforthcoming and it all could rebound on me personally. I didn't want to make things worse for myself so, for the moment, I did nothing.

I felt that some of the difficulties stemmed from there being too many family members in the company. Things had been working well through a combination of hard work and persistence but now there were all these competing individuals, each with their own agendas and philosophies. I was aware that, in other business families, I might never have been expected to join the company, but I had done what was asked of me – we all had – and now the whole enterprise was jeopardised by the addition of one more faction. It was hardly John's own fault – he was no upstart – but the irreconcilable differences in our personalities meant that it was simply not going to work any more. In short, I viewed his appointment as a huge mistake.

However, John was not the sort simply to let things fester around him. He was not passive or neutral in anything. He wanted to establish his own career path and he started to impose his will. The first indication that he meant business was when he moved me out of the first-floor office at Belper. He wanted the space to extend the Chocolate Department and I was relegated to a tiny room on the ground floor. Then he moved me again to a small windowless room in the personnel block. This claustrophobic box was a nightmare to work in and I was driven crazy for several years being confined in such a featureless environment.

I chatted to Mike one day about John's appointment as a director and what was behind it.

"Did you know that John has been appointed a director?" I asked.

"No, I knew nothing about it at all," Mike replied.

"Neither did I, and as far as I am concerned it is a disaster. John has been to see me and told me he will no longer take instructions from me about engineering matters. That is going to make my job impossible."

"Pete, I'm afraid that the Senior Directors still take decisions like that without any consultation with us. They *do* have control of the business, I suppose."

"Remind me what percentage of the voting shares they both hold, Mike."

Mike looked in one of the many folders he kept filled with papers adorned with his small but neat handwriting. "Norman has 43.5% and Stanley 42.2%, so they can do what they like really. Singly or alone they can out-vote everybody."

"Not that they would, but this means they could fire any of us if they ever wanted to," I stated. "I know this has always been the case since we joined the business, but it makes for a certain level of insecurity, particularly now I have reached the age of 39."

"Yes, it's doubly unfair when you realise that it is actually us running the company," agreed Mike.

"For everybody else that voting strength in the background really gives some people more power than others. We never discuss this but it is always there."

"I know," said Mike. "For instance, Tony has 6.85% and I have 5.0% whereas you and John have only 0.5%."

"What a ridiculous and unfair situation," I suggested. "This could provide some dangerous combinations if it came to the point of a vote."

Meanwhile, my affair with Charlie was exacting a heavy price on my honour and integrity. Our resolves to end the relationship were continually thwarted, I was becoming a serial liar and I hated the changes wrought on me. This mixture of infatuation and guilt meant that I was not really being fair to either woman. My time with Charlie was always wonderful but we could never be a complete couple. She often asked if I could leave Janet and I always replied that that was out of the question. There were financial reasons but mostly I couldn't bear to be apart from my children that I loved dearly.

We did manage to spend a weekend together during 1973. I drove her to lunch in Newark from where we journeyed to London and a room in the Cavendish Hotel. I was constantly afraid of being seen by someone who might know us. I took her to Beauchamp Place and I bought her an expensive designer dress which she immediately lost in a taxi. I hoped that there was nothing symbolic in that.

We went to see the musical *Evita* and I was enthralled to be in the company of such an attractive and fun-loving woman. In the hotel we repeatedly gave free rein to our physical feelings and eventually drove back, sated and exhausted, to Derbyshire on the Sunday afternoon. I returned to an empty house. The family had gone to an equestrian event. I looked around me and was overwhelmed by my own emotions. "I can't stand this any longer," I thought to myself, "I'm going. I'm getting out." I threw some clothes into the car and drove away, God knows where. Over the county border in Mansfield I checked in to a small and dingy hotel. This was just the place, I observed, in which to feel really miserable.

Despite Charlie's exhortations I had always resisted the idea of leaving my wife. Now, after the despair of that empty house, I picked up the phone and called Janet. I told her it was all over. I couldn't see her face over the phone but I could imagine the colour draining from her cheeks as I relayed the news. I didn't wait to discuss the issue. Instead I immediately phoned Charlie. "Listen, this is Peter. I'm in a hotel. I've left Janet and I want you to leave your husband. I want you to join me!"

I don't know if I expected her simply to rush away and into my arms, but I was taken aback by her response.

"Peter, darling, how can I do that? I'm not ready. I would need to get organised. I can't just walk out on my family without making some preparations, can I?"

This was not what I wanted to hear.

"Listen, sweetheart," I pleaded. "You're always asking me to leave Janet. Now I've done so. It's what you wanted. I went back home, there was nobody there. I thought about the beautiful time that we have just had together and I realised that I couldn't bear to be apart from you. I need you to be with me, so I left."

Charlie was starting to get tearful now. "Oh, darling, my darling. I just can't, I just can't." There was a pause, then she said, "Look, phone me tomorrow, will you ? Give me a few hours to calm down."

I stayed for three days at that hotel pleading my cause but she was adamant. She couldn't do it, she said, it would affect her daughter too much at an important time in her schooling, and she couldn't possibly sort everything out properly. I realised I had made a huge mess of things. In despair I decided to abandon all hope and go home. At the very point of my checking out, Charlie phoned the hotel once more. This time she was clearly in great distress. She was at last ready to leave her husband, she said.

"Well, it's too late for that now," I said dejectedly. "I'm returning home. I've telephoned and told them all. They're expecting me."

Janet and I had endless discussions to resolve the situation. I had definitely "burnt my boats" behind me and I had no option now but to make the marriage work. The next day at work I received a phone call from my sister Gill in New Zealand. It may have been intuition or a little bird within the family (our mother) had possibly had a word with her. Anyway, she invited me to go over there for a month and I grasped the opportunity as I thought this would help to put some distance, quite a lot of distance, in fact, between Charlie and me. After that sojourn in the Antipodes I took my family on a two-week holiday. I hoped that this would both fan the embers of my marriage and extinguish the flames of my erstwhile passion for Charlie.

The fact is, of course, that I was not certain about Charlotte. I never had been certain about her as a long-term partner for me, not certain enough to risk breaking up two families for the sake of my obsession. My reasons were all wrong. I was trying to escape from an unhappy marriage without first freeing myself as a person. Charlie continued to phone me at work and I continued to ignore her. It took some time and was very painful for us both, but eventually I was able get to her out of my mind, for a while, if not for good.

I had to adapt the same principle of self-denial which my GP had taught me as a means to combat my asthma. We'd failed with hypnosis so we fell back on the good old-fashioned moral approach of Christian values, putting others before self. It didn't always make me happy, but it was a start. Eventually, I came to see that, as in all things, it is a matter of balance. My needs were not to be ignored but I stood a better chance of being a fulfilled person if I worked positively on my relationships with others, helping them to feel secure and fulfilled with me.

This philosophy had implications for some specific work-related issues. During 1974 legislation was introduced to ensure that all businesses were obliged to offer company union recognition if even a small number of employees wanted it. The Trades Union and Labour Relations Act was, in my eyes, a most unwelcome piece of law and I was determined to limit its application and impact. I thought that my best strategy was to use charm on the Union representative, a Scotsman by the name of

McGavy. I invited him into my poky office for a chat against a background din of clanking machines and whirring fans.

"Please sit down, Mr McGavy," I said. He did so and we found ourselves face to face, no more than three feet apart. I'm not sure which of us felt the more intimidated. He introduced himself.

"I'm the new TGWU official for th' region and I would like ta see a Union branch opening here at Thorntons," he said, putting his cards firmly on the table.

"Oh, right, I understand," I said. "Is that why you've been organising meetings outside the factory in the early morning and evenings?"

"I dinna suppose you've heard about the new Trades Union Act, have yer?"

I was admitting to nothing. "Well, I'm not very good at these things, you know. I've read a bit about it in the newspapers but do tell me more."

This opened the flood gate and I sat there for some time while he told me about all the excellent new provisions within the legislation. I had actually bought a copy of the publication from HM Stationery Office in London but clearly each of us was reading a different document, but I sought to win his confidence.

"Mr McGavy," I said, "I don't really like the idea of your having to stand outside in all weathers, trying to talk to our workers. Would you like me to organise a meeting with our entire workforce in our canteen so that you can tell them all about it?"

His jaw dropped in amazement at this most unexpected suggestion. After a few moments hesitation he replied, "Oh yes, what date do you suggest?" We agreed the time of the meeting and it duly took place. I insisted on making my own speech to the workforce at the end and Betty Hall even got in on the act. We both received great support but Mr McGavy recognised that there was precious little enthusiasm for his offers and he realised he wasn't going to get anywhere with his proposals at that time.

Later that year at a directors' meeting Tony raised the possibility of opening franchises within other larger shops. He'd already found a greetings card retailer who would be interested in having a Thorntons outlet within his store. Stanley, who was not particularly *au fait* with contemporary marketing concepts, asked, "What exactly is a franchise?"

Tony explained it to him. "The idea is that a company sets up a format or template for a retail operation which they can sell to other individual business people. Those individuals then open up their own shop, or whatever it is, within the terms agreed. The franchisee benefits by having the use of a well-known brand with proven advertising and publicity."

Stanley thought about this. "Hmm, I'm not sure. It sounds a bit risky to me."

John, however, was in full support.

"I think that it's a good idea. Have you seen the Prontoprint business, Stanley? That's a franchise and it's very successful."

"At what price are we going to sell to a franchise?" asked Mike.

"Well, I think that we would have to allow about 25% off our retail," Tony replied.

"How can we make sure they stick to our quality and service standards?" wondered Stanley.

"We'll appoint Franchise Area Managers who will visit them, just as our Area Managers visit our own shops to check up at frequent intervals."

"What about deliveries?" I said. "They'll be more costly because there'll have to be smaller stock quantities sent out weekly."

"Yes, I admit there'll be some extra costs but I think it will be worth it in the long run."

After a good deal more discussion we agreed to run with the idea. The greetings cards shop was the first to take on a Thorntons franchise just before Christmas 1974 and soon established itself as a successful venture. Soon, Tony was opening up more franchises but naturally Dad remained apprehensive.

"What's all this franchise nonsense that Tony's doing?" he asked me one day. "He's not trying to swamp the country with this idea, is he? I don't like it at all."

"Oh, it's not such a bad idea," I reassured him. "It gives us the chance to trade in small towns where we can't have one of our own shops."

"No, I don't like it," he insisted. "We'll lose control of everything, you'll see. Eddie took me into one of these places the other day and the window display was awful. Tell Tony he ought to stop. He never comes to see me any more, so you'll have to speak to him."

"I'll have a word with him, Dad, and I'll tell him what you've said."
I knew I wouldn't actually do this as we rarely spoke to each other
outside of the directors' meeting but I didn't want to tell Dad that.

He went on. "I was over at Belper last week. There seemed to
be an awful lot of managers standing around with nothing to do.
Why have you taken on all these people?"

I took a deep breath. "It's quite a complicated business now,
you know. There are a lot of people to manage and we need
proper systems of quality control and material usage and all that
sort of thing."

He seemed to ignore this. "I've been looking at the figures," he
said. "The overhead costs are getting much too high and you'll
have to get rid of some of those people."

By now I was getting irritated. I didn't see why I had to take
such instructions. I was certainly not going to get rid of some of
our best employees.

Dick Smith was one of those people. He was a fellow TA
officer who had joined us in 1964. I had been very impressed
with his computational skills, unsurprising when I considered
that he worked in a bank. We had been on a fortnight's camping
expedition on Dartmoor and I got round to discussing the family
business and my latest contributions to it. He seemed
particularly interested in some of the new equipment I had
brought over from Germany.

"Dick, I desperately need somebody to help me at Belper with
all the administrative work," I said. "I'm really on my own there,
trying to do everything. You're just the sort of person who could
handle all that for me. How about giving up the bank and coming
to join us?"

He was rather taken aback by this job proposal. There we
were, walking along in military uniform, ready to dive into the
moorland undergrowth if somebody started to fire blanks at us,
and I just floored him with this question out of the blue. However,
he took it calmly and asked, "Well, what sort of things are there
to do?"

I put him in the picture. "I need someone to do the production
planning for me. I have this system worked out by a consultant but
it takes me the whole of each Friday to do it and I just can't spare
the time. It's all mathematical, adding up figures and using a slide
rule. I'm sure you'd be able to do it with no problem. Then there's

the buying of the raw materials. I have to do all that, along with lots of other admin jobs, form filling and that sort of thing."

He replied, "Well, I have to admit I'm getting very bored with the bank and I don't see a great future for me in it. What you say sounds interesting. I'll talk to Pam, my fiancée, and perhaps I'll come over to see you."

Dick was as good as his word and accepted my offer of a job with us. He moved from Sheffield to be closer to the factory, gave up the TA, married and settled with us for the rest of his career. Initially, he was our 'Commercial Manager', and later took over our expanding franchise operation.

Our policy of not selling our products to other retailers was still in place but we were keen to develop an export business. Dick had found an agent in Germany and in 1975 the coals truly returned to Newcastle when the agent showed our *Continental Assortment* at the ISM confectionery exhibition in February. When Tony and I went over to see how Dick was getting on he let us know that, yet again, he had been approached by an executive from Marks & Spencer. They had long been after getting a slice of our confectionery 'pie' and we had consistently declined. However, we felt that no harm could be done by meeting the executive, an energetic young man by the name of Ian Dunne.

"I can't understand what you're all so worried about," he told us. "Our customers know that we only buy high-quality products for sale under our label, and that we insist on very strict quality controls from all our manufacturers. To be seen as a Marks & Spencer supplier is an endorsement of your company's products and quality. It could do you nothing but good."

"What are these quality standards?" I asked. "How strict are they and what happens if we can't meet them?"

"Well, given the already acknowledged quality of your products, I don't think you would have any difficulty, but if there were problems we would help you to overcome them."

Tony came into the conversation. "Exactly what product range would you be looking for?"

"Why, the *Continental Assortment*, of course." Then he added, "This meeting with you is on my own initiative. I haven't discussed it with my senior management yet and I don't really want to do so until there is a positive indication that you would be interested."

Tony thought about this. "You realise we shall have to discuss this with our other directors before we go any further but, if we are interested, we'll arrange to meet up in London. What do you say?"

"That's fine," Ian replied. "I'll wait to hear from you and I suggest that our next meeting, if it goes ahead, should be at my local pub in Hampstead."

We thought that this was a bit odd but we agreed to it.

The next thing, of course, was to hold a directors' meeting. Dad would have been apoplectic if he'd heard about this idea so it was probably a good job that he never attended these discussions. Tony launched himself straight into the fray.

"Peter and I met this executive from Marks & Spencer at the ISM exhibition. He chatted with us and it seems they are very keen to sell our products under their own label. They're particularly interested in the *Continental Assortment*. I know we have a policy against this sort of thing, but we both think that this could actually help our retail sales or at least it wouldn't do any harm to the business."

This was controversial stuff and we knew there would be instant opposition. First off the mark was Stanley.

"I have to say I am completely against the whole concept and I know Norman will be, too. For years, long before you youngsters came on board, we held firm against this to protect our sales, not to jeopardise them. We saw other companies, Meeson's for example, who had done this very thing and ended up destroying their own business. And what about the risk to our highly-valued quality standards? Even a company with a prestige name like M&S cannot be guaranteed to treat our products as they might their own. There are bound to be compromises, you mark my words."

I had my answer ready. "There will be no risk of compromise. They already have a 'cool-chain' distribution system which is followed from warehouse through delivery to their stores, maintaining perfect storage conditions throughout."

"OK, but what about extra seasonal demand?" he wondered. "They're going to be claiming priority of supply at such times and we'll then be struggling to get stock out to our own shops."

"That's all accounted for," I explained. "We now have a production planning system which is working extremely well. Last Christmas, for instance, there was hardly any shortfall in supply and we were able to meet all outlet demands from the stocks here in the factory. Besides, they'll let us know their exact requirements in plenty of time, but, if ever there is a rush on demand elsewhere, they will just have to accept that they have no priority claim."

We made our case convincingly and Stanley begrudgingly permitted us to proceed to the next stage. We could have our meeting with Ian on the understanding that we would only agree to a trial arrangement over the Christmas season. There would be no commitment on either side until we saw how things worked in practice. We met up as arranged at the Jack Straw's Castle pub and put this limited proposal to Ian. He was delighted and immediately arranged for an inspection. Several hygiene inspectors from M&S descended upon us and looked at everything. They didn't like our old wooden floors or the bare steel girders in the ceiling but they let these pass. The firm was clearly anxious to get hold of our prized confectionery. It seemed to be a sensible alliance for us as Marks and Spencer was a solidly dependable British company, always buying British merchandise where they could. Clearly, a product with the reputation of our chocolate range was exactly right for their retail profile and would be far too expensive for them to import from Europe. However, that was not how Dad saw it when he finally learned of this new venture.

"What's this I hear about our stuff going to Marks?" he demanded to know. We were in the lounge at Greenways chatting before a roaring log fire. The flames seemed to mirror his petulance. "I suppose this is all Tony's doing, isn't it? He never tells me anything these days, you know."

"No, it's not just Tony's idea," I informed him. "It was mine, too. We both thought it would be good for the business."

"Good for the business?" he thundered. "Where did you get that crazy idea? You could at least have offered them something else, but no. You have to give them our best line, '*Continental*'. That's bound to damage our business. Why on earth should anybody come to our shops when they can buy our best product while they're in Marks buying their groceries along with their socks and knickers!"

"Oh, Dad," I despaired. "Can't you see that it helps with our image? Marks & Spencer is such a well-established name that it can only do us good to be associated with them. People will have an even better response to our products now just because of their endorsement. Why, they'll probably buy even more now."

He remained unconvinced. "No, it's not right. It's not what we should be doing. I'm losing sleep over it. I want you to tell the others to stop the plan right away."

"I can't do that, Dad. We've already agreed in principle and we're about to start a trial run. It's too late to change it now."

Despite Dad's reservations we went on to establish a very successful and mutually profitable retail arrangement with the high street giant and we never looked back. This link helped to consolidate and improve our existing quality control systems and, by 1977, we had a turnover of £460,000 just from our sales through Marks and Spencer alone.

Now, because I was thwarted in my ambitions in the engineering side of the business, I decided to leave that to John and re-direct my efforts elsewhere. Things had moved on and we needed someone to deal with job-related issues when they arose. We therefore employed Bill Sharman to be in charge of this aspect of the business. Today it would be called Human Resources but back then it was just plain old Personnel. He felt we needed a job evaluation scheme and I had to agree. If we could better establish the worth of each job, we could pay staff more equably as long as their council agreed. They did, and even though this entailed an awful lot of detailed work for Bill, it turned out be a very worthwhile thing to do.

In the mid-70s I was still actively involved in acquiring further property at Belper for the company and I eagerly went after the adjacent Maystock building, formerly owned by Sylcoto. I even went for official sanction from Dad and Stanley for me to put in a bid when the site came up for sale at auction. They limited me to £120,000 which wasn't really enough, I felt, for a modern single-storey building of this size, but I went nevertheless to the Lion Pub where the auction was to be held. I had got used to bargain-hunting at these sales, using my strategy of dressing up in old clothes and looking as if I hadn't two farthings to rub together. After lulling my fellow bidders into a false sense of security, I would then make my killer bid and usually would win the goods.

On this occasion, John came with me and we sat in the bar to observe through the serving hatch just who exactly was going into the auction room, weighing up the competition, so to speak.

By the appointed hour of 11 a.m. there was nobody there apart from the auctioneer and his assistant. We decided to make our entry and were immediately followed by a few others. The proceedings began.

The auctioneer asked for bids. There was a deathly hush. No one offered a penny. We were keen to get this property but we didn't want to play our hand just yet. When he saw that no bids were forthcoming the auctioneer said, "Well, gentlemen, I am very sorry, but I will have to withdraw this property from sale. If any of you are still interested come and have a word with me afterwards."

We did, and we asked him at what price was the reserve set.

"£110,000," he answered, and we tried not to show too much interest.

"OK," we said nonchalantly. "We'll meet the reserve." We then signed the contract and paid the customary 10% deposit. We returned to the factory and I was so pleased with myself I wanted to organise a party. I rushed out to get the entire stock of champagne from the nearest wine shop and supermarket and invited all departments to stop work an hour early and come to the canteen to hear the good news.

"I'm delighted to tell you that we have just bought the Maystock building," I announced to all who gathered there. "This will completely solve our storage problems on this site. Not only is it a high-quality building but it is adjacent to our existing premises – and we have paid very little for it! Now, help yourself to champagne and let's celebrate together!"

Not for the first time our enormously supportive workforce let out a loud cheer of approval and we then proceeded to have a great time. In a family business one of the great strengths is that the workforce seems almost to be part of the family. I regarded these people as my friends and they treated me likewise. Needless to say the entire stock of champagne was consumed very quickly. We then sent Graham Armstead out with a couple of other strong lads to see whether they could buy any more. They came back with their hand carts loaded with another 40 or 50 bottles and the party continued!

I was talking to Eddie Duffy one day after a Factory Council meeting. "How are things going in the Transport Department?" I asked.

"Those auld Bedford trucks we've got are allus breakin' doon an' they're only fit for 100,000 miles, you know. After that you might as well be throwing 'em away!"

"As bad as that, is it?"

"Och aye, an' you're sendin' out so much stock these days that the wee little things canna cope. We need much bigger trucks, something like the biggest ERF. Now *that*'s a real driver's truck, that is." He said.

"But I'm not really directly in charge of your Department, Eddie," I explained.

"What does that matter?" he asked. "You should just take over an' do something about it!" Before I knew it, I was directly responsible for the Transport Department! I went out on the lorries to our shops, ate breakfast in the transport 'caffs', watched our drivers and their mates as they delivered from the backs of the truck, across busy pavements, pushing their way through queues of people in the shops, up the back stairs and finally into the stockroom. I did calculations to see if it was worth having delivery depots in other parts of the country and finally decided that Eddie was right all the time. What we needed were much bigger trucks that could take three times as much stock and allow the drivers to make much longer delivery runs, staying away overnight if need be. It was crazy limiting ourselves to short daytime deliveries. We needed to be setting out from the depot much earlier in the morning to get stock to our shops *before* they opened.

Eddie pointed out that the drivers would need to be offered more pay if they were to be expected to adopt these new suggestions. I told him that I would put all this to the Job Evaluation Committee and the Factory Council and would seek a bigger transport budget.

"And you'd better talk to the drivers an' all, before you do anything," Eddie tactfully reminded me.

"Yes, of course. Would you be able to arrange a meeting for me?"

The meeting took place and there was plenty of banter but Eddie, in his eloquent Scottish dialect, persuaded the drivers that this was the way forward. I was extremely glad that he was on my side.

Financial control was in Michael's hands so the budget was no longer a problem. Then we had fun buying the trucks. Eddie remained very keen on ERFs with Gardner diesel engines. "These engines will do a million miles, ye know."

We went for a demonstration run and then placed an order for three of these beautiful machines and asked for them to be specially adapted for our needs. The new system was implemented and everybody was happy, even the usually recalcitrant drivers and their mates. Robin Eales became overall manager of storage and distribution, all under the one roof of the newly-acquired Maystock building.

During the 1970s the company was hit, as was everyone else, with inflation. In 1974 it reached a peak of 24%. We reluctantly had to make several price increases despite the fact that people's earnings were decreasing. It was forbidden by law to make pay increases to help employees keep up with inflation but we did so anyway. We persevered through the 'three-day weeks' in the spring of 1974 and John even installed generators at both factories to help during the power cuts. Remarkably, we still maintained our output despite the reduced working hours.

One of the effects of the three-day week was that bread was soon in very short supply. In our Chocolate Centre Department at Belper we had an ex-baker, Jeff Boultbee, and it was suggested that he could make bread dough in our mixers which could then be taken by other employees to bake at home. This proved to be an enormously popular idea and was all part of the wonderful spirit of co-operation and mutual support that helped our workforce to feel they were part of 'us', that we were all one family, united in business, driven by common goals and aware of our complete interdependence on each other.

We had by now acquired another chocolate enrober, this time from the Danish firm of Nielsen. On one of those occasions when we actually had electrical power a thermometer for testing the temperature of the chocolate shattered and particles of glass fell into the machine and the mixture. George Belfield and Graham Armstead worked heroically for 27 hours to clean the entire machine and get it working again while there was still electricity to power it. In an instance of supreme irony, the moment that they were able to restore it to full working order there was yet another unexpected power cut! Such was life in those heady days of the 1970s.

Apart from my interlude with Charlotte the greatest diversion for me during this time at Ashover was the local sailing club. Sailing racing dinghies became an escape from the stresses of work and my marriage. I needed some element of physical risk and excitement and sailing provided that. When I joined in 1964 I bought a 505, an extremely fast fibre-glass boat with a spinnaker and a trapeze. Planing along on the sea, crashing over the waves with the spray flying, my crew out on the wire in a 30 mph wind against excellent opposition, were among the most exciting things that I ever experienced. The threat of imminent capsize if the smallest mistake was made and the excitement of finishing in a good position, or on some occasions of just surviving, was wonderful. The sailing club was only a short distance from my home and I made many excellent friends there. Janet never came with me as she had no interest in the water whatsoever. She preferred her animals and I built some stables at Bath House Farm for her. She had an old Land Rover and a horsebox, and she and the children became very interested in pony-shows and show jumping. I had a similar disinterest in her hobby but unfortunately I still had to pay for everything.

So where had we got to by this time? Thorntons had grown to cover most of the country and we were undoubtedly supplying the best quality chocolate confectionery in the country and the best quality toffee. Nobody had anything to compare with our *Continental Assortment.* We had developed strategies to cope with our three big seasons: Christmas, Mother's Day and Easter. Our costs remained low as a result of mechanisation and excellent workforce management. The retail shops were beautifully laid out and were enticing ever greater numbers of people to go into them. We were, in short, a very successful and profitable company. The future looked assured and we had no premonition of the troubles that lay ahead.

Derwent Street frontage of Thorntons factory in Belper, Derbyshire where I started work in the summer of 1953.

Left: An atmospheric picture of 'Cole's Corner' in 1910 a year before the first Thorntons shop opened; the famous meeting place for generations of Sheffielders in the middle of the city.

Above: The maiden trip of Sheffield's first electric tram car (No. 1), on the Moor, Sheffield, September 5, 1899. On the driving platform are the Lord Mayor and members of the Tramway's Committee.

Right: My Dad, Norman Thornton when he was 15 years old. The picture was taken in 1911, the year that he started work as the manager of Thorntons' first shop.

Bottom: Thorntons first shop, 159 Norfolk Street, Sheffield which opened in 1911 photographed in 1970.

Opposite Page:
Top: Another shop on Norfolk Street this time on the corner with Change Alley. This photograph was taken just after the Sheffield blitz on 12th December 1940. In this case the building survived but as can be seen the display windows were damaged and there is a shop further down the street which had received a direct hit. I worked as a boy in this shop at Easter time writing names on Easter eggs.

Bottom: Our family home, Greenways, Whirlow Lane, Sheffield from 1938.

Inset: Stanley (left in picture) & Norman Thornton at Dad's wedding in 1926.

Top: Our first purpose-built factory situated on Archer Road, Sheffield. Photographed in the 1980s but almost unchanged since it was first built in the 1930s.

Bottom: The chocolate production line in the Belper factory, photographed in 1967. We assembled this ourselves that same year using second hand machines, the new OKA extruder and control panels and conveying systems which we had developed. It is manufacturing *Rum Marzipan* chocolates and is being operated by Stuart Adcock who had started his working life in the East Midlands coal mines.

Top Left: Dad in his late 40s. Top Right: Professor Peter Doyle who helped the company so much from 1979 to 1982, in typically engaging style at one of his seminars.

Centre Left: Our Belper Factory Manager, George Belfield, making a Safety Award presentation in the factory canteen.

Bottom Left: Three of our Retail Area Managers enjoy their short respite from the company in a Mediterranean hotel. Seated from left to right: Irene Mellors – Birmingham Area; Joyce Chapman – Sheffield Area; Veronica Simmons – Manchester Area.

Above Right: My Mum in her late 80s.

Top Left: This photograph was taken on the occasion of the Grand Opening of the new factory on 15th March 1985. Standing directly behind HRH the Queen and slightly to her right is my brother John, behind him and slightly to his right is the Lord Lieutenant of Derbyshire, Lt-Col Sir Peter Hilton (a WWII hero of great renown). I am standing to the left of HRH the Queen. Unusually, none of us is wearing protective clothing as it was impractical on that occasion and as a consequence all the demonstration products made on that day had to be scrapped.

Top Right: The Royal Visit, March 1985. From left to right: Lt-Col Sir Peter Hilton, HRH the Queen, Peter Thornton, John Thornton, my wife Jo (partially visible behind John), Mrs Mandy Thornton (John's wife), Michael Thornton, Mrs. Jane Thornton (Mike's wife), Stanley Thornton and my mum – Mrs. Muriel Thornton.

Above Left: Watching Walter Willen decorating Easter Eggs for the Royal grandchildren are, from left to right, John Thornton, HRH the Queen and Lady Winifred Hilton.

Aove Right: Our Swiss craftsman Walter Willen holds an armful of Easter Eggs for the Royal grandchildren.

Above: Peter Heaps who planned and built the new factory, 'Thornton Park' at Alfreton Derbyshire, improved productivity, increased output and organised the visit of HRH the Queen to open the factory in 1985. He left the company in 1993.

Top: An old-style
summer window
display.

Centre: The counter
display in Thorntons
English Chocolate
Shop, Water Tower
Place, 835 N.
Michigan Avenue,
Chicago, Illinois, USA.

Bottom: Iris
Muddiman with
Jamming Machine

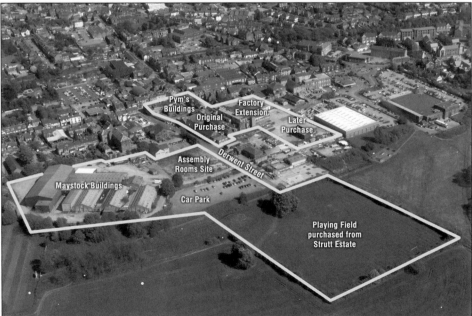

Top: 'Thornton Park' Alfreton, Derbyshire – The entire current factory and office premises.

Bottom: Thorntons Belper Site – The factory and office site at Derwent Street, Belper, Derbyshire showing all the adjacent property eventually acquired.

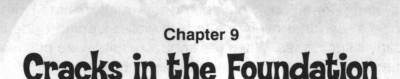

Chapter 9
Cracks in the Foundation

I was aware that things never remained stable for long within our family and the business. However, in 1976, there seemed to be at least a temporary remission, a sort of delicate equilibrium which could easily be upset by changing events. My personal life was more settled as Janet and I had learned to accept the realities of our life together. We took mutual delight in our three lovely children and a beautiful home. My duties at Thorntons were going very well and I would have been happy to spend the rest of my career doing nothing else.

We had enjoyed the most wonderful summer, several months of heat-soaked bliss. I had walked down the lane one Saturday afternoon from Bath House Farm to the centre of Ashover and had observed the field in the village centre where Ed Wilmot, our very neighbourly local farmer, had planted sweetcorn to feed his cattle. The weather was almost tropical and the sweetcorn had already ripened. Every evening we sat on the terrace outside our home, enjoying a meal in the open air and gazing over this idyllic landscape. It was all a far cry from the state of the nation's economy where inflation had hit very high levels and Prime Minister Callaghan was creeping off cap-in-hand to the IMF for an emergency loan.

The hot weather was also having a negative effect on Thornton's summer business. Parts of the country were drought-stricken and people wanted liquid refreshment rather than toffee and chocolates. Sales were very low throughout that hot spell and there was little we could do to improve matters. However, our factories were now all air-conditioned so we were able to keep production going smoothly. Quality was paramount. If anything was ever considered suspect it would be scrapped in fairness to our customers and everyone was encouraged to comply with this policy. It was always 'our firm' and 'our products' and the Thornton 'family' was seen to encompass the whole of the workforce as is often the case with family-run businesses. We had a lot of positive things going for us – our Representative Council, our improved Terms and Conditions, our personal relationships with our employees – so that everyone took a well-deserved pride in the company's successes. When the annual results were published in our magazine *Sweet Talk* the achievements were shared by all, and the rewards and promotions would be shared out accordingly. Most of our employees got a great buzz from their involvement with Thorntons. Friendships and loyalties were formed that have lasted to this day.

It is important to remember that many of these people, particularly those who rose up from the shop floor into my management team, were not just employees. They were individuals with interesting lives of their own and plenty of stories to tell. We've already met some of them. George Belfield was doing very well as Factory Manager, Trevor Fleetwood had come from the Sheffield factory to run the Toffee Department, Graham Armstead left school to work in the Chocolate Centre Department in April 1962 for £3-18s a week and then took over running the OKA from David Oliver before eventually running the entire chocolate production at Belper. Ivan Falconbridge moved up to run the Boiled Sweet Department, and David Varney went from the shop floor to be in charge of the enrobers and eventually the Packing Department. Ron Marsh took over engineering management when Colin Bridges left in 1968 and Pete Naylor oversaw all the electrical installations. Ray Gough became our

Personnel Manager assisted by Eva Kent who saw to all the recruitment, and then there was lanky Dave Bullock, a chemist who had started with us in 1966 and eventually supervised the increasingly complicated quality control and became keeper of all product records, standards and technical development.

Also I cannot forget Betty Hall, my mentor and 'second pair of eyes' from my early days at Belper. Like Iris in Sheffield, Betty died many years before her prime. She too succumbed to cancer and passed away in 1978. She was greatly missed by all those who had worked for her and with her.

I was in my office one day in that same year when the telephone rang. It was Paul Boswell from the loading bay. I could tell immediately that he was very upset about something.

"Mr Peter, can you come down to the loading bay immediately please? There's been an accident."

"What's happened?" I asked, alarmed. "Is anybody hurt?"

"Yes, Pete Williams has been injured. We've called an ambulance and it's on its way."

I immediately donned my white coat and hat and rushed round to the loading bay. Pete was on the ground, lying beside a truck which had backed up to one of the bays. A couple of our first-aiders were hovering over him. I feared the worst.

"Where's the ambulance?" I asked Paul. "Will it be here soon?"

Even as I spoke the sound of the emergency siren could be heard as the ambulance raced into the yard and two paramedics jumped out. They rushed over to Pete and immediately began resuscitation procedures for about fifteen minutes. Everyone else stood by, feeling anxious and somewhat helpless. Then one of the medics turned to us and said, "It's no good. I'm afraid his heart has stopped. He's gone."

We were devastated. We'd never experienced such a dreadful thing in our workplace.

"What happened, Paul?" I asked blankly. He told me what he claimed to have seen.

"Pete was standing in the back of the van, leaning round the side in order to give directions to the driver. He was trying to get the van as close as possible to the loading bay. Before he knew it, the van had reversed quickly and Pete was trapped up against the wall."

The news flew round the factory like wildfire. People were standing in small groups, talking about it, with shocked expressions on their faces. Pete's wife, May, worked in the factory, and George Belfield and Graham Armstead had already taken her into a private room to tell her what had happened and offer what comfort they could. They actually took her home and waited until her family could be with her. I phoned the local vicar and asked if he could come down to the canteen and offer some words of support and he agreed to do so. We stopped production half an hour early so that all those who wished to could attend this service – most did – and later, at the funeral, the church was packed with all of Pete's work colleagues and friends, paying their final respects. He had been halfway through re-decorating his house at the time of his death and it seemed the least we could do to arrange for the decoration to be completed professionally at our expense.

I was personally devastated and felt extremely responsible. How could we allow such a thing to happen in our factory? Not surprisingly, we had a visit from the Factories Inspector who, to my amazement, stayed no more than half an hour and asked a few superficial questions. There was of necessity a public inquest which I attended but I was rather dismayed by its superficiality. There was no real attempt to ascertain the true cause of the accident and a verdict of 'Death by Misadventure' was quickly pronounced.

This left me decidedly unhappy and I was determined to find out what had really happened. I spoke to every individual who had either witnessed the incident or, in one way or another, had been involved in it. I concluded that the exact cause was, as usual, a combination of several factors. Human error is often involved in such cases and so it was here. Paul Boswell had already established his own system for issuing driving licences to those who had taken a company driving test, so we immediately reviewed all the skills needed to obtain this licence. We discovered that there was a definite safety hazard in this particular circumstance which had gone unnoticed and so took steps to eliminate it. We also appointed a Safety Officer, Norris Thompson, who then reviewed all our "near misses" and managed a team of part-time Safety Officers looking for further hazards. This had to include close scrutiny of people's attitudes to risk before we could ever allow them to take on any duties which contained even the slightest element of danger or hazard.

We were determined that such a dreadful thing should never happen again. Thankfully, it didn't.

By 1977 the perceived stability of the previous year was proving to be transitory and we were facing new problems on all sides. Tony had become both Managing Director and Retail Director despite remaining in Sheffield, 30 miles away from the main production activity. My duties as Production Director were becoming increasingly impossible as I no longer had any say in the engineering side of things, and John, now my equal as a director, was forever questioning my decisions in public and in private. Father was by this time a grand old man of 81 with Uncle Stanley catching him up at 74. Neither of them had a practical role anymore but they were still directors and they still had voting control. They continued to have an intense interest in the business and my father particularly spent a lot of time at home talking separately to John, to Stanley and to me during his occasional visits to the Sheffield office, about the performance of the business, about decisions and actions that other directors were taking, causing greater dissent and stress in the process. By rights, the control of the business ought to have been passed to Tony, Michael and myself as we were actually managing things and had been making all the important decisions despite these being constantly questioned and sometimes overruled.

Production and retailing had always been managed as two separate businesses. They required different policies and strategies as they were dealing with two quite distinct arms of the company's operations. The needs of the production staff, their Terms and Conditions and the requirements of their individual roles, were completely separate from that of our retailing staff in our shops and other outlets. To try to unify things, the Board agreed that I should be Personnel Director for the whole company although this in itself was a cause of further conflict between us.

I had already shown interest in the work of Elliott Jaques and Wilfred Brown at the Glacier Metal Company and their so-called 'common ownership' which provided, among other things, a unanimous voting Representative Council system for their employees, so I decided to visit the firm of Scott Bader, another 'common ownership' company, to find out more about how such businesses worked. This came about because I was trying to find a solution to some of our 'family-ownership' problems. There I met

Bruce Reed, a tall, well-built man in his mid-50s with a hint of an antipodean accent, and I asked him a little about his background.

"As you can probably tell," he replied, "I started life in Australia where I trained first as an architect. But it was not to be. I found myself 'called to the priesthood' and decided that I would like to be ordained into the Anglican Church. I went initially to Moore College in Sydney and then served in the Sydney diocese."

"It's a long way from the Sydney diocese to helping Scott Bader," I stated, somewhat obviously. "How on earth did all that come about?"

"Well, I moved over to the UK to be chaplain of Fitzwilliam House in Cambridge with my wife in the 1940s and there I studied theology. This led to some research in group dynamics and then to the Tavistock Institute of Human Relations where I worked on the study of group and organisational behaviour. We started the Christian Teamwork Trust in 1957, backed by Sir Kenneth Grubb. It was a counselling service which converted in 1969 to the Grubb Institute of Behavioural Studies."

"And what does the Grubb Institute do now?" I asked.

"More or less the same thing really," he said. "We are now an Applied Social Research Institute and we work for governments and business organisations all over the world."

Listening to Bruce, I was beginning to see how he might be able to help with some of our problems.

"Would I be able to talk with you about some of the pressing organisational difficulties we have in Thornton's?" I asked him outright.

"Oh, yeah, no problem" he replied. "I've already worked with a number of similar family businesses. This is an area in which I have much experience and have done considerable research. I have a course running in London fairly soon on 'Organisational Role Analysis'. Why you don't attend that for starters, and then we could take it from there?"

Ray Gough was a young Canadian who had come to us for a temporary job. I had seen in Ray someone with more-than-usual ability in the area of human relations. He had a degree from a Canadian university and had come to England for some short-term experience. Bill Sharman had moved on and I had needed a replacement. Having Ray arrive on my doorstep was an opportunity that I couldn't miss as he was young and full of bright, perceptive ideas. I quickly transferred him from his job on the shop floor to become Personnel Manager. We worked so well together, seeing eye-to-eye on all personnel issues, as he was someone who wanted to make more of the relationship between the management and the workforce rather than simply carrying out orders and effecting dismissals.

I took Ray to London with me on Bruce Reed's course and we both learned much of fundamental importance. At the London seminar I heard about the concept of the 'Ownership/Management Conflict' where difficulties can arise between the two separate business dimensions, compounded further if a third element of 'family' is introduced, creating a three-directional pull. As a result, I asked Bruce Reed if he would come to Belper to talk to Michael and Tony and explore, with the three of us, ways to solve some of our family dilemmas. This meeting took place in March around our new smart boardroom table. I had persuaded Tony to attend but I could tell from the start that he was resistant. He had no intention of 'opening up' and having 'a full discussion' with Bruce or anyone else outside of the family. The meeting turned out to be a one-off but enough was said to sow the seeds of change and instigate some solutions to particular problems. Bruce recognised that John must be in a very difficult position and said so.

It's extraordinary when I look back to think just how completely this rather obvious fact had entirely escaped me. I had had no part in his joining the company and had seen him only as a 'spanner' in my particular 'works' and felt that his presence threatened my security. John had been in the business for nine years at this stage but must have been utterly frustrated with so little to do. There was nothing to be gained, I realised, by feeling angry and resentful about him, and resolved thenceforth to include him in all discussions on fundamental issues at Belper.

My relationship with Tony was improving and I managed to persuade him to come to Belper and get involved in production there, but then something happened which impacted seriously on his ability to do his job fully. We were aware that his wife's health had been deteriorating and there seemed little to be done for her deepening depression. Judith had even had electric shock therapy but with apparently no improvement. Then, at the end of April, she committed suicide in the kitchen of their home.

Tony – indeed the whole family – was utterly devastated. His concentration on the business evaporated and his whole attitude to life changed. He had been a great friend to me in his early adulthood. He'd been full of drive and enthusiasm, a risk-taker, quite open-minded and definitely good fun. We'd had great times at the Belper factory and had enjoyed our weekends sailing together until my showdown with Dad. Above all he was a fantastically good multiple retailer. Thornton's was a pioneer of the small shop chain and Tony was a master at knowing which shops to take, where to locate them, how to set up the leases and particularly how to fill them with effective staff and merchandise. After the loss of Judith he was a changed man, becoming much more introverted and losing much of his confidence. He also stopped coming to Belper and our relationship weakened further. This was at least in part because he knew that, on my visits to Sheffield, Dad was repeatedly complaining about him and all the things he was allegedly doing wrong. In the face of this constant tirade behind his back he must have felt completely undermined.

Not long after this Michael suddenly left his wife. Perhaps I shouldn't have been too surprised as I never felt that he and Marie were particularly suited. He often neglected her as he was a very outgoing, lively character, always cast in the role of 'life and soul of the party'. Being a director of a very successful family business meant that he was seen as rather an attractive catch by other women, and Marie could barely get a look in. My wife Janet had always been a good friend to Marie – perhaps they saw much in common in each other's lives – and she was bitterly upset when Mike left her. I then kept getting it in the neck about how awful it was and what a disgraceful person Michael must be and so on. It's very difficult to live with somebody on the premise of 'having made one's bed' and therefore 'having to lie on it' while at the same time hearing views that I really couldn't support. Yet, for the sake of marital harmony, I found myself starting to be critical of my cousin and his personal behaviour. If this had not been a family matter I would almost certainly have done nothing and said nothing about it. It would have been no business of mine. But objectivity is displaced by emotion and commitment, and it was mistaken of me not to remain aloof or neutral on this. So it was that my previously cordial relationship with Mike was compromised.

The business performance was fast declining and we were all getting very agitated. Each director had his own view as to the reasons why. What this produced was something known in business circles as 'triangulation', a phenomenon that often occurs in organisations, whether family-run or not, where there is a problem that is not properly understood by all parties. Two or more of them will get together and in their private conversations they blame a third member of the team for everything that's going wrong.

Father and Stanley had been fairly calm during our successful period but both were now getting quite anxious. Dad had always suffered from an anxiety complex, leading him to assume the worst if things ever seemed not to be ticking over smoothly. For him, this always meant bankruptcy. If he had retired at the usual age, say 65 or 70, a financial settlement could have been arranged securing his future and he would have been free to concentrate on other interests. He would be none the wiser if the company had temporary difficulties.

But Dad was not like that. He identified himself completely with the business. It had been his overwhelming passion and, as far as he was concerned, *he* was Thornton's. In earlier years he had played golf and bridge though without much confidence. Still, it gave him a social outlet of sorts, but all that suddenly changed when he was in London one weekend with Mum and his brother. She spoke to me afterwards about it.

"Your Dad seems to have had some sort of nervous breakdown."

"What do you mean?" I asked her. "Has something happened? Does he show any symptoms?"

"Well," she said, "You know we were staying at the Cumberland (a very smart hotel in Park Lane) and we'd been having such a lovely time. Dad had been arguing with Stanley but that was nothing unusual. We thought we'd treat ourselves to a lovely lunch at the Ritz. Midway through the meal, he went very pale and stopped eating. I said to him, 'What's the matter, Norman?'

"He said, 'I feel very peculiar, I think I must be ill. I shall have to go back to the hotel. I'm sorry, I can't face going out this evening for dinner or to the theatre.' We were all worried and a little disappointed as it rather spoiled the weekend, but now something even worse has occurred."

"What?" I asked. "You must tell me."

"Well, he's been to see old Dr. Rouse who has advised him to stop playing golf and only to play bridge occasionally with perhaps a few close friends. It seems he can no longer bear to go into public places." Mum looked at me with tears in her eyes. "What am I going to do, Peter? I know he's always been a bit of a misery and didn't really ever enjoy going to parties and such. But now he doesn't want to go out anywhere." Clearly her thoughts were as much for herself as for her husband. "Oh dear, if only I'd married a more sociable person. You know how I hate being cooped up in the house all the time. I shouldn't say this, I know, but I don't really love him, Peter. I often wish I'd never married him, but what can I do about it? It's all too late now."

"There is one thing you can do," I said, pressing her hand gently. "You can always talk to me about it, Mum."

From that time on, Dad never again went to a public place, neither restaurant nor board meeting nor theatre. He completely isolated himself from society. Instead, he took up painting and became rather good at it even though it clearly wasn't enough for such an active mind as his. His only social contact was with his children.

So here he we had an octogenarian with time on his hands and nothing to do except worry about the business. He would still visit the shops and factories – to him, these were places of work and not public spaces – but he was out of touch with the way things were changing so he often came away with the wrong impression.

His brother Stanley, on the other hand, had no anxiety complex of any kind. He remained extremely sociable and outgoing, captain of the local golf club, chairman of the board of the local girls' private school and still a very keen bridge player. To him, the business was more of a pastime. His interest in it was undimmed but he didn't harbour the same fears nor have the perpetual desire to be controlling and interfering. He would come to his office in Belper two or three times a week, have a quick tour of the factory *sans* white protective hat and then sit at his empty desk reading *The Daily Telegraph* and enjoying a cigarette or two. Occasionally, somebody – usually me – would come to seek his opinion on something and that would be it.

However, when things started to go seriously wrong in 1977, my father's agitation was so intense that it started to affect Stanley.

Even though the pair had no real managerial position anymore they still had their Monday morning meetings in the wood-panelled office in Sheffield where Norman would grumble about everything and blame each of us 'youngsters' in turn. Stanley was thus obliged to get more involved in the day-to-day business.

Meanwhile, the rest of us, far from doing everything 'wrong', were actually seeking ways to stop the slide and advance the company's fortunes in other ways. Clearly, we couldn't simply keep opening new shops. The number of towns without a Thorntons outlet was limited. Instead, we needed to think about diversifying and this was regularly the subject of discussions at our directors' meetings. Tony already had ideas in this direction such as the small chain of greetings card shops we acquired, but he was inclined to go off unilaterally and the rest of us were not always sure of his rationale. One such plan was to purchase a Dutch business called The Union Confectionery Company which may or may not have been a good idea but, because we were not fully in the picture regarding the benefits, the issue, as always, became an emotional one between us rather than purely strategic.

My father simply regarded such a possible purchase as unacceptably high capital spending. Along with the franchise operation and the deal with Marks and Spencer, he remained unconvinced of its business worth and ordered me to do something about these things.

"What can *I* do?" I pleaded. "I'm not running the company. Tony is the Managing Director – I can't tell him what to do."

This left me wondering about many things: my own situation in production management, John's position in the company, and whether Tony was possibly *not* the right person to be in overall charge. After all, he had a plateful of problems of his own, some personal and some to do with his lack of management skills. I felt that if he could resolve his poor relationship with our father – as I had done – he might at last be able to stand up for himself and demand to be treated properly as an adult. Maybe if I could 'push' him into an altercation, the two of them could sort out their differences without my being caught in the middle. I was fed up of being the go-between so I urged my father to raise his grievances directly with Tony so that each could clear the air, so to speak, and then they could attempt to re-establish a more positive relationship for themselves. I doubt that this ever happened though.

One evening in June, Michael's estranged wife came to see us and spent the time telling us how dreadful her husband was, about the tragedy of their marriage and about how distraught she had become. Rather foolishly, I felt that I must do something about it. Next morning I met up with Stanley in Sheffield and we talked about Michael's personal situation.

"Did you know that Marie came round to our house last night?" I asked him. "She talked at length about Michael and she can't understand why he's left her. She's very upset and says she's been a good wife to him and loved him very much. Both she and the two girls are absolutely devastated. Do you feel he's doing the right thing by leaving them like this? You don't think he's just being distracted by another woman, do you?"

I was not prepared for Stanley's reaction. He jumped to his feet and paced up and down the office with a face like thunder. "What's it got to do with you?" he demanded. "It's entirely between Michael and Marie. It's obvious you know little about it! Marie is quite dreadful and Michael has been having an awful time with her. In fact, he's scared stiff of her and I, for one, don't blame him at all for leaving her! He used to come home in the evenings and be too scared to go into the house because they were having such dreadful rows!"

I was absolutely taken aback by this. I suppose it *wasn't* really any of my business as Stanley said, but I had felt sorry for Marie. I just couldn't turn my back on them both. Thinking that it might be a total waste of time, I nevertheless felt that I ought to hear Michael's side of the story from the man himself. Some while later he popped into my office over some business matter and I seized my opportunity.

"Hi, Mike," I said.

"Hello, Pete," he smiled back.

"Mike, just take a seat for a moment. There's something I'd like to ask you. Marie came round to see us last night. She was in a terrible state, you know."

"Yes, I can imagine," he said, looking me full in the face. "It's been pretty rough for both of us."

I continued. "Janet and I listened to her for two hours. She went on and on about how dreadful everything was. She blames you entirely but would still love to have you back."

"That's all rubbish, you know," he declared, looking somewhat hurt. "It's a sad fact but we are just totally incompatible. I know I made a big mistake in marrying her but, in my defence, I was young and didn't really understand properly what marriage was all about."

"Now see here, Mike," I waded in with the voice of experience. "I've been through it all, as you well know. I was seriously involved with somebody else when I thought that I was unhappy with Janet. That went on for five years until suddenly I had to give it all up because the whole thing was such a mess."

"Well, I heard something about it," he conceded, "but what is any of that to do with me?"

"It's just to say that I coped with it. I sorted things out and now Janet and I are very happy together."

He looked at me disbelievingly. "Really? I *am* surprised. You two don't *look* compatible at all. Surely Charlie was much more your cup of tea."

"Oh, so you know who it was then?"

"Yes, of course I do," he admitted. "Everybody knew about it. All they had to do was watch you two when you were at parties together. Anyway, she was such a lovely woman in every respect."

Such remarks produced an instant pang of regret at my loss but I had now trained myself to suppress any such longings. Besides, I hadn't called Mike in to be reminded of my own folly but to help sort out his marriage and honour my self-imposed promise to Janet and Marie.

"I'll tell you how I dealt with it," I told him before he had time to refuse me. "I happened to be seeing my new doctor about the asthma which had been getting worse. He said it was all down to my emotional state and suggested I tell him everything. He explained that I had a typical 'Oedipus complex' where I would be looking for my mother's image in the women I met, and that I would have to acknowledge this before I could change my way of life to cope with it."

Mike's cynicism was complete. "I think that's a load of hooey. I can't imagine wanting to sleep with *my* mother but 'whatever turns you on'. *Do* carry on, doctor."

I ignored his sarcasm. "So what I do now is always put Janet and my family first. My priority is to make them happy before I consider my own happiness. It's hard at first but it's certainly working. Why don't you go back to Marie and give it a try?"

Now it was Mike's turn to explode with fury. I seemed to be good at lighting everybody's blue touch-paper today. He strode up and down in my office shouting at me.

"What the hell has it got to do with you!? This is *my* life and I am perfectly happy to look after myself, thank you very much!" Mike was normally one of the most affable people I know but my remarks had clearly upset him. He continued angrily. "This is *none* of your business and I've no wish to discuss it with you! I am extremely happy with Jane now. We *always* make sure that the other is content and satisfied. I have absolutely no need to act as her slave as you seem to be suggesting I do with Marie. I have no intention whatsoever of going back to *her* and you can make sure that she knows that! Everyone else is getting over it and she will have to as well!"

He stormed out of the office, slamming the door behind him. I sat there like some sort of deflated balloon. Our previously close relationship was at an end, at least for the immediate future.

There were more conflicts to come. Ray Gough, the young Canadian, resigned as Personnel Manager as he claimed that a senior member of the retail management was using undue influence with Tony to make his position impossible. Tony's proposal to purchase the Union Confectionery Company was discussed and rejected by the board in favour of a 'Trading Agreement'. He, in turn, felt increasingly isolated and blamed me for the decline in the company's fortunes, as did Stanley and my father who felt that I had inflicted far too many expensive factory overheads – things such as the Representative Council – upon the company. Their criticisms were put to me directly after they'd finished talking to each other behind closed doors. They had privately worked themselves up into a stew which, in Dad's case, meant a refreshing change, at least for Tony, from his usual *bêtes noir* of Marks and Spencer and the franchise retailing initiative. The extraordinary truth is that, after all these years of running the business together as a family, nobody really knew what the problems were so it was just easier to blame each other. New and different things were happening to the company and in the world outside. The old simple formulas didn't work any more. I was getting very upset about this and didn't see why I had to be the scapegoat for everybody's neuroses and anxieties. This was unfair and it was high time things were sorted out. I decided to confront the issues head on at the next Directors' Meeting.

It was the 4th of July and time for my own declaration of, if not independence, then at least justification. Stanley chaired the meeting and at an appropriate moment I stated my case for the defence.

"I have to say that I am getting well and truly fed up with all the company's problems being blamed entirely on increased factory overheads. Things like the Representative Council and Job Evaluation were set up deliberately in order to increase production efficiency and product quality with all incurred costs taken into account. These things were necessary and are having the opposite effect of what you claim. Just look at the weekly production reports to see the proof. On the other hand, I maintain that the Marks and Spencer business and franchising are not so profitable and are probably at the root of the decline in total profitability. These are areas that should be investigated."

This produced a storm of disagreement.

"No, you are quite wrong," said Stanley, emphatically. "I walk round this factory and what do I see? Loads of people standing around doing nothing, chatting and looking at products. What's that all about? – they aren't achieving anything." The arguments continued but we could agree on nothing and in the end the debate was set to one side.

Our roles as directors became a constant subject for discussion with everyone expressing dissatisfaction with their current responsibilities. It was becoming increasingly obvious that some sort of major change had to be engineered or this constant bickering would never cease and could eventually destroy the company. In an effort to move things forward I sent a note to Tony with some suggestions. These included allowing John take over my role as Production Director. Tony would be Chairman while I became Managing Director. To my pleasant surprise Tony agreed. He then went further and began to talk seriously about resigning and leaving the company. Without his wife he just didn't have the same interest and drive anymore, he claimed.

I arranged to meet with Stanley and John later that month in Belper to discuss Tony's suggestion. I arrived a bit early and John collared me.

"I've been talking to Tony," he said. "He doesn't really want to pack up, you know. It's only because he can't get on with you. So he thinks that one of you, either he or you, ought to leave the business."

"Oh no," I said despairingly. "Why on earth can't he make up his mind? Why does he tell me one thing and you another? This is ridiculous! He's using you to tell me what he really thinks, then when I meet up with him, and we talk about it, he says that he wants to resign. He sends me notes about it and what he apparently means is just the opposite! I don't know whether I'm coming or going."

"I suppose that he doesn't want to upset you."

"It upsets me a great deal more to be told by you."

"Well, that is what he really thinks anyway," insisted John. "Look, while I've got you, there are an awful lot of things wrong at Belper but I want to make sure I bring them up at the right time."

I was puzzled. "A lot of things? What are you on about? This place is very efficiently run, I thought. You'd better tell me what they are – now."

"No, it's not appropriate at the moment," he said annoyingly. "We'd better get on with our meeting with Stanley."

We all assembled around the big table in the Board Room. Stanley ignored the agenda and launched at once into his list of complaints: "I want to make my view perfectly clear right from the start. There are too many things wrong on the production side of the business and particularly here at Belper." He then produced a crumpled piece of paper from his pocket and proceeded to read from it.

"Too many 'indirect workers', too much time spent in Council Meetings, the Representative Council making all the important decisions, too rigid lines of management, too many people standing around in groups talking. Apparently we don't need to know what is in stock every day. And why do we have a fund to pay people to sue us? We have unnecessarily good Terms and Conditions of Employment, the wages are too high..."

Before I had any time to respond to this list, he turned on me. "I can see that you are trying to take over everything in this business, Peter. Let it be known that I, for one, am not having it, and neither is Norman."

With barely a pause for breath, he continued. "I heard that you threatened Dick Smith by having a confrontation with Robin Eales and now, as a result, we have a considerably worse delivery service to our shops." This latter remark made no sense to me at all; I'd no idea what he was talking about. "You are trying to extend Factory Terms of Employment and our high wages to all our shop staff. All that that will achieve is the raising of costs which will make the shops unprofitable." He then switched his attack to family matters. "And you are going to have to go very easy on Tony just now, Peter. You know he can't take it because of his personal circumstances."

John joined in the attack. "We have never agreed the Job Evaluation scheme in any Board Meeting, you know. You just went ahead and made the decision to install it on your own."

I could see that we weren't going to get round to discussing the real purpose of the meeting which was Tony's proposal to resign. Instead I had been thrown fully onto the defensive. Trying to control my own fury, I recognised, through gritted teeth, that all the initiatives which I had taken, and which seemed to many, both inside and outside the business, to have been extremely successful, were apparently seen by Stanley as the true cause of our imminent downfall.

"Frankly, Stanley, I don't know what the hell you're talking about and I'm not sure that you do either! If you speak to anyone in this factory, and to many people elsewhere, you'll find they give only glowing reports of my management and the progress of the business. Instead of being so uninformed and so critical you ought to be praising me for our great success. You should also thank your lucky stars that I'm still prepared to do this despite being constantly under threat and rendered powerless because you and father own all the voting shares!" At that, I decided that I had said enough. The meeting for me was over and I went back to my office across the corridor to cool off.

After a few minutes Stanley called me on the internal phone and asked me to go back into the Board Room. I thought that he might ready to apologise but not a bit of it.

"I want to have a word about Marie," he said.

"Go on then."

"Marie came round to Stanley Lodge last night. She created a terrible fuss. She was shouting and screaming about Michael and about how awful he is and how badly he has behaved and treated her. She became really hysterical. That woman is quite dreadful and I will never allow her to behave like that in my house again. I don't blame Michael at all for wanting to leave her."

"I see," I replied.

"You see? Then why do you condemn him?" he asked.

"I *don't* condemn him," I replied, "I just felt sorry for him and for you and Marie and the kids."

"Look, Michael has had a terrible time. Did you not know that he used to sit outside in his car, afraid to go into his own home because of all the constant rows? Marie had recently been very rude to Michael's sister Rosemary about her son Giles and he just wasn't going to stand for it."

Now I was beginning to understand why I had been under attack for my performance. It was to punish me for not supporting a family member.

By September things had changed again and discussions were now taking place between me and Stanley about my becoming joint managing director or perhaps taking over as sales director. I saw Dad in the Sheffield office and he didn't think that Tony would ever be capable of taking over full responsibility. Stanley joined us and he told him the same thing.

A few weeks later I called in at my father's house for a drink after work and found him in a surprisingly good mood. We settled in front of the lounge fire and he said to me, "I've been over to the Belper factory and things look very good there." This was pleasant to hear. "I've also been visiting some of the shops and they look much brighter. I'm feeling really relieved because at last things are sorting themselves out and all the clouds are lifting."

"I'm really sorry to disillusion you but I have to disagree," I said. "The clouds are *not* lifting and there are still many problems. As I see it, the company is not doing at all well and everybody is rushing round like madmen with no idea how to solve it."

This wasn't what he wanted to hear and his mood changed. He started to get angry with me and said, "Not one of us – me, Stanley or Michael – thinks that you should be Managing Director. We all agree that you are very selfish. What is it that you want? More money?"

I was nonplussed. "That's very strange," I pointed out. "Only a couple of weeks ago you thought that I *should* be Managing Director. You must admit there are major problems with the business. All I wanted to do was to discuss things with you."

My mother came home just then and he quietened down a bit. She had just been to see Tony at home. "He isn't well," she said.

"He's suffering terribly since Judith's suicide."

"That's not entirely the case," I said. "Tony's problem really lies with you, Dad. *That*'s what he cannot handle. At the beginning of this year, you talked to me endlessly about the problems of the business that you said were of Tony's doing. You can't expect to voice such opinions to me and then imagine I will just forget them or not repeat them. Tony just can't take it when he hears your disapproval of his efforts. I had really hoped that maybe the two of you could have got together to iron all this out, but I suppose that's completely out of the question."

I was now determined to thrust home my opinion, regardless of what he might think.

"The only really fair thing to do now would be to retire, Dad, so that you can no longer have an opinion about the business if you're not involved in it. In that way you will no longer upset Tony with your criticisms of him."

He replied very angrily. "I'm NOT going to retire! YOU retire! You silly, selfish boy – I mean, man." His slip of the tongue revealed how he still saw me. Nevertheless, he leaned forward in his armchair for emphasis.

"I can't rely on you, I can't rely on anyone!" he growled. "You just want your own way all the time. You want to control everything yourself. You keep introducing all these fancy modern ideas without referring to anybody and increasing our costs all the time. Tony keeps bringing up these daft ideas like Marks and Spencer, franchising, greetings cards and that awful business in Holland – and Michael doesn't seem to do much of anything! At least John seems to keep his head!"

"Well, if that's what you believe about us, then you really *should* retire!"

Getting angrier all the time, he thundered, "Don't imagine that you are essential to this business – you contribute nothing and I could easily replace you! I told Stanley that they will blame it all on us if things go wrong. Now see what you've done. I shan't sleep now. Don't come here any more in the evenings."

There was nothing anyone could say after that. I left at once.

From this it was clear that my father still saw himself in charge of the business and that he had recently saved us from bankruptcy by his own leadership, that his views about all of us were very far from the truth, that he was never going to relinquish full control and that he had absolutely no idea of the consequences on our feelings and personalities as a result of his autocratic behaviour. I realised there were four things I must do: first, hand over production to John; second, try to eliminate the continuous conflict between the directors and get them working together; third, find myself a more satisfying job; and fourth, maintain or improve my own status. But how on earth was I to achieve these objectives? It was time to have another meeting with Bruce Reed in London and we came up with this diagram to describe the relationships:

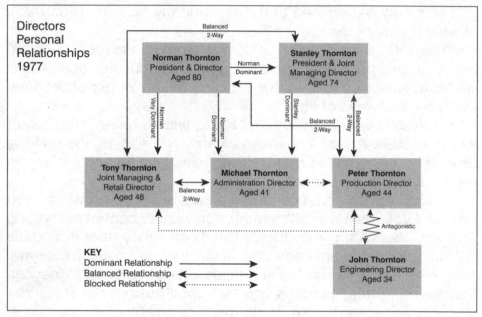

Bruce suggested that I should present this analysis of the problems to my fellow directors and propose a re-organisation of our jobs to try to resolve the apparent difficulties.

The idea of handing over production management was very painful to me. I was immensely proud of everything that had been achieved and couldn't bear the thought of no longer working with all those people I had nurtured, many of them initially from very lowly positions within the company. Our methods and systems, the unique products we had created, these were not things I could give up on lightly. And suddenly to change careers, to head off for completely unknown territories, was in itself quite daunting. So there is little wonder that I had resisted my brother John's involvement for so long. I accepted that he would benefit immensely from the proposal, as would Tony and the company as a whole. I would also be relieved of some of the frustrations that went with the current set-up, but what was I being left with? Sales management. Would that be enough for me? No directorship here, no involvement with marketing. I felt I needed more, if only to maintain some status within the group. Perhaps I could keep my involvement in human relations management, and retain computer and accountancy responsibility.

The fact that I had had this big bust-up with my father actually brought Tony and me back on to speaking terms again so this eased my efforts at re-organisation forward a little more smoothly. I presented Bruce's diagram at the next Directors' Meeting and, to my amazement, everybody understood it straightaway. Shown like that, I suppose it was fairly obvious. I formally proposed the re-organisation plan. This, too, was agreed with no difficulty (although I was denied 'computer and accountancy' as it was thought to be part of John's area of expertise) and it was decided that the new system should start from the coming January in 1978. Tony remained as managing director with additional responsibility for marketing.

Christmas was always the big event of the year for Thornton's. It was by far our busiest season, well ahead of Easter and Mother's Day, and the few weeks prior to the winter holiday were very exciting times for us all. The build-up would start way back in June when we began filling the Christmas chocolate boxes and putting them into deep-freeze. As the summer went on, we would hire extra packing teams from our regular supply of seasonal workers. These usually came from October to Christmas, but sometimes stayed on to the following Easter on their permanent 'temporary' contracts. Over the years, as sales increased, we found ourselves continually in need of more packers. I always knew how many people we required to keep our shops fully stocked right up to Christmas Eve and I relied on Eva Kent, herself one of our original 'temps', to select and recruit sufficient employees to see us through the peak times. For example, in 1976 she hired 106 extras just to work on the packing belts.

We used vacuum-formed plastic trays instead of paper cups in the chocolate boxes. Tony and I had seen these trays during one of our trips to Germany in the 1950s and had arranged for a British company to make something similar for us. We were the first confectionery company in Britain to use them and they were much easier to pack than paper cups. They held the chocolates in position better and an operator could use two hands while working instead of one hand to hold the paper cup and one to pack.

Each week's production was recorded and monitored very carefully to ensure that we were on target. If there was a drop in efficiency we resolved the issues immediately. We couldn't afford to get behind schedule. Christmas deliveries to our shops started six weeks in advance, and every available inch of space would be taken up with chocolate boxes – under the stairs, on the stairs, in bathrooms and cellars, in the break room – indeed, wherever space could be found.

In the week up to Christmas Day itself we would have the factory Christmas Lunch. There, all roles were reversed and the management would wait on the workers. I always tried my best to make a suitable speech, thanking everybody for hitting the targets, and eventually the directors and senior managers would sing a specially-composed song against a background of good-natured jeers and catcalls.

On this particular day in 1977, I had decided to take a last nostalgic look around the Belper factory to remind myself of all the sights, sounds and aromas that had been so familiar to me since my boyhood. I entered the Toffee Department and was assailed by that rich, warm smell of boiling toffee accompanied by the clanking of the boiling pans and the hissing of steam escaping from the pressure valves. Gordon Jennison was pacing beside the metal slabs, coaxing the exact amount of liquid toffee into each plastic tray. Stacked slabs of cooled toffee were moving through the metal detector and into the wrapping machine to be dressed neatly in its cardboard outer wrapper for its important one-way journey to the shops.

Trevor Fleetwood was standing there, looking very satisfied.

"How's it going today, Trevor?" I asked.

"Very well," he replied, smiling. "We should get 120 batches out today if we include the night shift."

"That sounds good, Trevor. You've probably heard that I'm giving up as Production Director now and I am moving off to manage the shops."

"I'm very sorry to hear that, Mr Peter," he said. "We've seen some real developments in the years since you first took over here. I'll be truly sorry to see you go."

"So will I, Trevor. I don't really want to do this, but I have to make way. I've enjoyed running the factory and knowing all the people who work here. We've seen lots of changes since I first came, haven't we? I think you only had two boiling pans at one stage on the shift and now you have five on a 24-hour basis. How's that for progress?"

"That's the way of it, Mr Peter. We keep managing to squeeze out more, one way or the other."

I went upstairs to the Chocolate Department where *Rum Truffles* – or *Rum Balls* as we used to call them – were pouring from the enrober, beautifully formed, the chocolate perfectly set and the markings standing up like chestnut spikes. I couldn't resist sampling one and it was perfect, an ideal combination of texture and taste. I walked up to the enrober itself, the same machine that I had originally installed with Leslie Charlesworth, Colin Bridges and his brother Ted. By now the whole system was electronically controlled and the OKA was churning out *Rum Truffle* centres at 60 rows per minute, 12 pieces to the row. That was 720 pieces a minute or 43,200 an hour! The concrete floor of the little extension was shaking every time the head of the machine moved up and down, and operators were frantically busy blending and rolling the centre-mix into neat 'sausages' to put into the machine's hopper. David Varney was looking very happy with himself. "We ought to hit target this week, eh?" he said to me proudly. "Been working twelve hours a day. It's all goin' very well."

"I can see that, David. Well done."

Joyce Blount was there at the end of the enrobing line, checking quality as she had been doing for the last twelve years. "Any problems today, Joyce?" I asked.

"No, Mr Peter," she replied. "Everything is within standard, I am glad to say."

By now we had three enrobers in the Chocolate Department. The two recent ones were in the building over the top of the new Boiled Sweet Department. Neither of these was second-hand and they were fed by two new OKA machines, one of which was the Rolls-Royce of enrobers, made by Sollich of Germany.

While I was watching the OKA in full swing I recalled that, only that summer, I had been put into the unhappy situation of having to taking disciplinary action although I always hated doing so. During our annual summer closedown Karl Jura, a German engineer from the manufacturers, came to rebuild our machines. They were in such heavy constant use that this servicing and maintenance was necessary to prevent breakdowns. I couldn't spare the time to act as an interpreter for Karl but I knew that Irma, who worked in the Boiled Sweet Department, could do this for us. Later I went into the department to see how they were getting on. The pair of them were taking a short break, leaning on the machine. Nothing wrong there except, to my absolute dismay, they were both smoking. This was totally forbidden anywhere in the factory, whether in operation or not, and Irma knew it. Now, there was little I could do to Karl except to say "*Nicht rauchen! Es ist verboten!*" I couldn't really dispose of his services or I would have been left with a machine in lots of tiny pieces. But with Irma I had no choice. "You're dismissed. You know that the penalty for smoking in the factory is instant dismissal." This action seemed harsh but was unavoidable. The memory of it left me rather saddened.

I moved on to the Packing Department in the extension at the back of the old building. In this huge area there were six packing lines, each with about twenty girls at work. Plastic trays were being put on each line at the beginning to be filled, two chocolates at a time, and then lifted into boxes, lids placed in position, ribbons tied on and the boxes put into their outer covers. The girls were all chatting or singing to the music coming over the PA speakers, adding to the jolly atmosphere of the place. There, as usual, was Betty Hall in her white turban, slightly breathless, pacing up and down to address each packing-belt supervisor, seeing that everyone was being properly supplied with trays of chocolates and that the completed boxes were being removed.

In the Loading Bay vans were being filled and Paul Boswell was ensuring that everything was safely and accurately stacked. "We're doing two trips a day this week, Mr. Peter, but the lads will be at the Lunch. In fact, they're all back now," he informed me.

The Christmas Lunch took place with the usual raucous fun and banter. Alcohol was traditionally not permitted but on this occasion we decided to relax the rule and allow everyone one drink each. Mike was adding to the supply by offering a tot of whisky from his hip flask to those nearby at his table. After lunch I stood up with John and, together with the senior managers, we offered our version of the Helston Floral Dance. Terry Wogan had recently popularised this melody by recording it with the Brighouse and Rastrick Brass Band and had even managed to reach No.21 in the pop charts. I hastily composed an alternative lyric which went as follows:

THE DERBYSHIRE THORNTON PLANTS
(AFTER 'THE HELSTON FLORAL DANCE')
As I drove to work on a winter's morn
In the fog and the rain feeling all forlorn,
Far away from my breakfast spare
Into the smelly and dirty air
Of a quaint old Derbyshire town.
Borne from afar in the howling gale,
Joining the noise of the traffic's wail,
Distant tones of a modern Plant,
Made by factory machines perchance
On the smoky air came floating down.
I thought I heard the curious whirr
Of a Sollich Automated Enrober,
OKA, Bottomer, Cooling Tunnel,
All of 'em seemed to be going like 'ell,
Far away as in a Trance
I heard the sound of the Thornton Plants.
As I drove slowly down Derwent Street,
The whole of the town seemed to be on its feet,
Out of buses and by their own car
Five hundred Thornton workers here they are
In that quaint old Derbyshire Town.
Into Reception past Jennie and Sharon
One was on Telex, t'other on Phone,
Past the department where they make Toffee,
Past the passage which goes to H.B.
Up the staircase and what did I see?
There was the machine with that curious whirr,
Of a Sollich Automated Enrober,
OKA, Bottomer, Cooling Tunnel
All of 'em seemed to be going like 'ell,
Each one making the most of his chance,
All together in the Thornton Plants.
Into the Packing Room in double quick time,

Where all the workers were talking in rhyme,
I said to someone, "This seems a bit queer,"
She said, "It's our grievance procedure,"
In that quaint old Derbyshire Town.
We have Absence and Sickness and Job Evaluation,
Appeals and Transfers and not much Promotion,
Computers and Maystock and other strange whims
And Management Services who fiddle at Pyms,
We also make chocolates which won us a crown.
Back to the machine with the curious whirr
Of a Sollich Automated Enrober,
OKA, Bottomer, Cooling Tunnel,
All of 'em seemed to be going like 'ell,
Each one making the most of his chance,
All together in the Thornton Plants.
Rum Balls here, *Alpini* there,
Thornton Mis-shapes everywhere,
Up and down, around the town,
Hurrah for the Derbyshire Thornton Plants.

With apologies to Terry Wogan, original composer Katie Moss and music lovers everywhere! It was a merry end to a difficult year but, as we all know, it didn't necessarily guarantee us a Happy New Year.

Chapter 10

Three Women and One More

And so I moved into Retail Management and found it much more difficult than I'd imagined. I was now nothing more than a basic manager with no control of the marketing strategies. These, I felt, were not without flaws but what could I do? The thought of spending the rest of my career so constrained was quite unbearable but I accepted that, at the very least, I needed first to uncover all the facts about the retail business and spent the first ten months of that new year visiting every one of our shops and franchises and getting to know the individuals who worked in them. Our Area Managers were all senior women and all very good at their jobs. They had started as shop managers and some had been with us for many years. They were each responsible for eleven outlets and clearly Tony's judgement was spot on in selecting them.

One of my first trips was to see Veronica Simmons in Manchester. Travelling from Derbyshire over the Pennines in January was never a good idea as the journey traversed the Peak National Park to Buxton which, as one of the highest market towns in England, could always be relied on to provide challenging driving conditions. If ever snow was forecast across the region, you could be certain that it would snow on Buxton, and the high winds blowing across the Cheshire plain meant that it would often drift into impassable conditions. My new car had a better front-wheel drive than most but I still cautiously carried a spare set of snow-tyres in the boot, just in case!

I recalled an occasion during a winter blizzard when, on my journey home from Sheffield, I drove smack into a 3 ft. wall of snow left by the snow-plough, the driver having suddenly turned from the main road to go off in an entirely different direction. My car had been lifted fully off the road and was stuck fast. I had no option but to walk, unsuitably clad, for at least a mile before I found any shelter, by which time I was on the verge of collapse, with hypothermia imminent. Ever since then I've carried extra clothing in the form of a ski-suit on all winter journeys. After all, once (frost) bitten, twice shy.

On this particular day there had been a light overnight dusting of snow as I drove up from Darley Bridge to Winster and then on to the old Roman road to Buxton. The sky was bright overhead and the Derbyshire hills, dotted with sheep, lay before me in all their magnificence. However, I observed the ominous grey clouds lowering in the distance, and the nearer I got to the town the deeper lay the patches of snow so that, by the time I was beyond Buxton and approaching Whaley Bridge, I was feeling apprehensive at the thought of what lay ahead. I had to drive with the utmost care until I reached the outer edge of Stockport and from there the journey was rendered painfully slow by the traffic congestion leading into the heart of the metropolis.

Thorntons had a shop at 67 Oxford Street and there was Veronica Simmons waiting to greet me with her cheery smile. She was short, in her late fifties and always ready to please, the very model of efficiency. I was welcomed and she promised to assist me in any way she could.

I had been to this shop once before but that had been thirty years earlier when accompanying my father. We had two shops on Oxford Street for "catching the trade", as Dad put it, from the patrons of the Gaumont Cinema, opposite No.67, and the nearby Palace Theatre, next to No. 95. The latter had been a very popular pre-war music hall but had fallen on hard times and it hardly justified our keeping the adjacent shop open at all. However, the shop had a low rent and we served from noon until seven in the evening.

I could sense my father peering over my shoulder as I checked Veronica's window and counter displays. It would have been easy to adopt his approach but I wanted to do things in my own way. And besides, there was nothing here to fault. It was all excellent – the shop was immaculate, the displays exquisite, everything was clean and proper, and Tony's *Continental* showcase was just how he intended it to be.

"How do you feel about running the shops, Mr. Peter?" Veronica asked in her light Lancastrian burr. "Quite a change from the factories, I suppose?"

"It certainly is," I replied, "but at least I know most of the Area Managers. I even know some of the Shop Managers too, and I guess I've been familiar with how everything works for many years."

"It's a big change for me as well. Mr. Tony has been looking after us for over twenty years," she pointed out. "He's a real gentleman and everybody respects him. They'd do anything for him as he is so kind and polite." She lowered her voice and, with a twinkle in her eye, added, "I think that some of them are even a bit in love with him really. They will actually go out and have their hair done in time for his visits! We've come a long way since he took over from your father."

This seemed to be setting some sort of template which I may be required to match.

"He's certainly done a good job with staff selection," I agreed. "Of all the Area Managers I can't think of one who isn't doing well."

"Well, we try to keep on top of it, you know," Veronica assured me. "We get an occasional problem with the odd manageress but normally we suss them out while they're shop assistants *before* we promote them."

"What about petty theft?" I asked her.

She frowned a little. "You know, with the old-fashioned manual tills, it *is* still a constant problem," she admitted. "If someone is willing to take just small amounts over a long period there's not very much we can do about it."

We walked through the noisy streets to our next branch. This Piccadilly shop, established before the war, was very tiny but extremely popular. We introduced ourselves to Miss Edwards, the shop manager who was busy behind the counter. She had a queue of customers stretching out on to the pavement. Many of them seemed to know each other and there was much carefree banter while they waited.

"Fred," one called to the other, "has tha come for thee *Striped Mints*?" (He pronounced it 'stripped mints'!)

"Nah, Mary," he replied, "Ah'm buying *Toffee* for the Missus and some of them *Nuggets*."

"Whaddya mean *Nuggets*? Them's called *Nougat* – Noogaar," she emphasised.

The assistants were serving as quickly as they could, weighing out a quarter of this and a quarter of that, chatting to the customers and adding up the cost in their heads as they worked.

"Hello, Fred. So you don't want your *Striped Mints* today but you *do* want half a pound of *Special Toffee,* a quarter of *Chocolate Nougat,* and a one pound box of *Plain Dessert Assortment*, is that right?"

"That's it, love."

"Let's see, that'll be £4.95."

"Hey, it's gone up since before Christmas!"

"Well, it's this inflation, love. Next please!"

Miss Edwards turned to me. "Do you want a nice cup of tea, Mr. Peter? It's time for my break."

"That would be lovely," I replied as we wound our way through to the back of the shop, squeezing between stacks of crates until we arrived at a small space, furnished with a small table and three chairs, which passed as the lunch room. There was the inevitable battered, old electric kettle on the table and the best china had been put out in readiness for our visit. Veronica and I sat down and Miss Edwards was able to join us, having filled the kettle from a tap somewhere in the depths of the shop.

"How's business been since Christmas?" I asked her.

"It's very good really. People still like their treats, you know, in spite of this inflation problem, and the offers we have on the *Misshapes,* the *Striped Mints* and other mint products seem to work."

"That's Dad's doing," I said. "It's a strange idea but his theory is that people indulge to such an extent over Christmas that afterwards they need the mint flavour as a counter to all the sweet stuff they've been eating!"

"Well, he must be right," said Veronica. "All the shops are pretty busy considering the amount of chocolates and toffee that customers will have received as Christmas presents."

"You probably have an awful lot of toffee chopping to do in this shop," I wondered.

"Yes, at Christmas time it *is* very hectic," conceded Miss Edwards. "We have a couple of 'temporaries' – they just chop all the time, smashing the slabs with those special hammers into exactly the right-sized pieces. That's quite a skill, you know, putting it into those plastic trays, and sealing the toffee cases in polythene bags until it's time to put them out."

"Yes, but it's essential to do all that," I reminded her. "You know how sticky it gets if you don't cover it up and, if you leave it around too long, it quickly congeals into a solid lump."

"I imagine that all adds to its hand-made appeal," observed Veronica. "Many customers think that we actually make it in the back of the shop and we don't want to disillusion them!"

I asked Miss Edwards how long she'd been working for us. "I started 13 years ago as an assistant here. Then I became the manageress and I have been here ever since."

"You obviously enjoy it."

"Yes, there's such a lovely atmosphere to the place. We're all good friends and we help each other out when we can. If we know that there is a busy period coming up we try to get everything ready in advance, even coming in when the shop's shut on a Sunday to get things prepared and laid out. That way we keep our customers happy and we know it keeps the business running successfully for you."

Veronica joined in. "All these people are my friends. If ever one of them's got a personal problem of some kind we all do what we can to help. It's not really like being at work when we come here. It's more like we're one big happy family and we all regard the business as ours."

"That shows through in the way the shops operate," I commented. "The fact that everybody works so hard and takes an interest in the products and the customers is the reason we are such a profitable company. But *why* is it so good, do you think? What makes it be like this?"

"It's because we're all treated with respect," answered Veronica. "People are promoted from the shop floor where they've learned their trade, and we see how the family is prepared to get their hands dirty and muck-in. The family are all friends with us and we're all friends with the family. It's the little things, like Mr. Tony always sending us Area Managers off on short holidays to Europe after Easter as a respite and a reward for working so hard."

Miss Edwards lived with her mother, and Veronica asked how the older lady was coping during the cold spell.

"Oh, she's not too good at the moment, but she is getting on a bit these days so we're not too surprised," came the reply.

It was pleasant but we couldn't stay there nattering all day, so we said our goodbyes and moved over to the more contemporary Arndale Centre where we had two more shops. As we walked I asked Veronica about her background with Thorntons.

"I started in 1945 just after the war as a shop assistant," she began. "At that time we only had five shops in Manchester because a couple had been destroyed in the bombing. Miss Dutton used to supervise all the company's shops for Mr. Norman back then, and had to then report to him every Monday morning. Mr. Norman used to come round quite a lot in those days and he always had plenty to say!"

"Tell me about it!" I said. "Just imagine what it is like for me being his son!"

"You know, it was just around the time that sweets came off rationing – or 'ray-tioning' as your father used to call it."

"Oh yes, I remember that well!" I said.

"Anyway, I soon became a shop manageress and then I was asked to supervise all the Liverpool shops as well. Miss Dutton left in the 1960s and I ended up with even more: seven shops in Manchester, three in Liverpool, two in Derby, two more in Stockport, plus Hanley, Macclesfield, Wilmslow, Middleton, Ashton-under-Lyne and Oldham. That was twenty shops altogether," she said proudly.

"Hmm, quite a collection," I said. "They'd make quite a business on their own." Anxious to get her opinion on a few things, I asked, "What do you think about our window displays? I'm constantly told that we really ought to cut down on the expense of it all it as it's not worth it, given the cost of window dressers and their expenses. What do you think? Would *you* say it was unnecessary?"

"Unnecessary? Mr. Peter, you must be joking! Look, every time we take out the window display briefly to re-dress it the sales drop by 20 or 30%. You should talk to your father about that. Not long ago, when he was on one of his visits, I told him. 'I'm a bit worried about sales of the truffles,' I says to him. 'They don't seem to be doing very well.'

"'Whereabouts have you put them in the window?' he asked and we went outside to have a look. 'There they are up, right up there in the top corner. That's your answer,' he says to me. 'Look, do me a favour and put them down here in the front corner by the door and see what happens.'

"Well, after he'd gone, I said to myself, 'What did you go and tell him that for? Now you're going to have to take out the whole window display and re-do it.' But he was right. When he came back the following week, he asked me how the truffles were selling now. 'Much better,' I told him.

"'There you go,' he says. 'That's all it needed. I'll let you into a little secret – never worry about those problems that have a solution. The ones to worry about are those *without* a solution!'"

"So you're as convinced as I am about it," I said.

"'Course I am," she agreed. "Look, if you want to get some real technical information about it why don't you talk to Angie Capel? She's based in Derby, that's near you in Belper. She's a fantastic window dresser. I gave her the first chance at it, you know. I wanted someone to do the window at Rugby and I thought that she'd be good at it. She was only 16 then and, the way things were, I had to go and see her mother to get permission to take her there!"

"Right," I said. "I'll see what Angie can tell me."

I decided to seek Veronica's opinion on Brian Leach. His background was in insurance but Tony had taken him on as Retail Sales Manager in 1976 despite my doubts as to his suitability for the job. He was a good friend of ours, articulate and intelligent, but without the necessary experience or sensitivity.

"Do you see much of Brian Leach?" I asked casually.

"Well, yes, he comes round visiting but I don't think he really understands the business," replied Veronica frankly. This confirmed my suspicion that here was another problem needing my attention.

We were welcomed at the Arndale Centre by Miss Lane. Such centres had been developed on the lines of the

American shopping mall and we felt provided a better retail environment. Dad insisted that the shop doors of all our branches be kept open constantly, even in mid-winter, but at least inside the Centre there were none of the freezing temperatures or dust blowing in from the High Street, nor was there the prospect of direct sunlight melting the chocolates in the window displays. Miss Lane offered us yet another cup of tea while we chatted in the back of the store after which we thanked her and moved on to Cross Street. While we were walking, Veronica continued the conversation.

"Your father always says that the *Special Toffee* is our 'bread and butter'. Is that still true?"

"Well, it accounts for about 45% of our sales but it used to be higher. It's gone down about ten per cent owing to the increasing demand for our chocolates."

I knew that Veronica had been involved with our earlier TV advertising campaign and I wanted to know more about that.

"Oh yes, that was in the late 60s," she recalled. "Tony got Dan Killip to organise it and he wrote the scripts. I had to go to the Capitol Theatre in Didsbury to help with the production. It was for a programme called *What's in Store* and the presenter was Doris Rogers."

"I remember it well and it was hugely successful," I informed her. "Our sales shot up dramatically in the Granada area."

"It was a wonderful opportunity to have a slot right next to *Coronation Street* and Doris came over as a friendly, homely lady who anyone could trust. She spent a lot of time describing our products and telling the audience how wonderful they were. I'd done a beautiful display for her on a silver tray so they looked really mouth-watering."

After Cross Street, Deansgate and Mosley Street we went on to our two shops in Stockport. The earlier snow had cleared but had now been replaced by a dreary fall of sleet in time for my return journey.

I had enjoyed visiting the shops and their managers and sought out some small identifying detail at each one that would allow me to recall it individually. I saw no immediate need for any re-organisation as everything was just fine and, besides, this wasn't yet my responsibility. However, I remained uneasy with the company's marketing strategy.

A few weeks after the Manchester visit, I acted on Veronica Simmons' advice and went to see Angie Caple. I tracked her down to the St James Street shop in Derby where we retired to the back for the inevitable cup of tea.

"So, Angie, how did you get into window dressing?" I asked.

She thought for a moment. "It would have been when I first started here as a Saturday girl on my 15th birthday. That was back in 1959." I could see in her face the memories flooding back. "I was chopping toffee and weighing chocolates, you know, making up toffee boxes and things like that. Then at Christmas, when it got really busy, they made me permanent. There was this woman – Peggy Shires I think she was called – who did all the window displays here in Derby. There were only two shops but it was a lot of work because there were four large windows to fill. I remember thinking that I'd like to do something like that so one day I asked Peggy if I could help. And that's how I started to learn all about it.

"One day Peggy was poorly so they sent me to dress the windows at the Market Place shop. I enjoyed doing it and I think it looked really good when I'd finished."

"What happened next?" I prompted.

"Well, Miss Dutton came one day to St James Street and asked me if I would go to Rugby to do their window. Naturally, I was delighted but Mrs. Simmons had to go and ask my mother first to see if this would be all right. Then later I went for a while to Manchester and did the windows there."

"How did you know what to do?" I wondered. "Where did you get your window dressing skills from? Did you go on any courses or training or anything like that?"

"Oh no," she said proudly. "I just picked it up from other people in the company. I learned as I went along."

"Did you have any important rules when you're doing a display?" I wondered.

"A lot of it came from what Mr. Norman and Mr. Tony told me. Mr. Norman always insisted that the *Toffee* had to be in the middle of the window and it always had to be there by 12 o'clock otherwise a lot of sales would be lost. I would build up the height of the window from the front to the back, using stacked-up empty tins covered with cloth. That meant that the most important selling place in the window, Mr. Norman says, was in the middle. Other important spots are the door-side low down and the opposite bottom corner of the window. On some days we would put the *Continental* in the middle of the window and then the *Toffee* would have to go in the bottom right-hand corner near the door. We always used a large silver tray for whatever is in the centre and smaller silver trays for everything else. Of course, the toffee in the window would go off very quickly so that had to be changed every morning.

"Talking about window displays," she continued, looking me full in the face, "did you know that Mr. Norman used to get quite jealous of Mr. Tony over it?"

"No. Tell me more?" I said, my curiosity aroused.

"Mr. Norman would come into the shop, turning his nose up. 'Tony did that window, didn't he? I can tell that *you* didn't do it. I don't like it – tell him!' Of course, I would do nothing of the sort."

"Angie," I said, "you've been around in this business for what, 18 years now? I'm sure you could tell me a lot more if you wanted to. I'd find it really interesting."

"Well, that's true, Mr. Peter, I could. For example, when Mr. Norman came round in his Rolls-Royce, Eddie would drop him off at the first shop and then take his picnic basket to the next one where the girls would ask what mood he was in. As he came in, Mr. Norman would always say, 'Good morning, do you keep the door shut on the *Continental* counter? Are the toffee boxes fresh every morning? Do you have any mice?' The manageress would always make him a nice cup of tea and I would have to go out and buy him two bananas for his dinner – always *under-ripe* ones!

"I was at the Market Place shop in Derby one day when he arrived and he asked these same questions. Then he asked me to get the cash book which was in the little back store-room down a long corridor. We were next door to a food shop and I knew that *they* had mice. I was rather worried that a mouse might be down this corridor and, sure enough, *there* was one! I stamped my foot very hard and it scuttled away. I really didn't want Mr. Norman to see it!"

"You don't still have that problem, do you?"

"Oh no," she lowered her voice to a whisper. "*Rentokil*," she said, knowing I needed no more detail, and changed the subject. "When I first started at Thorntons, the girls would bring old tables, chairs, cups and plates to put in the back-rooms, anything to make it feel more like home. At Christmas and Easter, they'd work late into the evening on a Sunday to get everything ready for the week ahead. They'd weigh out the chocolates, wrap the boxes, anything that would help the shop run smoothly. It was one big happy family – the shop was theirs.

"The window dressers travelled from place to place and helped wherever they could. They'd also work on Sundays if need be. Even the husbands would be dragged in if the Area Manager couldn't get to move stock around. Sometimes, you understand, one shop might be running low and another would have plenty, so they'd transfer it over until a proper delivery could be made from the factory.

"The windows would have to be cleaned every morning, and on Mondays we had to take down all the chocolate boxes, jars of sweets and bags of chocolates to clean the mirrored shelves and brasses. The scales had to be *Brasso-ed* or silvered every day; then we'd weigh up fresh bags of chocolates, make up new boxes and change the toffee in the window. At the end of the day we had to get out the mop and bucket to give the floor a thorough cleaning.

"We only had half a day off each week, and no time off at Christmas except for Christmas Day and Boxing Day. We'd have to go in on New Year's Day and we just had the Easter Monday holiday. We'd often be the only shop open on Good Friday.

"I've been to Sheffield and met Peggy Wood. She dresses the windows in Sheffield and Rotherham and she's excellent. She's the one who makes the cardboard rabbits and chicks for the Easter windows and the Santas and reindeers for the Christmas windows. She told me that, when she first started one Easter, she put real live yellow chicks in the window just like Mr. Norman used to do before the war.

"Thanks, Angie," I said, "and you continue to do all the Derby windows?"

"Yes, and quite a lot more in Mrs. Simmons area like she tells me."

"Well, keep up the good work. Thorntons would be lost without you."

Our staff were always our greatest asset and mention must be made here of Iris Smith – formerly Muddiman – who had been my friend, mentor, teacher and a wonderful Thorntons person for 36 years until she retired in November 1975. She finally succumbed to her lung cancer in the early summer of 1978 at the age of 53. I attended her funeral in the company of several other family directors. I penned a tribute to her in our company magazine and mourned her almost as if she had been one of my own family.

– ★★★ –

John and I no longer felt ourselves to be in conflict. We were separated by our different areas of responsibility. Although I still wasn't happy with my new duties, at least we shared the same concerns about Tony's overall management. That 'triangulation' phenomenon was in play with John and me now in cahoots over how to deal with this, although I still felt vulnerable and at risk from John's machinations.

"This is a serious problem," he said at one of our private meetings. "I've been analysing the recent accounts and comparing them to previous years."

"I know," I told him. "I've been doing the same. We're going to have to act – nobody else will. Stanley and Dad can't be relied on – they just make unhelpful comments all the time – and they don't really understand what's wrong. It's just that I'm not certain Tony is capable of handling everything."

"I'm sure you're right," agreed John, and he outlined the differences in our recent performance compared to that of just a few years earlier. Our turnover had all but tripled whereas the cash profits had increased but slightly. "Can you explain why this is so?" he asked me.

"It seems fairly obvious," I pointed out. "Our prices are just not keeping up with our costs. Tony seems afraid to raise them at a time of inflation but wages, materials and everything else keep going up. And as for cutting out TV advertising, well, that's really a bad move. We should be doing the opposite."

"I think that's all to do with Marks and Spencer," he suggested. "Tony has this idea that we're not allowed to increase the price of our stock to them, so he's keeping our general price down."

"Well, we *do* have this unwritten rule to keep our prices in line with theirs. We can't just put up the price without their agreement."

"True, but he'll just have to face that problem. He must tell them prices have to rise!"

"Can you actually see him doing that, John?"

"No, I'm afraid not," he replied Neither could I, yet it seemed that this was one of the essential changes the company needed, and I also took the opportunity to point out that my own job was quite impractical.

"How can Retail Management be separate from Marketing Management?" I asked.

"You know what this means, don't you?" asked John in reply. "We must get Tony to give up his role as Managing Director and Marketing Director. But who do you think should do what instead?"

The conversation was now getting close to the bone. I'd given a lot of thought to this and my objective was to become Managing Director and to ask John to be Deputy Managing Director. I was unhappy with his having equal status with me and decided to grasp the hot iron.

"Well, I suggest that Tony be the Chairman, responsible for company development, acquisitions, new marketing projects, property management and development. Yes?"

John thought about it. "Hmm, that's quite sensible," he answered, "and he could continue to run the greetings card business."

"Agreed! I think that we'd both be happy to have nothing to do with that!" I said.

"There's no problem about Mike's role, is there?"

"There's never been any problem there," I said with a wry smile. "Mike should continue as company secretary and look after public relations. He can help Tony with business developments and manage our cash investments."

"I agree with that," John said and then paused. "Now, what do *we* do?"

I took a deep breath. "I propose that I become Managing Director, looking after a number of services, and that you become Deputy Managing Director." (There, I thought to myself, I've said it.)

John's expression changed and the relaxed atmosphere suddenly chilled by a few degrees.

"I'm not having that," he said, sounding tetchy. "You know I just can't bear to work for *you*. You've known that since I started here."

"But why on earth not?" I asked, justifiably miffed. "I'm a perfectly reasonable person, aren't I? Others have had no problem working for me, and you must admit I've been in the business much longer than you. After all, I am your older brother by ten years."

"But that's just it!" he returned. "Other people are not your *younger* brother! We're just going to have to find another way round this!"

This hurt me somewhat as, only a year earlier, I had relinquished my much-loved Production Management role to John just because he *was* my brother. Yet now he was refusing to work for me and putting me under pressure to take a lesser role. How much longer was this absurd state of affairs going to continue? My days and nights continued to be troubled and sleepless. Eventually, after more soul-searching, I realised that compromise was the only way forward.

John and I met up again a week later.

"I listened to what you said," I told him. "I suggest we *both* take on the roles of Joint Managing Director. You can look after the manufacturing side and I will look after retail and marketing. What do you say?"

"Hmm, that's OK, so long as I can take over all the services as well," he replied.

"Oh, look," I said. It was my turn to get cross now. "You really are having your cake and eating it, aren't you? I really don't see why I should have to give up all these things, particularly the management services. I created them and I've been running them successfully for ages. This is going to leave *me* taking full responsibility for sales and marketing – which I'm happy to do, of course – but I've not really got the proper experience for it, and it does need some drastic action to get things back on to a proper footing. Meanwhile, *you* get to keep these well-organised sections of the business that need no re-organisation and are no real challenge. This is hardly fair!"

"Well, it's what I'm prepared to do," said John, unmoved. "It makes good business sense if you think about it because all the services really are related to the production operation."

Unfortunately I had no real argument here. He was in the stronger position. He already had a viable job and I didn't. I had to give in, and so this is what we agreed, but I remained distinctly bothered.

However, I tried to see things in a positive light and accepted that I could still have a definite role to play with some responsibility for the gross profits of the company. I knew that I was surrendering a lot of power to John who couldn't be relied on always to act in my better interests, but I knew that I would get little or no support from the other directors, so we agreed to meet with Tony and put this proposed new framework to him. I was very apprehensive about asking him to give up his Managing Directorship and become Chairman.

I went to his office in Belper one day. "Tony," I said, "the management organisation that we agreed a year ago is just not working. I'm finding my role impossible – it's really only half a job – and John feels that to do his work properly he needs control of Management Services. We've been discussing what can be done about it."

Tony looked remarkably calm. "What do you suggest then?"

"Well, the plan is this: that he and I become Joint Managing Directors. He will look after Production and all the Management Services and I will look after Retail and Marketing."

"And what do you propose that *I* should do?"

"We think that you should be Chairman. After all, Stanley's far too old for that job now." I then outlined all the separate areas of responsibility that the role would involve, including the greetings card business. He remained impassive, as if he had been expecting this.

"Well," he responded. "I suppose I *could* accept it if that's what you both think, and so long as it's properly agreed in discussion with the other directors."

We then had a crisis meeting and the new organisation was accepted to start from the beginning of 1979. After that, Tony hardly had any further contact with me and concentrated solely on the greeting cards, doubtless feeling rejected by Thorntons and so ignoring the company in turn. I, on the other hand, drove over to Belper on that first working day in January in a considerable state of relief. The familiar Derbyshire countryside looked more beautiful than ever and the world seemed altogether a much brighter place again. The fact that I actually knew nothing about the theory of retail marketing didn't bother me at all. I had developed such confidence in my own ability that I felt I could take on any new job and do it well. Suddenly I was happy again, stimulated and fulfilled. There was an enormous amount to do but I worked hard, and straight away I had a great piece of good fortune.

Tony had commissioned a report from Peter Doyle, a Professor of Retail Marketing at Bradford University. We'd all seen it when it was presented for discussion prior to the re-organisation but we'd dismissed it because of its largely critical content. Within a few days of taking over my new duties I read the report again and realised that it made a lot of sense. Peter Doyle was working for a year at INSEAD, the European Institute of Business Administration, in Paris so I called him and asked him to come over to see me at the weekend if possible.

"Fly over to East Midlands Airport on Saturday morning," I suggested, "and I'll pick you up and bring you back here. We need to talk."

I met him at the airport, a slim man in his early forties with an open face and a ready smile. We walked to the car park and he started to tell me about his career, first at the London Business School, then Bradford University and now at this international business school. We reached Belper and entered the silent factory offices. Seated in the Board Room, I began to discuss his paper and immediately came clean over our initial rejection of it.

"That was some weeks ago," I told him, "before I took over my current job. It's a different matter now that I'm in the 'hot-seat' and I need to do something urgently about our problems. I'm beginning to see you were saying some very important things."

Peter replied, "Well, in fairness to yourself, none of your fellow directors made any response either. I just assumed the project wasn't going anywhere. I'm pleased to see you're more enthusiastic now."

"It's more a case of trying to halt our business decline," I pointed out. "Your report noted our year-on-year increase in sales of about 17% between '74 and '78 but our net profit was increasing by a mere 5% each year. That's a substantial fall in our profit margin, isn't it?"

"Correct," he confirmed, "but remember, this is due to stagnation in your traditional core business, along with inflation, the Marks and Spencer deal and other things."

"What do you mean exactly by 'stagnation in the core business?" I asked.

"Well, you've cut out all TV advertising and, as a result, you've stopped telling your customers what you're about. In fact, I suspect that some individuals within your company have lost sight of what you're about. Where are the innovative products? Where's the focus for your promotional activity?"

"Hmm, I see what you mean," I admitted, "and I have been aware of some of these things myself. There's never been any effort historically to define our market position."

"Your prices haven't kept up with increasing costs and inflation," he stated, "and the franchise operation is also probably out of control."

"Regarding our prices, that's because of the Marks and Spencer factor," I reminded him.

"You mean that M & S keep their prices at the same level as yours by unwritten agreement? So to raise your own prices you'd have to get them to accept higher prices too?"

"That's it in a nutshell," I replied. "Furthermore they only sell our *Continental* line as it's our most prestigious product. But all our prices are related to that, so our entire range is affected."

"The solution's simple them," Peter said. "You're just going to have to inform them that the price is going up."

"Not so easy," I replied. "What happens if they say no and stop doing business with us?"

"Don't be wet, Peter. Of course they won't say no. They only go to British suppliers, and just think: who else is there in the UK who could possibly supply that range to them?"

"Well, nobody, of course!"

"There you are then. It seems to me you're not getting nearly enough management information to be able to do your job properly. This all needs serious improvement," he said.

"I agree with you there," I nodded. "You also said something about examining the manufacturing-retailing format to see if this remains viable for the future."

"Yes," he said, "I do think that you should look seriously at it. I know that was how the business started but it doesn't mean that is how it should continue. Just look at Burtons the tailor. They were founded on a principle of manufacturing their own stuff, but Ralph Halpern became their MD and did the unthinkable. He closed all their factories and started to buy from whoever offered the best quality and price. The result was that he saved the business."

"This is one area where I have to disagree with you," I said.

"Why? Is manufacturing your particular baby?" he asked, cynically.

"No, I think that I'm more objective than that. It's simply down to my belief that no other company could make our top products as well as we can. We have a very tight control of all aspects of a product's shelf life. As for innovation, any idea we might get from a customer enquiry can be turned almost instantly into a new product because we've got technologies exclusive to ourselves and we're not going to sign these over to any other business. Our workforce is loyal to us and prides itself on producing the best for our customers. This is what has kept us one step ahead of our competitors, even M & S."

"I can see that you feel very passionately about this," said Peter, "but you know, as mechanisation increases, you'll need heavier plant and machinery. You'll become less flexible and less able to develop those unique new products, won't you?"

"Not at all," I argued. "We keep ourselves very flexible and adaptable. We always have."

"Well, I still think that should remain an open question."

"Perhaps so," I conceded. "I'll admit that some products have become more commonplace on the market. Anyone can make good boiled sweets these days at very good prices so we could consider buying them in from elsewhere, I suppose."

This meeting left me with much to think about, most of it positive and urgent. It was clear that we needed to define this manufacturing-retailing relationship and I spent the next eight weeks, with Peter Doyle's help, devising an appropriate strategy. I produced it in mid-March and highlighted all the relevant factors: shop locations, physical facilities, products, pricing, service and promotions. The plan was to re-brand our market image, increase volume through extra shops, review the franchise operation and the Marks and Spencer partnership and seek further export outlets. In the process we could cut operating expenses while increasing prices and same-store sales with further discount promotions and a renewed TV advertising campaign.

This was a lot to do all in one go. Inevitably, we had to prioritise, and the first sensible thing was to appoint a proper advertising agency. The impact of the *What's in Store* promotion had been dramatic and initially inexpensive but, as costs rose, Tony appointed a Leeds-based company. Although we'd been one of the first in the field in TV advertising we'd never used a London agency as they were thought to be much more expensive.

To further my knowledge of retail marketing I decided to attend a three-day course run by Peter Doyle in London's Russell Square. The Russell Hotel was a slightly run-down, ornate Victorian building and I checked in with a mixture of excitement and apprehension. There were twelve of us at the first morning's seminar, seated in a U-shape facing Peter and his flip chart. His presentation was riveting as he strode up and down, brandishing his marker pen. The only distraction for me was the attractive young lady seated opposite whose name card bore the words, Alison Andrews.

During the coffee break I asked Alison why she was on this course.

"I work for the ad agency Mackinnon-Kent as an account manager," she told me. "My boss sent me as he thought it would be good for me to learn more about retail marketing. What about you?"

"Oh, I'm a director of Thorntons the confectioners. I've just taken on the retail and marketing side of the business, knowing absolutely nothing about it," I admitted. "I thought it was time to learn more – and fast!"

Alison showed a look of interest and respect at my mention of the company name. "Do you have an advertising agency?" she enquired.

"Yes, but it's just a provincial firm. I don't think they're quite suitable anymore and we're on the lookout for another one."

"Then you really ought to come and talk to us," she said, excitedly. "We've an excellent roster of clients. We're doing very well with them at the moment and I'm sure we could do something similar for you."

"That's probably so," I said, "but I generally look around and talk to a number of companies before I make any decisions about the business."

"Quite right. I understand," she replied. "But look, when you've done the course, we could arrange a dinner here in London some time and I could tell you much more about the world of advertising."

"That sounds like a good idea," I nodded enthusiastically. "Give me time to think about it and hopefully I'll give you a call."

The coffee break ended and I went back to my seat with my mind now on anything but retail marketing. I hadn't come here to make any amorous liaisons, far from it. Indeed, since my affair in 1973, I had established a much more settled home life, always putting Janet and the children first. Naturally, I had noticed other women from time to time but had always resisted any temptation to act foolishly. But with Alison Andrews, it was a different matter altogether. There we were, in the same hotel, attending the lectures together, sharing meals and drinks in the bar afterwards. It took every ounce of self-control not to surrender to my impulses and I certainly had a few sleepless nights in the hotel.

I was aware that, until recently, I had led a fairly provincial life. Apart from those occasional jaunts into Europe, the horizons since my Army days had extended no further than Sheffield and Derbyshire. I had seen little of life in the wider world, spending most of my time in the milieu of the factory and its offices. The cosmopolitan world of fancy restaurants and the big business community of the capital were all new to me. Here, people had more liberated attitudes and I felt very much one of the 'hicks from the sticks'. I felt dissatisfied with who I was and began to want something more. My cosy marriage now seemed exposed and I thought it was time to discuss things with my wife again.

Returning home, I raised this difficult topic tentatively, and Janet sensed immediately that something was up. "Is it another woman?" she asked coolly.

"Yes, I met this person on the course. I couldn't help it – I was very attracted to her. I resisted the temptation and I want to continue resisting, but it will be difficult now that I am moving in more sophisticated circles in London. You know that I want to put our marriage first, so I'm asking for help. Please, can we try harder to strengthen our marriage?"

I don't know what reaction I expected, but the one I got can be summed up in one word. Hysteria. So much for a calm, considered discussion.

A few weeks later I had to visit our Cambridge shop, and then went on to London for an overnight stay. I was exhausted and frustrated with Janet's refusal to talk, and the alternative of a stimulating dinner with an attractive and sparkling young woman was very appealing. I still intended to keep everything focussed on advertising rather than romance, so when I 'phoned Alison from the station and set up a dinner date it was with the express intention of remaining faithful and business-like. However, over the course of a delightful meal, our conversation drew ever closer to our personal lives. I threw discretion to the winds and told her all about my family problems and my unhappy marriage. It was wonderful to talk to somebody who was sympathetic rather than judgemental, and I was also intrigued to hear of the hard times she had suffered in her own past. She was a single woman, in her early thirties, with a string of unhappy, broken relationships behind her. She remembered my wish to explore a number of options in the ad agency world and gave me a list with about ten names including Mackinnon-Kent. We agreed to meet again next time I was in London and perhaps go to a concert.

A fortnight later I booked a couple of tickets for a programme of classical music at the Festival Hall. I rarely had an opportunity to go to such a concert at home. Venues were limited and Janet was no lover of the classics. However, Alison and I wallowed in this gorgeous, romantic music. Afterwards, at Alison's suggestion, we took a taxi back to the Holiday Inn at Swiss Cottage where I was staying overnight. The plan was simply to enjoy an after-concert drink in the hotel bar, but it was so noisy, in contrast to the harmonious melodies we'd just savoured, that it seemed preferable to continue our conversation from the comfortable chairs in my room. I naively imagined that this was all either of us had in mind, but once inside the room Alison showed me that she had another motive altogether.

As her clothes dropped to the floor, so did my jaw in amazement. Next, she started to undress me and I did absolutely nothing to stop her. My resolve to behave like a proper gentleman dissolved like so much mist as we took up positions on the floor, on the bed, on the chairs, anywhere we could embrace. The night was long and time stood still. However, the clock eventually read 6 a.m. and, our mutual passions spent, Alison said that she would have to return to her flat to get changed for work. She left me exhausted and in a daze. I had come to the capital thinking of myself as some innocent yokel from the North. Alison had truly awakened me to a whole new world. I'd never experienced anything like it.

The next day I wandered around with my head in the clouds. Ostensibly, I was checking out some potential locations for new shops, but my thoughts were dominated by Alison and how I could meet up with her again. My morals were completely compromised but I had no thought for the consequences. Somehow, I just had to find more reasons to come to London. There were further locations to look at, agencies to visit, all sorts of business meetings to set up…

Oh yes, London was definitely becoming the centre of the universe.

Chapter 11
Out of the Frying Pan

It came as a complete surprise in 1979 to learn that Tony had taken two of his sons, Mark and James, into the family business. Despite being Joint MD of Retail and Marketing, I had not been informed of this and I simply wanted to know what was going on.

"Tony, what's this I hear about your boys?" I asked him. "I didn't think any other family members were to be inducted into the company. I've no personal objection, of course, but it's not just a matter of hiring new employees. There are implications when it comes to 'family'. Surely you understand that?"

To my great surprise, Tony suddenly burst into tears. "That's it!" he retorted. "You're trying to destroy my sons now as well as me!"

I was completely aghast. "What? That's absolute nonsense, Tony. Oh dear, look, I'm truly sorry if I've upset you. It's just that I had no prior knowledge. Naturally, if they're now part of the business, I'll do all I can to help them. But where does that leave the rest of us? What about my own children, for example? Can I bring *them* into the business, too?"

He raised his eyes to look at me. "Peter, you don't understand. After losing Judith, they have been such a comfort to me. They've helped me in so many ways. I feel I must do everything I possibly can for them now. Can't you see that?"

It was difficult to deal with a *fait accompli* but I did what I could to incorporate these nephews into the corporate structure of the business. Mark actually didn't stay with us for very long but James made more of a go at it and I was quite impressed with him.

I was still getting to grips with marketing and felt that a manager was needed, but what sort of duties would this involve and what sort of person would best fill the role? I was ready to start meeting the advertising agencies in London and thought it sensible to take an objective third party with me. Dick Smith had been helping me throughout 1978 even though he had little experience or training in the field. He readily agreed to accompany me and remained a great help until such time as we could appoint someone to a permanent position.

We went up to the capital and set aside three days in which the ten agencies could make their pitch to us. We listened to them all and, even though I recognised the difficult position it would put me in, I had no doubt that Mackinnon-Kent was the best for us. I told Dick nothing about Alison. Indeed, I had told no one. The account director, Luke Stevens, suggested we do some market research before settling the details of our advertising plan and proposed a company called Specialist Research Unit run by Dennis Stevenson.

Dennis was a bright young man, fresh from Cambridge, who had set up SRU to employ, as he put, only "very bright people – brighter than myself!" His offices were in a rambling old building in Covent Garden and together we fixed the details of an appropriate survey and its subsequent report. Using this, along with what I had learned on Peter Doyle's course, I established a set of definitions for our company. Eventually, I found myself seated at my own desk with this unique document in front of me, and on a blank sheet of paper I wrote:

Thorntons' Differential Advantages
1. *Exclusive* (it was essential that customers should buy from our shops alone).
2. *Very good quality.*
3. *Unique products.*

4. *Innovative products.*
5. *Very fresh.*
6. *More wholesome.*
7. *Good value.*
8. *Made in a hygienically-controlled environment.*

I added another definition: *Target Segment.*

The market research had revealed that our customer base was allied to that of other recognised 'semi-lifestyle' businesses, such as Marks & Spencer and Waitrose, where customers valued these differences and were willing to pay that bit extra for a superior product.

Now that I had appointed Mackinnon-Kent it was essential that the affair between Alison and me should stop. The relationship had to be objective, particularly as Alison was appointed our Account Manager. We subsequently had many important business phone calls but everything was on a purely professional basis. This allowed me yet again to review the state of my marriage and what I really wanted from my union with Janet. I was wracked with guilt, felt a strong responsibility towards her and couldn't face the idea of separating from my children. The idea of a socially acceptable divorce was still a long way in the future. Indeed, society seemed to tolerate the deceit of a secret affair more readily than the admission of a failed marriage.

Alison and I devised a new advertising plan. Whenever I went to London we would meet for dinner or lunch together, and if I was in the office at Belper she would telephone me to discuss details. She was enthusiastic in her job and came up with some great ideas, along with a few not-so-good ones. In some ways, it was a pity that our business relationship had been clouded by personal issues. After some time spent talking about campaigns, Alison would then ask how I was getting on at home.

"Fine, thank you," was my non-committal reply.

"I don't believe you," she'd declare.

I would hesitate. "Well, it's a bit difficult, I suppose, after what's happened between us. It's not easy for me to relax."

"You know that you can always talk to me about your problems."

"Yes, I know, but we can't allow this to become personal again, can we?"

"How about the other directors? How are you getting on with them?"

"Well, as ever, it remains very difficult with John. I hardly speak to him but things are slowly improving with Mike and Tony."

"Don't they realise what a good job you're doing?"

This would usually solicit a laugh from me. "It's not like that in our business! They're always suspicious and my fellow directors never say 'Well done'."

"You poor thing, that's a shame," she'd say. "I think you're doing a fantastic job."

"Alison, I have to go now. It's seven o'clock and everyone's left the office. I'm going to be late home as it is, and that will make Jan suspicious, plus I need to see my kids."

"Do you ever think about *me*?" she'd enquire. "In *that* way, I mean?"

"Look, we mustn't talk like this. It doesn't help either of us and I really must go home now."

"I wish I could see you again, that's all."

"I know. I know exactly how you feel, but it's not going to happen." A pause. "Goodnight, Alison."

In spite of the distraction, working with Mackinnon-Kent was initially very exciting. Our 'Market Positioning Statement' described a Thorntons shop as 'a treasure trove filled with mouth-watering confectionery delights where you can treat yourself and others.' The idea of 'Retail Theatre' was paramount.

However, what Luke Stevens had proposed would use up the entire advertising budget for the year but I agreed to it because I was desperate to increase our volume of sales. A large proportion of the cash was to be spent on a TV promotional film to be shown in the run up to Christmas, and it soon became clear that the budget here would overrun our initial costs. It was very exciting to watch the film in production but I was acutely aware of all these people – producer, director, cameramen, continuity girl and many others – busily wasting our money.

After advertising, the next issue of concern was prices. The magazine *CTN*, published for the confectionery, tobacconists and newsagents trade, included a monthly list of retail prices for all confectionery products. Using this, I was able to do comparisons and felt that there *was* scope to raise the price of our specialist products by around ten per cent, maybe more for something unique as our *Continental* chocolates, but we were constrained by the deal with Marks and Spencer whereby all our products were inter-related by cost and dependent upon the store prices set by M & S. It was obvious to anyone who looked that their one-pound gift box was identical to ours apart from the name on the front. We had produced it, but we could hardly start selling ours at a higher price without asking them to follow suit. The question was: would they?

At that time the country was in the grip of rampant inflation. Our production costs were forever rising and it was essential to increase prices in line but, as always in such situations, there was an incredible balancing act to be done between potential benefits and possible losses. Sales could actually fall by volume if prices went up too much and we could end up in a worse position. There was much at risk in considering a price hike. M & S accounted for about 10% of our total turnover and we had benefited by association with such a prestigious brand name. They had insisted on strictly upheld quality standards, and dire warnings from some quarters of the family, predicting the demise of our own sales, had not come to pass.

John had already tentatively floated the idea of a price rise at a lunch with M & S's Stuart Rose in late July and had been given the impression that a modest increase, say, up to ten per cent, might be acceptable. Even so, when I arranged to meet their executive the following month to confirm our intent, I was extremely apprehensive. However, my courage fortified by a couple of drinks, I went to their Baker Street offices to meet Dan Jacobs.

I arrived early and was asked to take a seat. Somebody would be down shortly to take me to Dan's office. I sat with the other salesmen in the foyer, feeling embarrassed and pretended to check all the documents in my briefcase rather than look any of them in the eye. A smart young woman appeared before me and spoke in a very cultured accent. "Mr. Thornton? Mr Jacobs is ready to see you now."

I followed her silently to the lift and then down a long corridor to his oak-panelled office. It even had a carpet and, compared to our own office at Belper, might as well have been on another planet. Dan was a well-built man in his mid-fifties and he faced me from behind a very large desk in front of a very large window. Everything was very large and I, of course, felt small. My mind flashed back unhelpfully to my days in the Army when I had appeared in front of the two officers during my WOSB interview and had felt intimidated. Seated now in a low-level chair before this equally imposing figure, barely able to see above the polished surface of his desk, my image of him blurred by the bright window, I hoped that I didn't look too insignificant. More than that, I prayed that he wouldn't smell the alcohol on my breath. He spoke in a suitably upmarket London voice.

"Hello, Peter. So glad that you could call in. The business seems to be going well, I see."

"Yes, oh yes." I replied. "We're very pleased with it. It accounts for a significant part of our overall turnover, so it's quite important to us." First mistake, I thought, I should never have allowed him to know how important it is to us at this stage.

"Pleased to hear it," he said. "So, did you want to discuss any specific aspect?"

I answered, but it was as if someone else were speaking the words. I'd rehearsed the sentence so many times to myself as I came down on the train, but now it seemed hollow and far away.

"I'm really sorry about this, Dan, but our costs have gone up so much with inflation recently. We feel we must increase our prices to you so that we can raise our own prices of the Continental gift box." There was a pause, so I added. "By about 10%."

I waited, my heart pounding for the answer.

"OK, that's no problem," he replied, to my utter astonishment. "What new price are you going to charge us?" I told him and he accepted it, just like that. No question, no fuss. I sat up in my chair and suddenly felt a little taller. I started to relax and we then discussed other business issues of mutual interest. Afterwards, he accompanied me to the front entrance of the most important retailer in the UK and I hailed a taxi to take me back to St. Pancras and the train home. I went back to Derbyshire that afternoon feeling elated and I admit that I had a few more drinks on the way. I had achieved the breakthrough we needed, secure in the knowledge that our profit would now rise substantially.

1979 was not only a year of change for Thorntons but also for the country. The Conservatives were elected to government on the 3rd of May under the leadership of the first woman prime minister. As a businessman, I saw this as a turning away from some of the doctrines of former post-war governments that had supported inefficient nationalised industries at the expense of a weakened commercial sector. Too much power had lain with the trades unions, and taxation and inflation had risen out of all proportion. A monetarist policy had had to be adopted and interest rates remained in double figures until well into the 1990s. Top business earners were being taxed overall at rates above 90% so many took to receiving recompense in other ways through company cars and maximum expense allowances. There was little incentive for them to raise earnings through working harder.

After 1979 things changed rapidly. Interest rates remained high, but trade union powers were severely curtailed and a new Budget brought top rates of tax down from 83% to 40%. Privatisation began and miraculously those nationalised companies that had been sustaining great losses suddenly became profitable independent companies. The least efficient of them, of course, went to the wall and it was a painful time for many managers and employees, signalling the inexorable decline of Britain's place as a manufacturing country which has continued to this day. For the rest, a new dynamism was created, leading to continued growth and expansion right into the new millennium, only recently checked by the pendulum having swung too far. Britain, as the former 'sick man of Europe', beset with strikes and bureaucratic restrictions could face the 1980s with a renewed sense of optimism.

Of course, the new Government didn't have everything its own way. The miners' strike of 1985 saw to that. And we, too, were dismayed by the raising of VAT to a new high of 17½ per cent which naturally affected our new price structure, and by October our sales were down significantly. Only the increased profit margin helped to compensate.

I had been called to another meeting with Luke at the agency to commit to an even bigger advertising budget and I realised my strategy was not without its flaws. For example, we'd been rather tardy in starting our campaign but at least I felt I was learning from each new experience. I determined that the following year would see a much more detailed promotional plan with specific campaigns every few weeks.

We were also opening new shops and I commissioned a designer to establish a new look for them. At the same time, certain unprofitable shops had to go, seven in that year alone. The first new shop was in Covent Garden which was in the process of being transformed from a traditional vegetable market to a modern shopping centre. Tony did a great job in negotiating the lease as we were taking a bit of risk here. The premises were so tiny that we had no space to store stock in the back. We always felt that London was different from the rest of the country. We were an identifiably northern company and we weren't sure that our products were as well-known in the south. I was sad that Tony couldn't be at the opening and felt a bit of an impostor in his place, but the centre and the shop proved to be a runaway success. It confirmed that the Thornton brand was firmly established in the capital and raised our profile in the business world.

General sales were still struggling at the start of 1980 and I'd tried without success to get agreement on an increased budget for the coming financial year. I insisted that operating costs should be heavily cut but was under pressure to increase sales before anything else. Even more would have to be spent on advertising despite the likelihood of our allocation being wholly used up by June. The promotional film had not been the success we'd hoped for. It seemed with hindsight that no one involved in its making had had any real understanding of what would be effective. I think I'd been over-influenced by the agency and Tony had withdrawn himself from offering me any advice. The film merely showed some contented shoppers gazing into a Thorntons' shop window before going inside to buy the products. It didn't really focus in any tempting way on the products themselves. Subsequently, Tony broke his silence to offer constructive criticism and we realised that a new film, full of mouth-watering close-ups, was needed. Early in 1980, we made such a film at a fraction of the cost and it did the trick. So much for the clever boys at the agency.

Shortly after, I received a telephone call from a distraught Alison." I've been fired!" she exclaimed. "Luke called me into his office. He said he was dismissing me for having 'a special relationship with a client'. He named you, Peter."

"Oh, my goodness! That's grossly unfair," I responded. "No one was more dedicated to the job than you. We did some really great work between us, if we ignore that first film. Why didn't he just take you off the job and appoint another Account Manager if he was that concerned? He must realise that it will be bound to upset me. Is he not aware that he might lose the account as a result?"

"I don't know," she replied. "All he said was that 'someone from Derbyshire' had phoned and told him that we are having an affair."

"Well, well, well," I pondered. "Now who could that have been? Has this person demanded that you be fired?"

"I've no idea," she said, "but it's pretty bad for me."

"And most unjust, too. It's not as if we were actually having an affair, is it? Look, this is going to be bad for Mackinnon-Kent too. Now that I've learned a bit about the advertising business, I'm getting fairly dissatisfied with them and I guess I'll probably replace them before long."

"I wouldn't blame you," she said, "but don't act rashly and do something you'll regret."

"No, I'll try to keep calm," I reassured her. "What's gone wrong between Thorntons and Mackinnon-Kent isn't your fault, but I do feel that your senior management took advantage of my lack of experience and pushed me into an expensive and unsuccessful strategy. Anyway, try not to be too upset. I'll give you a call when I'm next up in London and we must get together to discuss it. I'm sure you'll get another job quickly."

We met as I'd suggested and she'd already taken a new position with Saatchi & Saatchi. We agreed not to resume things where we'd left off as it really wouldn't have helped my marriage at all. The business link between us was broken and there was no reason to prolong the distraction.

The financial year ending showed we'd actually taken a fall in profit from the previous year. Prices increases impacted on sales even as our production costs were going up, and I felt dissatisfied and vulnerable, but hope springs eternally to the optimistic businessman and I looked forward to a profitable recovery.

As 1980 progressed, John suddenly started to get panicky over the business and began to take unilateral action as I found out one day towards the end of April. I'd just called in at *Greenways* one lunch-time to visit Mum while Dad was out on his rounds of the shops. She was looking anxious as we sat down in the kitchen for a bowl of soup and a chat.

"How are you getting on?" she asked.

"What do you mean? At home or at work?"

"Both, really. I've been thinking about Janet. I've never really thought that she was the right person for you and I sometimes wish you'd married Alice instead. I know Dad and I disapproved of her and that's probably why it all went wrong."

"Don't blame yourself for that, Mum," I said. "It wasn't really your fault. There was a lot more to it. As for Janet and me, well, it's hard work at times but we're managing OK."

"I do hope that it doesn't fall apart for you," she continued. "You know I worry about the children. And I'm even more worried about the business. Your Dad seems very bothered, much more so than usual. He thinks you're making mistakes with the retail side of things. You see, John has been to see him, and I think he was trying to persuade Dad that you should be thrown out of the company."

My heart sank. Could I ever feel secure if one of my fellow directors was seeking to get rid of me?

"What did Dad say to that?" I asked.

"Well, he doesn't really want to see any of you out of the business. He gets very upset and goes off talking to all the others about it. He told John that he would have to see Stanley, Michael and Tony about it."

"That's something at least," I said, "but it's typical that none of them seems to appreciate what I'm doing. I'm actually solving our long-standing problems and doing what Tony should have done ages ago."

"I know that," Mum insisted. "I have faith in you, but it's very difficult for me. I can't take sides with anybody, can I? But I did think you ought to know what John is saying."

I was absolutely staggered. Here I was, working my socks off through the year to turn the business round. I knew I had made mistakes but was convinced now that we were on the right track. Just when light could be seen at the end of the tunnel they wanted to throw me out. I felt desperately lonely and needed a sympathetic ear but the only one I could find was Alison's. She was the one who'd supported me at times of weakness, not my wife. She had the positive outlook and the determination to make things work. I called her up and told her of my situation.

"Don't be aggressive with them," she advised. "That won't get you anywhere. In spite of what you feel, be friendly to them all. Disarm them with your charm." I took her advice and it worked. They didn't throw me out and everyone seemed to calm down.

Of course, I'd broken my resolve not to contact Alison and I met up with her again when I was next in London on business. We went to her flat in Chiswick. It was small and cluttered but that was no hindrance to two people who desperately needed each other. Our liaisons became a regular event despite the two hundred miles between us. We'd meet in various places, a Travelodge on the M1, a country location in Derbyshire, anywhere with a bed for us to share. I was becoming emotionally confused, a condition not helped by Alison's pleas when we were apart. My efforts to keep the whole affair secret were being compromised by midnight phone calls in which she would exclaim in desperation: "I love you. I need you. *Please talk to me!*"

I would slam the phone down, hoping Janet was asleep and unaware. Ten minutes later it would ring again. I would leave the phone off the hook, hoping to replace it in the morning before my wife got up.

If I hadn't been so blinded by my obsession I might have realised that there was something not quite right about Alison's behaviour. She was utterly and completely obsessed with me. I recognised my own infatuation but didn't think it was inducing any abnormal compulsive actions on my part. Perhaps she thought she could badger me into leaving my wife. Maybe she could see no alternative. I know I couldn't imagine life without her but that was the crux of the problem. I still had a beautiful family and a home that I wanted to keep. There were these three wonderful children who depended on me so much. Here was this lovely house that I had worked so hard to restore from its dilapidated state. This was my dilemma: I had a sexual addiction that could be accommodated only by throwing away everything dear to me, yet if I chose to remain true to my loved ones I would then have Alison constantly and desperately begging for my time and attention.

One Saturday in mid-July I went to the Sailing Club despite being in an evident state of distress. I took part in one race only and then packed up early and came home. The family had gone as usual to one of their weekend horse shows. I filled the car with as many of my belongings as I could pack in and drove away. I went straight to the home of two very good friends I'd got to know at the club.

Duke and Barbara had joined with me in buying an offshore boat and we'd had a great deal of fun and pleasure sailing it. Barbara was a lovely warm personality and a great cook besides. I arrived at their Nottinghamshire house unannounced but they suppressed their surprise and gave me a warm welcome. Of course, they said, I could stay at their home until things settled down. They asked no questions about what had happened, accepting what I'd done without judgement. I told them all about Alison and they said she could come to their house too if she wished. I telephoned her and she set off immediately to join me for the weekend. I phoned Janet who naturally was distraught in the extreme. She begged me to return whatever the situation, but this time I knew that it was out of the question. I'd burned my bridges behind me and was abandoning everything I'd formerly held dear. I could see the signs ahead pointing to unpleasantness and hassle. Everything was leading to that one dread word - divorce – and it all seemed inevitable. My only requirement was that I maintain the relationship with my children, if possible.

Alison arrived and we started to feel a little more relaxed. Duke and Barbara were extremely kind to her as they were to everybody. She returned to London that Sunday evening and I went off to work as usual the next morning. By chance I saw Mike quite early. I couldn't hide what I'd done and faced him with all my guilt and self-consciousness on show. He then actually shook my hand.

"Congratulations!" he said. "I don't know how it's happened but all I can say is that I'm delighted for you. You've finally left Janet."

"Thanks, Mike," I said in some relief.

"I've been talking to Tony, and he's very pleased too."

Immediately my relationship with them both improved. It seemed that they'd long harboured a dislike for Janet, and Michael in particular had strong reasons to do so. She and his ex-wife had spent much of their time talking about him and building up a general animosity towards him. Quietly, the idea of dropping me from the business was shelved. Things began to improve after the trials and tribulations of the late Fifties and early Sixties. We could now build a relationship based on warmth and mutual respect between us. Tony had tremendous practical experience of those parts of the business I was now running, and I was very happy to receive the benefit of his wisdom without compromising my own decision-making. John, of course, continued to complain about them both.

"What are you moaning about?" I would ask him. "You were the one who wanted them there. Their positions are supported by voting shares anyway, so there's not much that you can do about it."

I was beginning to assert my independence in both my personal and business lives. My secretary, Doreen Hunt, was extremely sympathetic to my situation and helped me to find a place to rent. After imposing on Duke and Barbara for the last three weeks, I simply had to move on but this, ironically, led me back to my *alma mater* at Repton where my son Miles was now a pupil. I moved into a little house in the village but it came with many drawbacks – it was dark and dismal, too close to the school – and besides, I knew nobody at all in the area. It wouldn't have been so bad if Miles had been keen to see me, but Janet didn't want that to happen and did everything she could to blacken my name and discourage him. Everywhere I went I felt people were staring at me and talking about me. I was utterly consumed with the shame of leaving my wife. In 1980 this was a matter of social disgrace. My friends in Ashover stopped communicating with me, I couldn't go to the Sailing Club, I resigned my membership of the many charitable associations with which I'd been associated as I couldn't face attending their meetings anymore. I was left with Duke and Barbara and, of course, Michael and his wife Jane.

Alison continued to come down every weekend but wasn't able to move in with me. All her professional commitments were in London. It was then that I began to see that this great love she had for me was nothing more than a neurotic dependency. I had allowed it to overwhelm me as it had her, and I recognised that there was no future in it for either of us. I had acted precipitately in leaving Janet but, in a way, I was grateful to Alison for providing the impetus to do what I should have done ages ago. We shared a mutual infatuation but I guessed it would cease, and I would be left alone. I could never return to my former life and had to accept the prospect of life without love, without hope, without personal satisfaction. The future looked bleak.

For a while Janet clung tenaciously to the hope that I might return to her. She wrote, she phoned; she contacted me in the office and at home. Her pleas slowly changed from anguished persuasion to bitter tirades against me. I tried at first to reply to her letters and spent hours concocting replies that I knew would lead nowhere but to further letters, distressing us both. In the end I just stopped replying.

Work provided its own daily distraction but every evening, returning to Repton, would see the gloom descend upon me. I agonised incessantly over the causes of my situation. How could I have let my marriage fail so spectacularly? Was it me? Was it us? Was Alison to blame? What could I have done differently? I was caught in a trap of my own making and there was no one around to get me out of it. The severe depression I had known in my earlier years was recurring and I would just sit there, unable even to make a meal for myself. One evening I called Duke in desperation and he dropped everything to come over and prepare the ingredients of a dinner for me. He was so supportive and kind.

Of course, Charlie had heard the news and called me up. We had a long conversation and agreed to a meeting but nothing else. She was still attractive in my mind but now I was riddled with doubts about any relationship I might have with anyone at all.

I was to attend a seminar in London and drove down the night before to stay with Alison in her flat. I felt as dependent on her as she was on me but I knew that this was an addiction, not love. I didn't follow a word of the seminar itself, being wholly preoccupied with my dilemma, and that evening I returned to the flat and confronted Alison with the reality. The relationship was finished, I told her, and now it was her turn to feel devastated. We were both plunged into the deepest pit of despair and loneliness that two people can share.

I telephoned Jane, Michael's wife. She calmed me down and said I must come to dinner as soon as possible after my return from London. She and Mike had bought a nice old house quite close to Ashover and I accepted the invitation. For the first time in weeks, I was able to feel human again. Jane knew of my emotional isolation and obviously thought the answer was for me to meet another woman. At the dinner party she introduced me not to one woman but two, Michelle Foster and Jo Thomson. Now I'm not certain that any therapist – if I'd allowed myself the luxury of such advice – would have recommended this course of action. He or she would have recognised the cycles of depression and elation linked to my failures and successes in life, may have concurred that the oral cortisone I took to treat my asthma didn't necessarily help, but wouldn't have considered rushing into the arms of another woman as necessarily wise. However, over the next nine months, that's exactly what I did – with three different women. For a brief time, this lifted me out of my emotional doldrums but was destined eventually to cause me even greater unhappiness.

What actually happened was this. First, I became friendly and then intimate with Michelle. She lived with her two young sons, her husband having abandoned her and their half-converted house a couple of years before. She wasn't bitter, she just got on with life and I think she was one of the kindest and most deserving souls I'd met in life. I used to love to brush her long black hair but I don't think I treated her as well as I should.

Next, Charlie would pester to come over to my house at Repton. I gave in and we rekindled our former passion. Then Alison was constantly telephoning me and, of course, I foolishly relented and allowed myself to sleep with her too on occasions. All three women knew of each other's presence so I didn't feel I was deceiving anybody. At least I was now having fun – a great deal of it. I had no idea now of what constituted a permanent relationship anymore. Sex ruled, OK?

After three months of living in Repton I could stand the house no longer and managed mercifully to get out of the one-year lease. Charlie knew of another small property in Bakewell which she thought I could rent and this seemed a much better idea as I already knew the town and some of the people there. She helped me to move in to the six rooms on three floors, and I felt much more comfortable at last. Michelle helped me through my first Christmas there on my own. Janet made sure that I did not see my children.

Throughout this personal upheaval there was still company business to attend. As we moved into the 80s the profits continued to decline for reasons mentioned earlier; prices rises, VAT increases and so on. I could add nothing to our market re-positioning and we simply needed to build on our new foundation. The gross margin was up 10% and we ought, I felt, to be able to increase profits by the end of the 1980-81 business year. Peter Doyle had contributed much to our tempered success but others worthy of mention in the company's roll of honour at the time included Jim Nolan, Jamie Dodd, Peter Crook, Geoff Cliffe, Graham Tidman, Elliott Jaques, Lord Wilfred Brown, Peter Doyle and Dennis Stevenson.

I terminated the agreement with Mackinnon-Kent and transferred our business to another advertising agency that I felt was far more suited to our profile. Our shop redesign exercise was finished by a London firm called Fitch, and we began a systematic refitting programme for all our outlets. New stores were added and I even maintained the franchise operation despite the criticisms of it that had come from within the family. With John McCaul of our Management Services Department, we had identified one of the most crucial factors determining sales from any particular shop, and that was to do with the type and number of customers within the shop's catchment. Each store had to be profitable in its own right whatever the company's fortunes. No shop could be a 'passenger', subsidised by more successful branches elsewhere. It needed a minimum average turnover of £150,000 annually to be considered viable. John McCaul had looked at the sales potential of every town in the country currently without a Thorntons branch – a further 120 shops (if they were ideally located) and 300 franchises seemed possible before we reached full coverage – and, if turnover looked to be less than that magical figure of £150k, we would opt for a franchise opportunity rather than a new shop. We didn't sell the franchises conventionally but preferred to select only the best outlets and then sell our products to them at a high margin. This ensured profitability for us independently of the franchisees' own profits. We continued to review our entire network, ready to prune away the deadwood.

Forever on the lookout for sales opportunities, I noticed that no British retailers at the time were making much out of St Valentine's Day. Too close after Christmas perhaps, no real market for something so openly sentimental. Yet in the autumn of 1979, on a trip to the USA, I had seen the huge, red heart-shaped boxes that retailers were stocking up for the next 14th of February. If the Americans could package up all that hearts-and-flowers stuff, then I could see no reason why we shouldn't do the same. I took a chance and ordered a few hundred of these boxes to be sent over for us to fill with Thorntons' chocolates. They went on sale on Valentine's Day 1980 and sold out literally within minutes. I guess we needed to order them in the thousands for the following year.

Easter remained a peak period for us and then trading eased throughout the summer until October when we charged full-tilt towards Christmas. During the mid-year slack I tried other promotions, such as Father's Day, but these never amounted to much. We pushed our boiled sweet lines but with little enthusiasm from the customers. Ice-cream, however, went down a bit better and that added a little more to our summer coffers.

At Christmas the shops were packed solid right through to the last minute. There'd be queues out to the pavements on Fridays and Saturdays. The stores at the back of the shops would be stacked so high it was almost impossible to move. It was a joy to visit at this time of year, assuming you could actually get inside. No one minded the crush as the season seemed to bring out a jovial spirit in everyone. It all led up to the big phone-in on the last day's trading. Each manageress would telephone the area manager at the close of the day with the takings. Then the area managers had to telephone head office where a team of people was waiting to take their calls in great excitement. I had got the business of Christmas supply and demand down to a fine art and the goal was to sell out of everything a few hours before closing on that last day. Occasionally we got it wrong and had some stock left over, but we didn't ape those retailers who deliberately overstocked in order to have something to discount in the January sales.

The phone-in was fantastic fun. Four or five of us would gather in the office at about 7 pm on Christmas Eve to take the calls. I loved talking to the excited area managers who were bursting to tell us how well they'd done. There were sometimes disappointments and we'd spend a few minutes talking about why a particular target had not been reached but we didn't dwell on it. Most shops easily reached, and often surpassed, their targets and the senior accountant would always be on hand with his adding machine. What a way to start the holiday season.

The impact of our window displays was always under review. I even undertook a whole day's market research of my own when I positioned myself outside our Change Alley branch in Sheffield and painstakingly observed the behaviour of everyone who walked past. I noted who stopped to look in the window and who actually then went in to buy something. Amazingly, I discovered that a good 60% of window-shoppers then went on to make a purchase. Obviously, the displays were doing their job.

We found ourselves briefly considering changes to allow some degree of self-service in our shops. After all, it had become a fairly widespread practice in most other retail outlets. However, I recognised that our customers liked the idea of 'being served', that it led to a positive interaction between them and the assistant.

Many regular patrons would look forward to a bit of banter and it made the whole transaction more informal and pleasurable. People felt they belonged more to a club than simply entering a shop. I didn't like the idea of self-service.

Everything was a delicate balance and I tried to get some of my marketing concepts committed to paper. I covered theories about branding, display, advertising, anything that could add to a successful organisation. That old bugbear, inflation, was necessitating at least three price rises a year. One wondered when it would ever stop.

How did other large retailers manage through this difficult time? I met up with Mark Souhami, the managing director of Dixon's and also the marketing director of WH Smith and studied their approach. Perhaps we should model ourselves along similar lines. I had let Brian Leach go, despite his being Tony's chosen retail manager. In his place, I appointed Martyn Prowse, an experienced retailer whom I felt would be right for the job. At the same time I separated marketing from management and created a new department headed by Stuart Vause. A more conservative budget was in place for the company for 1980-81.

During the latter part of 1980, Tony was at last acting properly as a Chairman. Thorntons was nearing maturity as a company in its present format and would, according to our calculations, reach its practical limit in terms of shops and franchises over the next eight to ten years. Maybe we should now seek ways to diversify beyond the two separate greetings card businesses - 'Mary Morrison' in Scotland and 'Wellwishers' in Yorkshire. Neither of these was performing particularly well for us. In all honesty, the latter was a loss-making disaster and we were able eventually to sell it on to another company.

By the end of the year I felt I deserved a holiday, a chance to get away by myself, maybe go skiing and reflect on my year, particularly on the women in my life. I needed to sort out which of them, if any, was really the right person for me – or perhaps I could even find someone new. I recognised that my promiscuous lifestyle had its attractions that some would envy, but I knew I couldn't sustain such a *modus vivendi* permanently. There was excitement, yes, but nothing deeply personal and satisfying. Where was the lifetime companion who would offer me intellectual commitment as well as physical exchange to the exclusion of all others? Alison and Michelle were single and available, but Charlie was not. This was no way to choose a long-term partner. I found myself idly drawing up a score card on the three of them, rating their plusses and minuses on a piece of notepaper from the Hotel Steffani in St. Moritz, how romantic.

However, upon my return, I received a phone call from Charlie which put everything on hold for a while. She had resolved finally to leave her husband in the following May. Here was the promise of security I needed but did she mean it? Anyway, I decided to ignore the other two on my list and wait for the outcome of Charlie's decision. In the process I committed myself to several months of celibacy although this was far from easy. I had kept in touch with Jo since that first meeting at Jane's dinner party but I kept everything on a level basis. The understanding was that we were just friends, nothing more.

But then Charlie *didn't* leave her husband when she said. Now the separation wouldn't happen till September, she told me, but curiously I was starting to be a little doubtful. In between, I did something decidedly reckless when, after leaving the Sailing Club one day, I took a corner too sharply near the entrance to Chatsworth Park and skidded the car into a large tree. I'd had half a lager at the club but I don't think that contributed to the accident. It was more my spirited mood and I was probably going a little too fast for the conditions. I sustained a heavy blow to my head and felt very dazed. The only person I could think of to rescue me was Jo who lived nearby in her cottage in Bakewell and she took me over to Newholme, the small local hospital on the outskirts of the town. Yes, they confirmed, it was a minor concussion. Best to stay in bed for a couple of days.

Jo took me back to my new home in Baslow and settled me down. I'd recently moved there to *Dunraven*, a flat opposite the Duke of Devonshire's Cavendish Hotel and, if I looked out of my bedroom window, I could see across to the famous House in the distance with its majestic Emperor Fountain reaching up to the sky and the wooded hillside beyond. My solicitor, Bertie Mather, insisted on calling the flat *Dunravin'* which may have been more appropriate for me but not for the property.

Jo and I stayed in touch and I firmly intended that we should keep our relationship platonic for the sake of Charlie. But early one Sunday morning she called round and told me she was off to buy the Sunday papers so we could sit and read them together over a cup of coffee. I'd not yet quite woken up, even when she returned with the papers, but I soon livened up when she took them into the bedroom, undressed and climbed in with me. This was an unexpected way to start the day, especially as I'd had no foreknowledge of her intentions. We had been, as they say, just good friends. Now we were lovers, and we were to remain so.

Of course, none of this eased my insecurity and guilt at leaving my wife. I missed my home, I deeply missed my wonderful children and, yes, in a way, I still missed my old life. I often thought about going back. After all, now I had no proper home of my own, very little money to live on, and a deep sense of failure over my marriage. Yet I couldn't return to a relationship that simply wasn't right for me, had never been right. Things had taken an unexpected turn with Jo but I was very, very wary of the future. What was I to do about her?

Chapter 12

...Into the New World

It's impressive the way that money flows in when you get things operating properly. In late 1980, because of the repositioning of the business, we'd been generating cash so fast that Tony, now responsible for the investment of surplus monies, had taken advice and decided to invest £731,000 into US dollars at the extraordinary rate of $2.30 to the £1, equivalent to $1.681 million – a more normal average rate is about $1.60 to the £1. Because of the very high interest rates he was then able to invest it at 18.5%, in other words $310,000 per year for doing nothing.

Having bought these dollars, the next question was what should be done with them? Tony's preference was to capitalise on the advantageous rate and keep them, investing them in America to make an even better return, but I thought that would be difficult to achieve. He considered starting an investment company but was advised by our accountants that we could be charged personally by the Inland Revenue for tax. However, if we had a trading business with an investment sideline we could avoid all that. This, together with our ideas on diversification, prompted

Tony and me to re-visit the United States. He was already fairly familiar with the American retail confectionery scene and believed that we had the experience to do well over there. We were all very proud of our company and saw it as a sophisticated business. Success was assured. What a naive thought!

I was concerned that Tony shouldn't be left to do this on his own. He'd already had ideas about buying European companies but he'd had rejected those in the face of our corporate doubts. Now that I was on good terms with him again, I didn't want him to suffer a similar rejection. I saw that the retail business was running well and could do without me for a time, so I arranged to accompany Tony to assess the possibilities for us Stateside.

We met at Heathrow Terminal One ready to check-in for the TWA flight to John F. Kennedy airport in New York. As money was at last very plentiful in the company we decided to treat ourselves and travelled business class which, if nothing else, helped to reduce the check-in time. This was my first flight in a 747 and we were ushered to two large and comfortable seats in the front section of the jumbo plane. It was quite exciting being served high quality meals and drinks whenever we raised a finger. For six hours we left the reality of phone calls and business meetings behind and it was wonderful. I was feeling a warmth towards my brother which I hadn't known since those early days working together at Belper. How extraordinary this is, I thought to myself. Here I am, at the age of 47, after all the arguments, disagreements and long silences, sitting next to my older brother and feeling this fraternal bond. Perhaps I shouldn't be so inclined, I wondered. He's made many mistakes, caused me great difficulty in my business life and yet I still feel good about him. Maybe I ought to be wary and not allow myself to be lulled into any hasty decisions which I may come to regret.

We chatted lazily as people do on aeroplanes, trains and at cocktail parties, just small talk to pass the time. We wanted to be friends, to say nothing offensive or challenging to each other. For the first time in ages I was relying on him, still the senior partner, to do something positive in America, to make sure everything was organised properly.

"What are our plans once we get to the US?" I asked him. "What have you arranged?"

"Oh, we're going to spend a couple of nights in New York to get over the jet-lag. That'll give us time to have a look round at the retailing scene. Then we're taking a flight up to Chicago where Tom Smith will meet us at O'Hare Airport and get us to our hotel. After that, we can discuss visits to various shopping malls."

"Well, that sounds all very enjoyable, I think. How are we getting into New York itself, and what hotel have you booked?"

"I'm getting a bit fed up of airport buses, trains and all that struggling through the subway," he admitted, "so I thought we'd go one better and take the helicopter. We're staying at the Ritz Carlton on Central Park. I've been to the Ritz in Chicago and that was great. So I guess this will be, too."

This is ironic, I thought. Here we are, lavishly spending all this newly-acquired money and how exactly have we acquired it? Mostly by *my* efforts, but why worry, it sounds exciting. "How long do you think it'll take us to get there?" I asked.

"About 15 minutes from the heliport at JFK to the one in downtown Manhattan, then it's a cab to the hotel."

This sounded a great improvement on my last trip to New York when I'd used the airport bus and stayed at the Grand Central Hotel to be kept awake all night by shunting trains and police sirens.

"Who's this Tom Smith? Tell me more."

"He's a senior partner at Ernst and Whinney in Chicago," Tony replied. "They're accountants but he's actually a lawyer and he specialises in Mergers and Acquisitions."

"I see. How did you come across him?"

"He's a contact of Gordon Brammer's, you know, the friend of mine who's done a great deal of work in America. He has a factory here."

"He should be good then, if Gordon's been using him."

"Yes, I'm sure he will be. By the way, do tell me. How are you managing on your own these days? Are you all right? Do you get to see the kids? And what about your social life – do you have one?"

I looked at him. "I can give you three straight answers," I said unequivocally. "No, no and no! And, compared to this pathetic flat I'm living in, the Ritz-Carlton is going to be a very welcome change."

As usual, it was rather intimidating entering the United States. We queued for half an hour to go through immigration and waited behind the customary yellow line where bold notices left us in no doubt that we were not to cross it until we were told to do so. Eventually we came separately to face the Immigration Officer with his mandatory interrogation about whether we'd ever had anything to do with the Communist Party and all the other national obsessions. Having satisfied him that we were not undesirable aliens, we stood for an eternity at the luggage carousel awaiting our bags. At this point, everything changed. Following the signs to 'Helicopter Transfers' and 'Helicopter Check-In', we handed over our cases, stood to be weighed and were then whisked off to a large Sikorsky helicopter. Every seat was taken and mine was beside the pilot. He gave me a pair of headphones and told me not to touch anything. We lifted off vertically, then tipped forward and accelerated very quickly towards the distant night-time Manhattan skyline.

The pilot was talking to air traffic control. *"JFK – this is helicopter November 301 Uniform Delta – departing your field for Downtown Manhattan Heliport."* This was exhilarating stuff, although it was actually my second chopper flight. Still, a quick hop from Belper over to Manchester hardly compared with this as the lights and skyscrapers of the Manhattan skyline loomed up before me. We banked, first to the east then back to the west, as the pilot pulled on the cyclic control, lowering the collective at the same time, and shifted his feet on the pedals. The machine tipped back and forward as we gently descended to the eastern tip of Manhattan Island with its brightly lit heliport. We hovered over the big H and touched down. The two jet engines slowed and stopped and that was it. We'd landed.

We exited the aircraft, walked into the Arrivals lounge and then out to a yellow cab. I could hardly catch my breath. "Tony," I gasped, "that was absolutely stupendous. I simply must learn to do that myself one day."

We arrived at the beautiful Ritz-Carlton overlooking Central Park. My room was luxurious in the extreme and large enough to accommodate ten people. We had a sumptuous meal and I forced myself to stay up till 10 pm, mindful that it would have been the middle of the night back home. The next two days were spent walking around shops in central Manhattan and in various shopping centres, taking in the metropolitan atmosphere. We paid particular attention to their candy stores.

As planned, we then flew on to O'Hare Field in Chicago where Tom Smith was waiting for us at the barrier.

"Hi, fellas!" he greeted us with his Midwestern lilt. "Great to see ya! Let's walk you out to the car park, then I can drive you to your hotel." We followed this pleasant well-built man who must have been about 60.

"How far is it into the city, Tom?" I asked.

"Oh, no more than 18 miles. Won't take long on the freeway."

I could soon see the tall buildings on the skyline which indicated downtown Chicago. One building stood out quite clearly above the rest and was topped by two huge aerial masts.

"What's the tall building, Tom?"

"That's the Sears Tower, Pete."

"Wow! Now *that*'s impressive," I said. "I'd love to go up that."

"Well, you're in luck, Pete, because that's exactly where we're going later. We're having dinner there tonight at the private Metropolitan Club on the 66th floor."

We'd not yet set foot in the city and already things were looking good and I was sure we'd get a lot of great business ideas too.

"Just how high is the Sears Tower, Tom?" Tony asked.

"1,725 feet to the top of the antenna. You know, even without the two aerial masts, it's still the highest building in the world. It was only completed seven years ago so that record is very new."

Tom drove us first to the Chicago Ritz-Carlton, another magnificent multi-storeyed building in which I had my customary palatial room. He told us that he'd collect us at about 6:30 to take us to his club. We soon discovered that the hotel was adjacent to a magnificent shopping centre, Water Tower Place, a very busy and quite upmarket affair, sadly without a candy store.

That evening we took one of the Sears Tower elevators and, with Tom, we were swept up to the 66th floor and into the Metropolitan Club. The huge restaurant section had an enormous glass wall stretching from the floor to an almost invisible ceiling and we were quickly seated at a window table to look out upon the tiny dots of cars and people moving way below us. I recalled a similar sense of isolation from the real world when I'd been in Salt Lake City but our attention was soon focussed on the excellent food brought to us. After that we began our business discussion.

"I've crossed everything out of my diary for the next two days so that I can show you two around the place. Tomorrow I'd like you to come to our office to meet a couple of people who might be helpful. One is Jeff Ross of Lehman Brothers who will be very good at handling investments for you, and the other is a very bright young lawyer friend of mine, Steve Slavin. Then we can take in some of the region's shopping malls so you can see what retailing possibilities there might be for you here."

We had a fascinating evening learning about the US business scene and discussing equally important matters such as golf. Later, as planned, we met both Jeff and Steve and began what was to become a friendly and productive business relationship.

Tony and I returned from this trip exhilarated by the exuberance of these Americans with their get-up-and-go attitude. It seemed that our best way in would be to get hold of an existing company so, by April 1981, after one more visit across the Atlantic, we gave Tom Smith a list of six companies and asked him to check whether any were interested in being sold to us.

After a time we'd heard nothing so we decided to go see these companies for ourselves. We flew back over and it was then that I started to get a bit worried about Tom Smith. Clearly, he was an absolute charmer and first-rate salesmen but he hadn't found out whether any of these companies were actually for sale. When we turned up on their doorsteps we found that their buying prices were astronomically high. Two of the companies were making no profit at all, one was already bankrupt and another was making a meagre profit. I was horrified at the prospect of being saddled with some tiny loss-making company in Hicksville, USA and paying a fortune for the privilege. I really couldn't see the other directors buying this particular idea.

We rejected all but one of these companies, but Tom then asked us to look at a manufacturing and retailing company in Missouri which might be on the market. This was a different kettle of fish altogether. It was profitable, well managed and had many positive things about it. Tony and I decided we'd like to negotiate and did some quick but detailed calculations. It seemed that $2½-3½ million was about right for it. We'd been commissioned to offer up to $5 million on a deferred deal by the directors. I felt extremely nervous about this but Tony went ahead and made the proposal anyway. It turned out they were after $10 million so we were very firmly rejected.

After further visits, investigations and rejections elsewhere, we ended up with a very short list of just three more hopefuls. The first of these was Fannie Farmer in the East, another was Fannie May based in the mid-West and the third was See's based out on the West Coast. The latter was already securely owned by Warren Buffet's organisation Berkshire Hathaway and therefore unavailable, Fannie May was an excellent business but also off the table, leaving just Fannie Farmer as a potential purchase but, after spending a week in the New York apartment of Ernst and Whinney poring over the accounts of the company, I wasn't so sure. I even visited their factory and several of their shops but came to the conclusion that we just wouldn't be able to make this business work for us.

We'd got nowhere. After all the travelling and discussion we were no nearer to acquiring an overseas company. I was beginning to think we'd be just as well promoting our own brand name instead. We were paying enormous fees to all these professional advisers and this was swallowing up what interest we were making on our investments. We were even being charged consultancy fees for having lunch with our adviser.

There were several points in favour of starting our own retail business in the US. There was a growing acceptance of the quality and variety of European food imports including confectionery but nobody yet was taking the trouble to market it effectively to our American cousins even though they showed great enthusiasm for anything British. They delighted in our accents and wanted to know more about the 'old country'. We knew we had a unique quality product with a 'European' profile and felt that the US market was just crying out for something like this at appropriate prices.

Campbell's, the famous American soup company, had bought Godiva, a one-shop confectionery retail business in Brussels, and were beginning to market their chocolate at $15.50 a pound. The local confectionery companies were selling it at $5.50, so I calculated that if we were to sell our *Continental* at $7.50 a pound then we could make a 60% margin and still be at a price befitting an imported European product. After all, an imported 'semi-lifestyle product' wouldn't be creditable if it was too cheap.

John and I were still Joint MDs dividing my retailing from his manufacturing and management services. My side of things was well under control with excellent managers in place and everything clearly understood. This freed me up to be over in the States working, or so I assumed, on the best interests of the business there. You can imagine how bothered I was when I heard that John had been making decisions in my areas of responsibility while I was away. I had to go and speak to him about this.

"Now look here. I'm still in charge of the retail operation, aren't I? I'm not really happy about you deciding things and changing them behind my back. If I happen to be away and you want to alter anything then please wait until I get back and talk to me about it." To me, this seemed fair and reasonable, and I wasn't expecting his reply.

"Quite frankly," he retorted, "this arrangement with us both as Joint MDs is just not working. It ought to be changed and it's obvious that I should be sole Managing Director."

Oh no, I thought, here we go again. Each time I make a good job of something John tries to take it off me. I could feel my anger rising.

"I think it's perfectly all right as it is," I protested. "The retail side's working extremely well now, surely you acknowledge that? I anticipate a brilliant year ahead after all the changes I've been making. My time in the States is not for myself, it's simply to protect the company's interest. I need to make sure decisions don't get made which may harm our prospects."

John started to get equally irate. "But it's impossible to do things when you're away so much. We need to do things *now* and we can't wait until you get back. I'm going to bring this up at the next meeting and insist that it's really time we changed the arrangement."

"I've had enough of this, John," I said. "It's always happening to me. I put all this effort in for the sake of the company and then it's all taken away from me! My achievements count for nothing with you! You expect me continually to start over with something else each time."

"Oh, and another thing," John interrupted. "I just can't work with you. I've told you before, I just can't bear it."

"Oh, come on now," I said, getting really annoyed with him. "That's your problem, not mine. I fail to see why I should have to give up *my* job just because you don't like 'working with me'." I made it sound pathetic and ridiculous, as indeed I felt it was.

"Oh, that's true. I admit that either one of us could do the job in its entirety," he conceded, "but if *I* don't do it then I'll have to leave the business. It's you or me, but not both!"

"Well, that's up to you, John. You have to decide what you want. Why not give up what you're doing at the moment and go over yourself to the States? Perhaps *you*'d care to explore some marketing possibilities for us. I'd be more than happy to stay here as sole M.D."

I hid my apprehensions about the true assessment for the year 1980-81 which was not yet yielding the outstanding results I'd hoped for. I knew that these things take time but I could sense a general belief amongst the other directors that maybe I was responsible for the temporary sad state of affairs and I suspected that John was doing everything he could to encourage such a view.

"Well, I'm certainly not going to do *that*," he said. "I couldn't bear the idea of spending all *my* time in the States. It's no use. If we can't persuade the other directors to change the MD role then I'll have to leave the business."

The meeting was held a few days later and John stuck to his word.

"I propose that the company should have just one Managing Director and that this should be either me or Peter. If it's not to be me, I shall leave the company – but I will still need my current level of salary to be paid by Thorntons."

I then put forward my point of view. "I see no reason for any change at all. Everything is working perfectly well as it is and there is no operational need to alter any of it."

John then made it personal. "Quite honestly I can't bear to work with Peter. There's no way I can get on with him."

"I have no problems at all like that," I pointed out. "All I can suggest is that if John feels that way then perhaps he *should* leave the company after all."

Tony was anxious to resolve this but totally failed to appreciate my position. "I've been very impressed with the job that Peter's been making of assessing potential companies in the States. I think therefore that he'd be an extremely good Group Development Director. I feel he should take on this role and give up being Joint MD."

Why, oh, why did I always try to make such a good job of everything? It would be much better if I failed from time to time. As before, I felt obliged to agree to Tony's suggestion but it was no compromise and I immediately wished that I'd not done so. We were stuck in a pattern whereby I'd be placed in yet another disorganised situation, would sort it out and then John would somehow manage to take it over from me. I'd no wish to see him forced out of the business even at his own instigation and, yes, I suppose I could accept the challenge of a new responsibility, especially if it had an entrepreneurial dimension. Anyway, John's attitude meant that there was practically no alternative. If this wasn't a family business things would have been sorted out more rationally. The possible expansion into the US would be more thoroughly investigated beforehand, but it seemed that each of our decisions was affected by the dynamics of our relationship as family members and the frictions and tensions that existed between us.

Why should I have been worried about John? His threat to leave the business seemed no more than emotional blackmail, especially as he was demanding to be fully paid even though he wouldn't be working for Thorntons anymore. You'd think I'd welcome his offer to leave, but it wasn't that simple. I was irrational and emotional where my younger brother was concerned and the blackmail worked every time. I still felt protective towards him and couldn't imagine what he'd do in the big world outside. And obviously the company couldn't justify paying him for doing absolutely nothing. There was no alternative; there was *never* an alternative, other than to put his interests ahead of my own.

The 1980-81 results came out in September and, against earlier expectations, it turned out we'd had an absolutely brilliant year. At £2.22 million our profits had almost quadrupled. It was perfectly obvious to me that this was entirely due to the efforts of our managers and workforce and to the steps I'd instigated on the advice of Peter Doyle. He was delighted, the management was delighted and so were our employees. People outside the company knew of our success and phoned us up to offer congratulations. Sadly, I received not one word of thanks from any of our directors. It was as if they'd never heard of Peter Doyle or the work that we'd done together. And, in future company discussions, this golden time was never mentioned again as though it had not really happened.

Peter Doyle wrote a case study on the whole exercise which he used on courses for the Institute of Marketing. He would ask me to attend to present the facts to the participants and I often got applause for taking such bold actions with our company. The study was used in universities all over the world and was printed, though without our permission, in an American book on marketing.

Towards the end of that year, now that I was the grand-sounding Group Development Director, I got together with Tony to devise a plan for opening our own retail stores in the US. I noticed a Crabtree & Evelyn shop in a shopping mall which looked very 'English' so I found the name of the designer. He was Peter Windett, based in London, and I commissioned him to provide some ideas for a period-style store for us with emphasis on a 'British' image.

Tony contacted a few competent mall operators and we were offered a perfect location in the Water Tower Place, the mall we'd visited on Michigan Avenue in the centre of Chicago. You'll recall that it had everything apart from a confectionery store. We were also offered a second shop in Woodfield in the city suburbs and decided to take them both although the latter proved to be a poor location and my estimates of turnover were over-ambitious.

Nevertheless, each store was fitted out, rather chaotically in the event, and cost us twice what we'd originally expected to pay. There was a lot of hassle and work for our staff but eventually the Water Tower Place shop opened on 2nd October 1982 and the Woodfield shop about two weeks later.

My original concept was that we should have a mid- to upmarket business and that we would exploit this imported European image in the design of the store and the packaging. There was nothing to compare us with in this area at the time, so no real competition.

Mike came with me for the opening and again I used the Ritz-Carlton. We'd employed Thom Meschinelli to be our American Vice President and General Manager. We could access the shopping mall directly from the hotel and we stood back to view the shop as we reached the top of the escalator. It was beautiful, too beautiful we soon realised. It was very quaint with lots of etched glass and mirrors, and the assistants were dressed like waitresses in an English tea shop. Gordon Jewkes, the British Consul General, cut the tape for us and we let in our first customers. Unfortunately, soon after opening, we realised we'd overlooked several potential problems which were to impact upon our overall success. More effective market research would have revealed that the footfall in these malls, that is the actual number of people passing through, was much lower than we'd anticipated so the opportunity for impulse purchasing was reduced. The smaller paned windows reduced the impact of our displays and the overall design of the stores should have been more subliminal. Perhaps we overplayed the Englishness too much at first.

Back at home, my divorce had finally come through. Under the financial settlement I had to give Janet the entire house even though I was still paying a rather large mortgage on it. There was maintenance to pay for our three children. Fortunately, I had retained my shares in the company but I now had negative capital coupled with crippling outgoings so I was not in any position to buy another house.

Janet remained unco-operative about access, and it took me and my solicitor a full twelve months before I could negotiate a meeting with the children. By then, of course, she'd ensured my image in their eyes was wholly negative and they remained uncomfortable with me for many years.

On the plus side, Jo and I were consolidating our relationship. She was bright, good fun to be with and we shared many interests. I remained unsure about whether or not I wanted this to be permanent and I felt an instinctive caution which was not customary for me. Clearly, the stress of the divorce and the hassles at work were having a deeper effect on my psyche, and it was Alison who suggested that I may benefit from some psychiatric support. To this end, I met up with Ben Blom, a gentle Jewish émigré who lived, impractically for me, in north London and with whom I had many counselling sessions. He provided that sympathetic ear I needed, discussing my symptoms objectively. I spoke to him of my ongoing dilemmas but nothing was ever resolved, and I continued to drift closer to a committed relationship with Jo. In September 1982 she came with me to Italy for a week in a beautiful hotel on the coast near Salerno. Our time there was so wonderful that it seemed ridiculous, on our return, for her to go back to her little house and me to my flat. The inner voice whispering into one ear said that it would make perfect sense to live together; the voice in the other ear said, hold on, perhaps she still wasn't the ideal partner you're seeking.

My working life now was divided equally between the USA and Derbyshire, spending two weeks at a time in each before jetting off back over the Atlantic. This was not the exciting business life that some may imagine. The flights were long and tedious and the jet-lag seemed constant. It wasn't as if I lived next door to Heathrow and could just hop on to a plane. Regularly, after my return flight, I would be faced with a further two hours' delay for an internal flight up to East Midlands airport to get back to Derbyshire. Sometimes it was quicker, despite having arrived on the overnight 'red-eye' flight, to drive myself back up the M1 when clearly I just needed to fall into a bed somewhere. To then go straight into my office at Belper was simply asking for trouble and one day I suffered a total relapse through exhaustion.

I still had my new role to keep me busy and I drew up a new Corporate Marketing Policy in February that year. It differed from its predecessor in one key aspect by dealing with the acquisition or creation of new businesses in other related fields. This was adopted by the Board and meant that, in addition to running the American business, I was now on the lookout for other manufacturing and retail concerns, in areas such as bakery. Our own production facilities at Belper and Sheffield were already reaching the limit of their capacity even though sales of chocolates and chocolate boxes for Christmas were still increasing rapidly. Accordingly, John started scouting around for more factory space. We had a series of meetings to discuss this over the summer months of 1982.

At the first of these meeting John made an announcement.

"I've come across a large piece of reclaimed coal-mining land at Swanwick near Alfreton. It's about six miles away and is owned by the local council. The company could get this at a very attractive price and I think it would be a suitable site on which to develop a whole new production facility."

He looked around to gauge our response. No one spoke, so he continued.

"This would be a much better alternative than trying to develop new production buildings here at Belper. It would also allow us to have a 'state-of-the-art' plant, much more efficient and hygienic than the present set-up. I'd like your agreement to go ahead with this deal."

"What is it all going to cost?" Stanley asked, this being the primary issue in everyone else's mind.

"I am proposing a budget of £4 million for the whole development."

Now then, I thought to myself, how can I be tactful here? This goes counter to everything we've ever done in the past.

"I have to say I'm opposed to this idea," I said, and proceeded to outline my objections. "Our business has been extremely successful so far on the principle of buying adjacent land, keeping factory costs low by using and improving existing buildings, buying second-hand machines to re-build and adapt. That's how we've always done things – maximum use of our assets to keep costs low. What you're proposing will reverse that principle in one fell swoop."

John turned to me. "We really have to get out of this site. We all know how old some of these buildings are. Logistically, it's a nightmare, hygiene is difficult to maintain, and everything could be made much more efficient if we moved to a new site where things could flow through smoothly, all on the same level."

"Yes, but a project like this will eat up far more money than originally budgeted," I explained. "We'd probably use up our entire surplus cash and end up having to borrow a great deal. It would severely limit our potential to spend on other projects and we've all agreed that diversification is sorely needed."

"Then what do *you* suggest, Peter?" he asked, barely able to disguise the irritation in his voice.

"I think we should consider the possibility of buying and converting an existing building somewhere, not necessarily here, possibly in an area where there is high unemployment and where grants are available. But before that, have we thoroughly checked all the possible alternatives here on our current site, perhaps putting up another facility or buying more adjacent land?"

"None of that will do," John said emphatically. "We need to look to the future. Efficiency, strict hygiene – those should be our goals."

"But this will tie up so much money in one big production unit, I insisted. "We'll become rigid and inflexible. How will we react to sudden changes in the business environment?"

John was getting impatient with me now. "You're just trying to impede everything. If we don't act soon, we'll lose this opportunity and may never get the chance of another."

"So what do you propose we do with *this* place?" I asked, gesturing to the buildings around us. "It'll become completely redundant and therefore of little value."

"Oh, not yet," he replied. "It'll be a long time before we stop using it altogether."

"Anyway," I added, "we've not actually given any real thought to whether we should continue to make every single product ourselves. It seems to me the only things we really need to manufacture here are those items we couldn't possibly obtain from anyone else at the same cost, you know, the products where our methods and recipes are to remain strictly within our own control."

"Oh, we could never allow anyone else to do that!" agreed Stanley.

"On the other hand, we have to think of our reputation with the customer. I'm not certain but I would think that most customers have a higher regard for our products because they know and trust that *we* make these ourselves. We don't just licence them out to any Tom, Dick or Harry to make for us."

"Yes, yes, I'm sure that's true," Stanley agreed again.

"In other words," I continued, "I think there's a whole lot of things we ought to consider before we make a decision as big as this."

"We'd better leave it to another meeting," suggested Tony.

I then carried out some research of my own and obtained a list of buildings which were currently available at low cost and presented it at this later meeting, but the properties were all dismissed as unsuitable, too far away or whatever.

John appeared extremely annoyed by what he saw as my obstructive attitude and he persuaded the Board to go ahead and adopt his proposal anyway. Accordingly, the new site was purchased and a planning application made. I thought this was a grave error at the time and feared that there were many negative implications for the future of the company.

For a long while I'd had the sole services of my superb secretary, Doreen Hunt, but when John and I became Joint Managing Directors it had been agreed we should share her. One day, shortly before one of these important meetings, I'd been discussing some work with her when John came charging into her office and threw some papers down in front of her as if I wasn't there. Doreen immediately looked flustered and upset.

"Hang on a minute John," I protested. "We're in the middle of a conversation here. Please have the goodness to wait till I've finished. We'll only be a couple of minutes."

John stormed out again.

After this, it became obvious to me Doreen couldn't be expected to work jointly for two masters and so, with the directors' agreement, I interviewed some new secretaries. But when I returned from my next trip to the States I found a note from Tony saying that I was not to go ahead until the matter had been discussed further.

A few days later we had an impromptu meeting. It was Wednesday 2nd June 1982, and Tony, Mike, John and I were present to discuss a paper I'd put forward entitled 'Growth Strategy'.

John had not arrived for the start so we filled the waiting time by talking about our salaries. We'd just had another very profitable year and were considering paying ourselves much higher salaries. Traditionally, we'd received relatively low remuneration when company results had been poor or worsening, but profits had quadrupled now and it seemed reasonable to award ourselves a comparable increase, particularly in the light of the new lower tax rates.

John eventually arrived in a very irritable mood. Tony asked him what the problem was, assuming it was some management issue.

"Look, I've just come back from holiday," he glowered. "I have a mountain of work to do and I don't like being called into impromptu meetings on my first day back."

This shows how little regard he has for the work I'm now doing, I thought.

Tony, as Chairman, said, "I've called this meeting to discuss an important document Peter has proposed in his role as Group Development Director. It needs us all to consider it and commit to it as we think fit."

"Yes, I know," said John, "but I'm far too busy to talk about such ideas at the moment."

Tony went on. "Well, we *do* need to discuss it, John, but just now we were filling in the time talking about our salaries. We think it's perfectly justified, in view of the current success, to increase them substantially..."

John interrupted him angrily. "If you're prepared to pay my salary and let me go and do something else, then I'm quite happy to do so. In fact, I would *like* to!"

The rest of us looked very puzzled at this remark and we assumed that he wasn't being serious, was he? I imagined that now he was Managing Director he felt it was unfair for him to have the responsibility of generating these high profits which were then paid out in salaries to all the family directors.

"Calm down, John," pleaded Tony. "I, for one, don't understand what's behind your statement. You don't really mean it, do you?"

"Yes, I do!" he retorted. "I'm fed up with being the only one who works flat out to generate profits."

"Well, you did want it that way, John," I reminded him. "You can't be too surprised." Turning to Tony, I said, "Can we now get on with the subject of the meeting, please?"

In order to calm things down, Tony asked me to propose a policy on salaries for the next meeting. "I also think it would be a good idea if everyone could write down their personal objectives within the company as they now see them," he added.

We all agreed to this, John calmed down, and we started to look through the agenda that Mike had prepared. I said to him, "Oh Mike, you haven't included the item about cost budgeting."

Because of my anxiety about the continuing and escalating fixed costs I had produced some proposals for a new cost budgeting system based on ideas put forward by Peter Doyle.

John got extremely angry again, turning red in the face and shouted, "The system will *not* work! All the Senior Managers think so and I don't have time to waste considering it. Perhaps in six months, but not just now!"

He looked round at the three of us. We were dumbfounded. What could we say? Then suddenly his expression changed and he stood up.

"That's it. I resign. I cannot be constrained in this way."

I didn't know what to make of these continual offers to resign. What was wrong with the man? Did he really not care whether he was in the business or not? Or did he feel in such a strong position that he could use this as a blackmailing tool to get whatever he wanted? I suspected the latter so I decided to call his bluff.

"Don't be ridiculous, John. Sit down." He did so.

We then had a silly argument about secretaries. This resulted in my losing Doreen, not being allowed to employ a new secretary and having to make do with an inexperienced individual who I didn't think would be good enough.

John then said that he was too busy and would have to go. We never did get to discuss my paper on 'Growth Strategy'.

All this was very threatening to me personally, and I really didn't want to contemplate how things would be if John took to treating the workforce in this same fashion. Maybe it was time to sublimate those feelings of 'brotherly love' and stand up to him. Perhaps then I might earn a bit more respect. I went on several occasions towards the end of 1982 to discuss my concerns about the immediate future – how could we maintain our improvements?, were costs being properly controlled?, what was likely to happen to our profit margin with the ongoing Swanwick project?, did we have a proper rationalisation plan for the shops? – but all he would say was: "No-one knows what this business is about."

Even though my father was now in his 86th year his interest and anxiety about Thorntons was not at all diminished. He would frequently misuse the power he so desperately clung to. One Monday morning in November 1982 I happened to be dealing with three simultaneous crises in the business, namely, a possible legal action against us in the States, a breach of our and Peter Doyle's copyright for the Case Study which had been published without our permission in America, and an unexpected large loss in one of the small subsidiary businesses. In the midst of this, Dad telephoned.

"Peter, I want you to go straight away to the Moor shop in Sheffield," he ordered. "The greetings cards are extremely overstocked and badly organised. You must go and sort it out at once."

"OK, Dad, I will sort it out," I promised. I didn't bother to explain to him on the phone why I could not do this immediately. Under the new arrangements I was now responsible for a small subsidiary business called THS (Thorntons Holdings Sheffield) which had originally been set up to hold certain freehold properties but we now used it to manage the large greetings card units we had in some shops. Tony's son James was working in this business and I had made him Managing Director so really he was responsible for it all, but shortly afterwards I called in to see my parents for a social visit and a meal, the first thing my father said to me was, "Did you visit the Moor shop like I told you?"

"No, Dad, I didn't. In the first place, *we* are now running this business, not you, regardless of your controlling interest with your shares – we can't be at your beck and call. And in the second place, if I'd done as you asked, I would have undermined James's authority as well as the Area Manager and the Retail Manager. Finally, I was thoroughly occupied with three other major problems and you can't expect me to break off in order do something of relatively minor importance."

At this the old autocrat in him exploded.

"I don't really care what you think! All I know is that the shop is in an absolute mess and something needs to be done about it – at once! James has no idea what he's doing. He's totally inexperienced and the Retail Manager is useless and John never goes anywhere near the shop!"

"*I* didn't introduce James into the business!" I protested. "I'd no idea he was coming in until after the fact. Even so, he ended up working for me and I've tried to do the best by him. He's been under great pressure himself because he's had no assistance and he's stuck in the middle, trying to create a new greetings card selling concept which, if you ask me, is very successful so far."

Father had no answer to this, so I continued. "I'm not surprised the operation's been unsatisfactory given the circumstances. I'm sure with time and help James is capable of getting it right. And if the Shop Manageress has any problems with it, she can always complain to the Area Manager or go direct to James himself who I'm certain will deal with it for her."

About three or four weeks later in early December I returned from yet another trip to the States and found a memo on my desk from John headed 'THS Greetings Card Franchise Division'. It transpired that Father had applied pressure on John to visit the Moor shop in my place. All this seemed at once typical but also unnecessary, solely a manifestation of the tortuous dynamics that existed within our family. Where things should have been straightforward business matters, for us it was always personal and complicated. I suppose I should have ignored the memo. After all, this was commonplace among us and I should have been used to it by now, but no, it upset me as it was probably calculated to do, and that night I lay awake into the small hours, contemplating my lot. Perhaps if I got up and wrote it all down, externalised my feelings, so to speak, maybe then I could see my way through this mess of relationships and family crises.

"What should I do about my father?" I wrote. "I have to stop him influencing John against me. So how do I do that? John will do whatever he pleases and it's quite impossible to stop him. I feel so resentful to know that he's 'gone behind my back'; I don't think I can speak to him any longer. He's been brought into the management which should never have happened, and I can't do a thing about it. There's just no easy way out of this mess for me. Here I am, now nearly 50, with years of desperate hard work behind me. I've lost my wife and my family, I've lost my home and most of my money through the divorce, and now I keep losing my job to my brother, Dad's favourite. So what have I still left? Well, there's always my business skill. I guess I shall have to look for other ways to use it."

That same November evening in 1982 I'd had dinner with my parents at their house and, in a rare moment of calm between us, I let slip that I was thinking of getting engaged to Jo. I later went over to her house and thought that I better tell her the same news. She was deliriously happy and the next day we rushed over to my old TA friend Mike Frampton at the jewellers H.L. Brown in Sheffield. We bought the ring and I also spoke to my three children about it. Their reaction was what you'd call 'grown-up' but hardly enthusiastic.

I was still beset with occasional doubts and apprehension and uncertainty but we went ahead anyway and rented a house together in Bakewell in time for Christmas. I tried to be coolly analytical about my feelings. "I have an emotional uncertainty about this relationship," I wrote. "It's not perfect but it is pretty good. I desperately need security. I either go ahead with it on this basis or I give it up and return to my little flat where I have nothing but utter loneliness." I chose to go ahead and fervently hoped it would bring a measure of stability to my life.

This was the time when I'd been reporting back to the employees on our overall progress since launching our American outlets. The two shops in Chicago had done well enough but nowhere near our original expectations. Nevertheless, this seemed to be a considerable achievement and had required a tremendous effort on my part, helped by Thom Meschinelli and others in our US and UK companies. We recognised that there were a few basic flaws with these stores, such as the shelving being too narrow to allow proper self-service and the display windows not being quite suitable for purpose, and we had big problems complying with the American food regulations which resulted in limiting the range of products we could offer. Getting the goods over from Belper to Chicago had been quite a feat, too, as we had to send stuff in deep-freeze air freight containers to avoid heat damage. All this was extremely expensive and my initial optimism turned out to be somewhat misplaced. We'd set up the Water Tower store on a budget of $300,000 but only received $200,000 in takings during that first year. The Woodfield store took in an even measlier $120,000. These figures were not the ringing endorsement I'd hoped for.

Chapter 13
Home and Away

It was good that I had finally decided to take the plunge and settle down with Jo. Our wedding was arranged for the 8th April 1983 at the Registry Office in Bakewell. A small number of close friends attended and my old chum Duke acted as Best Man. There was a short solemnisation ceremony in the little chapel of St. Elphin's School where Jo worked part-time, after which we all went to a celebration lunch at the Riber Hall Hotel near Matlock. It was a lovely occasion, a pleasant interlude in what was turning out to be my most traumatic year with Thorntons. Ongoing tension between the directors was making the business of planning and decision-making almost impossible. There were also increasing apprehensions on my part because the fact we were losing money in Chicago meant it was increasingly risky venturing to other American cities.

The year started pleasantly enough with a skiing holiday in Italy with my children. Sarah was now 19, Samantha nearly 18 and Miles 14, and we all loved the mountains, the brilliant blue sky, the crystal clear air and that liberating sensation of flying down the mountain slopes. They were already very competent on skis as they'd learned at an early age and I was the one having difficulty keeping up. This was the first time we'd been together since their mother and I had split up, nearly three years ago. Now, at last they were beginning to understand what had happened between us and our contact and communications began to improve from that time despite the obstacles placed in our way. My sincere hope was that they hadn't been too deeply harmed by what had befallen their parents.

Next, it was off to Puerto Rico with Jo to attend the convention of the Retail Confectioners International of USA. The RCI was the trade organisation of the prolific *Mama and Poppa* stores, run by Tom Sullivan whom we had recently met in Chicago, and we, along with a single Australian company, had been allowed to join as foreign members, thus justifying the 'International' part. The convention itself was undemanding, merely voluntary meetings each morning, so there was plenty of time to enjoy the beautiful weather, the comforts of the hotel and each other's company. After this Jo returned home and I went on to New York and Chicago.

However, things started to go sour early in the year when a special meeting was convened to discuss the future of the American operation and Thorntons Holdings Sheffield. These issues were weighing heavily on the directors' minds and I felt I was being put into an untenable position. I explained my frustrations and the reasons behind my actions so far. We all sensed that, as members of a family, we were trapped in ways that wouldn't apply to unrelated directors of a public company.

"So, coming to the point," I said, "what I really need is maximum co-operation from you all to make the American business succeed."

John immediately chimed in with another of his emotional interjections. "Look, we can switch Managing Director roles if you want."

"Oh no, that's not what I'm after at all," I said. "It's just that I feel my efforts in this direction are such that I should be awarded a personal shareholding in the business. That seems reasonable to me."

"*That* might remove *my* incentive to co-operate altogether!" replied John, churlishly.

"Listen," I said to him later when we were alone. "I don't want you thinking I'm unwilling to take the Managing Director job if you really want to give it up, but I don't think that you've thought it out fully, have you? You're just reacting emotionally."

"No, it's not that," he said. "The real problem is that there are three important people heading this company and the old adage about 'three's a crowd' applies. It's an impossible situation." The 'three of us' – John, Tony and me (Mike was safely out of it in administration) – were admittedly caught in an awkward triangulation. "But there's no need to worry about America," he re-assured me in a rare moment of apparent understanding. "I'm sure it'll all work out if you spend enough time over there. And if you don't want to do that, then to hell with it, I say. Shut it down, cut your losses and come back here. You don't want to spend all your life living in hotel rooms. And, as for a personal shareholding, I have no objections at all. However, there are still too many of us in the business, don't you think? Things would be easier if we were one fewer, but who do you think should go?"

"I actually agree with you," I pointed out. It had been some time since the pair of us had held such views in concert. "That's the central issue, isn't it? We can't really lose either Michael or Tony – they have too many important skills – so it comes down to just you or me, doesn't it?"

I'd already publicly stated my views on the impracticability of my own departure and I knew John had similar thoughts for himself. It seemed now as if, between us, we were strategically focussing our sights elsewhere – perhaps on Tony.

Tony himself was still pursuing the acquisition of a manufacturing and retail company in Wisconsin. The idea had come from Tom Smith but I thought I'd successfully argued him out of it. However, Tony phoned from the States in early March to say that he and Tom were still thinking along those lines and, if Thornton's weren't going to follow it up, then he might consider buying it himself. I now had to take this idea more seriously because, if he went ahead with the purchase, he would have to give up as Chairman, wouldn't he?, leaving an important vacancy which possibly I could fill. Did he mean it? Had he considered the reality of this idea? Would he later renege and slump back into his old frustrated ways?

Tom Smith had valued the Wisconsin business at about $3 million, I thought a little less. I wasn't keen to get too involved as I feared the plan would keep me out of the UK for too long, leaving

John in an ever more powerful position at home. When Tony returned from the United States even he wasn't as enthusiastic as he had been and was now more pre-occupied with issues such as his early retirement.

"We have to be much more logical than this," I told him. "It's about time we stopped trying to please everybody and concentrate on what is right for Thornton's. How do we get the best return on our assets and resources? You know, each time we're away, things are going off here which neither of us knows about. Things just sort of happen and John gets more and more powerful."

"What things?" he asked.

"Well, as I see it, he's taken complete control and is making whatever decisions he wants and taking whatever actions he likes. By the way, did you realise that if you buy the Wisconsin business yourself then it'll be difficult for you to remain as Chairman?" We talked further and it was clear that there were many potentially explosive issues arising

John called us all to a meeting in the middle of March on the subject of management reorganisation. No prior papers were issued and I'd had only the briefest of discussions with him but he suddenly proposed that we demote some of my long-standing and excellent managers and replace them with new ones for no good earthly reason. Placating them with the same pay, titles and terms and conditions but in lesser roles wouldn't compensate, I thought, and would only create the same sort of job insecurity that I knew so well, but most significantly for John, he would have extended his overall control through the new appointees. Naturally, Michael agreed straightaway with the proposals and Stanley didn't seem bothered one way or the other.

"Look," I pointed out, "yet again you're forcing me into a corner. If you do this, you'll cause irreparable damage to the positive culture we've taken years to establish. Production and performance will be bound to suffer."

Tony nodded in agreement at first but, as the discussion went round and round in circles, I felt myself becoming distanced further from the others. In the end, because the meeting had to close, I reluctantly accepted the proposals even though I shouldn't have. Unfortunately, I was off to the States again in the morning and still needed to get ready. I didn't leave my office till

9.30 that night and then at home I found I couldn't sleep. These ideas were preying on my mind and, in the small hours, I set down in writing my concerns and discontent at having accepted them. I'd been under duress, I felt, and I urged Tony to hold back any actions upon them until we'd all had a chance to discuss them further. I put the note on his desk in the Belper offices at 7:30 the next morning and set off for Heathrow.

Around 10 o'clock John called me on my new car 'radio-phone' and I could tell he was very agitated and angry. "You have no power of veto," he stated tersely. "You agreed with us yesterday and it should stand."

"I know, but I regret doing so. It was late and I'd still got four hours of work to do. You have to concede the subject was not properly introduced, was it? You gave me no prior knowledge of it."

John wasn't listening. "This is not good enough," he protested. "You can't do this."

"Well, go and talk to Tony then and see what he says. I'll phone you back in ten minutes and, if he agrees with you, then I shall just have to turn round and come back!"

I called as promised. They had talked and it was agreed that I should return. I aborted my flight to the US and began the long drive back to Belper. I found them both surprisingly calm. We all apologised to each other, they for not giving me notice of the plans and I for agreeing with them when I meant otherwise. We then had a constructive conversation out of which came the following consensus: we were wasting my resources and instead should spend up to £4 million acquiring a worthwhile business here in the UK to maximise the return on that capital; we would make a bid for the Wisconsin company and I would employ a manager with sufficient acumen to run it dynamically; and, most significantly, from now on we were going to pursue our goals objectively rather than subjectively. A further two hours were spent discussing the details of the changes.

"Well, I don't like specific parts of it," I had to say finally, "but you must run the business as you see fit. So I will *accept* rather than *agree*." The next day I returned to Heathrow and eventually crossed the Atlantic.

By the time I returned home late March I was very miserable. The management and staff in Chicago were receiving conflicting instructions from the designer, from myself and others including Tony, and I was in constant disagreement with him over it. He wanted to be involved, I wanted to please him but it all impacted on my ability to run the overseas business independently.

Tony and I continued to discuss various issues of contention. For example, we wanted to sort out the problems affecting his son James, but John kept bringing the focus back on to Tony himself. He was clearly agitated, and was manifesting some of the characteristics of my own situation.

"Tony is being so subjective and emotional. I keep agreeing with him just to keep him happy, but it's not what I want to do," he complained to me.

"That's a common problem in our business, John," I replied, thinking this was a bit of an understatement. "But, you know, he's under a lot of stress within the family, isn't he?"

"Yes, but we really need him out of the business."

"Sadly, I have to agree with you, and I'm not sure he'd be too unhappy about it if only we could make a good arrangement for him."

"A possible solution would be to buy him out," John suggested and we discussed how this could be done. Over the next few days there were many more discussions, together and separately, over the viability of the American arm (no one really wanted to see it go, but it hadn't proved itself yet), the possibility of acquiring another company closer to home, the tortuous dynamics of having four active directors and, most particularly, Tony's position as Chairman. We often seemed to be singing from the same hymn sheet but, just when I thought consensus had been reached, someone would change his mind or say something to the others in contradiction of what he'd said to me. This level of inconsistency and contrariness was enough to induce paranoia.

By the end of April 1983 my mood was forever swinging from optimism back to depression. Tony had made $200,000 on investments with our charming stockbroker friend Jeff Ross which would compensate for much of the trading loss. We'd found a more secure and satisfactory way to buy the Wisconsin Company and were asking our advisors to work out a deal. Tony proved me wrong by demonstrating excellent skills of Chairmanship at this time and I realised he was still too valuable to lose.

However, I was still compromised by him in my own decisions. He'd encouraged me to overspend on changing the Woodfield store. It was the wrong decision and I had to back-pedal and confuse everybody further. He was investing surplus cash in the American stock market which seemed risky to me. Our half-share purchase of the Wisconsin business would need at least half-a-million dollars down payment. If it wasn't for his continuing enthusiasm I would have dropped this project to concentrate on existing commitments.

My counselling friend Ben Blom had been aware of these mood swings and explained them as a partial consequence of jetting back and forth across the Atlantic. He took a piece of paper and drew a 'sine wave' with the word 'Euphoria' at the top and 'Depression' at the bottom, like so:

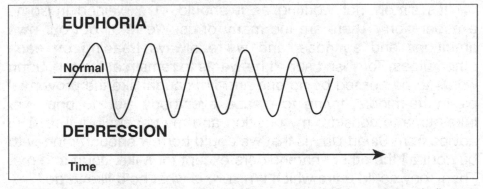

"When you feel yourself getting euphoric," he advised, "cut it off, don't allow it to happen. Try to calm yourself and you'll then find that any subsequent feelings of depression won't seem so deep. It's like a pendulum and you must try not to let it swing out so far. Eventually your moods will settle down and you'll not suffer such extremes in the future."

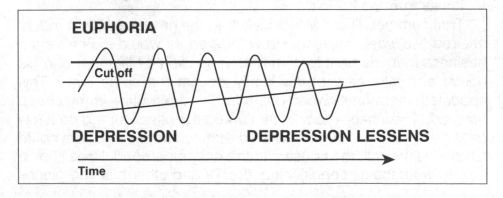

I thought of what he'd said and tried to control these feelings, at least when I was aware of them, and things did seem to improve for me.

However, we were getting no nearer to a resolution of our family squabbles. By June I secured an agreement that we would seek a management buy-in to focus control on ourselves as the younger directors, leaving Tony free to retire with some financial security. We approached Stuart Urry of the accountants Binder Hamlyn to take these ideas further, but when I informed Stanley, as of course I had to do ultimately, he immediately poured cold water on the whole thing.

"Why are you constantly squabbling with John and Mike?" he asked impatiently. "Here you all are, running a successful business. You're all very well paid and yet still you have to fall out with each other. What's wrong with you all?"

"It's simply not working as it should," I explained in some exasperation. "There are too many of us. We've all got our own ambitions and agendas, and we're always treading on each other's toes. Tony isn't sure if he wants to remain at the top, John wants to be bossed by no one and I'm caught like the proverbial pig-in-the-middle, trying to please everybody. Yet no one ever takes time to consider my position and my uncertain future. The advice from Stuart Urry is that we could borrow enough money to buy out all the other shareholders except for Mike, John and me. Then Tony could retire which I'm sure is what he'd like to do."

"Oh, I just don't understand any of this," he replied. "You're all being selfish. What about the wider family? They value their shareholdings immensely as it allows them to identify with the company. And how on earth would we explain all this to Norman? It would just about finish him off! And I bet you've not even thought about things like Capital Transfer Tax, have you?"

It was true, we hadn't.

That summer, Thom Meschinelli told me he was taking a much-needed two-week vacation. He wondered if I would look after the business management for him and, if so, would I like to live in his house and take care of the family dog at the same time? This appealed enormously when compared to the routine in my cheap hotel and I was happy to take him up on the offer. I turned up a few days before he was due to leave so that he and his wife Judi could familiarise me with the house and the neighbourhood. I was shown how to work the air-conditioning, the TV and other bits and pieces of equipment, and to get used to the daily routine of dog-walking. I noticed there was the large cellar, so often a feature of American homes, in which Thom stored all the packaging stock for the business, having room for it nowhere else. Judi prepared a lovely meal and we enjoyed a couple of bottles of wine between us.

I set off back to my hotel in Thom's company car, feeling quite cheerful about the prospect of two weeks in their very pleasant home. I had nearly completed my journey when I became aware of a car racing past with flashing lights and a blaring siren. Goodness, I thought to myself, this *is* rather exciting. Am I going to witness at first-hand one of those famous American gangster shootouts?

You can imagine my surprise when the overtaking car suddenly pulled sharply in front of me, forcing me to a sudden halt. Damned careless driving, what does he think he's doing? No sooner had the car screeched to a halt than two police officers leapt from it, brandishing revolvers. Oh my God, I thought, they must have mistaken me for some dangerous criminal.

The two officers rushed to either side and yanked open the car doors. I was grabbed by my left arm and pulled violently out of the vehicle. Both arms were then pinned behind my back and I was thrust forward on to the car's bonnet – or was that 'the hood'?

"What's this all about, Officer?" I asked, attempting a look of injured innocence befitting a stranger in an unfamiliar land.

"Have you been drinking, sir?" I was asked.

"Well, I've did have a couple of glasses of wine over dinner," I replied in my best upmarket English.

They frisked me for weapons and decided I was not armed. I was allowed to stand up but they still held their revolvers in readiness for that other weapon I undoubtedly had hidden upon my person.

"You were weaving!" said the first officer.

"What do you mean, I was weaving?"

"You were *weaving* all over the road. That's usually the first sign of drunkenness." Oh hell, I wondered, am I going to be breathalysed?

"Look, officers, I assure you I feel perfectly fine, not in the slightest bit drunk. Besides, I'm British, you see. I'm afraid I don't really know much about your regulations here." I was trying to sound as deliberately 'English' as I could.

"Hmm, well, that's not really any excuse, you know. If you drive here on our roads you need to know that it's an offence to be 'D.U.I.'."

"What's that?" I asked innocently.

"It means being in charge of an automobile under the influence of alcohol," he replied.

"All I can say to you, Officer, is that I'm not under the influence, as you put it, of anything. And I certainly hope that you're not thinking of arresting me or anything like that. I *do* have friends here in the British Embassy, you understand? And I'm sure they'd be able to help me out."

"OK, sir, if you insist. We'll let you off with a caution this time, but please remember not to drive when you've been drinking."

"Thank you, Officer," I said, hoping I didn't sound over-relieved. "I'm sure you're making the right decision. I am a very responsible British citizen, I'd like you to know."

With that I drove away very carefully, doing my utmost not to 'weave' anymore, aware of the two pairs of police officers' eyes keenly following me.

I soon settled into Thom and Judi's house and took the dog for its walk every evening as instructed. He certainly seemed to enjoy it. Early one morning the sky was so beautiful I decided to go for a run and thought that the dog might like to come with me. After running for about a mile I turned and realised the he wasn't with me. I stopped and looked round to see him sitting on the ground, panting heavily, some distance back. I jogged back to him and gently encouraged him to get up and follow me. "Come on, boy!" This he did, but he kept stopping and I was rather surprised to see that he couldn't keep up as I wasn't really going *so* fast. Usually, I was the one trying to catch up with *other* runners.

Naturally, I didn't bother to take him with me on subsequent runs, and I was very sorry to learn, several weeks later, that the poor thing had died from a heart attack. I secretly felt quite guilty about this and hoped that it had been nothing to do with my exercise regime.

Jo and I had had enough of the rented house in Bakewell and we managed to scrape together enough between us to buy a lovely old Elizabethan house back in Winster which I remembered so clearly from my time there during the War. The Dower House wasn't for sale as such but the owners were willing to negotiate privately and we agreed a price and moved in two weeks later. No survey, no fees, just a private transaction, So here we were, in this classical three-storeyed building at the end of the main street, when one day I received an unexpected phone call. Fortunately, I was alone in the dining room when I heard this female voice, English with a slight German accent, coming through the earpiece.

"Hello? Hello? Is this Peter?"

"Hello, yes. Peter Thornton speaking."

"Ah, Peter, this is Sonja. I'm calling you from Germany. Do you remember me?"

My heart missed a few beats just then. Of course, Sonja. No, I'd not forgotten her nor our romantic time together in Bremerhaven. Why, I suddenly wondered, had I not thought of her when I was in my emotional wilderness?

"Sonja, of course I remember you. How lovely to hear from you. How are you? What's happening in your neck of the woods?"

"I'm…well, I'm not very happy at all, but never mind that. How are you? And those lovely children of yours? They were so sweet."

"Well, I'm fine – and the children are all grown up now, you know. It must be….let me think…15 years since I last saw you. Your English is really good now. We always had to speak German back then, didn't we?"

"I know, but you see I didn't marry my dentist fiancé after all. The engagement finished a few months after I came back to Germany. After a while I met a soldier in the British Army and in the end I married him. But it couldn't last and I've been divorced about a year now. But that explains why I speak my English so well now!"

I was saddened to hear of this, and felt slightly put out that she had not contacted me sooner.

"Sonja, you should have told me when the engagement was over. You know I always loved you very much."

"I know, Peter," she said kindly, "but you *were* married and I was ruining it for you."

"I only wish you *had* ruined it," I said ruefully. "I actually left Janet three years ago and now we're divorced. But tell me, how did you get my phone number?"

"Well, after *my* marriage broke up, I longed to see you and your children again so I came over to England to find you. I spoke to your old neighbour at Over Asher and he found the phone number for me."

"Sonja, this is all very strange, but I don't think it was 'meant to be', do you? It was probably just as well that our affair finished when it did."

"Oh Peter, I really did love you," she implored, "and now I regret things so much."

"But it's all too late, Sonja," I told her. "I've been on my own for three years, and now I've just re-married. And I have to say that I'm very happy with my new wife."

We ended the conversation with a few further pleasantries and I put the phone down, feeling quite disturbed.

"Who was that?" Jo wanted to know as she came into the room. I'd already told her about Sonja and she was rather bothered by this call out of the blue. It took me two or three weeks to forget about it.

To make matters worse, we then heard that Charlie and her husband had bought a house just a few doors away from us here in Winster. They were going to convert the old shop at the end of the terrace back into a house again, but why on earth would they want to do that? Admittedly, it was a good deal in property terms but there were several others equally good that were not directly opposite *us*. Was she seeking to spy on us? Was this a sinister plan to unsettle me? Surely not, but I couldn't help wondering about it. Strangely, our paths never crossed until the occasion of her daughter's wedding when I had the chance to ask her quietly what had prompted the move to this street.

"It was such a good deal and we liked the place."

"Hmm, really," I said.

As the year went by Tony was still thinking about retiring, but that was all. None of our ingenious ideas to compensate him fully satisfied. It took until the end of September before we all finally agreed to the details of his leaving. He would resign on 31st October 1983 from all companies except THS and his pension would be funded by the company from the age of 55 the following year. His voting shares would be sold to me, Michael, Stanley and John who was further entrenched in his belief that he alone should be king of the castle. I felt things had gone on long enough and decided finally to "have it out with him".

It was the 4th October 1983. I sat down in his office. He was already looking very agitated. My opening remark was not calculated to help him.

"I think you're trying to take over everything, aren't you?"

"On the contrary, it seems that *you* are the one trying to take over everything," he countered. "And I know why. It's because you feel insecure about the US business, am I right? I wish you'd stop thinking that your position depends entirely on the success of that!"

"No, I don't actually believe that any more."

"We *are* going to make the American business work, aren't we?"

"Of course."

"Well, then," he continued. "I'll admit I may have been wrong about the marketing stance there".

"Perhaps you should go over there and assess things for yourself, then your arguments could be based on facts."

"Hmm, I really must do that."

"After all, we need to look at the bigger picture to assess where we may be several years down the line. The point is, there are three of us in this business, all striving to do what's right for the company. If you control everything and put all the company's eggs in one basket, it impacts upon what the rest of us are trying to do." I was thinking here of his current interest in the private confectionery business, Bendicks.

"Well, you become the Development Director," he suggested, "and then you can develop new projects such as that."

"I already *am* the Development Director," I reminded him. "That's actually my responsibility and you know perfectly well that I'm against such things. Just because something's for sale doesn't mean we have to buy it. It needs to be part of an overall plan before we start looking for those kinds of opportunities."

"Bendicks fits perfectly into Thornton's marketing plan," he insisted, ignoring the fact that this was his own Corporate Development Plan and nothing to do with Board policy.

"It's not the job of your Executive team to plan our corporate future," I argued. "The corporate future of the business is to be planned by *all* the directors as we've agreed."

This discussion was going nowhere. It was plain that John had made up his own mind and was going to do what he wanted regardless of any other decisions. Both Mike and Tony were convinced of his intention to strengthen his own power base at our expense. We agreed we needed to be much tougher with him, but how?

At a mid-October meeting where we were finalising the arrangements for Tony's retirement, John threw his own particular spanner into the works.

"I can't agree with this deal unless the rest of us find a way to sort things out between us. What if one of *us* is made to leave too? If I agree to these terms for Tony now, the opportunity for a decent deal for me is reduced."

There was an astounded silence for a few moments. Then Stanley spoke up. "You can't get out. Who would manage the development of the new factory and run everything?"

"Oh, there's no problem with that," I interceded. "I've run everything in this business before and I'm completely capable of doing so now."

"Exactly what are you saying?" asked Stanley. I repeated my words and Mike nodded in agreement.

"There is another way," said John. "We could go on the Public Market now."

"That's a very poor alternative," I replied. "You know that Dad would never agree to that while ever he was still alive."

Everyone except John accepted this. He insisted on his right to dissent and the meeting broke up without agreement on the settlement. Tony had specifically absented himself from the meeting for obvious reasons and was shocked and very frustrated when he learned how John had behaved.

"Why don't the four of you just agree my deal between you?" he asked when we were later driving to a company lunch in Derby. "You have a voting majority. You don't need John?"

"It goes deeper than that," I told him. "John will not accept anything unless he is in total control. We can agree as many compromises as we like but they won't work because he will prevent them from doing so."

"Who would run the company if John actually left?" Stanley asked Tony.

"Peter's quite capable. So is Michael."

The lunch was to honour a long-serving employee and was a surprisingly relaxed affair. It briefly took our minds off this insoluble conundrum, but on the drive back we were still looking for a way out of the morass.

"Look, let's phone Barrie Smith," I suggested (he was our auditor), "and see if there is any objection to us agreeing between ourselves to this deal."

I phoned Barrie from the car.

"Yes, you can do that," he confirmed, "but it'll have to be on the basis of a vote of no confidence in John and then he will have to resign."

He suggested a figure to offer in settlement but Stanley was still nervous about the whole thing, especially the new factory development. Maybe we'd have to keep on with Plan A which was to work as constructively together as John would allow.

Before I knew it I was back in Chicago once more. For reasons of economy I'd forsaken the plush Ritz-Carlton when I was there on sole business trips for a cheap motel in the suburbs, but when I had my fellow directors and executives with me I felt we should have the benefit of the city's downtown attractions. This area, forming part of the Lake Michigan waterfront, was a delightful spot and I would, when given the chance, join the early morning joggers along the shoreline. We had become known in the various restaurants there and were regarded almost as honorary citizens.

Chicago was justifiably proud of its Opera House, home to the famous Lyric Opera, on Wacker Drive. You would never guess from its undistinguished exterior but, once inside, you were in a centre of cultural excellence to rival any of the great opera houses of Europe. The Lyric Opera was able to meet its outrageously high costs of staging performances by the private patronage of its very wealthy benefactors and business sponsors, far exceeding the humble subsidies given to the likes of Covent Garden Opera by the Arts Council of Great Britain. This is how it was able to afford top international talent and to put on some of the most prestigious productions from the global opera repertoire.

Steve Slavin, our Chicago lawyer, was a member of the Lyric Opera and was keen to take us to a performance while we were there. Naturally, I accepted his invitation despite the fact that the scheduled show would be almost as soon as I'd touched down at the local airport after an 8-hour flight. My 'body-clock' would also be six hours ahead but it would be churlish, I felt, to decline on these grounds. Accordingly, after a quick shower, a bite to eat and a bottle of California Chardonnay in Gordon's, my favourite restaurant on North Clark Street, I went along with Steve to the Lyric Opera for a performance of Wagner's *Die Meistersingers*. However, despite having one of the best seats in the house, my natural weariness, combined with the darkness of the auditorium and the lengthy but beautiful music, induced an overpowering drowsiness in me. I'm of the opinion that Wagner can have that effect and I'm deeply ashamed to recall that I was probably conscious for no more than the first thirty minutes. Afterwards I apologised to Steve but he re-assured me that it was all right, he understood and, more importantly, I hadn't snored, even for a moment.

The Executives with me on this trip were Nigel Etchells and Jon Chidley. Nigel, a bluff Lancastrian, had been with the company for some years, originally as Property Manager although John had since re-appointed him as an executive in charge of retail, not, I felt, the most appropriate use of his talents. Jon Chidley, too, had been taken on by my brother to replace another of my appointees. In each case, the outgoing individual was retained but demoted. This was particularly annoying to me, but both men were pleasant company on this trip abroad.

We were taking breakfast together on the Monday morning after our arrival. The breakfast room at the Ritz-Carlton had a wonderful panoramic view of the city to the lake beyond. The breakfast buffet was an outstanding array of every conceivable food one might like to eat first thing in the morning with the obligatory pots of coffee and orange juice to wash it all down.

"Have you heard of the 'Retail Standards of Performance'?" Nigel asked me, innocently.

"Of course, I have," I replied. "I devised them."

"Oh, did you?" Jon joined in. "So what do you think of Thorntons US adopting a different market positioning to Thorntons UK?"

"Well, I'm more or less bound to agree with it, aren't I? It's my decision and my policy. I don't think it's any sort of a problem. The Americans won't believe that a quality imported confectionery range could be anything other than higher priced. They see it as a lifestyle thing."

It was not their fault, I suppose, but neither Nigel nor John had the slightest idea of the position I was in. I tried not to let their remarks bother me. Fortunately, there was no mention of Tony or the directors' jobs while we were away.

It was another matter as soon as we were back home. There, on the 24th October, was John's handwritten resignation, accompanied by his proposals on the financial deal for himself together with a possible alternative management structure. Two days later, we all gathered for yet another meeting. Stanley absented himself but the others were still suggesting their own ways forward. Tony wanted a compromise. Michael thought we should have both a Group Board and an Operating Board. I still sensed that John wanted to cut me out while he remained paranoid that I was out to 'boss' him. If only these energies could be directed into the business rather than into forever defending our own positions.

As before, we'd reached the point where we trying to iron out the details of Tony's cash deal. Perhaps we needed an Ironing Board! Suddenly John froze and looked remote. The discussion stopped and we looked at him quizzically.

"What happens if I want to get out?" he asked. "You know, I really would quite like to do my own thing."

"Well, that's OK," I said, "except the money you asked for was quite ridiculous, you know, far too much."

He froze again and became even more detached. Hell, I thought, perhaps I shouldn't have said that.

Afterwards I sought him out to apologise for my remark. He was clearly very upset.

"Peter, I'm terrified of getting locked in."

"I understand," I said, "and I'm very sorry. You know, if it really wasn't right for you I'd do my level best to get you the best deal possible."

We all met again the following day. This time Stanley was with us and we agreed the deal proposed by Michael with the caveat that I would be Chairman for a trial period of six months. Right, I thought, I can accept that. But how will John take it in practice?

As 1983 shuddered to an end it was apparent that we still hadn't got the mix right to suit everybody. There were several more heated exchanges. Tony came to regret the concessions he'd made and was quite unhappy about the THS deal. John continued to accuse us all, but me in particular, of trying to run things simply for our own benefit. He complained to Tony that we had all made financial sacrifices to fund his settlement. Poor old Michael was kept out of the loop on more than one occasion. We were all hurt by these stinging comments.

By the end of the year the real issue had become one of raising finance. Arguments shuttled back and forth over the relative wisdom of if and when to go public with the company. By trying to keep calm and remaining totally honest and frank we eventually reached the following agreements:

i)   Tony would resign with a suitable retirement package;

ii) I was to be acting chairman with Mike as acting vice-chairman;

iii) the acting appointments would be confirmed next April;

iv) the management structure and family directors' duties were to be as proposed by Mike;

v) and Tony was to remain as a non-executive director.

I thought the latter would be difficult and I also felt I'd have to keep an eye on John's move to go public in the New Year. This, I thought, would be terribly premature and ill-advised.

Dad and Stanley signed the necessary documents within a few days and things appeared to calm down dramatically. However, in January 1984, we discovered that errors by our pension fund managers meant that Tony's pension payment with its 5% escalation was far too high. We were forced to drop that clause which, not surprisingly, upset Tony a great deal. After all, this is what we'd agreed, but it was increasingly apparent that, in the family business world, agreements were often not worth the paper they'd been written on.

Chapter 14
Endings and Beginnings

"A way to rid yourself of anxiety is to use it as nervous energy in some physical activity."

This was Ben Blom's advice when I consulted him on the state of my life in early 1984. Everything was conspiring to induce in me a state of extreme anxiety. All the attendant issues – the relative difficulties with the US operation and my sense of personal responsibility for it, the promise to Tony for the company to 'go public' allied to the sheer impossibility of doing so while ever Dad remained implacably opposed to it – all contributed to this drain upon my nervous energy and confidence. Michael and John had differing ideas about how we should develop the American business – they favoured a cheaper, more down-market approach where I felt success would come from the more select 'lifestyle' approach – and I was concerned that cash reserves for the US company were falling dangerously low. I felt we needed further market research to determine the true position of the operation even while we were asking for loans from US banks to finance the opening of more stores. This was hard for me as I'd routinely been a cheerful and optimistic person, always achieving some measure of success in whatever I did professionally. I wasn't used to the idea of commercial failure and I was unsure of how to cope with it.

Meanwhile, the relentless routine of meetings and transatlantic travelling continued. Every fortnight Jo would take me to East Midlands Airport for the flight to Heathrow and on to the BA or TWA check-in for my economy class journey to Chicago. The airlines had not yet cottoned-on to the idea of over-booking so there were always plenty of empty seats. I would take my reserved place on the plane until I heard the doors closing and then I'd move to another spot with plenty of unoccupied seats around it. Although normally a social person I hated long conversations on planes with someone I'd never met before, preferring to immerse myself in documents and snoozing, though not necessarily in that order.

Arriving at O'Hare, Thom would usually pick me up in his company car and take me straight to the office over in Schaumburg. He was always cheerful no matter how difficult things seemed.

"Hi, Peter. How was the trip?"

"Not bad really. Not too busy – and not too many nosey-parkers trying to talk to me."

"Typical reserved Brit!"

"Not at all. I just don't like talking to people on aeroplanes that much. Anyway, how's the business doing?" I would ask.

"Not bad. Not bad at all, really. I think we're slowly getting regular customers and they all love the quality of the products. Toffee is a bit strange to them, though. It's not really known over here, so we have to train them to enjoy it."

We would go up to the office over a shop in 'the strip' and look at the sales figures after which he'd take me on to my usual cheap motel. Although it offered only basic and minimal accommodation there was at least a good bedroom with all the facilities, but no restaurant, just a do-it-yourself breakfast bar. Thom would return after I'd settled in to take me to a local diner where I was always overwhelmed by the choices on offer.

"What dressing will you have with your salad, sir?"

"What have you got?" I would reply, naively.

"Well, we've got Thousand Island, Blue Cheese, Italian, Ranch, Caesar, Vinaigrette, Cheddar, American, Hawaii, Spinach and Ham…"

"OK, OK," I would break in, "that's enough. Bring me Blue Cheese."

"What would you like to drink, sir?"

"Oh, just bring me a beer, thank you."

"What sort of beer do you want, sir?"

"What have you got?"

"Well, we've got Coor's, Beck's, Budweiser, Harpoon, Anchor, Blue Moon, Dixie, Root Beer, Lone Star…"

"Yes, that's enough. I'll just have a Beck's, thanks."

Totally exhausted, I would fall into bed at about nine o'clock with a sleeping pill and, if I was lucky, I'd sleep through the night. Next day we'd go to our shop at Water Tower Place. A beautiful shop, a very classy mall, very well looked after, I thought, but where were all the people? I estimated that there'd be four times as many in an equivalent location in Britain. Here, it was difficult to catch that 'passing trade'. The staff were very good, doing their best to sell to the few customers who did come in and slowly the store was increasing its trade. Then we'd go on to Woodfield, a beautiful indoor mall with fountains, waterfalls and lovely shops but even fewer people, and finally on to Oakbrook, an outdoor shopping area with wide open spaces and hardly any customers at all.

My flights back to the UK were always worse for being overnight but I'd still look for a seat away from other passengers where hopefully I could stretch out and get a bit more sleep. On one occasion I was awake and reading a book entitled *Nine American Lifestyles* when a middle-aged woman suddenly seated herself next to me.

"Hi," she said.

"Hi," I replied, never the great conversationalist of the air.

"That looks like a mighty interestin' book you're reading. I saw it from the other side of the cabin and I just had to come over to ask you about it."

This was a novel way of introducing oneself but hey, she was American, so what else could I do but reply?

"Uh, yes, it's a marketing book," I said, trying to be as uncommunicative as possible without actually being downright rude.

"How faaaa….scinating! Tell me all about it," she gushed.

I attempted a simple outline of the theme of the book. She seemed satisfied with that and proceeded to ask me all about myself, what I was doing on the plane, where I had come from, where I was going and so on. I hadn't prepared myself for such a personal inquisition so I tried to answer without giving too much away.

"Wow! You must be a very successful and intelligent guy," she trilled. Natural modesty compelled me to deny all. Then, "Are you married?"

"Yes, I'm happily married, I'm pleased to say. How about you?" Oops, gone too far, I thought.

"Oh gee, that's a shame. No, I'm divorced. About a year now," she told me.

"What a pity," I said.

"I thought that maybe you'd like to meet up in London. You see, I'm on my own now."

"Oh no, I couldn't possibly do that. My wife wouldn't like it, you understand," I replied.

"Well, never mind. Perhaps you might know someone else who'd love to meet a lonely and sexy divorcee in London?" she persisted.

Thinking that here was a way to get rid of her, I said, "Well, I do have a friend who might be interested so give me your business card and I'll pass it on to him."

She gave me her details and then, satisfied with her efforts, she heeded my suggestion to go back to her seat so that I could continue with my book.

It was now mid-1984 and I decided to implement another bit of Ben's advice. He suggested I needed to 'share the responsibility' more with my co-directors and, at the next meeting of the Operating Board, I told them frankly of all the current problems with the US business and made it clear that any suggestions would be greatly appreciated. John proposed a variety of promotions and I urged that we consider taking some extra outlets in 'higher sales' areas on the East Coast. I asked that a further half-million US dollars be invested to put the American business on to a more secure footing. At another meeting the appointments of myself and Michael as Chairman and Vice Chairman were made permanent, but the transfer of further monies into the American operation was vetoed, pending further calculations.

As for John, the period of sweetness and light seemed to coming to an end. He was still taking matters into his own hands, unilaterally deciding things and showing little patience for anyone else's suggestions. His conviction that we should lower prices in the States remained firm and, when Thom Meschinelli flew over in July to discuss our strategy, John simply took over the meeting and declared everything was *fait accompli* in his favour. We *were* going to experiment with lower prices and that was that. When I tried to extend the discussion he would exclaim airily that he had other things to do and would leave. I felt flattened by such behaviour and resented his giving direct orders to Thom who actually worked for me. I certainly didn't think we'd made a mutually acceptable decision about any of this.

Phase Two of the Swanwick Factory Development was set to proceed but we had to delay the machinery installation for a year. This decision was driven by major changes in Inland Revenue tax rules. We had to construct the building immediately or lose a lot in tax allowances. We also had to agree to borrow £6 million to cover both this development and our Christmas stock situation.

Against this background of acquisition and new business projects I proposed that we should now consider seriously the idea of retailing further afield and it was with some enthusiasm that it was agreed for John and me to visit Hong Kong and Japan later in the year. I'd already begun looking at the possibilities for opening up in France. I'd met John Hardcastle, a consultant based in Paris and Jersey who spoke fluent French, understood the culture and was very well connected in the French capital. John sensibly proposed that we should carry out the customary market research project to see how well the idea of British confectionery would go down with French focus groups. We accepted his quotation for a project to be undertaken using students from a couple of universities in Paris and left him to get on with it and report back to us the following year.

Tony had now formally retired at the age of 55 although he remained in the background as a very important voting shareholder. I wrote an article for *Sweet Talk*, the in-house magazine and made it clear that he was now a consultant. He didn't want any sort of retirement party even though I'd had a presentation silver casket, in the style of Thorntons' *Nougat Caskets*, made for him. I suggested instead that a small dinner party could be held, just for those with more than ten years service, but he flatly refused all my offers. I guess he was just too upset. Of course Stanley, at 81, and Dad, even older at 88, clung on to their positions as directors.

And what of Janet? Apparently, she now had a regular man friend and I believed that they were effectively living together despite her having stewardship of our old home at Bath House Farm. He, I gathered, was a farmer and there seemed to be no reason, as far as I could see, why she shouldn't move into his place with the children and sell our former property. In that way I would be relieved of the hefty maintenance payments. However, the lawyers told me that my children still loved our family home and wished to remain there, which is why Janet needed to receive maintenance from me on their behalf. This I understood, but it didn't do much to improve my own position. If only I could prove that Janet and Farmer Rob were now living as one they could be expected to move in together into his farmhouse and I could then stop the payments. This was quickly achieved and I soon heard that my beautiful old home was being sold to an old friend of mine who had always had his eye on it. The mortgage was paid off and the remaining substantial amount of cash went to Janet as part of the settlement.

This was indeed a perfect solution because Rob also had a flat in an old building over the road into which the girls moved while Miles moved into the farmhouse with his mother. I was saddened to think that my children were never again to live in their old home, but in other ways this was an ideal outcome. I particularly hoped that Janet, with her love of animals, could now find happiness on this farm with hopefully a more compatible partner. Also, it left me more directly able to help my children financially when they needed it.

Jo and I were still getting on well even though I was an absentee husband for much of the time. She desperately wanted a child and I was more than happy to oblige. Being in the States made this a little difficult but I would 'double my efforts' on those occasions when I was back home. This was a particularly harmonious time in my private life but then, in June, my father fell ill. He'd been a bronchitis sufferer for as long as I could remember, probably asthmatic as I was but made worse by his lifelong smoking. Antibiotics had usually kept the worst of it at bay but no longer. His faithful chauffeur, Eddie Unwin, had set up a bed for him by the fire in the downstairs sitting-room where he used to sit in bygone days and talk about the business. By October he had worsened and could no longer get out of bed. He lay, propped up with several pillows, and was well aware of moving into the final stage of his life. He told our mother that he was ready to go, he'd had his years, it was time to sleep, and on November 3rd, 1984, he got his wish.

Even though it was distressing to see him fading away, I tried to visit as often as I could during those last weeks, but afterwards I didn't feel a great sense of loss. For a long time now I'd been my own man and hadn't felt particularly close to him. My maternal grandfather, on the other hand, I had loved dearly. He'd been a gentle, creative, considerate person, and I was devastated when he died, but my own father was cursed with inherent emotional problems that prevented him ever from relinquishing control or delegating responsibility fully to his family. He'd established a fantastic business but clung to it with an iron grip long after he should have eased off and trusted his sons to safeguard the name and the company's fortunes for him. I sat at his funeral and hoped that we had already 'done him proud', as they say, but I doubt if he or his brother Stanley ever saw it like that. They were simply not made that way.

Father's passing, of course, signified much more than our personal family loss. For a start, it meant the end of the constant criticism of one director against another, his strategy of 'dividing and ruling' was suddenly removed. This was undoubtedly a relief to us all but it facilitated a re-focussing of our own attitudes and behaviours towards each other. More importantly, there was no longer so much resistance to the idea of 'going public' and the balance of voting shares was also changed. In a way, I felt I was even more vulnerable than before.

One thing my father certainly would not have done would be to use his voting shares to force me out of the business. He simply held on to his shares so that no one could sell the business without his consent, not to retain his authority to hire and fire. A settlement of his will was still 18 months away but clearly redistribution would create an imbalance of power which could lead to some very unfair and threatening decisions being taken by certain parties in the future. Tony, Michael and Stanley would each end up as majority shareholders. John would have fewer but equal shares with me. My position would be substantially weakened within the hierarchy.

As the year neared its end we were still searching for that elusive success in the US. We all agreed that the American market was a "a very tough nut to crack", but with persistence we felt that we could realise its potential excellence. We now had six shops trading Stateside: three in Chicago, one in Boston, one in Washington D.C. and one in New Jersey with a second N.J. location to open shortly. The parent company had eventually invested a sum of $320,000 to expedite the operation there, useful but not quite the half a million dollars I'd hoped for. Once again Thom Meschinelli was asked to come over to Belper to devise a new business plan with our US company accountant, John Lawson. This envisaged an eventual chain of about twenty shops to make the whole enterprise a successful concern.

By this time differences of opinion between John and me regarding the price positioning of the US company had developed into serious conflict. We had a meeting to discuss this question when we were over in New Jersey but couldn't reach any fundamental agreement. At that point John deferred to me and my calculations, but then demurred over the content of the report of that meeting. I challenged what he claimed to have said about the pricing policy. He was committing us to an unacceptable lower price structure and I tried to get him to change it. However, the report was then published along with this factual error. I sent a message to his secretary in which I pointed out what I assumed to have been a mistake, but at a mid-December meeting back home I noticed the error was still there in the report. I went to see John about it.

"I expected a memo from you to correct that misleading statement," I said. "Why haven't you issued one? Honestly, I'm getting very tired of this and I'll tell you straight. If you don't issue that memo very soon, then I will!"

He hardly lifted his eyes from his desk. "If you *do* issue a memo correcting the mistake, I will simply issue another saying yours is all b***s," he replied.

"That's not very helpful, is it?" I said. John then started to get angry with me.

"You don't understand the business at all," he shouted. "We should have a shareholders meeting about your remark."

John did eventually issue the memo, the error was corrected and the report was accepted. However, we still needed to discuss other aspects of the pricing policy and store locations among other things. So, on the following Tuesday, I approached him again but was not prepared for what followed. I remember it well.

There he stood, behind the desk in his large office, bellowing at me, red in the face. He was incredibly angry, shouting and swearing.

"Get out of my f*****g office! Just p**s off, won't you? You've made a complete mess of everything as usual! You overspend on advertising; you've wasted all this money on shopfitting and design…"

I tried to remain calm. "Now look here," I countered. "The effect of those changes back then was to make the best profit since 1974. I was returning the company to its former financial glory. Can't you see that?"

John continued shouting at me.

"You don't understand how the business works," he repeated. "It was going downhill when you were Joint Managing Director and all the other directors wanted to take you out of that job. You disagreed with me about the new factory and your disagreement delayed its start by six months."

"To be frank John," I said, still remaining calm, "it seems to me that, in the report of our meeting, you tried to trick me deliberately, simply to make it fit your point of view."

"That is totally unreasonable!" he continued angrily. "Of course I never tricked you or deceived you! I certainly didn't put that sentence in on purpose. I'm sorry about it."

Eventually we agreed that a 'low price' experiment would be tried in the new shop opening in January at Paramus, New Jersey.

Sales were well up in the original Chicago shops during the run-up to Christmas and the last two days before the holiday had been excellent. This was encouraging but served to underline the realisation that time was needed to build these business successfully. As the other shops continued to prove, success could not be established overnight.

While in the US, I got to know Peter Revers who had gone out from England on behalf of Laura Ashley, started their retail business in their first store and had been the company's President there. He remained a very successful 'hands-on' manager with his great retailing and merchandising skills and had built it up into a 400 million dollar business by the time he left in 1990. I had dreams of trying to persuade him to take over our American business but it probably wouldn't have been fair to ask him as there wasn't the attendant financial commitment from the UK that he would have been looking for

Sending our products to the USA was also a serious issue. The costs were high and dehydration during the flights was a constant problem, aggravated by the frequent delays caused by the FDA inspections. We considered having our own warehouse over there so that we could send stock in bulk by container ships. This led to a discussion on the possibility of an out-of-town retail outlet as a joint venture with Laura Ashley, possibly to include living and office accommodation. I promised my fellow directors and executives to investigate, but what could be done without commitment and money?

At the January 1985 meeting of directors John announced, "It's been decided to switch all our shops to self-service wherever possible. It's been shown that it leads to a much more efficient customer through-put."

Thorntons had held on to the concept of counter service much longer than most retail shops in an attempt to retain that traditional intimate and friendly atmosphere. I felt apprehensive about the change. There were obvious advantages but I thought that total self-service might change the image of the shop to the detriment of the business. It would become just another mini-supermarket with pre-packaged products and minimal personal service.

In September I was invited to assume the Presidency of the Confectioners Benevolent Fund. I was already the President Elect and it was agreed that Mike and I should attend the CBF Ball in London. I announced all this to our fellow directors but expressions of pleasure or congratulations were not forthcoming. However, another statement made by John was thought to be of great importance. Under the heading of New Projects, normally my preserve, he announced that he was working on a Forward Marketing Plan which was going to touch on many of those areas for which I was actually responsible. Again, he was trespassing into my managerial territory but I let it ride at that stage.

We next met to discuss the financial estimates for a Mainstream Business Plan to cover a five-year period commencing 1984-5. I was delighted to see the quality and ambition of this planning but was very concerned about the cash requirement, particularly as it would starve my own areas of responsibility of cash. Without diversification, such major expansion would come to a full stop when full store capacity was reached within the UK. Added to this, the development of the major new facility at Swanwick continued to cause anxiety as it swallowed up so much capital. The company's seeming inflexibility and John's unbridled ambitions contributed to my headaches and it is little wonder that some of this inner conflict was spreading to my relationship with Jo. Outwardly we were still very happy but I had a secret apprehension that some obscure difficulty was lurking just beneath the surface.

Against this background I was still trying to keep in touch with the main business by walking round the factories and by visiting the shops. In February I'd agreed to look at a possible new location for us on Princes Street in Edinburgh but I also wanted to go in the opposite direction to visit London. I'd encountered Peter Gorb, a charming man who taught Design Management at the London Business School, and we'd agreed that we would meet, with our wives, for dinner in the capital. The plan then was to fly to Edinburgh, spend the bulk of the day there and fly on to London in the late afternoon and have dinner with the Gorbs in the evening.

With Jo, I flew up to Edinburgh one afternoon and we had a very pleasant evening in an Edinburgh hotel. The next morning we visited our St James Centre shop in that beautiful city. While I was talking to the area manager I noticed, out of the corner of my eye, that Jo seemed to be instructing the manageress about the merchandising in one of the showcases. I didn't want to correct her while on the premises but as soon as we were outside I felt I had to say something.

"Jo, with all due respect, you may know plenty about display and merchandising, but please remember that you're here as my wife. It's definitely *not* your role to give instructions to members of staff, particularly when their senior manager is present."

She took this extremely badly and refused to speak to me for the rest of the day, not even on the flight down to London. We arrived at our next hotel with Jo in an extremely bad mood. This did not bode well for the evening ahead and I tried, without success, to lift her out of this ill humour. We went ahead with the dinner but the evening was completely spoiled and the Gorbs must have been quite disappointed. Sadly, we never met them again and I wasn't even able to call Peter to explain what had happened. Even more sadly, Jo and I now seemed unable to work together as a team, our period of harmony seemed to have finished and I began to realise the reasons for my original apprehension.

A Grand Opening for the new factory at Swanwick, now known as Thornton Park, had been on the cards for some time. Through Mike's influence in the county, particularly with the Lord-Lieutenant, Colonel Sir Peter Hilton, it had been arranged for Her Majesty the Queen to open the factory on the 15th March, 1985. The planning for this was done by a committee under Peter Heaps, the Operations Executive and the member of the new executive team for whom I had the greatest of respect. He was a very mature individual with considerable experience who had been taken on by John to replace my old friend and colleague, George Belfield. I had to admit that Peter, very independently minded, had the skills and training to carry out the much increased duties that the expansion now required.

He did a fantastic job of organising the whole event with its complex security and logistics. Only one chocolate enrobing machine was operational in the new factory so this left plenty of space for a complete grandstand to be erected for a thousand guests including staff. A budget of £50,000 had been set aside for the event and probably more was spent on the luncheon and entertainment. The royal visit lasted a mere half hour but was enough to show the Queen around the place and to make a presentation to her. As Chairman it fell to me to take the leading role. This was undeniably a very great honour for me but I couldn't help being aware of the irony that I had always been against this project, especially in the extent to which I had been sidelined by John over it. However, I did my best to live up to the duty bestowed upon me and spent many hours thinking about an appropriate speech for the occasion, ignoring any personal feelings I might have about it. When speechmaking, I usually preferred not to have anything written down, choosing instead to stand up in front of my audience with a host of ideas, phrases and situations in my mind, selecting those that seemed right for the moment. From my experience of other speakers, reading from a prepared text, it often seemed that they came across as remote from their audience and unaware of their surroundings. This time, though, I really couldn't risk such an informal approach and very carefully wrote out the lines and learned them, word for word, off by heart. I think it came over quite well but one is never sure of such things.

I spent a few minutes talking one-to-one with the Queen as I walked her to the podium and found her to be a very pleasant relaxed person, able to communicate extremely well. After all, that's what she does. It goes with the job. The occasion was deemed to be a spectacular success, thanks to Peter Heaps and his team.

Ever since the 'turnaround' exercise with Professor Peter Doyle, I'd been invited by him to take part in courses that he ran for the Institute of Marketing. He'd use the case study written with my assistance, after which I would then make a presentation to the students about what had actually happened. This was unpaid work but it was very rewarding in a personal sense. However, there had been some discussion in Operating Board meetings about directors appearing at functions to make speeches and so on. It was felt that advance approval ought to be sought from the Board as to the content of such speeches. It was with some reticence that I therefore asked about my next scheduled involvement with Peter Doyle and his courses. Agreement was reluctantly given on the following terms:

Peter Doyle course. It was agreed that there would be no objection to PNT participating, as previously, in the Marketing Course run by Peter Doyle, if he decided to do so. This involved the case study about the Company which was now becoming rather historic. It was expected that this would be the last time this took place.

Once again I had been put in my place. More fool me, I thought, for bothering to comply with this rule which, in my opinion, really shouldn't have applied to the Chairman.

John Hardcastle had now finished his market research in France and came to see us with the results. He showed us videos of the Focus Groups doing blind tests on confectionery from many sources, including our company. The French people in the videos could somehow recognise that our confectionery had been made in England and turned their noses up in very French gestures of disgust when they tried our products.

Cultural attitudes to food are very strong in France and, even where there is the presence of ethnic restaurants, their overriding preference is for French cuisine. The abhorrence of British confectionery apparently dates back to the immediate post-war years when, because the French confectionery industry had not yet re-established itself, considerable quantities of cheap British chocolate confectionery were imported. They bought it because there was nothing else but it was soon removed from the shelves when French companies started to produce the more popular indigenous products. The result was a national revulsion for British chocolate allied to their spirit of independence regarding all culinary matters. All else was automatically and disgustedly rejected. These videos, together with the thousands of questionnaires completed by people in the street, made it abundantly clear that it would be a disaster for Thorntons to attempt to retail in France.

Meanwhile, the picture from across the Atlantic was no more encouraging. The US operation was being seen as wayward, a badly managed subsidiary needing close control and firm action. There was great concern in the April 1985 meeting that the 'low pricing' experiment had been tried at the Paramus shop in New Jersey and had been a complete failure. This topic was not discussed further.

The following month Thom made his scheduled visit and yet again I was embarrassed by John's behaviour at our meeting. He arrived 75 minutes late and treated me with no more respect than before. I was evidently his subordinate and he continued to make statements that were not policy and which ought to have had prior discussion by the Board.

"We should put no more money into the US company." "You should cut out $100,000 of cost." "It's taking a quarter of our cash flow." He assumed that no-one else had sufficient intelligence to tackle the problems; he would not admit that he'd been wrong on the price strategy and lengthened and delayed the meeting considerably to the detriment of my own contribution.

A few days after this meeting, Stanley asked me to his office.

"Pete," he said, "I think you ought to go off and run Sayers in the States." Sayers was a large, once successful confectionery company but now in administration. I'd considered it once before and the idea of resurrecting it had given me the shivers.

"Stanley, you have me completely mystified," I replied. "Here I am, fulfilling an important role as Chairman. Why on earth would I want to go off to the USA on a permanent basis to run a defunct confectionery company that we don't own and are certainly not going to buy?"

"Well, it seems that there's so much conflict between you and John, and I thought, in the light of the new factory and John's importance in managing it, that it would be better for you if we bought Sayers and you could go off and run it."

"It's nice of you to think about my well-being," I said, "but I don't think that either Jo or I have any interest in doing that, thank you very much!"

After the June meeting, during which we had discussed improved methods of working together, John and Stanley suddenly disappeared to have a private conversation. John returned to announce, "Stanley and I both feel that there's a lot of dissent and we want to talk about it."

My heart sank when I heard this. Not again, I thought. What dissent?

"It's about 'Mary Morrison'," John continued.

"I don't understand. What about it?" I asked.

"I don't agree with our decision on these improved methods for working together," he replied, not answering my question, "and neither do the others."

"Then why the hell did you all say you *did* agree then?" I asked, dumbfounded. "I tried to be as open and unemotional and flexible as possible. If you'd all said you disagreed then I would have accepted that!"

"Mike was upset," he said.

"Well, it won't do him any harm," I replied.

Then came that old familiar line: "It's impossible for you and me to work together, isn't it? What do you want to do about it?"

"I'm perfectly happy to be Chairman of the company," I said. "I don't need any projects to keep *me* happy. Any future projects will be proposed completely on the basis of their viability. Alternatively, I'd be quite happy to be managing director, but I have accepted that's out of the question because of you."

He continued to press the point that one of us might have to get out.

"Well, the only way for that to happen would be to go public. Then we'd have to decide which one of us would go."

"Yes, on that I agree," he said. "It wouldn't affect Michael because the difficulty is between the two of us, isn't it."

Sadly, there was no denying the truth of that.

When I thought on what I'd said I wondered if I had left it too open for myself to be manoeuvred out. As far as I could see it, there were three possible options: John accepts and fulfils my policies on working together which we had just agreed, or we buy Sayers and he goes to run it which he said he'd like to do, or we go public and get financial ability to buy him out. This would provide long term security for the company from the money raised from the Issue and, in the event that this might happen, we'd already engaged the services of Nicolas Moy, the senior partner at Granville, the Merchant Bank, to oversee the arrangement. However, nothing further was said for the time being.

I thought it was time to canvass the views of some of the minority shareholders within the family and met up with two of my cousins who lived locally, Shirley Thurman and Rosemary Chambers. They were extremely proud to be associated with the company and wished to retain their investment. They would like to have some say as shareholders but had no desire to change the current management. They disliked the idea of the voting shares being limited to just a handful of individuals. It seemed they preferred the company to stay private or for Stanley's daughters to have more voting shares or perhaps create a trust with carefully appointed family trustees. They believed that if we did nothing then it would be very likely for the voting shares to fall into the wrong hands, a less attractive outcome than having all shares enfranchised.

Although the Dower House was a big improvement on the small rented house in Bakewell it still had its serious disadvantages, particularly the lack of space for Jo's children to be on their own. It had been difficult at first for them to accept me and vice versa, and this was part of the conflict arising between Jo and me. For this reason I felt we should move somewhere else. I was also missing my former home in Ashover that I had so lovingly converted and wanted desperately to recreate that sort of environment. If I could find another dilapidated farmhouse like Bath House Farm we could start over again.

I had managed to increase my capital by investing borrowed money in 'call options' on US Treasury bonds at a time when interest rates were falling dramatically. This was an extraordinarily risky thing to do but worked perfectly at the time, leading me to think of myself as an investor of some genius, an impression which I later learned to my cost was altogether erroneous.

I was driving along my usual route to work from Winster to Belper. Passing through the village of Wensley I observed a very run-down farm building standing well back from the road on a small hillock. Immediately I noticed two things: it seemed to have a magnificent view to the south, and, more pertinently, there was a 'For Sale' sign at the top of the drive. Instinctively I broke my journey and turned off to inspect this property.

The place was deserted and I was able to walk round to the south side of the building to confirm that indeed the aspect was splendid. There the house stood, on its slight elevation, in this commanding position above the fields, each delineated by the familiar dry-stone boundaries, leading down to the Derwent in the valley below. The town of Matlock could be glimpsed in the distance and beyond it, the brooding presence of Smedley's folly, Riber Castle, whose imposing outline stood sentinel-like over all.

I turned round to look at the building before me and was persuaded that it would be ideal for conversion. At once I knew I must buy this property and went to the agent's office in Bakewell. The house was due to be auctioned in two weeks time and I asked for details and the guide price. The entire site consisted of about 40 acres divided into separate lots and I told Jo all about it when I got home. I didn't heed too much her apparent lack of enthusiasm which, in hindsight, was another error on my part.

I then telephoned Andrew Sebire, an architect of some talent with whom I was acquainted. I described the property and asked him to visit it with me to consider the potential for, and the cost of, a suitable conversion. Upon seeing the place he was as enamoured as I was and, on being unfairly pressed to estimate how much would be required to turn it into the place of my dreams, he came up with the very loose figure of £70,000. This convinced me to offer an equal sum for the house and the six acres surrounding it. Thus, I figured, I would acquire a wonderful new home for a mere £140,000.

I couldn't go to the auction personally as we were hosting a meeting with some VIPs from the States at the time. I asked another agent to bid on my behalf and found my mind drifting constantly from the meeting to what I imagined was happening at the auction. What, in fact, did happen is that the agent exercised the latitude I allowed for him to go slightly above my bid price and consequently he purchased the property for me for the sum of £75,000.

Previous experience had taught me that conversions always cost more than I anticipated, in the case of Bath House Farm, three times my original budget. With this newly-acquired Field Farm it turned out to be only twice as much and I did end up with a beautifully-designed house, a wonderful ambience within it and spectacular views around it. The conversion took nearly a year and we needed almost as much time to sell the Dower House as the market had gone into one of its regular periods of decline. The Winster property had few viewings and we eventually sold it at some loss. But no matter, we now had a perfect home to share, with space for the children and everything seemingly idyllic. Doubtlessly, Jo must have been content with it?

Her response was terse. It was beautiful but she would rather be back in Bakewell.

Chapter 15
The Big Rumble

Dora Fleetwood telephoned me at the Dower House one Saturday morning in late June 1985. Her husband Trevor, a long-standing and loyal servant of the company, was manager of our toffee department. Dora was dreadfully distressed.

"Trevor is too upset to speak to you and didn't want to bother you," she sobbed, "so I said I was going to call because I knew that you'd do something about it."

"About what, Dora? Whatever is the matter?" I asked her, genuinely perplexed.

"Don't you know about it, Mr Peter?" she asked. "Trevor was told on Friday afternoon by Peter Heaps that he was being made redundant and would be leaving on the 19th of next month. Is there anything you can do about this?"

This was certainly news to me. Trevor was one of the stalwarts of the business and I was personally shocked.

"I'm afraid I can't tell you anything Dora. I didn't know about this but I'll try to find you out for you and I'll call you back."

I telephoned John Culverhouse, now the Personnel Executive.

"Trevor Fleetwood is a nuisance," he said. "He really has to go. The best thing is to advise him to see John on Monday morning and try to get a better deal."

"He's a nuisance?" I asked, nonplussed. "I never found him to be a nuisance; I thought that he was a very good man. Anyway, you can't make someone redundant just because they are a nuisance."

"Why don't you get him to talk to George Belfield?"

"How about *you* talk to him?" I suggested.

"Oh no, he and I have a bad relationship. I'm afraid that wouldn't work."

I phoned Dora back but this time Trevor answered. "I can't understand it," he said. "I feel guilty but don't know what for. What have I done wrong?"

I didn't wish to burden him further by repeating all this 'nuisance' nonsense and simply said, "I've no idea, Trevor. I'll try to find out more on Monday."

I let him carry on talking for a while. I knew this would help.

"I had a first-class appraisal six weeks ago," he reminded me. "I'm saving the company thousands of pounds. How can they possibly manage the job without a manager? George hasn't the time to do it. Besides, I'm 53 now; I can't possibly get another job. I've been with the company since 1952. That's 32 years, did you realise that? I came over to Belper at Thorntons' request to start things off. I can't possibly manage on what's been offered me. I've just bought a new car and….oh, I feel so ashamed." I could picture him at the other end of the phone, his head drooping in dismay.

"Well, at the moment I can't really help you, Trevor, because I don't have any of the facts," I said, trying to sound as sympathetic as I could. "I understand what you've told me about your appraisal but that doesn't really count for anything if it's been decided your job is no longer necessary. I'm afraid that's what redundancy means in its literal sense. But I'm with you on one thing. I don't see how they can run the department without a manager."

I'm not sure Trevor was actually listening to me. His mind was overwhelmed by the distress and ignominy of it all. "All Belper is talking about it," he confessed. "I was in the supermarket and this woman said to me, 'I hear you've been sacked'. I didn't know where to put my face, especially when she said, 'I thought

Thorntons was your life'. Dora told her in no uncertain terms, 'He *is* Thorntons'."

It was true that Trevor was a well-known figure in the town of Belper and word would quickly get round.

"The grapevine will soon pick up on this and it'll not do the company's image any good," I told him.

"It was so unexpected," he said, still lost in his own thoughts. "I had absolutely no idea this was coming. Peter Heaps called me in 'for a chat' on Friday afternoon and said, 'We've come to the end of the road, Trevor. We have to make some changes. That means we're going to make you redundant'. I was completely shattered. I would rather have resigned than be treated like this."

"I can quite understand," I said.

"Please don't mention to John that we've spoken," he urged. "I'm scared about what else may happen."

"You needn't worry about that," I reassured him. "I'm merely the Chairman now, you know. I'm not in any executive role."

"Yes, I know that," he replied. It was plain that he simply needed someone to turn to at this critical moment in his life. I shared his distress but mine was compounded by the inability to help him in any practical way.

'Thornton people' – this phrase would apply to just about everybody who had ever worked for us – had the name of the company written on their hearts. Each to a man, and woman, was dedicated to what they thought of as 'our business'. They spoke of 'us', they were proud of their contributions, whether in the factories or the shops or the vans or the offices or just cleaning the floors. Most people never forgot their experience of working there. To them, it was not just 'any old job'. If they were suddenly dismissed, as Trevor was, the hurt would stay with them for the rest of their lives.

The following Monday brought young James Thornton into the office to see me.

"When are you going to issue a statement?" he demanded to know. "And what are you going to do about it?"

Once again, I was completely in the dark. "Do about what?" I asked.

"Well, is it true that we are going bankrupt? Because that's what everybody thinks."

"What absolute nonsense!"

"I'm not so sure," he said. "Morale is at its lowest ever, people are totally confused and no one can understand what's going on. Everyone is terrified, and the danger is that the good ones will leave along with the bad ones. You've got to explain things to them."

I admired him for coming to talk to me about it, but pointed out that John was the one to be urged to take the appropriate action. I asked John to come in and listen to what James had to say. He stood in the doorway, obviously displeased, and remained silent. Clearly, he had no intention of doing anything.

"I believe what you've told me, James," I said after John had gone. "Thank you, and I assure you it'll not rest at that."

I followed after John, mindful that he now was running the business and therefore could only challenge the manner of his actions, not the decisions themselves.

"Look, John, I accept that you have a right to do what you're doing, but let's not destroy totally all we've created. Whatever's happening, you need to inform people about it as soon as possible."

He looked at me. "I'll do something by the end of the week."

"No, that's not good enough," I said. "People need to know now!"

"The insecurity will do them good," he said without a trace of compassion. "Besides, there are more things to be done yet."

He was evidently determined not to do anything to ameliorate the situation today. I had no choice but to stand by and accept his stance.

"The company has reached the depths of despair and despondency as a result of recent events," James reported to me later. "It's not the action itself but the way it's been undertaken. Everyone agrees with reducing inefficiency but no-one understands the reasons for the dismissals. Therefore they invent reasons, and rumours spread. People are meeting in little groups and there is even talk of unions and so on. Everyone believes that Michael and you have no idea what's going on. The only secure ones are the executives because they are fully informed. The rest believe their jobs are under threat but they're terrified to do anything in case they're wrong. It used to be a company that cared for people but that's all changed. It's just a joke now. It started with the dismissal of Cynthia Linton. People are thinking that if *she* can be made redundant, then no one is safe."

This is desperate, I thought to myself. The culture of the company is at risk. I need to be fully in the picture. Talking to John is hopeless, but positive action is required from *someone*.

At home that same evening, I mulled over what I could possibly do to help my colleagues. I was due to go back over to America the next day but I didn't want to leave with all this on my mind. Michael was away on business in Scotland and I tried, through his secretary, to get hold of his hotel number. I also called my own secretary, Doreen, and told her I intended to put up a notice which I had just written out. She was very apprehensive about my doing this. "Don't you think you ought to talk to John first?" she suggested.

"Yes, perhaps you're right," I concurred. I would leave a note for John and then phone him from the airport to see if he would allow this notice to be displayed.

So the next day, Tuesday 25th June, I did everything as planned and set off to East Midlands Airport. From there I called Stanley – he agreed with my action apart from a single change to one word in the notice – and I managed to speak to Michael who was also in full support.

Then John phoned me. It was 8:50 a.m. He was very angry. "It's despicable leaving such notes for your secretary and involving her in your machinations."

"Well, I think it's despicable that *you* should open notes addressed to *my* secretary," I pointed out. "I've got the right to post this notice in such circumstances whether you agree or not."

"I certainly do not agree and will definitely prevent it being posted."

"In that case," I said, "I'll just have to cancel my US visit and we'd better have a Board Meeting to resolve this."

By now I was hearing of another dismissal, this time of Peter Tickle, one of our shopfitting team. His manager, Doug Phillips, had called him into the office and said, "You're being made redundant. You're to pack up your things and go. You have ten minutes to do this, and don't talk to anyone at all."

Doug then stood over him while he gathered up his stuff just to make sure that he complied with this edict.

There were three other staff members in the shopfitting department. They, too, were called in and told that the department was finished. "It's being closed down," Doug informed them, "and there's no job for either of you two." Pointing to the third employee, he said, "There *may* be a job for you but there will be other applicants."

I suppose that Doug was simply carrying out orders.

My flight plans were aborted, I returned from the airport and immediately called for a Special Board Meeting to be held the next day. On the notification for this I wrote:

This meeting was called by me because of John's disagreement that I should post a notice designed to relieve our employees' insecurity. However other things now need resolution, e.g. director's relationships.

The priority item for discussion was the insecurity felt by many of the staff and I attempted to summarise the situation as I saw it, but John persisted with his dissatisfaction over the letter I'd left for Doreen Hunt. I countered this by pointing to his unprofessional behaviour in opening mail addressed to someone else.

"I'm perfectly happy to discuss the contents of the letter if you wish," I offered. "It was simply an instruction to my secretary."

"But I had decided on Monday night that I'd post a notice myself to alleviate insecurity," explained John, "and I also intended to have a meeting with the Representatives and Managers."

My proposed notice was carefully scrutinised and found to be satisfactory as was John's further proposal. I took the opportunity to put the others in the picture about the dismissals of Trevor Fleetwood, Peter Tickle and others. I pointed out that these had been very insensitively handled and had caused much shock and distress. John promised to investigate, but there was no intimation that the redundancies might be annulled.

Next we turned our attention to the problems between ourselves.

"John is usually too busy to discuss any differences of opinion," I said. "Any alternative viewpoints are never even considered, and if I then act unilaterally it always leads to conflict and confrontation."

I proposed that we needed a set of regulations to govern our working relationships, urging John to set aside some of his precious time to share decision-making with Michael and me. I also felt strongly that all the directors should have input to the company's policies, but John was having none of it.

"In my opinion," he stated boldly, "it's impossible to agree a set of rules. Why? Because basically it's a question of personality differences and different management styles. It becomes a question of the practical impossibility of liaising on every little detail with the other directors."

There were the expected mutterings from the others, leading John to add, "All right then. I volunteer to tender my resignation on the basis of two years' pay or declare that we should sell the company and let someone else decide how to run it."

Michael nodded reluctantly. "You're probably right. Agreeing a set of rules is practically impossible and maybe it is time for someone to leave."

"A set of rules such as you suggest, Peter, is largely unworkable," agreed Stanley. "We should seriously think about John's offer to resign or sell the company. We know that Rowntrees are interested; perhaps we should sell it to them."

John then announced that he had to leave the meeting for some other purpose. "You make the decision," was his parting shot as he walked out of the office.

Four hours later John sought me out again.

"It's all unresolved, isn't it? No-one will make a decision."

"That's not so," I argued. "Everybody is ready to make up their minds."

"We really ought to sell the business," he continued, "let someone else make the decisions and get our capital out while we can."

We beat around the bush as we always did. I tried to play it cool while he got more and more aerated. I was certain that his emotions were getting the better of him and felt that he didn't really know what he wanted. He seemed to contradict himself at every turn and was probably regretting some of the things he'd already said. However, we couldn't function properly as working executives in this no-win situation. The board, I believed, really had to resolve the ridiculous stalemate between us.

The story of the redundancies had reached the local media and John wrote a letter to *The Belper News* about it. I received a report from John Culverhouse concerning the dismissals of a long list of loyal long-serving employees. These included Norris Thompson, Bill Mould, Jim Willis, Peter Pratt, Jill Goodwin and many others. I was shocked by the way these people had been forced out when there was no real reason to lose them. I made the following note in early July 1985:

The Company has been run very badly this year; optimistically budgeted, costs too high, margin not achieved due to changes in policy, high depreciation and high interest costs.

And so it turned out. We made less money than we had in 1981 despite achieving nearly twice the sales. John seemed intent on stifling initiative and changing the whole nature of the company. Stanley and Michael were equally despairing and I was fed up with the Executive Board making policy decisions. I could no longer pretend that I would like John out of the way. Any sympathies I'd had for him were now entirely spent. He *could* work with us, but apparently didn't want to.

I was back in the US by September and I asked Thom whether there was anything else that we could do to give us extra sales as we weren't making enough in the retail business. We were passing Marshall Fields, a well-known department store in Chicago, and noticed they were selling 'big truffles', similar to our *Rum* and *Coffee Truffles* but much larger. "How on earth does anyone get a thing like that into their mouths?" I asked.

"Well, you know the Americans," replied Thom, laughing. "We like snacks in large portions! Why don't you try to make some back in Belper?"

"I see no reason why we couldn't," I replied. "Do you think you could wholesale them for us?"

"Yeah, sure. I'd love to have a go. We could probably improve on them and at a much better price too. You can see how expensive *these* are."

"Hmm, do you know, there's a fantastic idea in this," I said. "I'm not sure where you would store them but I bet we could market them quite profitably."

"They could be kept at the back of the Woodfield store or in my basement," Thom offered.

"Right. I'll get on to it as soon as I return," I promised him.

However, the atmosphere back in the UK was so negative that I could generate no enthusiasm or co-operation to get large truffles produced. In the days when I'd been in charge of production I would have had samples ready within a week, but now everyone thought the business was doomed and this, of course, had a knock-on effect on the motivation of staff on the other side of The Pond.

In desperation I began to think of finding a new manager for the US business. I'd always liked Thom and his wife and he'd put enormous effort into achieving success for us but the lack of support was wearing him down and with great sadness I eventually did a deal with him and he left. His replacement was Connie Whiting, another very experienced retailer.

Over the next few days I spent some time gauging opinion from others in Belper. I talked to Doug on the shopfloor.

"I am very disgusted with the change in management," he said, completely unprompted. "I don't think that Thorntons will ever be the same again."

There was considerable disappointment over the recent pay award. Trust and loyalty had been compromised, I was told, and everybody believed that the executives were a barrier to stop information reaching those at the top. The profit share scheme hadn't paid out that year because of the poor performance which, in itself, was discouraging.

"Things are still extremely poor," Doreen commented. "Maybe the discussions that John Culverhouse and Peter Heaps have been holding will do some good."

She described a meeting that she'd attended and had noted that most people were too afraid to talk openly. Some pertinent thoughts had been expressed however.

"Close the USA side," someone said.

"Michael got himself a new car on the same day that people were being made redundant" complained another. Everything was grist to the mill – the 5% wage increase, the credibility of executives, trust in the management – were all challenged. Even the company's support for Michael's elected charity, the NSPCC, was questioned. James expressed his own frustration once again. "Morale is still very bad. Nobody is accountable, no action is taken when errors occur, and no capital appraisals are done."

George Belfield said pretty much the same thing. "Morale is very low. If Cadbury's opened a factory along the street everyone would go along there. It'll never be the same again. If there'd been a profit share the 5% wage increase would have been more readily accepted."

Michael was obviously very frustrated with the overall situation, and I asked Jo if she would come with me to see him and his wife for a private chat one Saturday in October. Out it all poured.

"The whole philosophy of the company is being destroyed. The way we cared about our people has just been squandered. You know, Peter, we are abandoning our principles."

"I agree with you entirely, you know that," I said. "It shocks me deeply."

"Our prices are now way too high. We can't justify that 11% increase in September, can we?"

"Not really," I admitted. "It will alter our image in the High Street radically. I suppose John's trying to claw back from a poor year, but we should stick to our old pricing formula. It's no good covering our mistakes by putting the prices beyond our customers' reach."

"I used to enjoy going into our shops up in Scotland," Michael added, "but I won't go now as all I ever get is endless complaints about things I can do nothing about."

"That's really bad, Mike," I said.

This outpouring of doom and gloom continued for a while and then turned into a tirade against John.

"He delegates everything away from us," he complained. "I can't work this way. Neither can you. We need to be hands-on in this business."

Inexorably we were moving towards a showdown and the date of December 6th loomed large. This was when the next review of the Operating Board was scheduled and it offered the chance to determine John's future as MD of the company once and for all. For all our brave talk, we decided to do nothing more for the moment.

The conflicts within my new marriage were also developing quietly but inevitably. We were still each having difficulty relating to the other's children and my pre-occupation with work could not be ignored.

"You just sit there every evening with the business papers all over the sofa," complained Jo. "Your mind's elsewhere – it's certainly not with me. Things were much better before we were married. What's happened since Puerto Rico or Italy? We were really together then, if I ignore the exception that when we went to Greece, you had to go off sailing all the time."

This mention of Greece recalled an image of sitting with Jo on a beautiful beach in Khalkidhiki, the sunshine beating down gloriously on us, a lovely breeze blowing along the shore, catamarans lined up ready for hire on the beach – and a beautiful young topless attendant who tempted me to go sailing by offering to accompany me.

We raced off over the waves, me at the helm and she leaning over to balance the boat. We planed out for perhaps a mile until we reached the stronger waters around the reef where I was able to turn the boat round with some difficulty. This manoeuvre was repeated six or seven times until we were exhausted. She then thanked me for the ride and we parted company. This had been an uplifting experience in its combination of excitement and sensuality it was inconsiderate and I wasn't unduly surprised that Jo was upset about it.

"I'm sorry, darling, you know I'm having a pretty hellish time with the business at the moment." She gave me a withering look. I could tell that, in her mind, this justified nothing and I vowed to do better.

My own politics, which had formally been as conservative with a large 'C' as Jo's, were now more allied to the policies of the SDP which I had formally joined in 1981. I'd always been frustrated by the governmental swings from left to right during the last two decades which I felt had led to unnecessary turbulence and discontinuity in our national life. With a centre party, I believed, we could secure the best of both worlds and dispense with the wastefulness engendered by the extremes of either side.

I'd been very much persuaded by the SDP's promotion of 'proportional representation' and I was determined to do what I could in my own small way to assist the new party. I joined a fundraising committee based in London, chaired by David Sainsbury, with luminaries such as David Putnam among its members. I felt my contribution couldn't match theirs with their greater wealth and connections, but at least it got me involved.

Then, in the spring of 1986, Matthew Parris, the journalist and broadcaster, decided to resign from his seat as the Conservative Member of Parliament for West Derbyshire, our constituency, to take up journalism full-time. This naturally meant there would have to be a by-election and the local Alliance organisation felt that they had a very good chance of overturning his large majority in favour of the Lib-Dems. A win for them would be most significant, not just locally but for the whole country.

I really wanted to get involved but I knew this wouldn't sit easily with Jo or with my fellow directors at Thorntons. After all, the Conservatives had traditionally been the party of the businessman and I wasn't sure how they'd take to one of their own supporting a political rival. Nevertheless, I canvassed around the constituency on behalf of the Alliance and put up posters everywhere including in our own garden in Winster. I made appearances on platforms to show solidarity with the candidate, Chris Walmsley, and even made a few speeches for him. As the election date approached I drove him around the area in my Range Rover plastered with Alliance posters – by which I mean the vehicle, not us.

Unavoidably, this increased the antagonism between Jo and me. We found it almost impossible to agree to disagree. There was no good humour to be found in our opposing stances. She countered my poster displays by putting an equal number of Conservative posters around the Dower House garden. I then went one better by displaying a load more around the frontage of our new house, Field Farm, which was still being converted. However, I could not convert Jo to my cause and when she insisted on matching my display of support at Field Farm with a similar one for the Tory candidate, I had to point out to her that the new property was wholly in my name and that she had no legal right to put up *any* posters there. She duly removed them but this was hardly likely to bring us closer together.

Election Day came. It was 8th May 1986 and we worked separately for our chosen parties throughout the day before coming together for the count late that evening in the Town Hall with our own groups of party workers. We didn't actually meet up during the day at all and even came home separately afterwards. When the result was announced the Alliance supporters were devastated by the way the democratic process worked. Chris Walmsley had increased the Alliance vote by a magnificent 12.3% while the Conservative vote had actually gone down by a whopping 16.3%. Yet the Tory candidate still won by a mere 100 votes. But, as James Callaghan once said, just one vote more is enough to constitute a majority and we had to contain our grief and disappointment. The SDP's profile suffered a lot after that and it was eventually subsumed wholly into the Liberal party.

As for me, my enthusiasm to play politics was dealt a severe blow. I'd taken a big risk personally which did harm to my already weak marriage and put me in a questionable position with my fellow directors. I did what I thought to be right at the time but probably did myself more harm than good by it.

Rowntrees of York, still an independent public company and one of the best British confectionery companies, had approached us with the idea of a buy-out. We'd been talking about this in meetings since early 1986 but were not entirely persuaded by the arguments. I got to know one of their directors, Kurt Haslinger, very well. He was soon to retire, having reached the age of 65, and wondered if there might be an opportunity to become a non-executive director with us.

I got on with him extremely well and thought he'd be a great asset. He was Austrian-born but had worked for most of his career in Britain for Rowntrees. He had relevant experience, was a mature and sensible man, and I thought he'd be just the right person to make our Board Meetings more objective and take the emotional heat out of them. However, despite my enthusiasm to bring him on board, we dithered over the decision to appoint by which time he'd made alternative plans. This was a great missed opportunity as he would have been particularly helpful, with his established contacts in the USA, in sorting out our problems in America.

The US results came out in August for the business year to June 1986. This was our fourth year of operation and sales had now reached almost a million and a half dollars with a corresponding loss of about four hundred thousand dollars, equivalent roughly to £270,000. This was more than regrettable but wasn't actually disastrous. We'd finally established a strong foothold in that most difficult of retail markets and there was the potential eventually to achieve sales in excess of $200m if we persevered. We now had the infrastructure in place and the brand recognition to go into franchising and wholesaling.

For the UK company, despite all its woes, 1986 turned out to be quite a good year. Sales had only slightly increased but the profit had more than doubled as the customers loyally absorbed the effect of the price increase. After five lean years of flat profits things were now moving in the right direction and, of course,

John's profile went up with it. All the mistakes of the previous years were forgotten.

The pressure was now even greater to go public and our discussions with Granville's had led us to this inexorable conclusion. Tony was pressing for it and John saw it as a way out. We agreed at one of our meetings that we should seek a public listing in the fairly short term. Two to three years would be preferable in order to build up the size of the company and consolidate the sort of performance we required.

It was strange that, despite everything that had passed between us, John would occasionally seek out my opinion and advice. He approached me in December in a perfectly reasonable, if somewhat emotional, manner to talk about the organisation. He felt that the company should be split into two separate entities, Production and Retailing. We discussed this for over three hours but came to no firm agreement.

Then things took an emotional twist when we turned to the issue of financial control. He had full responsibility for this and did not want to share it in any way, least of all with me as Chairman. He insultingly asked what jobs I thought I was supposed to be doing. This surprised me but I told him anyway. He kept coming back to the idea of his resigning, but we both accepted that, at least until after the public issue, this would have complex implications regarding his shareholding.

A few days later he came to me again. He'd made up his mind to divide the company in two after Christmas.

"Look," I said, "I know we've talked about it but it has still to be discussed by the Board." I don't think he'd even considered that.

"We discussed it at a meeting with Mike," he said.

"No, we certainly did not!" I contradicted.

"Look, we *must* tackle this organisation problem," he groaned. "Do we *have* to go that meeting with Granville's next Monday? I want to talk to you privately about it all."

"OK," I said. "I'll cancel the Granville meeting so we can discuss splitting the company and everything else with Michael, if that's what you want." I suspected he didn't really want to include Michael but he accepted my offer.

Accordingly, we met on 15th December as agreed. Michael said my proposal for the Board organisation was perfectly logical. John complained that it was an unsatisfactory compromise and signalled, in his view, my attempt to take charge once more. Yet again came his *cri de coeur* that he'd better leave the company but he still laid down his terms: two years salary with a written guarantee that the company would go public within that time.

The discussions continued the following day. I'd received some top-level advice from the likes of Brian McGowan, Group Managing Director of the Williams Group and Sir Peter Thompson, Chairman, National Freight Corporation, who had been extraordinarily helpful with tips on how they successfully managed their public companies. My suggestion proposed roles for each Director with myself as Chairman, Michael as Vice-chair and Chief Executive of the Greetings Card Division, John to be Chief Executive of the Food Division, with a Finance Director to be nominated and Stanley Thornton to be President along with non-Executive Directors. I also proposed that the duties of the Group Board would be fundamentally to do with strategy, financial management and acquisition opportunities.

It was getting close to Christmas. Michael had lunch with Tony on the 23rd and they continued to debate the finer points.

"Tony definitely wants to go public," Michael confided to me. "Full issue, as soon as possible given the state of the market and the political situation. He made it very clear that that he's firmly against any break-up of the directors but, if it came to such, he'd have to support John because of the apparent success under his management."

It was also apparent that Michael's support of me had considerably weakened. "I'm caught in the middle really, you know," he said. "The fight is between you and John, and has always been so."

"I'm not trying to fight with anyone," I protested. "I just want an organisation which will allow us to work together for the success of the business."

"I admit that John's proposals would virtually give us non-executive status," he conceded, "although he has offered to come up with a compromise solution, if he can find one."

In the light of these remarks I was even more fearful for my own position. John had had one good year and was now being spoken of as having 'a good track record'. He would obviously seek to strengthen his position and, if he didn't get me to abdicate my remaining authority to him, not for one moment did I think he would carry out his threat to resign. Instead he would press for a vote. On the basis of our voting shares I would lose and would ignominiously have to leave.

Wishing to push things forward, I issued my proposals in a formal document to confirm our agreement to the public issue on 29th December 1986. It noted that three executive directors had agreed to seek a public market for the shares of the company with a full listing on the Stock Exchange within the next 18 months, most likely around October 1987. It went on to define the organisation of the company as a Public Company based on the proposals I'd already put to Mike and John and included the objectives and duties of the Group Board. It acknowledged that all the existing Directors were competent to fulfil the roles envisaged.

After the Christmas break I came across my old colleague Dick Smith in the corridor.

"Morning, Dick," I greeted him. "How are you doing? Was your Christmas OK?"

"Christmas was great and I'm just fine," he replied, smiling. "John has told me he wants to split Retail and Manufacturing and that he will need me to concentrate entirely on Franchising and hand over all the Commercial Sales work I've been doing."

"Yes, John did mention that to me," I said. "I suppose there is more potential for Franchising now that things are going so well. At one point, you know, we were talking of opening a further 300 franchise shops."

"That's quite possible," he replied. "In the meantime, we're meeting a Mr Ward from Hong Kong to discuss retailing over in the Far East shortly." This was good news for him but less so for me as, once again, here was a part of the business that was meant to be my responsibility.

Everywhere I turned I was facing the same brick wall. Proposal followed by counter-proposal. All attempts to be rational and calm were being met with temperamental outbursts. The others stood by, meekly watching as John and I moved ever closer to the final act whereby I was to be out-manoeuvred. I could easily imagine how Caesar felt on the Capitol steps with Brutus standing behind him.

"Mike, this is just completely unacceptable to me," I said. "I'm having to employ every conceivable strategy just to protect myself. The whole situation is disgraceful – it's unreasonable and unfair and I'm damned if I will accept it!"

John went on to produce his so-called compromise proposal, virtually identical to mine save for the insistence that he retain full control. No surprise there.

Everything hinged on the upcoming meeting on 23 January 1987. Nick Harvey from Granville's was mooted to act as an intermediary. I didn't want to seem obstructive so I went along with this. However, all it achieved was further confusion and distress and the scheduling of yet another meeting a week later.

Stanley: I've had enough of all this. I don't think that we should go public. None of my three daughters wants this. It's not in their interest to do so. But Tony's done so well out of his deal that *that* is all he wants now.

Michael: I'm really confused about it all. John saw me on Friday evening after the meeting and said that he was concentrating entirely on organisation of the Board for the public issue and leaving everything else to the executives. He wants to spend all day Monday talking to me about it. He says that, as Chief Executive, he's got Nick Harvey's support. He's also suggested that you should be non-executive or, better still, retire completely. Then we should bring Tony in as Chairman. He claims the City won't be happy about the issue if the Chief Executive, who has the 'track record', has resigned *before* the issue. You know, he really has this psychological block which prevents him from working with you.

Peter: That's his problem, not mine. It's high time the other directors saw this.

Michael: John will never change his mind, you realise that, don't you? It looks as if we'll need an Extraordinary General Meeting. I've talked to Tony and he feels we'll be forced to keep John as CEO because of this 'track record' of his.

Peter: What 'track record'? What about *our* 'track record'? *I* turned the company round in 1980, *I* set up this business system, John has merely exploited it. What about all our earlier creativity?

Michael: My wife and I have come to the conclusion that all we can usefully do is sell the company.

Peter: Why on earth should we do that? Just because of the obstinacy of one person who wants to run everything himself? You know very well that if it were just us two running things, there's no way I'd insist on being Chairman, would I? We'd settle all matters between us with no hassle.

Michael: Of course, we would.

In view of what Stanley had said I felt it was important for his daughters to be fully informed of what was being planned and why. They needed to see how they would personally benefit so we could get their support. This wasn't particularly easy as they remained convinced they'd lose their shareholder status and that the business would be taken over, but I think I left them a little less concerned and, in the main, they seemed more supportive of the decision to go public.

Nick Harvey also wanted to talk privately to me before the meeting on the 30th and we met up in Derby's Midland Hotel where he was waiting for his return train to London. This was an uncomfortable meeting, largely because the room had no seating and we were obliged to stand awkwardly facing each other.

Nick: The company has invited me to find a solution to the current problems so I'd like to discuss a few of my ideas with you.

Peter: That's fine. John suggested that we should talk.

Nick: The purpose of all these discussions is to establish a proper Group Board suitable for a public issue, right? Well, I've talked this over with my other partners in Granville's and come to some conclusions.

Peter: And they are....?

Nick: Everyone I've spoken to has accepted that we should call in an independent part-time Executive Chairman. You would then be free to develop new ideas and so on.

Me: Did you talk to Peter Doyle as I suggested? He helped, you know, with the turn-round exercise in the early 80's. It's very important to me that you get an outside opinion from someone like him.

Nick: No, I haven't done that. The fewer people who know about the current problems the better. We have to think about your shareholders and employees. I imagine they're already talking about it on the shop floor, and we shouldn't delay a decision simply to talk to someone from the dim and distant past.

Peter: But Doyle has a useful insight into....

Nick: I'm sorry. I'm telling you this now to avoid giving you a shock at the next Board Meeting. You have certain strengths which would make you very good for the role I'm proposing. Granville's might even ask you to be a Regional Director for them.

Peter: That's a bit of news. Do carry on.

Nick: Well, Stanley's told me that none of you has ever done anything for the business – except him!

Peter: That's a load of bloody rubbish! I hope you didn't believe him. Let me tell you some facts. Tony and I actually built this company from the early 50's onwards. Joseph William was the one who started it, and Dad and Stanley developed it awhile until we effectively took things over. It's what we were required to do until John came along to take everything away from us.

Nick: He categorically denies that. Anyway, it's been agreed that I should phone Tony as obviously he is very much involved.

Peter (laughing contemptuously): I haven't *agreed*. Anyway, what's it to do with Tony? He's not a director any longer.

Nick: But I have a proposal from everyone.

Peter: You don't have one from John. He's withdrawn it.

Nick: Oh, well, I'll ring him tomorrow and tell him to put one in.

Peter (getting angrier): No, you're not listening! I don't agree with any of this, *and I will not accept any of this!* I've already been pushed into a 'non-executive' role before. I'd just turned the business round and what did they do to thank me? They took my job away and made me Development Director! *Development Director* – I ask you! I'll never do that again. No, I just don't think this idea will work. Have you proposed to John that *he* be Development Director?

Nick: No, of course not. After all, there *is* his track record.

Peter (shouting): *What track record? I* was the one who turned the company round in 1981. *(Repeats the story in full detail.)* I had tremendous battles with John about cutting costs. Why we did so badly in the first year of the exercise was all to do with things beyond our control such as the VAT increase. Now just consider. How ridiculous would it be bringing in an outside Chairman when I am perfectly capable of doing the job? This suggestion from John is simply because he, for some reason best known to himself, refuses to work with me. Why should I accept any compromise of his? He's simply out to get total control!

Nick and I had had a good relationship. It was I who had brought him into the debate. But now things were turning personal and we parted angrily. I was in a fair stew as I drove back to Belper.

Anyway, his proposal didn't get enough support at the subsequent meeting and he didn't pursue it, conceding that the Chairman ought to come from within the family. Instead, we asked him to draw up, in conjunction with our independent lawyer Michael Jelley, a list of Chairman's duties to which we could all subscribe. They did this, producing a perfectly acceptable summary of the responsibilities involved, but the others wouldn't go along with it.

Nick (clearly irritated): You won't be able to get an outside Chairman to take on the job without having at least a similar level of commitment. Anyway, I can't hang around much longer. I have to go – I've another train to catch…"

Michael J: Peter, a private word in your ear. You know, before you sign anything here, you really ought to take legal advice, if only to protect your employment rights and income. I strongly urge you to consider this.

Peter: Thank you, I'll take it under advisement.

(I didn't.)

Nick went further and produced a paper entitled *The Chairman's Role* which was then discussed and approved in a February meeting. We also at last agreed a management structure for the whole company under which I would remain as Chairman and John as Chief Executive. He would have his own Executive Committee to help him manage the business. We agreed formally to recommend to shareholders a full public listing of the company in 1988. The Chairman could now enter into detailed technical discussions with Granville on all aspects of this decision and keep the main Board informed. I noted at the time:

It goes without saying that this agreement is a complete fudge and is designed to give John total control of the company. I have accepted it because at least any agreement is better then no agreement.

It was time to go visit my Mum who was now living in a lovely bungalow in Dore, that delightful rural suburb of Sheffield. She was well settled and, if truth be told, was more relaxed without Dad's constant moaning to deal with. Her own health was quite poor though and she suffered very badly from delicate skin on her legs. Her years of taking cortisone had resulted in a thinning of the epidermal layer and she had sustained some appalling lacerations needing frequent hospitalisation. She required constant help in the house throughout the day.

"How are things, Mum?" I asked.

"I'm happy, Peter. I really am so long as you keep coming to see me. I do see my old friend Elsie Nunweek quite often. As you know, she's a lot younger than me and in much better health, but there you go."

"But you're doing fine," I told her. "At least you don't have Father's grumbles any more, do you?"

"No, you're right. I know I shouldn't say it but I'm relieved really, you know."

"Yes, yes, I *do* understand, Mum. But your legs must be quite a problem for you though."

"They are, that's true. I'm so stupid because when I use them I keep walking into things and cutting myself quite badly. Just look at what I did a week ago." She unwound a huge bandage and exposed this horrific injury to her left leg.

"Oh, that's awful, Mum," I said. "I hope you're getting proper attention?"

"Yes, I am, thank you, Peter. But can I ask you to do something for me?"

"Of course. What is it?"

"Well, you know that your nephew Richard is getting married in May in New Zealand?"

"Yes," I said, "I received an invitation but it's an awfully long way to go for a wedding."

"I know, but someone from the family ought to go. Your sister Gill would be so delighted if you went as I'm certain that none of the others would bother."

"No, I don't suppose they would."

"The good thing is, if you *did* go, I could go along with you! Stanley came round the other day and he said that if *we* went he'd come along too."

"Are you sure that you really want to do that?" I asked. "It's a terribly long way and a very tedious flight. Do you think you'd be able to cope?"

"Oh Peter, I so long to go! It'd be just wonderful to see them all and to be at the wedding. Richard is such a lovely boy and so clever as well – he's going to be a surgeon, you know."

She clearly had her heart set on this journey which, after all, might be the last chance she would have to see this branch of the family.

"Look, Mum. I'll think about it and let you know as soon as I can."

After talking to Jo we decided it was time to put family matters above all else and so, in mid-May 1986, off I flew to New Zealand with these two elderly passengers in my care. We had a lovely few days there and my mother was the happiest person alive. Stanley stayed with us a short while and then returned on his own as Mum had decided to stay for several weeks longer with Gill arranging to bring her back to England.

Once I was certain she was in good hands and being properly looked after, I flew home and returned to the office on Wednesday 20 May, happy but exhausted. I went over to the new factory at Thornton Park and realised that John was entertaining visitors. He didn't appear to want to talk to me about Mum, the wedding or anything else. Mike was away in the USA and not due to return until the 22nd. However, as he soon as he was back on Derbyshire soil (or so I thought), he came straight to see me.

Michael: We have to sort out this question of directors' roles.

Peter: Oh, for goodness sake, Mike, not again. We've had endless meetings about this. It's been thoroughly dealt with.

Michael: I was asked to go to Granville's in London yesterday to meet Mr DeFriezz of Warburg's.

Peter: You what? I thought you were still coming back from the States yesterday. Honestly, I don't understand this. I know we've talked about Warburg's being a *possible* co-sponsor but we haven't actually appointed them yet.

Michael: John was there and he said that the arrangement between the directors was not working and that he ought to be appointed both Chairman *and* Chief Executive.

Peter (mouth gaping): And what about me?

Michael: You will be asked to resign.

(A moment's shocked silence.)

Michael (hastening to clarify his position): This has been fully discussed with Tony. He's being invited to be non-executive Chairman and he's accepted. I've been delegated to discuss this with the voting shareholders. The basic problem is that John still has this 'hang-up' about you and it's impossible to go ahead with the public issue while this remains unresolved. A meeting of the shareholders has been arranged for next Wednesday in order for them to accept these new proposals.

Peter (utterly flabbergasted): Mike, this is just deceitful. It's both unlawful and disgraceful. I will certainly *not* resign as there's no justification for it. Look, I'm going to have to consider my position, but there's no question of a meeting next Wednesday because I will be on holiday. I've been really unfair to Jo recently with all this preoccupation with the business and my trip to New Zealand so I've booked to take her to France for a week and I'm not going to cancel it.

(John then appeared at my door, giving no indication that anything was afoot.)

John: Would you please spend a few minutes with my visitors, Peter, because I have to go and make a phone call?

This I willingly did, John returned from the phone, but by then I had to go to Derby to present a trophy to the winner of the annual Milk Race, a cycling event which we had sponsored. Obviously nothing further was said. However, that afternoon I decided I'd have to ask Nicholas Harvey to explain to me what was going on. After a great deal of difficulty and insistence, I managed to speak to him at about 4.45 p.m.

Peter: Nicholas, I'm shocked and disgusted by what I've been told today. Will you please explain your actions to me?

Nick: I've been told that the voting shareholders have unanimously agreed that the present system of management is not successful and will have to be changed and you will have to resign. On this basis, I've agreed to have a meeting with John to discuss the matter.

Peter: The voting shareholders do *not* unanimously agree! *I am a voting shareholder and I've not even been asked*. I was completely unaware of it. And I can't believe that Stanley has been asked. He's another major voting shareholder *and was still in New Zealand at the time*. Also, you're forgetting my mother who is a minor voting shareholder. Look, Nicholas, this isn't the first time you've been misled. A meeting should not have been requested on this basis and you shouldn't have agreed to one.

Nick: Well, they all say they're in agreement except you.

Peter: I find this very hard to believe, and even if they did say this, John has no right to request such a meeting without informing me. You're forgetting that the formal relationship between our two companies is between you and me, and anyway this is a Board matter, and the Board has definitely not been informed. I'm astounded by you. This is totally unethical for you and John to meet with someone like Alistair De Friezz.. This man is from another Merchant Bank – he's not been appointed by us. There's no way that such matters should be discussed in his presence.

(Michael enters.)

Michael (to Nick): "Tony *is* able to attend the meeting of voting shareholders next Thursday or Friday.

Peter: Oh no, hold on. Not so fast. I am going on holiday. I can't attend a meeting on Thursday or Friday and besides, this is not a matter for voting shareholders or Merchant Banks! We're operating under an Agreement drawn up by the Board of Directors. If John has a complaint to make under the terms of that Agreement he should do so in a Board Meeting. I'm prepared to resolve the problem there and nowhere else. I could attend on the 2nd or 4th of June. Is that OK? This whole situation is beyond the pale. How could any Chairman think otherwise?

I told Jo about all this when I returned home. She was as appalled by this behaviour as I was, at least we were now on the same side and fighting as a team together.

"It's extraordinary, isn't it?" I said to her. "I agree to take my mother and Stanley to New Zealand to Richard's wedding, wholly for family reasons, and while I'm away John uses the opportunity to set up a plot to get me out of the family business. It's nothing less than a coup!"

So anyway, Jo and I went off on holiday to Brittany as we'd planned. I was a bit numb from the drip-drip effect of all this chicanery but somehow we managed to have a good time.

On my return I found an 'Agenda' had been prepared by John and Michael Jelley, requiring my resignation. I told them I refused to sign it because obviously we hadn't *all* agreed to it, had we?

I went back to my office for business as usual and met Stanley. This was on Friday 29th May. His attitude seemed to be one of utter dismay and confusion. I'd written to him about the unethical behaviour of the directors but he couldn't quite take it all in, so I explained it fully to him. He simply shook his head with a look that seemed to say, I don't know what the world is coming to these days. He seemed determined to sit on the fence and maintain a position of detachment from it all.

I also saw Tony on that Friday. He claimed that everything was a complete surprise to him but I couldn't get him to budge from his view that John was to be supported because, well, look, he's been so *successful*.

So what of Michael? Surely he could see through all the bullshit? He was my natural ally, wasn't he? I went to lobby him.

Peter: I'm very concerned, Mike, not just for myself but for the company. I'm *extremely* concerned for you and Jane. You'll have no security if I go and you'll find yourself next in line, you mark my words. John is just using you to get rid of me. Then, some time in the future, he'll use someone else to get rid of you. He'll get stronger and stronger and no one will be able to stop him.

Michael: I know, and I'm absolutely fed up with all the hassle over these past ten years. But look at it this way. John seems to be able to make the business work, and I am at least involved with what's going on now. I know it seems terribly unfair but I guess I'd better go along with it. What other option is there? A compromise just seems out of the question.

Peter: Not so, Mike. A compromise is perfectly possible. All that's needed is for John to toe the line. It's *he* who has the 'hang-up', by his own admission. I believe we should have this Board Meeting, stick to a simple agenda and get it all ironed out. He should play the game fairly and accept that *he* needs me, the company needs me, and he can't rule it as if it's his own private fiefdom. We could work things out amicably if we all stood together. Listen, I'm not suggesting this as the only alternative, but you and I could do exactly what John is trying to do if we wanted to. Then you could be the Chairman and I would be Chief Executive. What do you say?

Michael: (no reply)

I was getting completely desperate by now. I felt like a cornered animal when all the hunters' rifles are trained in its direction. Once more I appealed to Stanley and Tony over the telephone but to no avail. Jo tried to lobby Michael on my behalf and got quite angry with him. I appreciated her effort but it achieved nothing.

June 2, 1987. It would be an overstatement to talk of signing one's own death warrant but there were similarities. Here, at this most dreadful Board Meeting, I was required to do something completely against my will in offering to resign. This was wrong, it was not what I wanted to do, it was not going to do the family or the business any good, yet this 'obligation' was being made of me, and I had to sign. The meeting devolved into a negotiating session between us all with me continually referring to my lawyer over the phone.

Eventually a form of words was agreed on paper wherein I tendered my resignation subject to reasonable terms and a legal promise to go public with the company. The voting share majority was in their hands and they had all decided to back John's 'track record'. My negotiating position in all this was non-existent. There was nothing I could do but try to obtain the best deal possible (which turned out to be considerably worse than Tony's). There was some comfort to be drawn from the obligation to go public as this would ensure some financial security for me and many others in the future. Whether it would be a good deal for the public shareholders would remain to be seen.

But for now – this was it, and on Saturday, June 6, 1987 I went into my office for the last time. I had left early that morning from my beautiful converted farmhouse in the Derbyshire village of Wensley because I wanted to get to the office before anyone else arrived.

Epilogue

The Story So Far

In January 2009, as I drive across the hills of East Devon taking my two young children, Rebecca (13) and William (11), to their school, I turn to look down on the sparkling estuary of the Exe, shimmering in the early morning sunshine and dotted with small boats resting at anchor. My wife, Julia, has already left to go to her new job as a teacher, having qualified in the previous year once she'd realised there was little future in pursuing her stage management career in this part of the world.

My mind goes back to that other sunny day in June 1987 when I made my last trip to Thorntons in Belper and I reflect on the many things that have happened in the 22 years since. In particular I ponder the circumstances that brought me to that fateful day.

I had been so deeply traumatised by my forced resignation that, in the following decade, I couldn't bring myself to enter the doors of a Thorntons shop. For the first five of those ten years I was so ashamed at having been ejected from a seemingly successful enterprise. How was I to explain to anyone why I'd suddenly left the family business? Eventually I decided to tell the truth about it and say simply that I'd been thrown out due to a 'family conflict', but it was a long time before I felt able to talk to any of my old working colleagues. Indeed, I didn't make any sort of contact with them at all until just a few months ago.

The only way to overcome all this back in 1987 was to find some new position, possibly in an organisation under my personal ownership. Searching for a job elsewhere would be so humiliating, I thought, as my reputation would seem irreparably tarnished. Having achieved the status of senior company director, it was unthinkable to go back to being 'a nobody' once more. It wasn't a question of money as I now had an assured pension with the likelihood of a dividend income and capital from Thorntons, the public company. It was simply that I did not know what to do with myself. I couldn't bear to sit at home doing nothing, so I put myself to work in my new office together with my secretary, Doreen, who had gallantly resigned with me, and started to consider what else I could create.

I was, of course, in no fit state to create anything. Hindsight taught me that I needed at least a year to get over what had happened before I could usefully do anything new. Perhaps taking a very long holiday would have been a good idea, anything to avoid making important decisions.

Unfortunately, I went ahead and made a number of *very bad* decisions. Thorntons eventually went public in May 1988 for £78.6 million but, until then, I couldn't get any money from the public issue so I had little capital with which to make any investments. In spite of this, within a few months I had purchased one small business, started a second and invested in others, but I soon found myself locked into a number of business situations where I was either losing money or had to sell them. These set-ups had been hurried and ill-thought out having no differential advantage and the whole picture was far from satisfactory.

You see, I now had this 'big business' mentality and no longer wanted to 'get my hands dirty' at the lower levels where I should have been focussing my attention. Also, with so many businesses to look after, I didn't really have the time to attend to the detail so I appointed people to manage them for me. Most of the time this didn't work and I remained tied to these businesses for quite a while. Eventually I tried direct management of my biscuit business in Devon, but it was very weak and after years of trying it failed. Altogether I lost a great deal of money as a result.

At least in my private life I didn't feel so driven by irrational needs. I continued to do my best to make the marriage work but my problems with Jo worsened. I did my utmost in my own behaviour to ensure that I always walked on eggshells but it was impossible for me to live this way and so, after deliberating on the difficulties for at least six months, I decided in late 1990 that after Christmas I would gently suggest to Jo that we stop trying and agree to separate. We had a short conversation and, to my surprise, she said, without any anger or rancour "Yes, I agree" and that was that. No one else had been involved and it had simply been a case of insoluble incompatibility. How fortunate that we had not had a child after all.

As part of the settlement I agreed to buy her a house back in her familiar Bakewell. She found a suitable property and moved into it in April 1991. Living together in the one home but in separate rooms had been a very unpleasant experience for both of us, if only for three months. We tried to be adult about it, doing our own shopping separately, preparing individual meals and going our own ways socially, but it was more uncomfortable than we could have ever imagined.

Jo took back all the furniture she had brought to the marriage and also some of what we had acquired together. This rendered the house very empty and hollow, and it was almost with a sense of panic that I rushed around madly buying replacement items to fill up the rooms again. It took me about four weeks and a lot of cash but it made me feel better.

This separation was totally different from the earlier experience with Janet. Jo and I dealt with it in an organised and mature way and, when she left, I still had a lovely and comfortable home. Admittedly, the separation was costing me a lot of money but I still had enough to live on. So, hopefully, we parted with no bad feelings.

Nevertheless, I was troubled by my poor marital history. To misquote Oscar Wilde, losing one wife may be regarded as a misfortune, but to lose two looks like carelessness. Why, I wondered, was I continually forming unfortunate relationships with women? Whatever faults each of them may or may not have had, there seemed to be something inherently abnormal about my own behaviour. I was suffering again from those 'sine-wave' mood-swings, going from depression to elation and euphoria in a very unsettling way. As soon as I was released from my commitments I determined to spend at least three years living independently at Field Farm, with perhaps only casual relationships, and I would use the space to get some proper therapy to work out the basis of my problems. Ben Blom had been a great mentor to me in many ways but he had never attempted to work out what lay behind my fundamental emotional difficulties.

I needed a new therapist, but who would be right for me? Searching through the Yellow Pages eventually led me to a bureau in London that seemed to offer some solutions. From there I was referred to Keith Tudor who occupied a converted bedroom in his terraced house in nearby Sheffield. This room was sparsely furnished with two sofas and a large white-board and, over the course of ten sessions there with him, he provided me with the theory and led me in a very structured way to explore my early childhood and reach some understanding of the problems arising from it. As the child of a cheerfully extrovert mother and an introverted depressive father, it is no surprise that I grew up with the attributes of both. Keith believed it was impossible to change my fundamental disposition but, by being at least aware of these conflicting traits, I should be able to focus more on the one and suppress the other. By recognising the interludes of anxiety when they were imminent I could employ strategies that would reduce or eliminate them. It sounds simple when put like that but, over time, I really did manage to get ownership of my emotions so that I became increasingly less neurotic. These days I hardly ever allow myself to drop into those former depressed moods and remain upbeat and cheerful for most of the time.

"But," I asked Keith, "why, oh why do I keep seeking out relationships with individuals who aren't really suitable for me?" Even as I framed the question the answer was beginning to form in my mind. I was too ready, it seems, to succumb to infatuation with beautiful women, supposing that my love for them was based just on their physical attractiveness to the exclusion of those deeper needs within a relationship. "She is beautiful because I love her," and not "I love her because she is beautiful." Infatuation is always short-lived and conveniently overlooks the elements of a two-way loving and caring relationship. A marriage, I now realised, required mature behaviour, common interests and outlooks, a sense of fun and an ability to empathise, to know without needing to be told of the other's needs and concerns. Superficial beauty was truly only skin deep and of relatively small importance. I'd never known such a relationship before but, within a year of my sessions with Keith, I met Julia and all that changed.

It may have taken me a long time to realise that most of the problems we face in our society are based on our inherent emotional instability and immaturity. Doctor friends have often commented to me on the number of patients presenting physical symptoms when the real underlying problems are emotional. It is hard for some individuals even to acknowledge that they *have* a problem and much more investment is needed in our times to develop a support network through health authorities to help such people. Yet the benefits in terms of reduced illness, absenteeism, suicide, alcoholism, drug taking, child abuse and many other ills of modern life are self-apparent.

A few days after separating from Jo, I decided it was time to follow through the idea I'd had in the back of my mind since the occasion I had flown from Belper to Manchester in a small helicopter and then later from JFK Airport to the helipad in Manhattan. I wanted to learn to fly a helicopter.

I had my first flight training in April 1991 but it wasn't until late December, and 64 flying hours in between, that I finally qualified. I guess a young person would have done it in considerably less time. Nevertheless, I was now able to buy a two-seater Robinson R22 with my friend Gary Cunningham. Together we enjoyed a lot of aerial excitement until a later disagreement put paid to that partnership.

In time, I put in about 550 hours in the air, having a truly wonderful time with my remarkable new wife beside me. Julia also became a pilot and we flew all over Britain and Ireland and even over parts of the Continent. It was this experience, together with re-building my personal life, that at last restored my confidence in myself and my self-belief that I could always achieve more. This was not done through business activity.

Julia and I had first met in the conservatory of Field Farm when she had been working on the 1992 Buxton Festival. Susie Jarrett, the festival manager, was a mutual friend and had insisted that Julia and I get together, partly because she felt we were well suited and possibly to stop me pestering Susie herself. The idea seemed ridiculous at first as Julia was 28 years younger than me. What on earth would a 31-year-old see in a 59-year-old ex-confectionery businessman? However, I had recently started another small chocolate business and the Buxton opera that year required a box of chocolates as a stage-prop. Susie thought that Julia could charm me into providing the necessary item. Why they couldn't simply go to the nearest sweet shop and buy one was beyond me, but who was I to resist such an approach?

Susie arrived with Julia at Field Farm one sunny afternoon and we all chatted pleasantly in the conservatory. I'd already gone down into the town that lunchtime to buy in a nice selection of sandwiches from Boots. These were arranged decoratively on plates to disguise the fact that I hadn't just thrown them together in the kitchen, but I don't think either of them noticed or cared. Julia's main focus was on getting the box of chocolates and, at the time, that was all there was to it.

A couple of weeks later the Buxton Festival Ball was to take place at the Palace Hotel. I had arranged to take a table for twelve and had invited a female friend from Gloucestershire to partner me but, for reasons of expense, she bowed out at the last minute and left me in the potentially embarrassing position of being 'unaccompanied' in front of my guests. I immediately gave up the work that I was attempting to do that afternoon and got out my address book in order to telephone everybody on my list of single women friends to see whom I might persuade to accompany me.

Suddenly I remembered Julia. Surely, it would be out of the question, but I was desperate. I could think of no one else. I called her in the middle of managing something or other on the actual Opera House stage.

"Sorry to interrupt," I said, "but I don't suppose you'd be willing to come to the Ball with me, would you? I know it's short notice and all that, but I'm in a bit of a fix. So what do you think?"

There was not even a moment's hesitation.

"Oh yes, I'd *love* to come to the Ball with you. Let's meet at the bar, shall we? The Palace Hotel at about 7.30?"

Prince Charming couldn't have got a commitment from Cinderella any more quickly.

We had a remarkably pleasant evening. I was amazed that we related to each other. We had such a lot in common. I'm afraid I had rather too much to drink and Julia very kindly volunteered to drive me the 18 miles home to Wensley in her Nissan Micra and dropped me off at my front door. Naturally, I thanked her profusely for such a lovely time but didn't think there was any mileage in a 'May-September' couple such as ourselves taking things any further. However, I did wish at least to take her out to dinner one evening to thank her for her kindness so later I called her and invited her to my favourite 'local', the Peacock Hotel at Rowsley. She was happy to accept and we had a delightful meal during which I discovered that she also spoke the same foreign language as me. We were mildly amused to see the expressions of our fellow diners as they overheard us conversing in German.

I told Julia that my new satellite TV system at Field Farm could receive broadcasts from Germany and asked if she would like to come back with me and watch something. That is how the two of us ended up in front of a James Bond film in German *without* English sub-titles and I realised that Julia, laughing at jokes that I hadn't understood, was the first English person I'd met who could speak German better than me. My admiration increased.

A couple of days later I had the daring thought to invite her on a flight with me to the Lake District. I said we would be staying the night at Grasmere and then flying the next day to the Sellafield Nuclear Power Station as part of a Helicopter Club tour. Again, she seemed delighted to be invited and we set off above the trees to the north of my house and headed towards the Yorkshire Moors. At one point I flew into a cloud, a dangerous thing to do in a helicopter, but I managed to get out of it safely and Julia was completely unfazed. I had a new a GPS navigation device which I hoped she could cope with, but neither of us properly understood it so we relied on the tried-and-tested methods of flying on a compass-bearing for a measured distance and 'looking out of the window' to see where we were. We eventually reached our destination, landed at Pooley Bridge for lunch with other members of the Club at the famous Sharrow Bay restaurant and then took off again for Grasmere.

Once in the garden of the Waterside Hotel I realised that, despite my considerable embarrassment, I would have to bite the bullet.

"Look, Julia," I said, "I didn't know what to do and I didn't have the nerve to ask you beforehand. I've booked two rooms here in the hotel. One is a single bedroom, the other is a double. What do you want to do?"

"Oh, there's no point in your paying for two rooms," she replied, jauntily. "I don't mind sharing a room if you don't." We checked in and I have to admit that by the time we appeared for supper in the dining-room I was wearing a very large grin. I probably never even noticed the other guests as we ate and talked together. I was in my seventh heaven and our relationship really took off from there. Since then I have never looked back – I had found my perfect partner. By January 1995 we were we were on our way to the Caribbean to get married. Our Airbus landed in Antigua from where we took a local plane to the British Virgin Islands and finally aboard the hotel launch to the Peter Island Resort.

However, it wasn't all wine and roses. For years I'd been plagued with asthmatic problems, or so I thought. However, my new ENT specialist at the Chesterfield Royal Hospital had confirmed that the real trouble lay with my sinuses and that an operation would really make a huge difference.

"But I'm going to the Virgin Islands to get married on New Year's Day," I pointed out.

"No problem," he said. "Come in on the 27th," (he meant December) "and you'll just need to stay in overnight."

I came home the following day as promised but felt pretty ill from the procedure. Arriving at our island resort a few days later I still felt decidedly not how a prospective husband should feel. The doctor had told me I shouldn't need to keep taking cortisone after the operation, so I made my own decision to stop taking it and was then left me completely drained of energy for at least eight days.

"Are you sure about the cortisone?" I asked him by phone from the hotel.

"Oh, have you already stopped? That could be really dangerous. Your adrenal glands may be suppressed and making no cortisone at all. You could die. You'd better start taking it again immediately!"

I did and at once felt better. However, upon my return to England, he told me that the operation had not been completely successful and he would have to do it again. This he did in April and from then on I had a new lease of life which has continued to this day. Derek Cullen, another consultant, found that my adrenals *were* suppressed beyond recovery so I now have to take small regular maintenance doses of cortisone. I bless my medical advisers who at last revoked my previous poor advice about 'asthma' but felt aggrieved that I'd taken all that cortisone, with its side-effects, when all the time the problem was to do with my sinuses.

Stanley Thornton died in February 1992 at the age of 88. He was very proud to have outlived his brother by one year. Despite what had happened at the time of my leaving the business I remained very fond of him and made sure that I went to his funeral.

Then in August 1995 my lovely mother died. This time I was very sad. I loved her dearly for the warm and kindly person she was. She had relied upon me for help and support after my father had gone and we'd been able to afford 24-hour nursing care at home in her last few years. I was aware that not everyone is able to live out their last days in such comfort and security.

Mike retired from the business in April 2003; he was very upset also and not ready to leave. As far as I was concerned his departure at least allowed me to resume our friendship because I couldn't do that while he was still in the business. We've had great times together visiting his home in the Channel Islands where he resides very happily with his third wife. We've shared skiing holidays and have been made very welcome by his lovely daughter and her family at their home in Kenya. I'm very happy to be on such good terms with all his sisters and it's a real pleasure for me and my family that we see them so often.

My brother Tony and his wife 'Scilla now split their life between their homes in London and Arizona. Our paths don't often cross but Julia and I have had the pleasure of visiting them, both in Arizona and in France where they lived for a short time. As always, it's great to remain in touch with Tony and to see him when I can.

My three older children have their own families now and I'm very pleased to see them regularly and, of course, my seven grandchildren.

It's been wonderful re-building friendships in the last few months with many of the people who were working colleagues while I was at Thorntons. Many of my old friends have given me invaluable assistance in recalling events, dates and people that had slipped from my mind.

Charlie remains married and tells me she is very happy. I'm glad she stayed with her husband. They deserve each other as he is indeed a stalwart and faithful man. I apologise to him for being brazenly deceitful and for the hurt which I caused him. Indeed, I apologise to Janet and to my children for the same reasons and trust that they have in them the power to forgive me.

I forgive my close relatives for what they did to me in the business. The real problem was that we were all victims of our circumstances. There were too many Thorntons, too young and inexperienced, thrust into a situation not of our choosing. I don't blame any one person. We were all put under the most appalling strain and each of us might have achieved great success in any other organisation away from family rivalries. Neither do I blame Dad or Stanley as we were all operating in the dark in the early days. There was no business theory to guide us at first and, by the time we were able to see what was happening, the seeds of discontent had been long sown.

There is no doubt however that a family business is on the average more successful than a non-family one and, in spite of everything, this remained true of Thorntons. A group of closely-related people are thrust together on the basis of their blood relationship alone. They are not selected to work together and they will probably have very different strengths and aptitudes, as we did. In order to survive and be successful they have to find a means of working constructively together. The result is a group of people with disparate abilities, working in a 'chaotic' system. It's probably more effective and creative this way compared to a 'normal' hierarchy where individuals are selected on merit, but it is much more difficult to manage.

To all of you reading this who may be contemplating bringing later generations into your business or who already have a family business I hope that this is a cautionary tale.

The first generation of a family business generally has few problems. Typically the entrepreneur brings in someone to help out who is trustworthy, perhaps a close relative of the same generation such as a spouse or sibling. There can be problems of ownership, leadership and decision-making but this is fairly easy to sort out on a one-to-one basis.

So it was with Thorntons. Dad had made a very good start, realising early on that he couldn't work with his brother Frank as the latter didn't have the right kind of ability to help run things. He paid him off when the business was still very small and before Frank could get 'locked-in' with very high expectations. Dad looked after him well, all things considered.

Then he realised that a small miracle had been presented to him. His younger brother Stanley was very intelligent and happened to have complementary talents, being mechanically and technically-minded whereas Dad's skills were on the creative and financial side. This was the right combination to develop the business. They had contrasting personalities too, but had worked out how to get along together as long as Dad always in charge.

It is at the stage when the entrepreneur and business partner are approaching middle-age, now with a well-established business and with their children nearing the end of their education that they need to consider with their families what they want to do.

Do they want to sell the business and give themselves enough to live on for the rest of their lives, leaving their children to make their own way outside the business? Or do they want to keep it permanently within the family to benefit future generations with jobs, an income and assets? Or perhaps do they want a combination of the two?

If they decide on the long-term family business route then an appropriate business adviser will be a great help. He, or possibly she, will have the skills, knowledge and experience which the usual entrepreneur doesn't have, with the additional advantage of being an objective and impartial outsider.

When Thorntons reached this stage in the late 1940s there were no family business advisers. They didn't come on to the scene in the U.K. for another 50 years. Only then was there sufficient knowledge and science of the subject to allow people to become specialists.

If such a person had been available to the brothers, and if they had wanted to call him in, he would probably have proceeded as follows: "You've decided that you want to keep this as a family business. Now you need to decide what top jobs there might be in the future in the period while you two continue to keep control. Then you have to start considering which of your children (all the children, not just the boys) might turn out to be suitable for which job. I also need to interview each one of them separately, even if they're really young, and find out what they think about the business and what sort of job they'd love to do when they're grown up. Particularly I need to find out whether they'd be happy to work for each other, particularly if one of them eventually becomes Managing Director. Would the others still be prepared to work with him?"

This would give the adviser a list of potential jobs and he'd have a good understanding of who would like to do what. He'd then need to talk to Stanley and Dad about education, higher education, technical or business training and external working experience for each individual candidate child.

Technical training would be paramount to gain an inherent knowledge of the product, and being 'brought up with the business' (going to the office, warehouse and elsewhere with Dad) would provide those necessary extra insights which are a real advantage, as I experienced.

Work experience beyond the family business is another essential. It gives the individual much more independence, authority and value to the company when he or she eventually joins. A first class MBA, not available in the 1940s but widely available now, and gained at one of the top schools after external work experience, is a further important advantage.

The adviser might then say to Stanley and Norman: "Now we need to decide on selection, training and induction procedures for each person. When will they be expected to take over their designated roles? When are you going to retire and give up control? This ought not to be beyond the age of 70. What will the financial arrangements be for you after retirement? You'll have to hand over voting control and shareholdings. Have you thought how this will be done? When are you going to take action about a Family Constitution and Council and how will these be organised? Who are we going to appoint as an independent non-executive director to mediate between the family members as individuals?

"When you've decided all this, you should be set up for a spectacular future which will benefit everybody as long as the family is able to keep things going successfully, be of good disposition and support to their staff, and allow you a restful and secure retirement and benefit society through charitable donations."

In the case of companies which took no such advice and brought in second generation members without any planning, as happened with Thorntons, and are now experiencing great conflict as a result, they really need to agree that a business adviser is essential to help them through the morass. The adviser will interview each individual director, shareholder and family member to get a consensus on their views, aspirations and ambitions, even though, at this late stage, it will be extraordinarily difficult. The complexities and dynamics of the relationships, evolved over many years, will make the process much more awkward.

If it has been agreed to continue as a family business it'll probably be fairly obvious that one or more of the existing directors should really be encouraged to leave. The adviser will then work on behalf of the business to make mutually satisfactory arrangements for this. If conflict still remains, he might turn to techniques outlined in the excellent book by Edwin A. Hoover and Colette Lombard Hoover, *Getting Along in Family Business: The Relationship Intelligence Handbook* (Routledge, 1999). This will ensure that the remaining directors can still get along with each other. The authors say that sometimes these techniques reveal the extent of the impossibility of the directors working as a group in which case there might have to be further departures.

Once the relationships have all been sorted out, the adviser will assist the company to make decisions, set up the rules and institutions as outlined above.

During the last few years of my time at Thorntons my pre-occupation had always been the need for the company to diversify and stop being so dependent on its own UK retail shops if we wished to continue to expand. I could see that there was a limit to the expansion of the shop chain here. I'd calculated that we couldn't go above 275 shops because we'd then be operating in smaller shopping centres and towns where the potential for high enough sales simply wasn't there. The economics associated with each outlet vary between locations, but the general principle that each shop must generate sufficient gross profit on its sales to pay its share of whole business costs and still make a good enough net profit remains central. We had a target profit margin for the business of between 10-15% on sales which by extension applied to each shop. The amount by which a very profitable outlet could subsidise a less successful one was a matter of a few per cent and nothing more.

We knew what affected annual sales in a shop – catchment population, their spending power, its location, size of the shop front, street position and so on – and from this we could work out quite accurately what the sales of any potential outlet in any location would be. If therefore we opened shops in poor locations we would gradually weaken the company's profit margin.

This wouldn't happen if we were to open only franchises in such locations because franchises made a consistent contribution without adding any extra retailing cost. In fact, at the time I did these calculations I worked out that "franchise' was actually much more profitable for us than 'retailing', but even then there was a natural limit to the number of franchises we could successfully supply. In my view this was about 300.

At that time I had proposed that we should look very carefully at retailing abroad in other countries and we should invest in the US Company, diversify its activities and give it time to become profitable. I also thought that we should experiment with selling non-competitive snack products to the major retailers in the UK and consider buying some compatible but non-competitive businesses. I felt, too, that we should consider expanding beyond our confectionery range in our shops to take advantage of our very strong brand name.

After I left Thorntons, and before the public issue, the US business was dissolved. I imagine there had been pressure from the Merchant Bank to get rid of this loss-making activity. Once the company had gone public it continued expanding the retail chain up to 263 shops. The franchise chain was also increased to 286 by 1995 and profits rose likewise.

I'm sure that John and his management team were under great pressure from the money-men in the City to keep this expansion going and to use the funds raised by the issue as fully as possible. An attempt was made to achieve this by the purchase of two French retail businesses along with a Belgian chocolates company. Unfortunately these ventures were not successful and resulted in considerable losses by the time they were closed or sold.

Thorntons then employed a new Chief Executive, Mr Roger Paffard, an extremely well-qualified and experienced retailer. Enthused by Roger's apparent skill (perhaps over-enthused might be a better word), the directors embarked on a programme of mass expansion taking the number of shops to over four hundred by the turn of the millennium and increasing the production and distribution facilities substantially in order to supply them. Many of these had to be in low-volume locations and accordingly the number of franchises was reduced. This seemed to work at first but the plan impacted on profitability levels and Mr Paffard left the business to be replaced by Mr Peter Burdon in 2000. The latter acknowledged the errors of the former strategy in his annual report and, in March 2002, he began selling non-competitive snack products to Tesco on a one-year exclusive deal. This was successful and the new management has continued this strategy to very great effect except that non-competitive gift lines are also now sold in the major retailers. The idea had traditionally been resisted by the family directors fearing that it would damage the sales of the retail shops and possibly the brand image. It's uncertain whether this damage has actually occurred and it's quite possible that our original view was wrong and that the strategy will continue to be successful and can be built upon.

John von Spreckelsen was appointed Chairman of the company in June 2006. He had a successful record as Chief Executive of Budgens for nine years before turning Somerfield round under his Chairmanship.

John Thornton retired in August the same year and Peter Burdon left the business at the end of September.

A new Chief Executive, Mike Davies, was appointed in October. His background was "with that other family confectionery business – Mars," he told me. We have met on a few occasions and I like him very much. He has a positive outlook, is highly motivated, and has the experience, ability and charisma necessary to do the job.

As for me, my vision of what the business should be remains clear. There have been many changes to it over the last two decades and it's possible that some things need to be looked at closely. The price structure, for example, needs to be reconsidered, and I don't think the shops are any longer 'the people's lifestyle shops' they used to be. The business has moved upmarket and I doubt that it appeals to a cross-section of the public in the way it did. This could easily be addressed by measures such as the re-introduction of simpler gift boxes at more attractive prices.

I think there needs to be a return to the company's original retailing format. A Thorntons shop was a "treasure trove of confectionery delights where you can treat yourself and others".

They ought to be fun once more with that friendly banter between customers and shop staff. I wouldn't advocate a complete return to counter service as customers now expect a certain measure of self-selection, but it seems a pity that those old standards of personal service seem to be long gone from the High Street.

At the very least, those beautiful window displays of the past should be restored. This alone would give a considerable boost to sales. The bi-weekly promotions could be brought back to build interest in individual lines, and the old 'family culture' needs to be encouraged among the shop staff, recreating that warm atmosphere which made it such a pleasure to be served by them.

And what happened to *Thorntons Special Toffee*? Personally, I think the current method of selling it is quite dreadful. I would abandon all pre-packaging and return to the old practice of breaking the toffee in the shops before carefully packing it in fresh boxes. Loose product could still be offered to the customers by the self-select method mentioned above, but it's not my place or intention to go into details here.

John Thornton must be credited with the creation of a state-of-the-art production and distribution facility at Thornton Park. This is a major achievement and is probably the best of its kind anywhere in the world. Even when it reaches full production capacity there is plenty more land available to increase things further.

The current management has done an excellent job of consolidating Thorntons as a national brand. It is sufficiently well-recognised to be at No.18 in the list of 'superbrands', a very valuable placing, and has exceeded the sales of Cadbury Dairy Milk, one of its biggest rival products in the market.

High Street and Shopping Centre retailing has suffered a serious decline since I was in the business but I refuse to believe that it will ever die completely. In these recessionary times the need for little comforts and treats is even more important and confectionery sales throughout the current downturn have remained solid, even increasing. 'Going shopping' is still a major leisure pursuit for many people and Thorntons needs to be a part of that. The company may need to slim down a little and lose a few less- profitable stores, but it could actually broaden the range of pleasant experiences it offers in the more successful outlets by including a patisserie or other closely related products where premises permit.

Once this is all re-established the company could then consider once more the idea of retailing abroad, but should pay great attention to the 'what, where and when' aspects. I would start with just with one shop in a very prime position in an important city in the target country. It wouldn't be profitable at first because it would need a top-class manager, and supplies would have to be air-freighted from England at very high cost, and the business would yet have no reputation in the new market. However, once it was well-established, profitability could be achieved by expansion on this basis. The mistakes we made in America could be avoided as there'd be no need to have fancy uniquely-designed shops. We would instead be building upon an already recognised international brand – same chocolates, same packaging, same values – extending to a chain of outlets and franchises just like in the U.K.

This is all hypothetical, but I see a very bright future for Thorntons. It will take time, patience and a high level of managerial control. But it can be done, and profitably so. The confectionery lovers of the world deserve it, and while ever customers keep that special 'sweet tooth' of theirs, Thorntons will be there to keep them happy.

Appendices

Glossary
Some business terms as used in Thorntons

Shares
In common with all companies, ownership was divided into 'shares', nominally, in our case, of a value of £1 each. In virtually all companies each share carries one vote which can be used at general meetings of the company. However in our business there were two classes of share; Ordinary and 'A' Ordinary. The Ordinary shares carried a vote and the 'A' Ordinary did not carry a vote. All shares carried an equal right to dividend payments. In the 1950's the 'A' Ordinary shares had been distributed between Norman and Stanley Thornton, their spouses and their children, there being a bias in favour of those working within the business. However the majority of the Ordinary (voting) shares continued to be tightly held by Norman and Stanley until Norman's death in November 1984.

Annual General Meeting
There is a legal obligation for every company to hold an AGM every year. All members (shareholders) have a right to attend. Amongst other things the accounts are approved and directors appointed including those who are retiring by 'rotation'. In our case only the holders of Ordinary shares had a right to vote so as a result the 'A' Ordinary shareholders never did attend.

Directors
The directors manage the company on behalf of the shareholders and are appointed at the AGM by the members. They also have statutory responsibilities. They can be dismissed at a General Meeting by a majority of shareholders.

Directors and Non-Executive Directors
Directors commonly have a dual role; 1. Statutory and representing the interest of the shareholders and 2. Acting as an executive of the company. Thus there can be; Managing Director, Finance Director, Production Director, Sales Director, HR Director etc.. Directors who have an executive role are normally known simply as directors and those who do not have an executive role are known as non-executive directors. The Chairman can be

anything from non-executive but responsible for the operation of the Board and its Managing Director to executive additionally responsible for company strategy, City relationships etc.

Board of Directors
The 'Board', as it is commonly known, has the collective responsibility to manage the company on behalf of the shareholders. There is a statutory requirement to hold a minimum number of Board Meetings every year and the Minutes of these meeting must be recorded in the Company Minute Book. Many companies limit the number of Board Meetings to perhaps a quarterly meeting and otherwise use an Operating Board or an Executive Board to run the company. Generally non-executive directors only attend Board Meetings and not Operating Meetings or Executive Meetings.

Officers of the Company
The Chairman, Company Secretary, Managing Director and other Executive Directors are appointed by the directors. However the Executive Directors are usually responsible to the Managing Director and the Managing Director to the Chairman. In effect this means that the 'appointment by the directors' really means the appointment is nominally approved by the directors. In our case because the company was under the control of Norman and Stanley Thornton who virtually never took action to make appointments then all that the younger directors could do was to seek to change responsibilities by their own means. In our business because of its family nature, the 'managing' aspect of the Managing Directors role over the family Sales and Production Directors roles was very difficult to apply.

Joint Managing Director System
The concept is that the Managing Director role is split into two parts, one director taking responsibility for one half of the business and the other for the other.

Job Evaluation
This was a scheme whereby we put a points 'value' on every job. There were certain categories for which points were awarded such as; level of responsibility (how long term would the effect of a

mistake be on the company – Time Span of Discretion in terms of Elliott Jaques theory), degree of skill required, experience required etc. The total number of points would then put the job into a certain wage or salary band. Within that band the wage rate would be varied according to the individual's performance against certain criteria. A committee of the Factory Council would discuss and agree on a unanimous basis the points value attributable to each category.

Representatives
In the context of our business, representatives to the Factory Council were elected by secret ballot to represent each level of work as determined by the Job Evaluation scheme within each department.

Same Store Sales (or Like-for-Like Sales)
It is normal for the number of stores operated by a retail company to increase year by year. This is a phrase commonly used by retailers in order to compare one year's sales with the previous year's. If last year we had 100 stores and turned over £1,000,000 in total then the sales per store was £10,000. If this year we have 120 stores then on the same basis the sales should be £1,200,000 to be the same. If sales are actually £1,500,000 then we have increased sales by (£1,500,000 - £1,200,000) /£1,200,000 x 100% = 25%.

'Going Public'
The act of changing the structure of the business from that of a private company to that of a public company with any member of the public being able to buy shares. There are quite a large number of different statutory requirements required for this process and much more transparency about the company's affairs. On the other hand a much higher price is usually achieved for the company's shares and raising new capital is much easier.

Annual Budget
Each new financial year was operated based on an 'annual budget'. We drew up predictions for every aspect of the operation of the business. From this targets for sales for every category of the business down to the individual shop were established and control figures for every aspect of cost.

Financial Year
The financial year for the business ran from the beginning of June to the end of May until the company went public when it was changed to the end of June.

Depreciation
Is the system whereby the value of the company's assets is reduced each year and a charge for the reduction made against the profit and loss account.

Net Profit before Tax
The net profit of the company is arrived at as in the following simplified example:

Business category	Sub-category	£	£	%ge
Sales or Turnover (ex-VAT)			100	100%
Cost of Sales or Variable cost				
	Raw materials	15		
	Packaging	15		
	Workforce	15		
	Transport	5		
	Total	50	50	50%
Gross Profit			50	50%
Overheads or Operating Expenses				
	Salaries	10		
	Occupancy costs	10		
	Repairs and renewals	3		
	Other costs	2		
	Interest charges	5		
	Depreciation	5	35	35%
Net Profit			15	15%

OBITUARY: LORD BROWN
Industrialist and Former Labour Minister.

Lord Brown, PC, MBE, who died on March 17 1985 at the age of 76, was an experienced and innovative industrialist who served as Minister of State at the Board of Trade in the Harold Wilson Government, from 1965 to 1970. As chairman of the Glacier Metal Co Ltd from 1939 to 1965 he had initiated significant developments in management practice and factory management and from 1966 to 1981 he was the first Pro-Chancellor of Brunel University.

Wilfred Banks Brown was born on November 29, 1908 and educated at Rossall School. He joined the Glacier Metal Co. Ltd, then a small firm, in 1931 and became managing director eight years later.

He had himself already published (with Mrs W. Raphael) *Managers, Men and Morale* in 1947 and to help himself, as he put it "to become clearer about the basis of my conduct as an executive", he sought the advice of social scientists.

From 1948 to 1950 a team from the Tavistock Institute, under the guidance of Elliott Jaques, worked in the firm. Their findings were made public in 1951 in *The Changing Culture of a Factory*, an original work that was first in a series of publications which marked the Glacier Metal Co. as a significant centre of studies in the social sciences as applied to industry.

There followed Wilfred Brown's own *Exploration in Management (1960)* and *Piecework Abandoned (1962)*, besides other writings by Elliott Jaques and members of the original Project Team.

The firm spread its experience beyond its own walls and set up a training institution, GIM, which organised courses for senior managers from industry. This activity made an outstanding contribution to thinking about management and industrial organisation in Britain and overseas, particularly in the USA where the University Of Illinois made him a Doctor of Law.

He was interested in education at all levels and accepted an invitation from Acton Technical College to join its governing body as chairman. This was no sinecure at a time of change. Later, when the Brunel College of Technology was established in 1957, he joined its governing body and became chairman after the College of Advanced Technology was created.

A committed socialist, he had contested St George's Westminster for the Common Wealth Party in 1945. He remained active for Labour outside Parliament and in 1964 he was invited by Harold Wilson to join the Government and, after being created a Life Peer in 1964, he became a Minister of State at the Board of Trade with a brief to stimulate the United Kingdom's exports.

To this he devoted his energies during the remainder of the life of Harold Wilson's two administrations of the 1970s, attempting to bring all his own experience of the psychology of industry to bear in an "on the factory floor" approach to his task, with the aim of attempting to get British companies to see beyond their obsession with home markets.

Throughout these years in politics he was deeply involved in the planning of the new Brunel University to whose foundation and development his contribution cannot be overestimated. He became its first Pro-Chancellor in 1966 and received the Hon. Degree of DTech.

Later books include *Organisation (1971)* and *The Earnings Conflict (1973)*. He had been appointed MBE in 1944.

He is survived by his wife Marjorie and three sons.

© The Times, March 1985

Reproduced with the permission of the Times

PROFESSOR PETER DOYLE, 1943-2003

It is with great sadness that Warwick Business School reports the death of Peter Doyle. For some time, Peter had been fighting cancer with great courage. On Sunday, 30 March 2003, he lost that battle.

Peter's teaching skills were envied by many and his sessions were renowned. His research prowess and his record in services to the profession were equally strong. Few in the United Kingdom have mentored more PhD students and junior colleagues who subsequently became professors.

Peter Doyle was Professor of Marketing at Warwick Business School, holding PhD and MBA degrees from Carnegie Mellon University, and an Honorary DSc from Aston University. Previously he had taught at London Business School, INSEAD and Stanford University. He published extensively on marketing strategy and brands, including the best selling textbook, *Marketing*

Management and Strategy and widely referenced articles on *Building Successful Brands* and *What are Excellent Companies?* His last book was *Value-based Marketing: Marketing Strategies for Corporate Growth and Shareholder Value.*

Peter consulted for many top international companies. These included such suppliers as Coca Cola, Mars, J&J, IBM, Nestle, Cadbury-Schweppes, British Airways, British Telecom, Novartis, Diageo, Unilever, Shell, Philips, AstraZeneca and Hewlett-Packard. He also worked extensively with leading retailers including Tesco, Dixons, Marks and Spencer, Asda, Safeway, Boots, C&A, W H Smith and Woolworths. He consulted with many advertising agencies, including Saatchi and Saatchi, Ogilvy and Mather, J Walter Thompson, BMP DDB, Abbott Mead, Lowe Howard Spink, Howell Henry and Interbrand. He has also advised the Cabinet Office, DTI, CHI, IPA, Andersen Consulting, KPMG, Institute of Chartered Accountants and the Pacific-Asian Management Institute.

He wrote a regular column on business matters for the Guardian newspaper and has published in most of the leading international journals. Described by the Marketing Society as the *"undisputed doyen of marketing"* in this country, he was voted Outstanding Teacher on numerous programmes and conferences throughout America, Asia and Europe.

Peter was an exceptional academic and a wonderful colleague. Our thoughts are with Sylvia, and with their two sons.

02/04/2003 © Warwick Business School, Published with the permission of Professor Howard Thomas, Dean of Warwick Business School.

LEADING PSYCHOLOGIST OF LAST CENTURY, DR. ELLIOTT JAQUES, DIES AT 86
Legacy and Study of Work Continues

Dr. Elliott Jaques, one of the world's leading psychologists and a pioneer in human development theory, died on March 8th 2003 in Gloucester, Massachusetts. He is survived by his wife, Kathryn Cason, as well as three children and grandchildren.

Dr. Jaques, who graduated from the Johns Hopkins School of Medicine and earned a Ph.D. in social relations from Harvard University, became well known for identifying and coining the phrase "mid-life crisis" and his breakthrough discovery that a person's capability to perform complex tasks is both a lifelong evolution and predictable.

During his extensive work with disparate organizations such as the U.S. Army and corporations, Dr. Jaques was the first to develop an objective scientific process for testing and measuring human behaviour through a numeric and provable methodology. This breakthrough approach has been used for the selection of generals for our armed services, political leaders as well as managers in some of the world's largest businesses. This science is now recognized as one of the most important discoveries in its field, making Dr. Jaques one of the most referenced psychologists.

"What's most important is that his work be carried forward," said Kathryn Cason, Dr. Jaques wife. "It took 25 years for Elliott's work on midlife crisis to be accepted; we don't want to have to wait that long for recognition of his other work. Through the individual work of psychologists and the Requisite Organization International Institute (ROII), we hope that Elliott's ideas will be discussed - even debated - in order once again to improve upon human growth and understanding and to create superior working environments. This is what Elliott always strived for."

Dr. Jaques is the author of more than 20 books, including *The Life and Behaviour of Living Organisms* (2002), *Social Power and the CEO* (2002), *Requisite Organization* (1996), *Human Capability* (1994) with Kathryn Cason, and *General Theory of Bureaucracy* (1976). Dr. Jaques is recognized throughout the world for the discoveries he made in the social sciences, contributing in a significant way to our understanding of human nature and social institutions. His life and work has been a great gift to the world.

Noteworthy awards include the Joint Staff Certificate of Appreciation presented by General Colin Powell on behalf of the Joint Chiefs of Staff of the U.S. Armed Forces for "outstanding contributions in the field of military leadership theory and instruction to all of the service departments of the United States" and the Harry Levinson Award of the Consulting Psychology Division of the American Psychological Association for "a distinguished career and impressive accomplishments."

Dr. Jaques' contributions are multi-disciplinary and include fundamental developments in our understanding of the meaning of work and in the evaluation and development of individuals engaged in work, as well a method for objectively measuring the complexity of work roles. Further, his contribution to the social sciences include an objective understanding of the nature of human potential capability and of its maturation throughout life from infancy through old age.

Nearly 60 theses have been developed based on the work of Dr. Jaques and more continue to be developed and written around the world. His work has changed and advanced family and business relationships dramatically over the past half century.

His Life and Times
Born in 1917 in Toronto, Canada, Dr. Jaques graduated with a B.A. Honors Science degree from the University of Toronto at the age of eighteen in 1935, an M.D. from Johns Hopkins Medical School at age twenty-three in 1939, and a Ph.D. in Social Relations from Harvard University. He was a Fellow of the Royal College of Psychiatry and was a Visiting Professor at George Washington University in Washington, DC, and Honorary Professor of the University of Buenos Aires.

Jaques served as a Major in the Canadian Army Medical Corps during WWII and acted as liaison to the British Army War Office Psychiatry Division, whose members developed the War Office Selection Boards.

He remained in England after the war where he was qualified under the renowned psychoanalyst Melanie Klein, and became a founding member of the Tavistock Institute, later moving away from the group-dynamics model toward a rigorous science-based model of human development and maturation. In 1964 he created the School of Social Sciences.

The Rev. Bruce Reed
The Rev Bruce Reed, who has died aged 83, was a charismatic problem solver who applied his Christian values to some of the day's most pressing social issues. His counselling service, the Christian Teamwork Trust, which later evolved into the Grubb Institute of Behavourial Studies, an applied social research institute much relied upon by government and business worldwide, will be his lasting legacy.

It was while serving as chaplain at Fitzwilliam House, Cambridge, between 1950 and 1954, that Bruce's gifts emerged for analysing in depth, from a Christian perspective, the paradoxes and dilemmas that face ordinary human beings, and for offering concrete and practical ways to address them.

This rare talent led him to leave academia in 1954, and offer his services to the Billy Graham Evangelistic Association. He realised there were many decision-makers in British life who were confronted by issues of truth, justice and peace at every turn. The challenge they faced was to handle their daily work with integrity, and seeking ways to be of use to such people set Bruce's agenda for the next 50 years.

Several distinguished laymen, including Sir Kenneth Grubb, backed him in 1957 in setting up the Christian Teamwork Trust. From this sprang a series of charities, many of which still exist today - the Richmond Fellowship, supporting the mentally ill; Langley House, rehabilitating ex-prisoners; the Abbeyfield Society, providing homes in the community for the elderly. For more than 30 years, Bruce and his first wife, Mary, were involved in the Lyndhurst Club for disadvantaged young people in Kentish Town, north London.

Born in Melbourne, Bruce trained as an architect before studying theology at Moore College, Sydney, becoming ordained as an Anglican priest and serving in Sydney diocese. His brother Don later became Archbishop of Sydney, while he himself moved to Cambridge with Mary, whom he married in 1948.

It was while studying theology there that Bruce learned about the theological concept of corporate personality. This led him to seek ways of understanding group dynamics at all levels, an inquiry that brought him, in 1962, into contact with Ken Rice and Pierre Turquet, of the Tavistock Institute of Human Relations. Working with colleagues, including Jean Hutton, who was to be his second wife, Bruce became an influential figure in the development of the thinking and practice of the study of group and organisational behaviour.

Another result of his relationship with the Tavistock was the transformation, in 1969, of Christian Teamwork into the Grubb Institute of Behavioural Studies. This marked a move from a counseling service to an applied social research institute, working for government departments, businesses and other bodies around the world.

Bruce led studies of the transition from childhood to adulthood, looked at ways of supporting the young unemployed and enhancing the leadership and management of schools, and explored how the spiritual resources of the YMCA could be harnessed in its work with young people and others in the community.

His talents were in demand as a consultant on major leadership and management questions at senior levels for multinational companies, including ITT, IBM, Philips and Ericsson. Among areas of government policy that drew on his insights were the probation and prison services. His passionate and continuing concern for the marginalised led to work which directly influenced criminal justice policy. He also worked on the troubles in Northern Ireland in the early 1970s, and his widely circulated working note analysing the dynamics of the situation still bears examination today.

He maintained work with churches and advised senior figures in both the Anglican and Roman Catholic churches, helping Cardinal Basil Hume in the late 1970s, for example, to restructure the archdiocese of Westminster's education service. His grasp of psychoanalytic and systemic thinking, and Christian theology, led him to publish his seminal book on oscillation theory, The Dynamics of Religion (1978), which the Archbishop of York sent to every Church of England bishop.

From 1980, Bruce designed and led conferences for parish clergy which transformed the way they understood their roles as servants of whole communities, not simply their gathered congregations. In 1990, he was awarded a Lambeth degree of MLitt for his "very valuable services to the church" by Archbishop Robert Runcie. Those close to Bruce experienced his passions, which grew from his lived faith in God.

He is survived by his second wife, Jean.

· Bruce Douglas Reed, cleric and organisational analyst, born February 2 1920; died November 4 2003

Thorntons Financial Statistics Page 1

Year	Turnover £ ''000's	Company owned Shops Sales £ ''000's	pre-tax Profit £ ''000's	Company owned Shops Units	Franchise Units	Marks & Spencer Sales £ ''000's	Franchise Sales £ ''000's	Commercial Sales £ ''000's	Thornton Direct £ ''000's	Royalty £ ''000's	Gross Margin
66/67	£1,739	£1,739	£219	87							N/K
67/68	£1,874	£1,874	£217	95							N/K
68/69	£2,191	£2,191	£234	100							N/K
69/70	£2,262	£2,262	£237	107							54.81%
70/71	£2,566	£2,566	£277	110							52.97%
71/72	£2,890	£2,890	£348	122							54.50%
72/73	£3,759	£3,759	£558	126							54.00%
73/74	£4,313	£4,313	£622	130	1						52.99%
74/75	£5,635	£5,625	£601	128	2	£3	£1	£6			49.56%
75/76	£7,091	£6,669	£709	130	14	£236	£85	£176			53.92%
76/77	£8,821	£7,731	£587	130	23	£612	£373	£186			50.50%
77/78	£10,887	£9,197	£678	132	56	£588	£927	£297			50.80%
78/79	£12,826	£10,968	£770	138	N/K	£427	£1,206	£360			52.35%
79/80	£15,534	£13,252	£644	148	N/K	£803	£1,165	£344			53.75%
80/81	£18,876	£15,677	£2,217	155	N/K	£1,795	£1,192	£214			55.80%
81/82	£20,620	£16,867	£2,176	155	N/K	£1,881	£1,410	£465			55.10%
82/83	£24,916	£19,413	£2,579	155	N/K	£2,402	£2,458	£644			54.71%
83/84	£30,926	£22,550	£2,506	156	N/K	£3,100	£3,970	£780			N/K
84/85	£35,667	£25,936	£2,132	157	78	£2,877	£4,170	£880			N/K
85/86	£41,528	£29,163	£4,788	152	N/K	£3,394	£5,140	£1,200			N/K
86/87	£45,419	£31,361	£6,183	164	N/K	£3,775	£5,884	£1,600			N/K
87/88	£52,497	N/K	£7,545	177	103		N/K	£6,900			N/K
88/89	£63,920	N/K	£10,089	188	117		N/K	£8,500			N/K
89/90	£76,170	N/K	£11,311	205	138		N/K	£9,800			N/K
90/91	£79,911	N/K	£11,880	211	165		N/K	£12,400			N/K
91/92	£84,325	N/K	£6,274	224	180		N/K	£14,800			N/K
92/93	£92,476	£54,000	-£7,601	237	221		£12,900	£15,000			N/K
93/94	£93,095	£64,088	£12,107	243	276		£14,000	£16,900			N/K
94/95	£92,607	£65,882	£10,482	263	286		N/K	£17,200			N/K
95/96	£96,407	£62,900	-£13,485	269	222		£11,200	£17,600			N/K
96/97	£111,288	£80,227	£11,541	300	202		£10,900	£18,100			N/K
97/98	£132,678	£105,900	£12,583	344	151		£9,500	£17,400	£200		N/K
98/99	£141,267	£117,200	£10,513	390	110		N/K	£16,600	£800		52.71%
99/00	£153,487	£123,210	£5,512	410	127		N/K	£15,800	£2,000		52.90%
00/01	£159,921	£127,410	£6,085	400	163		N/K	£15,231	£2,400		52.00%
01/02	£163,800	£130,350	£7,110	395	181		N/K	£13,936	£4,200	£200	53.40%

Year	Turnover	Company owned Shops Sales	pre-tax Profit	Company owned Shops	Franchise	Marks & Spencer Sales	Franchise Sales	Commercial Sales	Thornton Direct	Royalty	Gross Margin
	£ ''000's	£ ''000's	£ ''000's	Units	Units	£ ''000's	£ ''000's	£ ''000's	£ ''000's	£ ''000's	
02/03	£167,100	£133,800	£6,400	389	198		£12,300	£15,700	£5,000	£500	53.10%
03/04	£178,750	£136,800	£7,010	378	203		£12,900	£23,700	£5,300	£400	52.40%
04/05	£187,700	£134,100	£8,080	369	216		£13,400	£35,200	£5,300	N/K	51.40%
05/06	£176,630	£127,000	£5,160	367	212		£12,900	£31,200	£5,500	N/K	52.00%
06/07	£185,989	£129,200	£7,081	368	218		£13,000	£37,000	£6,800	N/K	53.70%
07/08	£208,122	£135,100	£8,470	379	250		£14,900	£49,500	£8,600	£649	50.50%

Notes

This data has been obtained from many sources and should not be relied upon for perfect accuracy

N/K = Not Known

Marks and Spencer sales are included in Commercial Sales from 87/88 onwards

Figures do not include VAT

Thorntons Financial Statistics   Page 2

Year	RPI Inflator Index	Turnover at 2008 value	Profit at 2008 value	Annual turnover increase	Annual profit increase	Net margin	Sales per shop	Sales per shop at 2008 value	Chief Executive
		£ ''000's	£ ''000's			£ ''000's	£ ''000's		
66/67	1.0250	£23,484	£2,957			12.59%	£20	£270	JS Thornton
67/68	1.0470	£24,171	£2,799	2.93%	-5.36%	11.58%	£20	£254	JS Thornton
68/69	1.0540	£26,812	£2,864	10.93%	2.31%	10.68%	£22	£268	JS Thornton
69/70	1.0640	£26,016	£2,726	-2.97%	-4.81%	10.48%	£21	£243	AH Thornton
70/71	1.0940	£26,976	£2,912	3.69%	6.84%	10.80%	£23	£245	AH Thornton
71/72	1.0710	£28,369	£3,416	5.16%	17.30%	12.04%	£23.69	£233	AH Thornton
72/73	1.0920	£33,790	£5,016	19.11%	46.84%	14.84%	£29.83	£268	AH Thornton
73/74	1.1600	£33,422	£4,820	-1.09%	-3.91%	14.42%	£33.18	£257	AH Thornton
74/75	1.2420	£35,159	£3,750	5.19%	-22.20%	10.67%	£43.95	£274	AH Thornton
75/76	1.1650	£37,977	£3,797	8.02%	1.26%	10.00%	£51.30	£275	AH Thornton
76/77	1.1580	£40,796	£2,715	7.42%	-28.50%	6.65%	£59.47	£275	AH Thornton
77/78	1.0830	£46,492	£2,895	13.96%	6.65%	6.23%	£69.67	£298	AH Thornton
78/79	1.1340	£48,301	£2,900	3.89%	0.15%	6.00%	£79.48	£299	AH Thornton
79/80	1.1800	£49,575	£2,055	2.64%	-29.12%	4.15%	£89.54	£286	PN & CJ Thornton
80/81	1.1190	£53,834	£6,323	8.59%	207.64%	11.75%	£101.14	£288	PN & CJ Thornton
81/82	1.0860	£54,151	£5,714	0.59%	-9.62%	10.55%	£108.82	£286	C.J.Thornton
82/83	1.0460	£62,556	£6,475	15.52%	13.31%	10.35%	£125.25	£314	C.J.Thornton
83/84	1.0500	£73,947	£5,992	18.21%	-7.46%	8.10%	£144.55	£346	C.J.Thornton
84/85	1.0610	£80,380	£4,805	8.70%	-19.82%	5.98%	£165.20	£372	C.J.Thornton

Year	RPI Inflator Index	Turnover at 2008 value	Profit at 2008 value	Annual turnover increase	Annual profit increase	Net margin	Sales per shop	Sales per shop at 2008 value	Chief Executive
		£ ''000's	£ ''000's				£ ''000's	£ ''000's	
85/86	1.0340	£90,511	£10,436	12.60%	117.19%	11.53%	£191.86	£418	C.J.Thornton
86/87	1.0420	£95,002	£12,933	4.96%	23.93%	13.61%	£191.23	£400	C.J.Thornton
87/88	1.0490	£104,678	£15,045	10.18%	16.33%	14.37%	N/K	N/K	C.J.Thornton
88/89	1.0780	£118,233	£18,662	12.95%	24.04%	15.78%	N/K	N/K	C.J.Thornton
89/90	1.0950	£128,668	£19,107	8.83%	2.39%	14.85%	N/K	N/K	C.J.Thornton
90/91	1.0590	£127,467	£18,950	-0.93%	-0.82%	14.87%	N/K	N/K	C.J.Thornton
91/92	1.0370	£129,708	£9,651	1.76%	-49.07%	7.44%	N/K	N/K	C.J.Thornton
92/93	1.0160	£140,006	-£11,508	7.94%	n/a	-8.22%	£227.85	£345	C.J.Thornton
93/94	1.0240	£137,640	£17,900	-1.69%	42.74%	13.00%	£263.74	£390	C.J.Thornton
94/95	1.0350	£132,288	£14,973	-3.89%	-16.35%	11.32%	£250.50	£358	C.J.Thornton
95/96	1.0240	£134,489	-£18,812	1.66%	n/a	-13.99%	£233.83	£326	R. Paffard
96/97	1.0310	£150,580	£15,616	11.96%	2.14%	10.37%	£267.42	£362	R. Paffard
97/98	1.0340	£173,619	£16,466	15.30%	5.44%	9.48%	£307.85	£403	R. Paffard
98/99	1.0150	£182,126	£13,554	4.90%	-17.69%	7.44%	£300.51	£387	R. Paffard
99/00	1.0300	£192,117	£6,899	5.49%	-49.10%	3.59%	£300.51	£376	P. Burdon
00/01	1.0180	£196,631	£7,482	2.35%	8.44%	3.81%	£318.53	£392	P. Burdon
01/02	1.0170	£198,034	£8,596	0.71%	14.89%	4.34%	£330.00	£399	P. Burdon
02/03	1.0290	£196,330	£7,520	-0.86%	-12.52%	3.83%	£343.96	£404	P. Burdon
03/04	1.0300	£203,901	£7,996	3.86%	6.34%	3.92%	£361.90	£413	P. Burdon
04/05	1.0280	£208,279	£8,966	2.15%	12.12%	4.30%	£363.41	£403	P. Burdon
05/06	1.0309	£190,120	£5,554	-8.72%	-38.05%	2.92%	£346.05	£372	P. Burdon
06/07	1.0320	£193,987	£7,385	2.03%	32.97%	3.81%	£351.09	£366	M.Davies
07/08	1.0430	£208,122	£8,470	7.29%	14.68%	4.07%	£356.46	£356	M.Davies

Notes

This data has been obtained from many sources and should not be relied upon for perfect accuracy

N/K = Not Known

Marks and Spencer sales are included in Commercial Sales from 87/88 onwards

Figures do not include VAT

Index

Note: We have not included entries in the index for the Thorntons company or for individual Thornton family members, as these are covered extensively throughout the book.

Acknowledgements

I had wanted to write this story for 18 years before I eventually made an effort to get something written down. There were so many reasons not to get started – no time to do it properly because I was too busy, there were still family members working in the business, I had no definite publisher or agent and, crucially, I'd never done any writing of this sort before.

However, at the point when we decided to move down to Devon in 2005, my wife Julia said to me, "Why don't you just dictate it on to tape and then I will type it up for you?" Thereupon I decided, in the light of her generous offer, that whether it ever got published or not was unimportant; the story was crying out to be written down and I would just do it.

So it was that I lay on my back on a lounger in the very small garden of our first rented house in Devon and, using my notes of the events of many years ago, began to dictate. By the time that I had recorded 20 tapes, and Julia had not even started to transcribe anything because she was now too busy herself, I decided that the job was all down to me. Thus I began typing or 'voice dictating' to my computer.

Nevertheless, my first thanks must go to Julia for prompting me at last to do this thing, but also for much more - being my sounding board, putting up with me being shut away in my study at weekends until the early hours, and maintaining a happy and cheerful family home at the same time.

By October 2006, when I had written three quarters of the story, I was seriously 'running out of steam' when I happened to meet Richard Graves at an Institute of Directors meeting. Richard is an author himself and when he expressed great interest and offered his support I became even more motivated. I completed my first writing by May 2007 by which time Richard read the script as did a very good friend of ours, Paul Kearney, as well as my son Miles and my cousin Mike Thornton. The enthusiasm and very important comments of these four people further inspired me, so my sincere appreciation to them all. They were very important in getting this story finally on paper.

It was a year later that I came across my publisher, Bruce Sachs of Tomahawk Press. Bruce proposed that I should re-write the book and that we should co-opt Kenneth Bishton to review and reconstruct where necessary all that I had written. I give my sincere thanks to both these individuals who have been enormously helpful.

I have used the Family Tree which was commissioned by my brother Tony Thornton as a source of important information and I would like to thank him for having done that for us all.

During the final period of writing I have received great help with reminders about events that I had forgotten, pictures and company magazines from some of my old friends at Thorntons particularly Margaret Beachim, our original PA at Belper who put me in touch with many others: Walter Willen, George Belfield, Graham Armstead, Dick Smith, Angie Capel, David Bullock, Joyce Blount, Joyce's daughter Susan and Veronica Symonds. All these and many others I met at the pensioners' dinner have given freely of their time and memories for which I thank them sincerely.

Edward Neather, Professor of Linguistics, who with his wife Elisabeth are good friends of ours, was invaluable in checking the 'German bits' and also helped with the bits of British dialect.

A big 'thank you' is due to Sylvia Doyle for all her help, particularly for her photos of Peter; and my appreciation also goes to the Warwick Business School for Peter's obituary and the archetypal picture of him in mid-lecture. Further thanks must go to Joan Heaps who sent me the photograph of her husband Peter along with his CV, to John Bazelgette and Colin Quine of the Grubb Institute for the obituary of Reverend Bruce Reed, to the Times newspaper for the obituary of Lord Wilfred Brown, to Kathryn Cason, the widow of Elliott Jaques for permission to use his obituary and to Karen Dolman, then of the Sheffield Local Studies Library for the wonderful pictures of old Sheffield and early Sheffield shops.

John Wagstaff, a pal of many years standing (and still an excellent helicopter pilot well into his 70s), flew with me over the two factory sites so that I could take the pictures that appear in the book, so my gratitude is extended to him also.

I remain indebted to Mike Davies, Chief Executive of Thorntons Plc for reading and commenting on my book, for providing me with pictures and for granting the right to use them and other material under the Thornton copyright. I am very grateful for the company's support of the project.

Thanks too to Steve Kirkham for excellently designing the book.

Finally Bruce Sachs made a fine choice in commissioning Kenneth Bishton as my 'review writer'. He did an outstanding job of checking my facts, polishing my grammar and fine-tuning every aspect of the text. To him I extend my most sincere thanks.

OTHER GREAT BOOKS FROM TOMAHAWK

Will Hay
by Graham Rinaldi
Foreword by Ken Dodd

*"A meticulously researched and
richly entertaining biography of one
of the most popular and influential
comedians Britain has ever
produced."*
The Daily Express

**BIOGRAPHY OF THE MONTH
(June 2009) – Foyles Bookshop**

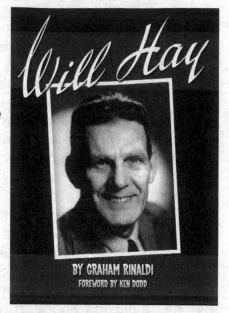

Every British comic actor that
followed Will Hay owes Hay a debt
of gratitude – for it was Hay who defined the modern essence of
British comedy. Working closely with Hay's family, Graham
Rinaldi's definitive tribute to the respected comic actor, takes a
close look into Hay's on-screen and off-screen personae.
Drawing upon Hay's own writings: - newspaper articles, notes
from his astronomy observations and pilot's logbooks and
extracts from his unfinished and previously unpublished
autobiography, the book gives a unique insight into Hay's
childhood, his continuous thirst for knowledge and his passion
for aviation, astronomy and comedy. In addition, the book is
illustrated throughout with previously unpublished photographs
from Hay's family albums.

**To order and for all the latest information
visit www.tomahawkpress.com**

Patrick McGoohan – Danger Man or Prisoner?

by Roger Langley
Foreword by Peter Falk

FEATURING OVER 450 RARE AND EXCLUSIVE PHOTOGRAPHS

Patrick McGoohan changed the history of television with his landmark series *The Prisoner*. Many TV series since have cited *The Prisoner* as an inspiration, including *Lost*. But there is a lot more to McGoohan than *The Prisoner*. This renowned actor has an impressive CV of stage, screen and TV productions, and is often declared to be one of the best actors to have ever come out of Britain. Yet, his obsessive protection of his privacy and the often conflicting and provocative remarks made to the press over the years have created a need to set the record straight. This first ever biography of McGoohan does just that. It chronicles a career that begins on the Sheffield stage and ends with international stardom. The book details McGoohan's classic television series *Danger Man* and *The Prisoner*; it explains why McGoohan was top choice for James Bond, and why he turned down the role; it explores the impact he had on both actors and directors he has worked with; and highlights McGoohan's friendship with Peter Falk (who has written the foreword for this book) which has gained him two Emmy Awards.

In *Patrick McGoohan: Danger Man or Prisoner?*, Roger Langley unravels the myths, separating the man from his on-screen creations. McGoohan attracts thousands of admirers around the globe and this book reveals why!

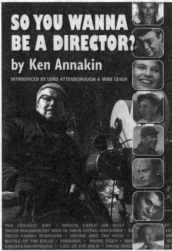